July 2020

The
Sociological
Review
Monographs

Contents

TERF Wars: Feminism and the fight for transgender futures

Edited by Ben Vincent, Sonja Erikainen, and Ruth Pearce

T0349468

Afterword

Acknowledgements 215

The
Sociological
Review
Monographs

TERF wars: An introduction

The Sociological Review Monographs
2020, Vol. 68(4) 3–24
© The Author(s) 2020

DOI: 10.1177/0038026120934713
journals.sagepub.com/home/sor

⑤SAGE

Ruth Pearce
University of Leeds, UK

Sonja Erikainen
Centre for Biomedicine, Self and Society, University of Edinburgh, UK

Ben Vincent
Open University, UK

Keywords
exclusionary politics, feminism, gender ideology, post-truth, trans feminism

In the academic year of 2017–18, one of the editors of this volume convened a course on gender and sexuality at a UK university. The course elicited overwhelmingly positive feedback from students. However, following examinations an invigilator expressed concern, communicated via management, with the language some students used in their answers. Specifically, the invigilator took issue with students employing the acronym 'TERF' (Trans-Exclusionary Radical Feminist) to criticise a range of ideological positions, because they considered the acronym a misogynist slur. The course convenor's line manager subsequently asked whether the term was used within teaching materials.

The convenor had not, in fact, used the TERF acronym at all in any of their teaching, nor explicitly engaged with questions of 'pro' or 'anti' trans[1] positions within feminism. A lecture on trans feminism had focused specifically on understanding transphobia as a manifestation of misogyny, drawing on the work of writers such as Julia Serano (2007), and media analysis of films, including *Silence of the Lambs* and *Ace Ventura*. It was the students themselves who applied what they had learned from contemporary popular discourse to their exam scripts. They had chosen to use the acronym to reference a series of increasingly fraught disputes over how feminism should conceptualise and respond to trans identities and experiences, and did so because 'TERF' was part of their everyday vernacular in discussing the politics of gender, sex and inclusion/exclusion in feminism. The invigilator's objection to the acronym, meanwhile, is indicative of wider

Corresponding author:
Ruth Pearce, University of Leeds, Woodhouse Lane, Leeds, LS2 9JT, UK.
Email: r.pearce1@leeds.ac.uk

disagreements over the deployment of language and, indeed, the very terms of debate when it comes to disputes within feminism.

This anecdote illustrates an experience that we have had on numerous occasions as feminist scholars working in trans studies. We have not sought out the TERF wars; rather, the TERF wars have found us.

We consider a sociological understanding of this phenomenon to be vital, because it is difficult to comprehend what happened even in the minor disagreement described above without understanding how and why the convenor, invigilator, and students all effectively talked past one another. Intense debates over trans issues, feminism, anti-trans ideologies, and the very language employed by various agents in these debates are not just terminological disputes or about how sex and gender should be conceptualised. They are also debates about information, and how people relate to it in a time of information overload; they are debates about truth, and how people relate to truth in a 'post-truth era'. The trans/feminist conflicts we refer to as the 'TERF wars' reflect the current conditions of our time in which public discourse is dominated by political polarisation, deepened by the proliferation of misinformation and distrust in 'experts' whose knowledge may not speak to individuals' cultural common sense. These are contemporary phenomena with deep historical roots, which must be interrogated to make sense of the current landscape.

Analyses of trans-exclusionary rhetoric provide an important contribution to sociology. This is not only because they offer an insight into the production of ideologically ossified, anti-evidential politics (including within academic environments), but also because of what can be learned about power relations. Questions of whose voices are heard, who is found to be convincing, what is considered a 'reasonable concern' and by who, and how these discourses impact marginalised groups are key elements of sociological enquiry.

In this introduction, we set out the political, social and epistemic context in which this edited collection is located and into which it intervenes. We consider the current backlash against trans rights, the political landscape of anti-trans politics, and their relationship to older discourses of gender, femaleness and womanhood. We also examine the construction of knowledge about trans phenomena within feminism and more widely, the uses of 'science' in trans-exclusionary arguments, and the broader ideological landscape in which these arguments are made. In so doing, we show not only why a critical social interrogation of the TERF wars is necessary in 2020, but also why this interrogation should be a trans feminist one.

Trans-exclusionary politics and 'gender ideology'

In the UK context in which we write, a significant upsurge in public anti-trans sentiment has taken place since 2017, when Prime Minister Theresa May announced the Conservative government's plans to reform the Gender Recognition Act 2004 (GRA); a proposal that was also supported by other major UK political parties. While the GRA enables trans people to change the sex marker on their birth certificates from 'female' to 'male' or vice versa, the process involved is frequently experienced as unduly medicalised, bureaucratic, invasive and expensive (Hines, 2013). This is because changing one's birth certificate sex marker requires, among other things, living in one's preferred gender for two years and having a medical diagnosis of gender dysphoria (or homologous older term such as 'transsexualism'). Trans people in the UK can change their name and sex marker on nearly every other relevant record via a process of self-determination without first changing their birth certificate (including with the National Health Service, Driver and Vehicle Licensing Agency and Passport Office[2]). Doing so usually only requires a simple statement of intent to be henceforth known by the new name and/or sex/gender. Yet, as a form of legal recognition, the birth certificate continues to have symbolic importance for many people. The GRA reform plans were largely driven by a proposal to allow trans people to change their birth certificates via self-determination as well. These plans were welcomed by many trans people and LGBT organisations.

In 2018, the UK government held a public consultation on GRA reform. The effect, however, was a backlash against the proposed changes. Leading up to the consultation, multiple campaign organisations were founded to specifically resist self-determination as the mechanism by which birth certificate sex marker can be changed. Organisations including A Woman's Place UK (WPUK), Fair Play For Women (FPFW), Mayday4Women, We Need To Talk and the Lesbian Rights Alliance held meetings across the UK, building a new trans-exclusionary feminist movement that also rapidly expanded online through digital platforms, such as Twitter and the Mumsnet 'feminist chat' message board. The activities and views of these groups have also been widely reported by the media. GRA reform has not materialised at the time of writing. On 22 April 2020, Women and Equalities Minister Liz Truss delivered a speech to the Women and Equalities Select Committee, where in reference to GRA reform, she indicated that the future of the Act would be reported by summer 2020. Truss emphasised three priorities in relation to this: the 'protection' of single-sex spaces (erroneously implying that the GRA has or would have interplay with who may use them); 'maintaining the proper checks and balances in the system' (implying a gatekeeping model for trans adults' autonomy); and 'protecting' under 18s from 'decisions they could make', raising serious concerns regarding the already highly constrained ability of trans people under 18 to access medical care related to gender, but also an implicit threat to bodily autonomy for all young people.

To understand the nature of the backlash, two important points are worth unpacking regarding what, exactly, is being opposed and espoused by groups like WPUK and FPFW. The first concerns how sex and gender are being operationalised: a central concept mobilised by these organisations is 'women's sex-based rights', and this concept is used in ways that emphasise the distinction of sex (as 'biological' or material reality) from gender (as social role or ideology). Organisations opposed to gender self-determination have argued not only that there is a clear distinction between sex and gender, but also that UK laws such as the GRA and the Equality Act 2010 should be interpreted in such a way that trans women are understood as 'male', trans men as 'female', and non-binary people as implicitly delusional (Fair Play for Women, 2017). That is to say, the view of these organisations is that while 'gender' may be subject to change, 'sex' is immutable. Notably, this position ignores decades of feminist scholarship which argue that gender and sex are discursively co-constituted (a point to which we return below), along with the fact that 'sex' and 'gender' are not actually independently defined within UK law (Jenkins & Pearce, 2019; Sandland, 2005).[3]

The second point concerns what self-determination is argued to render possible. Organisations resisting self-determination discursively position it as 'dangerous', arguing that it enables 'men' (a category frequently presumed to encompass trans women and non-binary people assigned male at birth) unfettered access to women-only spaces. Trans people and allies often describe proponents of this approach as 'TERFs' because they tend to support trans women's/girls' *exclusion* from spaces such as women's toilets, changing rooms, rape crisis centres, shelters and feminist groups.

The backlash against the proposed GRA reforms, and the trans-exclusionary feminist movement that has taken shape in the UK in relation to it, did not emerge in a vacuum. Rather, they are a contextual expression of a wider trans-exclusionary political climate with international dimensions. For example, in 2016, the US state of North Carolina introduced a law requiring individuals to use public bathrooms corresponding with their 'biological sex'. The aim was principally to prohibit trans people from using toilet facilities consistent with their gender. Subsequently, similar laws (so-called 'bathroom bills') were proposed in other US states (Barnett et al., 2018). Proponents of anti-trans 'bathroom bills' argued that they were required to protect the safety of cis[4] women, who could supposedly become victims of harm committed by trans women and non-binary people, who, in turn, were (implicitly or explicitly) positioned as 'men' who 'identify as' women.

This kind of argument is a contemporary manifestation of older sex/gender essentialist discourses: trans women have long been positioned as a threat to cis women's safety, especially in Western societies, because trans women's bodies have been discursively associated with dangerous male sexuality and potential sexual predation (Westbrook & Schilt, 2014). Women-only facilities like toilets are often positioned as 'safe spaces' granting (cis) women protection against gender-based harm, and especially sexual violence (see Jones & Slater, this collection). Yet, this notion of toilet 'safety' is part of a wider protectionist politics around (cis) women's bodies that function to protect idealised notions of white female vulnerability (Patel, 2017; see also Koyama, this collection). The cultural positioning of trans women as dangerous to cis women relies on gendered conceptualisations of (cis, implicitly white) women as necessarily fragile in relation to (cis) men, who in turn are conceptualised as having superior physical (and sexual) prowess. By positioning (cis, white) 'females' as a category *uniquely* vulnerable to the threat of 'male' violence (and especially 'biological' male sexual violence), trans-exclusionary arguments around toilet access – including those advanced by self-proclaimed feminist groups – lend support to the gendered and misogynistic discourses that have long positioned (white) women as the 'weaker sex' needing protection (by men, from men).

These discourses have racist undertones, as the implicit whiteness of the women who are the subject of protection means that racialised and especially Black women and non-binary people are more likely to be considered dangerously masculine (Patel, 2017). This is due to the enduring colonial legacies that have long defined racialised women as the unfeminine or 'masculine' contrast to white women's presumed 'natural' femininity (see e.g. McClintock, 2013). Racialised women (cis and trans alike), non-binary and intersex people are especially likely to be rendered 'gender suspect' due to discourses that position bodies of colour as gender deviant in relation to white body norms (Gill-Peterson,

2018; Snorton, 2017). Moreover, discourses that position trans women and non-binary people as a 'threat' to cis women elude how (white) cis women's ability to claim a position of vulnerability in this context is, itself, a reflection of the power that (white) cis women have over trans women (as well as racialised subjects of all genders). One's ability to be recognised or awarded a position as 'vulnerable' is conditioned by whiteness and gender normativity. It is often trans women and non-binary people, especially trans women and non-binary people of colour, who are most vulnerable to gender-based violence in women-only spaces in material terms (see Jones and Slater, this collection). It is disproportionately cis people (both women and men) who are dangerous to, and perpetrators of violence against, trans women, not the other way around (Bachman & Gooch, 2018; Hasenbush et al., 2019). In this way, trans-exclusionary feminist politics can work to erase forms of gendered and racialised violence.

Notably, while many (but not all) trans people and allies describe trans-exclusionary feminist campaigners as 'TERFs', the campaigners themselves generally object to this acronym. In recent years, many have preferred to call themselves 'gender critical' – a term that denotes, less a critical approach to gender, and more an emphasis on claiming 'biologically defined' notions of femaleness and womanhood over gender identity and social concepts of gender. In addition to attacking trans people's right to access public toilets in line with their sex/gender presentation, 'gender critical' feminists have criticised social developments such as LGBTIQ-inclusive school education and positive media representations of trans people. Increasingly, they argue that such developments result from what they call 'gender ideology' (see e.g. 4thWaveNow, 2019).

The language of 'gender ideology' originates in anti-feminist and anti-trans discourses among right-wing Christians, with the Catholic Church acting as a major nucleating agent (Careaga-Pérez, 2016; Kuhar & Paternotte, 2017). In the last decade the concept has been increasingly adopted by far-right organisations and politicians in numerous American, European and African states. They position gender egalitarianism, sexual liberation and LGBTQ+ rights as an attack on traditional values by 'global elites', as represented by multinational corporations and international bodies such as the United Nations (Korolczuk & Graff, 2018). In this context, 'gender' is made to stand in for identity politics and notions of social malleability: '*Gender* provides the theatre for the struggle for hegemony . . . a contest for redefining liberal democracy where "gender ideology" embodies numerous deficits of the so-called progressive actors' (Kováts, 2018, p. 535, emphasis in original).

Mallory Moore (2019) traces the first appearance of 'gender ideology' in a 'gender critical' context: a comment responding to a 2016 blog post on trans-exclusionary feminist website *4thWaveNow*, which shared material from conservative advocacy group the American College of Pediatricians (not to be confused with professional body the American Academy of Pediatrics). From this time the concept saw increasing circulation in trans-exclusionary feminist discourse, especially following its use by 'gender critical' activist Stephanie Davies-Arai (who has been interviewed and profiled on *4thWaveNow*), at a London conference attended by anti-trans campaigners (Singleton, 2016).

Yet, what is actually meant by 'gender ideology' (along with anti-feminist uses of terms such as 'genderism' and 'gender theory') has not been clearly defined: as Elżbieta Korolczuk and Agnieszka Graff (2018, p. 799) argue, 'these terms have become empty signifiers, flexible synonyms for demoralization, abortion, non-normative sexuality, and sex confusion'. This makes them an effective tool in conjuring a moral panic around the breakdown of conventional notions of sex/gender, as evidenced for example in the increasing visibility of the trans liberation movement. Meg-John Barker (2017) observes a range of contradictions within the moral panic over trans existence within the UK media, with trans people blamed for both dismantling and reinforcing the current gender system, and trans women's status as women questioned on the grounds of biology in some contexts, and socialisation in others. The proposed solution is frequently to set aside questions of 'gender' in law and policy, and instead define women and men in law on the basis of 'birth sex'. In 2020 this became a legislative reality in several jurisdictions. In March the US state of Idaho banned trans people from changing their birth certificates, and in April the government of Hungarian dictator Viktor Orbán (an outspoken critic of 'gender ideology') moved to legally redefine sex on the very same day the far-right leader was granted the power to rule by decree.

Ultimately, the growing social acceptance of trans and non-binary people has challenged immutable, biologically derived conceptualisations of both 'femaleness' and 'womanhood'. 'Gender critical' opposition to this can be understood as an emotionally loaded, reactionary response to reassert essentialism, resulting in interventions such as the 'Declaration of Women's Sex-Based Rights' (see Hines, this collection) which effectively echo the demands of far-right, anti-feminist actors.

Trans/feminist relations

While trans subjectivities and feminism are sometimes positioned as oppositional, especially by 'gender critical' writers, this way of framing their relationship is not the dominant (nor an accurate) understanding of the landscape of feminist thought. The starting point for the relationship is often identified with the publication of Janice Raymond's *The Transsexual Empire* (1979), which positioned trans women as violent male subjects infiltrating women's spaces and appropriating women's bodies. Eleanor MacDonald (1998, p. 3), for example, described Raymond's work as 'the classic (and until quite recently, nearly the exclusive) feminist statement on the issue of transsexualism'. Yet, Raymond's depiction of trans people is neither the first nor the exclusive feminist account of trans issues. Indeed, Susanne Kessler and Wendy McKenna's *Gender: An Ethnomethodological Approach* (1978) was published a year earlier. This work extensively discussed transsexualism, not in terms of transsexualism-as-misogyny like Raymond, but as an example of how we are all 'doing' or performing gender.

MacDonald's own approach to transsexualism was not hostile, but rather, like Kessler and McKenna's (1978), curious about what trans perspectives 'might have to contribute to the understanding of gender experience, gender relations or women's oppression' (MacDonald, 1998, p. 4). While MacDonald noted that many feminist writers had ignored trans phenomena because of their apparent rarity and association with medical literatures, feminist approaches to trans issues were beginning to change when she made this observation. By the late 1990s, trans subjectivities and gender diversity became feminism's entry point to understanding the social construction of gender more generally in many feminist accounts. This was especially due to the advent of postmodern feminism and queer theory – particularly Judith Butler's (1990) interventions that theorised binary notions of sex and gender as culturally constituted – along with the emergence of transgender studies as a field in the 1990s (Stryker & Aizura, 2013). It also followed from trans people's everyday involvement in feminist movements, which has been a reality in many countries for decades (Cutuli, 2015; Enke, 2018; Garriga-López, 2016).

Mainstream feminist thought has generally seen the relationship between feminism and trans phenomena as a locus for enquiry into the construction and manifestation of gender relations and systems. For example, the preface for the 2011 special issue of *Feminist Studies* on race and transgender studies opens with the claim that 'for some time now feminists have struggled with the challenges that transgender subjectivity brings to sexuality and gender binaries, especially in the understanding of the category "woman"' (Richardson & Meyer, 2011, p. 247). Richardson and Meyer do not imply, however, that these struggles concern whether or not feminism can be trans-inclusionary or whether trans being threatens feminist praxis. Rather, they highlight the challenges of centring marginalised voices in feminist scholarship, and the need to address the predominant whiteness of transgender studies, both of which remain highly relevant issues (Green & Bey, 2017). While there have been a few relatively prolific trans-exclusionary radical feminist scholars (e.g. Jeffreys, 1997, 2014), they have generally not been in dialogue with contemporary feminist theory, especially that written by trans women and allies with trans-inclusionary politics (with the exception of Hausman, 1995). Rather, trans-exclusionary feminists have generally sat outside decades-long trans/feminist productivity, partially due to convictions that (biological) notions of shared 'femaleness'/'womanhood' are necessary for feminism, and trans bodies and subjectivities pose a threat to these notions (as discussed in this collection by Hines, Koyama, and Carrera-Fernández and DePalma).

In understanding the current landscape of trans-exclusionary feminist politics, the terminology used by different parties in the debates is central, and constitutes a challenge for analysing trans-exclusionary discourses. This is because language is being deliberately used to include, exclude, and/or denote power relations: for example, trans-inclusive feminist writers tend to prefer the term 'trans women', because this implies that a trans woman is a kind of woman (like 'gay woman'). 'Gender critical' writers, however, generally use 'transwomen' and avoid using 'cis', which can (implicitly or explicitly) exclude trans women from the general category 'women', by conflating 'women' with 'cis women'.

Similar debates surround the acronym 'TERF', which was originally used in the late 2000s by some cis women to explicitly distinguish their own radical feminism from trans-exclusionary approaches (Smythe, 2018). 'TERF' is now employed by many trans-inclusive feminists and rejected by trans-exclusionary campaigners. Individuals who object to the acronym 'TERF' often argue that it amounts to a misogynist slur, as in the case of the external examiner in the opening vignette. Certainly, TERF (like 'cis') is often used in angry commentaries online by both cis and trans feminists, either as an accusation (e.g. 'you're a TERF') or an insult (e.g. 'fuck off TERF'). Yet, it is important to understand and account for the power dynamic at play here. In examples such as those above, members of a marginalised group and their allies seek to identify, and express anger or frustration at, a harmful ideology that is promoted primarily by and in the interests of those who are systemically privileged *as cis* (men as well as women). That is not to say that this is a helpful process without qualification. For example, a well-meaning but poorly-informed individual may be unfairly labelled a 'TERF' due to their lack of awareness or understanding of the realities of trans lives. This does not, however, mean that 'TERF' actually functions as a *slur*. Christopher Davis and Elin McCready (2020), for example, have argued that while the acronym can be used to denigrate a particular group, this group is defined by chosen ideology rather than an intrinsic property (in contrast to trans people for instance, or women). It is this denigration of a group defined by an intrinsic property that is necessary to constitute a slur. Moreover, in the case of 'TERF' the act of denigration does not function to subordinate within some structure of power relations (in contrast to acts such as misgendering, and sexist slurs such as 'bitch').

More confusingly, debates exist over the appropriate use and actual referent(s) of the 'TERF' acronym. Recent years have increasingly seen 'TERF' used to refer to transphobia or transphobic individuals in general, losing sight of its original meaning (trans-exclusionary *radical feminism*). Trans communities and their allies are often divided on when and how anti-TERF language might go too far; notably, trans feminist writers have criticised interventions which use excessively violent imagery, especially when this is propagated primarily by male and/or cis individuals. For example, Beth Desmond (2019) criticises a viral video in which a male video game character repeatedly stabs a female character labelled as a 'TERF', observing that 'trans women have nothing to gain from a man delighting in inflicting violence against women'.

Simultaneously, a growing number of anti-trans campaigners associated with radical feminist movements have openly aligned themselves with anti-feminist organisations. For instance, from 2017 US group the Women's Liberation Front (WoLF) have partnered with conservative organisations The Heritage Foundation and Family Policy Alliance, both known for supporting traditional gender roles and opposing abortion rights, comprehensive sex education and same-sex marriage. This raises the question of whether groups such as WoLF might properly be considered 'radical feminist' (and hence, 'TERF') organisations at all. However, it is important to acknowledge that such organisations *do* explicitly draw on the language of women's liberation, and effectively represent the legacy of radical feminist writers such as Raymond (1979) and Jeffreys (1997). Feminists – and especially radical feminists – must contend with this: hence the creation of the 'TERF' acronym in the first place. In this work, we therefore seek to focus specifically on trans-exclusionary ideology and action that is associated with feminisms, rather than attempting to draw a boundary around what does or does not 'count' as a feminist intervention.

The TERF wars, then, are best understood as a series of complex discursive and ideological battles *within* (rather than *against*) feminism. Feminist histories and debates over language are central to this contested landscape. So too are notions of 'truth' and 'neutrality', which are invoked alongside trans-exclusionary feminist discourses to undermine trans activism and research.

'Gender critical' feminism in the post-truth era

It is increasingly argued that we are living in a 'post-truth' era, where conventional notions of expertise and the epistemic status of facts are fragmenting, exemplified by the proliferation of so-called fake news especially in digital spaces (Marres, 2018). As an unprecedented number of people have access to the internet and social media where they can read and circulate information of all kinds, numerous differently positioned knowledge claims now coexist digitally. Indeed, it has been argued that many people are abandoning conventional criteria of evidence in favour of alternative knowledges and beliefs (Lewandowsky et al., 2017). This 'post-truth' environment is frequently invoked by 'gender critical' writers, who argue that trans people's knowledge claims are endorsed by media and legislative bodies in a manner that is difficult to oppose (Brunskell-Evans & Moore, 2018; Davies-Arai, 2018; Moore, 2018). For example, Heather Brunskell-Evans and Michelle Moore (2018, p. 5) claim the idea that young transgender people are 'born in the wrong body' is 'relentlessly promoted by transgender lobbyists within a cultural climate where challenge is silenced'. Others identify 'silencing' factors such as 'fear of criticism or controversy' especially around 'allegations of transphobic bigotry' (Kirkup, 2019), cancelled event bookings after venues received complaints about transphobic content (Doward, 2018), and individuals refusing to participate in public discussions with those they feel are transphobic (Bindel, 2018). There are assertions that anti-trans campaigners (usually positioned as 'women' and/or 'feminists', although many journalists writing on these issues are men, and/or contributing to publications that have not historically favoured feminist perspectives) face opposition specifically for their commitment to truth. For example, Julie Bindel (2018), writing for *Quillette*, insists that 'a feminist such as myself refuses to accept the idea that a penis is a female body part, or declines to mouth Orwellian mantras that completely equate trans women with biological females'.

It seems, however, that claims of 'silencing' are heard loud and clear in mainstream media and political events held across political lines. In the UK, 'gender critical' opinion pieces are regularly published in both left- and right-leaning outlets including *The Observer, The Guardian*, the *Daily Telegraph* and *The Mail on Sunday.* A Google search for articles on 'transgender' published in *The Times* in 2018 alone yields approximately 230 results, with headlines such as 'Girl Guide leaders expelled for questioning trans policy' and 'Picking and choosing gender is demonic, writes churchman'. Multiple 'gender critical' events have also taken place in the UK Parliament and the Scottish Parliament, hosted variously by Conservative, Labour and Scottish National Party politicians.

Both 'gender critical' and Christian conservative writers frequently position trans communities and inclusive feminisms as a monolithic 'cult' (e.g. Davies-Arai, 2018; Hendley, 2019; Trinko, 2019). Often, this assertion relies on implication rather than argument: for example, Stephanie Davies-Arai's (2018, p. 30) writing on 'the transgender experiment on children' includes a section titled 'recruitment into a cult?' but does not explain how/why trans communities might be understood as a cult. Instead, she argues that UK organisations which run trans youth groups, including Gendered Intelligence and Mermaids, 'validate and reinforce a transgender identity' by providing 'vulnerable adolescents with the "tribe" they were looking for . . . [they] will find, perhaps for the first time, approval and belonging in these groups, as long as they identify as transgender' (Davies-Arai, 2018, p. 31). In a highly-read blog post for *Feminist Current*, Alicia Hendley (2019) adds:

. . . while I'm reluctant to call trans activism a 'cult,' I'm aware of many disconcerting similarities: the absolute refusal to allow anyone to criticize issues; silencing, smearing, and ostracizing those who do ask questions (in this case, labeling them 'transphobic') about the ideology of transgenderism; and pressuring individuals (from parents to health professionals) to blindly adhere to the view that some people are 'born in the wrong body,' and that the only way to 'fix' this error is through medical intervention.

Importantly, these claims fail to engage with the extensively documented ideological diversity of trans knowledges, communities and activisms (e.g. Boellstorff et al., 2014; Ekins & King, 2006; Halberstam, 1998; Prince, 1973). For example, through qualitative interviews and participant observation within trans communities in India and the UK over 10 years, Surya Monro (2007) has demonstrated that trans people's views on sex and gender are diverse. They include accounts centring or de-centring the body, supporting or opposing gender abolition or 'degendering', relying on female and male identifications and/or seeking to occupy a non-binary space. Trans people may also strategically position themselves as more or less transgressive depending on their social positioning and circumstances. For instance, transgressive gender expression may result in loss of one's support network, or be the basis for being kicked out of one's family home. This can have profound economic impacts, with the cost of coming out or transgressing transnormative expectations being too high for many. Monro therefore argues for a 'gender pluralist' model of trans identity which acknowledges multiple approaches to identification; a model which is ultimately reflected in the community dynamics of many trans spaces (Pearce, 2018; Pearce & Lohman, 2019). Similarly, numerous trans feminist writers have extensively critiqued the so-called 'wrong body' narrative (e.g. Bettcher, 2014; Lester, 2017), along with the pathologising cis medical models of trans identity from which it arises (Gill-Peterson, 2018; Riggs et al., 2019; Stone, 2006).

'Gender critical' accounts are therefore often at odds with how trans people themselves theorise, identify, and describe their experiences. This is not to say that 'gender critical' claims are always entirely inaccurate. For example, Alicia Hendley (2019) argues that within 'trans activism' there is a 'silencing, smearing, and ostracizing [of] those who do ask questions . . . about the ideology of transgenderism'. Hendley does not describe exactly what these questions are, but it is quite reasonable to imagine that a given query might be perceived as an innocent enquiry by Hendley, but (depending on the framing of the question), could be experienced as transphobic by trans persons. For example, Hendley implicitly questions the fact that trans youth are at high risk for suicide ideations and attempts, describing references to this within trans activism as 'scare tactics'. To trans activists who have experienced multiple friends dying by suicide in their youth, this might quite reasonably come across as a transphobic question particularly considering empirical evidence regarding trans suicidality more generally (Adams & Vincent, 2019; Pearce, 2020). They might therefore seek to shut down the discussion or avoid future contact with Hendley rather than continue the discussion. While this disparity could be understood simply as an epistemic problem caused by different but coexisting forms of knowledge, Hendley's and her trans interlocutors' differing perspectives can also be understood in terms of misinformation and power (Lewandowsky et al., 2017). As we have shown, the insistence that there is one definable '(trans)gender ideology' regarding sex, gender and trans phenomena is demonstrably incorrect. Consequently, the continued circulation of this idea can also be regarded as transphobic, as it is associated with inaccurate (and often prejudiced) views towards trans people rather than a commitment to genuine dialogue.

Even where 'gender critical' writers appear to engage with trans theory, these engagements are generally partial. For example, Michele Moore (2018, p. 225) criticises a 'proposed coalition of disability studies and transgenderism' without explaining what this coalition might look like, and without citing any trans writers beyond the introduction to the *Transgender Studies Reader 2* (Stryker & Aizura, 2013). The growing literature on intersections of disability and trans theory and activism (e.g. Baril, 2015; Chung, 2011; Mog & Swarr, 2008; Puar, 2014; Slater & Liddiard, 2018) is entirely absent from Moore's account. Some writers sympathetic to 'gender critical' positions have also made entirely inaccurate claims about trans authors' arguments. For example, David Pilgrim (2018, p. 309) argues that the 'blurred line between the personal vulnerabilities of individual trans-people [*sic*] and their collective societal position, as a social movement, can prompt trans-activists and their supporters to reject these gender critical feminist arguments for being bigoted and 'transphobic' (e.g. Pearce 2018)'. Clara Greed (2019, p. 912) states that 'Transgender and gender non-binary toilet users may find GNTs [gender neutral toilets] provide them with a valuable alternative (. . . Pearce, 2018).' Neither of these arguments are actually made in Pearce (2018). Rather, it appears that Pilgrim and Greed chose Pearce as a token trans author to cite, without having read her work, which raises wider questions about the kinds of truth claims that are being made in the pursuit of trans-exclusionary agendas.

Mobilising 'science' and 'neutrality' in exclusionary politics

The uses (and abuses) of truth claims in trans-exclusionary arguments raise questions about both the forms of evidence that are being used to justify these arguments, and the epistemic alliances that are being formed between self-proclaimed feminists and what have historically been 'gender-conservative' organisations (Krutkowski et al., 2019). As noted above, 'gender critical' feminists' arguments often run against (and ignore) decades of feminist theorising on the ontological and epistemic status of 'womanhood' and 'femaleness' (see also Hines, 2019). Gender scholars (e.g. Butler, 1990; Laqueur, 1990; Snorton, 2017; Warren, 2017) have shown how biological conceptualisations of sex are mediated by wider gendered as well as colonial and racialised norms that direct the social positions ascribed to different women and men, including one's ability to claim a position as a 'man' or a 'woman' in the first place. Western colonial narratives have not only constituted colonised racialised subjects as less than human, but also framed 'womanhood' and 'manhood' (defined in terms of white, European heteronorms) as characteristic of human culture, which colonised subjects were seen as unable to replicate due to their 'primitive' status. They thus remained female and male, at best, but were not granted the status of women and men (McClintock, 2013). This means that female and male are, themselves, socially constituted categories, changing over time and meaning different things in different contexts and for different people. Moreover, feminist science studies has demonstrated that gendered and racialised language appears throughout contemporary biology (e.g. Birke, 1999; Haraway, 1991; Hubbard, 1990), making it worthwhile to distinguish between biology as organisms' material organisa-tion, and biology as the scientific discourse about that organism (Birke, 2003). In appealing to 'femaleness' as a 'biological 'truth', 'gender critical' arguments fail to account for how sex difference has itself been produced as binary through socio-biolog-ical discourses shaped by gendered and racialised ideas about 'womanhood' and 'man-hood' (Fausto-Sterling, 2000; Laqueur, 1990). Yet, currently, 'gender critical' feminist groups are actively re-claiming 'femaleness' as a fixed, undeniable biological reality, and arguing that regardless of whether trans women are (socially) women, they cannot be 'female', because femaleness requires a particular biological makeup that one is born with (see Hines, 2019).

Essentialist arguments about sex difference are not restricted to 'gender critical' femi-nist groups, or to discussions around specifically 'trans bodies'. They also extend to higher level political and policy discourses. In international sports, for example, new regulations were recently introduced that restrict the right of some intersex women with high testosterone levels and XY chromosomes to compete in women's running races, regardless of their legal or social status as women, or possession of other female sex characteristics from birth (World Athletics, 2019). Sport regulators posit that these regu-lations are based on biological truths about sex that social considerations cannot over-come. Women with XY chromosomes and high testosterone levels are, they claim, 'biologically male athletes with female gender identities' (Court of Arbitration for Sport, 2019, p. 71). These claims were supported by self-proclaimed feminist commentators, including former competitive athlete Dorian Lambelet Coleman (2019), who stated: 'when we are told that 46, XY males [*sic*] with DSD ['Disorders of Sex Development'] who identify as female are no different from us because identity is all that matters, the effect is to erase our deeply significant, sex-specific experience both on and off the track'. Sport regulators have a long history of anti-feminist stances and excluding women, including via implicitly ascribing inferiority to (all) women's bodies for over a century (Erikainen, 2020). This exclusion has, however, disproportionately impacted racialised women from the Global South, in many ways because of the enduring dis-courses in the West that pre-position racialised (and especially Black) women and their bodies as unfeminine, failing to manifest normative 'womanhood' of the Western, white and middle-class form (Erikainen, 2020). Despite this, an alliance has emerged between powerful sport governing bodies and some 'gender critical' women's rights advocates. The effect is that new iterations of older, gendered as well as racialised boundaries between 'biological' femaleness and 'social' womanhood are being drawn. Yet, it is women's rights advocates such as Coleman herself who erase a deeply significant reality that has long been recognised in feminist (and especially Black feminist) politics: there is no single shared experience of female embodiment or 'womanhood' (Combahee River Collective, 1983; Koyama, this collection) – and neither chromosomes nor hormones 'determine' sex (Fausto-Sterling, 2000).

Both trans and intersex women, and racialised trans and intersex women in particular, face heightened levels of discrimination and exclusion from sports due to narrow con-ceptualisations of biological 'femaleness'. The most prominent cases have focused on intersex women and, most visibly, Caster Semenya, whose womanhood has been questioned publicly since 2009, in inherently racialised ways that are intertwined with her position as a 'butch' Black woman from the Global South (see e.g. Erikainen, 2020; Karkazis & Carpenter, 2018). Trans women athletes have, however, also become the object of 'gender critical' media commentaries. For example, following the involuntary disclosure of her trans history, MMA fighter Fallon Fox's right to compete with other women was publicly questioned, including by fellow competitors who made public remarks about presumed advantages she may have due to having been assigned male at birth. Media coverage included depictions that pathologised and marginalised her identity in biologically reductionist ways (Love, 2019).

The sports example illustrates how notions of science (and especially biology) are mobilised to exclude some women from the scope of 'femaleness' (see also Karkazis & Carpenter, 2018). By appealing to 'biology', authorities lay claim to the 'neutrality' and 'objectivity' of science – a claim that has public appeal even if it has been contested in social scientific and humanities scholarship for decades (e.g. Haraway, 1988; Spanier, 1995). Yet, the authority of 'science' allows 'biological truths' about sex difference to be presented as incontestable realities trumping (merely 'social') gender. The alliance between self-proclaimed feminists like Coleman and powerful sports authorities further shows how the mobilisation of 'biology' as a basis for trans (and intersex) people's exclusion currently transcends traditional political positionalities. Moreover, science is used strategically rather than 'factually', in selective ways that enable trans-exclusionary groups to foreground their pre-existing political views upon something 'immutable', even while the immutability of sex is itself established discursively, via political means. As Hubbard (1990, pp. 15–16) argued three decades ago, the world of scientific facts is 'contextual not only in that it depends on who we are and where and when but also in that it is shaped by where we want our "facts" to take us'.[5] 'Gender critical' feminists are constructing and mobilising very particular, contested versions of biological 'facts' that are also lending support to the politics of anti-feminist organisations.

It is important to acknowledge, however, that we ourselves do not write from a position of neutrality for our own sake, nor for this collection as a whole. Instead, and in many ways like the trans-exclusionary voices we critique, we write from a located position that is both political and personal. We are trans and gender diverse feminists who centre personal and bodily autonomy as an uncompromisable value, while also being attentive to structures of power and inequality in ways that are led by the stated experiences of marginalised people. We write from perspectives shaped by our own gendered histories, and the circumstances of our 'entry into knowledge' (Hook, 2005, p. 23) about sex, gender and feminism through personal experiences and educational trajectories. Following Donna Haraway (1988), we conceptualise our writing as situated knowledge, where recognising situatedness also implies recognising failure in political innocence. Our social locations are epistemically and politically salient, and we are therefore not 'neutral' observers or outsiders looking into the TERF wars. Rather, these 'debates' are waged on our lives and bodies, as well as those of our friends, colleagues and loved ones. This has shaped our motivations for collating the articles that follow, as well as the trans feminist voice with which we speak collectively in introducing this collection.

Outline of this monograph

This collection brings together a range of peer-reviewed interventions into complex debates over trans inclusion within (and beyond) feminism. As editors, we intentionally sought contributions from a diversity of perspectives. On some points, contributors take different approaches, use different language to one another, or draw different conclusions. We did not request that authors adhere to any given ideology or worldview, other than a commitment to recognising trans people's stated experiences as worthy of respect and recognition. Rather, what unites the essays in this collection is a commitment to evidenced critique, and an interest in building genuine solidarity within and between trans and feminist movements.

We begin with a look at the historical background to these debates. Part One, *Navigating Feminisms from Past to Present*, traces the entwined histories of feminism and trans activism and thought, examining how these have shaped contemporary debates within scholarship, activism, and the wider public sphere.

In 'Sex wars and (trans)gender panics: Identity and body politics in contemporary UK feminism', Sally Hines parses contemporary UK debates through examining the history of feminist thought. She explores the concept of 'womanhood' and debates on the 'proper' subject of feminism, revisiting feminist conceptualisations of the sex/gender distinction to contextualise the emergence of calls for 'sex-based rights'. Hines argues that this approach dismisses decades of feminist critiques regarding the social construction of sex, and risks reducing womanhood to reproductive capacity. She further insists that 'womanhood' becomes a productive category when it is freed from questions of 'sex' as essentialised biology, enabling allegiances across lines of difference for all people oppressed by patriarchal forces.

The second article, 'The ontological woman: A history of deauthentication, dehumanisation, and violence', critically unpacks the politicised constructs of 'womanhood' used to justify the exclusion of trans women from feminism. Cristan Williams focuses on the animating question that has inspired decades of trans-exclusionary politics – namely, whether womanhood is nature/God-given, or defined by the material conditions of one's life. She maps how trans-exclusionary arguments mobilise a specific rhetoric that then supports a specific morality in an attempt to justify harmful practices. Williams ultimately argues that the moralities and practices enacted by trans-exclusionary individuals and groups are toxic to both trans and feminist communities.

The third contribution is a reprint of Emi Koyama's 2000 essay 'Whose feminism is it anyway? The unspoken racism of the trans inclusion debate'. Stryker and Whittle (2006, p. 698) describe it as 'a stinging rebuke of both lesbian-feminists and transgender activists' for 'predicat[ing] their arguments on racist practices and assumptions'. Much of the language and discourse surrounding trans identities and bodies have changed in the 20 years since its authorship. Yet, the central tensions, illustrated through a critical account of the Michigan Womyn's Music Festival's trans-exclusion policy and the social, political and psychological threat that trans heterogeneity can pose to white, middle-class women (potentially both trans, and cis), remain powerfully illuminatory.

In 'Feminism will be trans-inclusive or it will not be: Why do two cis-hetero woman educators support transfeminism?', María Victoria Carrera-Fernández and Renée

DePalma deconstruct arguments that support trans-exclusionary ideologies and provide contrasting insight into trans feminist and queer approaches to education. Showing how schools act as agents of socialisation, Carrera-Fernández and DePalma position pedagogy as a potent political tool for combating heteronormativity and gendered violence. They not only propose that an emancipatory pedagogy can contribute towards the creation of more equitable societies, but also argue for a critical queer pedagogy that rejects exclusionary discourses and incorporates trans experience as part of a broader feminist educational agenda.

Part Two of this book, *The Medical is Political*, explores the relationship between 'feminism' and medical 'science' in the context of debates over how trans experiences are defined and conceptualised. In 'Autogynephilia: A scientific review, feminist analysis, and alternative "embodiment fantasies" model', Julia Serano analyses the theory of autogynephilia, according to which trans women's gender identities are a by-product of their sexual orientation. The article charts the significant body of evidence that exists to dismantle the theory and shows how and why autogynephilia continues to be invoked by anti-trans actors. Challenging these mobilisations, Serano proposes an alternative 'embodiment fantasy' model as a better explanation for the evidence that has been used to support autogynephilia. She argues that the concept relies on essentialist, heteronormative, and sexist presumptions about women and LGBTQ+ people that are inconsistent with the basic tenets of feminism.

The next article, 'A critical commentary on "rapid-onset gender dysphoria"', dismantles the concept of 'rapid-onset gender dysphoria' (ROGD), a pseudoscientific diagnostic category for young people who supposedly believe mistakenly that they are transgender. Florence Ashley politically and historically contextualises the emergence of ROGD as a category, and deconstructs the evidence base and arguments used to support its use within scholarly contexts and by campaign groups such as 4thWaveNow. Ashley argues that ROGD reflects a deliberate and politicised weaponisation of scientific language to dismiss the overwhelming evidence that exists to support gender-affirmative approaches to care provision for trans teenagers.

The article by Rowan Hildebrand-Chupp, titled 'More than "canaries in the gender coal mine": A transfeminist approach to research on detransition', offers methodological insights to inform research on the fraught topic of detransition. The figure of the detransitioner is often invoked by people on all 'sides' in trans/feminist debates, but the voices of detransitioned people themselves are almost entirely excluded from academic studies. There is a discursive defensiveness around detransition within many trans communities, due to concerns that individuals who imply (or state) that they experience regret following transition will be used to justify greater restrictions around access to gender-affirming medical services. Hildebrand-Chupp addresses these issues by unpacking concepts that are subsumed under the term 'detransition', and suggests categories to allow clear specificity when conducting detransition-related research. Through a critical engagement with how detransition is often poorly represented in research (including, and perhaps especially, 'trans-positive' research), the article creates space for a narrative that recognises the mutual need to acknowledge factors that contribute to negative experiences around gender non-conformity and transition.

Part Three, *Contemporary Discourses, Debates, and Transfeminist Resistance*, turns to questions of feminist activism and contestation in the current moment. These frequently hinge on debates that have unfolded primarily in the Anglophone West, but have influence far beyond, through the unequal hierarchies of knowledge in the postcolonial context. This is demonstrated in the article 'Disregard and danger: Chimamanda Ngozi Adichie and the voices of trans (and cis) African feminists', in which B Camminga shows how the consequences of a question asked on UK television reverberated through the African continent. Camminga explores responses to Nigerian feminist Adichie's televised suggestion that trans women are not women, and shows how this resulted in intense media interest, during which African trans women's voices were erased. Camminga seeks to amplify the voices of these trans women in questioning Adichie's definition of 'womanhood', which is seemingly at odds with the lived realities of both trans and cis women in African countries, and indicative of the unequal flow of feminist discourse between the Global North and South.

The next piece, 'The toilet debate: Stalling trans possibilities and defending "women/s protected spaces"', considers how gender-segregated public toilets have become a prominent site of debate and politicisation for 'gender critical' feminists, who position women's public toilets as safe spaces for cis women, and argue against trans people's right to access gender-segregated toilets. Drawing on data from the Around the Toilet research project, which explored the extent to which toilets can provide a safe and accessible space for everyone, Charlotte Jones and Jen Slater show how the very spaces that gender critical feminists politicise as safe for cis women become sites of danger for trans and non-binary people. They argue that trans-exclusionary politics and practices do nothing to improve toilet access, put trans people at a greater risk of violence, and contribute to a harmful homogenisation of 'womanhood'.

In the tenth article, 'Sex work abolitionism and hegemonic feminisms: Implications for gender-diverse sex workers and migrants from Brazil', Lua da Mota Stabile examines the consequences of Western radical feminist discourses around sex work and human trafficking for trans and gender-diverse sex workers from the Global South. Focusing on Brazilian sex workers migrating to Europe, she explores how Western feminisms often represent migrant sex workers in ways that reproduce colonialism, cissexism and racism. Concurrently, Western feminist politics have influenced international anti-trafficking and anti-prostitution discourses in ways that impact negatively on trans and gender-diverse sex workers. da Mota Stabile argues for the importance of recognising sex workers' self-determination, capacity and conscience, and proposes the development of regulatory and rights frameworks that are receptive of migrants, especially vulnerable groups from the Global South.

Finally, in 'The transfeminist and the liberal institution: A love story', Jay Bernard offers a critical reflection on their experiences of producing the 'RadFem/Trans: A Love Story' event as part of the BFI Flare London LGBTQ film festival. They consider the challenges of negotiating tensions between radical trans feminist politics and liberal cultural institutions, where the default approach is not to take (political) sides. They reflect on questions of representation, exclusions and inclusions, along with their own and others' social locations, in ways that offer lessons for navigating and transcending antagonistic politics.

Across these interventions, our aim is to advance understanding of the TERF wars, their place in the feminist past and present, and their relationship to 'science'. While we do not claim to address every topic of debate in this multifaceted field, we aim to contribute to an unravelling of exclusionary discourses within both feminist *and* trans communities. Our hope is that one day these entrenched debates over 'trans-exclusionary' and 'gender critical' politics will become entirely irrelevant, so that we might instead unite around a shared interest in sex liberation and feminist freedom for all.

Acknowledgements

We thank Steven Brown and the reviewers for *The Sociological Review* for their useful comments on an earlier daft of this article.

Funding

This scholarship was supported in part by the Wellcome Trust (grant number 209519/Z/17/Z).

Notes

1. We use trans as an umbrella term, synonymous with contemporary uses of transgender, or trans*, to roughly capture people whose gender identity/sense of selfhood does not correspond to the assignment made at birth (or in cases of genital ambiguity, slightly later). We recognise the term as leaky and imperfect; and that disidentification with sex/gender assignment does not infer trans identity. Trans identity also does not depend upon dysphoria, transition, or gender expression.
2. A doctor's letter is required to change sex marker on passports, where a person doesn't have a Gender Recognition Certificate, or a birth/adoption certificate with the acquired gender.
3. While 'sex' and 'gender *reassignment*' are separate protected characteristics within the Equality Act 2010, these categories would function in the same way even if named as 'gender' and 'sex reassignment'. The former category is used in measures to prevent unfair treatment on the basis of an individual's status as a woman or a man, while the latter is used in measures to prevent unfair treatment on the basis of an individual having undergone a social and/or physical sex/gender transition.
4. Cisgender (or cis) is a descriptive term indicating people who are not trans and/or whose experience of gender corresponds with their assignment at birth. In use since as early as 1992, the term has come to replace terms such as 'not-trans', 'born-women/men', 'biological women/men' or 'natural women/men', ultimately serving a neutralising function. In resistance to this, many 'gender critical' activists claim that cis (like TERF) is a slur. Recognition of the limitations of a trans/cis binary have been academically articulated (e.g. Enke, 2013).
5. See also Gill-Peterson's (2018) work on the eugenic histories of trans and intersex medicine.

References

4thWaveNow. (2019). *Gender health query: New LGBT organization will address the 'child/teen medical transition movement'.* https://4thwavenow.com/2019/07/28/gender-health-query-new-lgbt-organization-will-address-the-child-teen-medical-transition-movement/ (accessed 24 May 2020).

Adams, N. J., & Vincent, B. (2019). Suicidal thoughts and behaviors among transgender adults in relation to education, ethnicity, and income: A systematic review. *Transgender Health, 4*(1), 226–246.

Bachman, C. L., & Gooch, B. (2018). *LGBT in Britain: Trans report*. Stonewall. www.stonewall.
    org.uk/lgbt-britain-trans-report (accessed 24 May 2020).
Baril, A. (2015). Needing to acquire a physical impairment/disability: (Re) thinking the connec-
    tions between trans and disability studies through transability. *Hypatia*, *30*(1), 30–48.
Barker, M.-J. (2017). *2017 review: The transgender moral panic*. www.rewriting-the-rules.com/
    gender/2017-review-transgender-moral-panic/ (accessed 24 May 2020).
Barnett, B. S., Nesbit, A. E., & Sorrentino, R. M. (2018). The transgender bathroom debate at the
    intersection of politics, law, ethics, and science. *The Journal of the American Academy of
    Psychiatry and the Law*, *46*(2), 232–241.
Bettcher, T. M. (2014). Trapped in the wrong theory: Rethinking trans oppression and resistance.
    Signs, *39*(2), 383–406.
Bindel, J. (2018). *Silencing women in the name of trans activism*. Quillette. https://quillette.
    com/2018/10/31/silencing-women-in-the-name-of-trans-activism/ (accessed 24 May 2020).
Birke, L. I. (1999). *Feminism and the biological body*. Edinburgh University Press.
Birke, L. I. (2003). Shaping biology: Feminism and the idea of 'the biological'. In S. J. Williams,
    L. Birke & G. E. Bendelow (Eds.), *Debating biology: Sociological reflections on health,
    medicine and society* (pp. 39–52). Routledge.
Boellstorff, T., Cabral, M., Cárdenas, M., Cotten, T., Stanley, E. A., Young, K., & Aizura, A. Z.
    (2014). Decolonizing transgender: A roundtable discussion. *Transgender Studies Quarterly*,
    1(3), 419–439.
Brunskell-Evans, H., & Moore, M. (2018). The fabrication of 'the transgender child'. In H.
    Brunskell-Evans & M. Moore (Eds.), *Transgender children and young people: Born in your
    own body* (pp. 1–15). Cambridge Scholars Publishing.
Butler, J. (1990). *Gender trouble: Feminism and the subversion of identity*. Routledge.
Careaga-Pérez, G. (2016). Moral panic and gender ideology in Latin America. *Religion and
    Gender*, *6*(2), 251–255.
Chung, J. J. (2011). Identity or condition: The theory and practice of applying State Disability
    Laws to transgender individuals. *Columbia. Journal of Gender and the Law*, *21*, 1–45.
Combahee River Collective. (1983). The Combahee river collective statement. In B. Smith (Ed.),
    Home girls: A black feminist anthology (pp. 264–274). Rutgers University Press.
Court of Arbitration for Sport. (2019). CAS2018/O/5794 Mokgadi Caster Semenya v. International
    Association of Athletics Federations. CAS 2018/O/5798 Athletics South Africa v.
    Internations Association of Athletics Federations. www.tas-cas.org/fileadmin/user_upload/
    CAS_Award_-_redacted_-_Semenya_ASA_IAAF.pdf (accessed 24 May 2020).
Cutuli, M. S. (2015). Travesti associations, state policies, and NGOs: Resistance and collective
    action in Buenos Aires, Argentina. *Sexualities*, *18*(3), 297–309.
Davies-Arai, S. (2018). The transgender experiment on children. In H. Brunskell-Evans & M.
    Moore (Eds.), *Transgender children and young people: Born in your own body* (pp. 16–40).
    Cambridge Scholars Publishing
Davis, C., & McCready, E. (2020). The instability of slurs. *Grazer Philosophische Studien*, *97*(1),
    63–85.
Desmond, B. (2019, May 5). *Sonic Fox and trans allyship*. The Social Review. www.thesocial-
    review.co.uk/2019/05/05/sonic-fox-and-trans-allyship/ (accessed 24 May 2020).
Doward, J. (2018, October 14). Women's groups claim 'silencing' on transgender concerns. *The
    Guardian*. www.theguardian.com/society/2018/oct/14/women-claim-intimidation-silencing-
    gender-recognition-act-debate (accessed 24 May 2020).
Ekins, R., & King, D. (2006). *The transgender phenomenon*: Sage.
Enke, F. (2013). The education of little cis: Cisgender and the discipline of opposing bodies. In S.
    Stryker & A. Z. Aizura (Eds.), *The transgender studies reader 2* (pp. 234–247). Routledge.

Enke, F. (2018). Collective memory and the transfeminist 1970s: Toward a less plausible history. *TSQ: Transgender Studies Quarterly*, *5*(1), 9–29.

Erikainen, S. (2020). *Gender verification and the making of the female body in sport: A history of the present*. Routledge.

Fair Play for Women. (2017). *Biological sex differences: bones and muscles*. https://fairplayfor-women.com/biological-sex-differences/ (accessed 24 May 2020).

Fausto-Sterling, A. (2000). *Sexing the body: Gender politics and the construction of sexuality*. Basic Books.

Garriga-López, C. S. (2016). Transfeminist crossroads: Reimagining the Ecuadorian state. *TSQ: Transgender Studies Quarterly*, *3*(1–2), 104–119.

Gill-Peterson, J. (2018). *Histories of the transgender child*. University of Minnesota Press.

Greed, C. (2019). Join the queue: Including women's toilet needs in public space. *The Sociological Review*, *67*(4), 908–926.

Green, K. M., & Bey, M. (2017). Where Black feminist thought and trans* feminism meet: A conversation. *Souls*, *19*(4), 438–454.

Halberstam, J. (1998). *Female masculinity*. Duke University Press.

Haraway, D. (1988). Situated knowledges: The science question in feminism and the privilege of partial perspective. *Feminist Studies*, *14*(3), 575–599.

Haraway, D. (1991). *Simians, cyborgs, and women: The reinvention of nature*. Free Association Books.

Hasenbush, A., Flores, A. R., & Herman, J. L. (2019). Gender identity nondiscrimination laws in public accommodations: A review of evidence regarding safety and privacy in public restrooms, locker rooms, and changing rooms. *Sexuality Research and Social Policy*, *16*(1), 70–83.

Hausman, B. L. (1995). *Changing sex: Transsexualism, technology, and the idea of gender*. Duke University Press.

Hendley, A. (2019, April 10). I supported trans ideology until I couldn't anymore. Feminist Current. www.feministcurrent.com/2019/04/10/i-supported-trans-ideology-until-i-couldnt-anymore/ (accessed 24 May 2020).

Hines, S. (2013). *Gender diversity, recognition and citizenship: Towards a politics of difference*. Palgrave Macmillan.

Hines, S. (2019). The feminist frontier: On trans and feminism. *Journal of Gender Studies*, *28*(2), 145–157.

Hook, D. (2005). Genealogy, discourse, 'effective history': Foucault and the work of critique. *Qualitative Research in Psychology*, *2*(1), 3–31.

Hubbard, R. (1990). *The politics of women's biology*: Rutgers University Press.

Jeffreys, S. (1997). Transgender activism: A lesbian feminist perspective. *Journal of Lesbian Studies*, *1*(3–4), 55–74.

Jeffreys, S. (2014). *Gender hurts: A feminist analysis of the politics of transgenderism*. Routledge.

Jenkins, K., & Pearce, R. (2019). *The Gender Recognition Act: A trans-inclusive feminist approach*. www.nottingham.ac.uk/policy-and-engagement/documents/gender-recognition-act/briefing-gender-recognition-act.pdf (accessed 24 May 2020).

Karkazis, K., & Carpenter, M. (2018). Impossible 'choices': The inherent harms of regulating women's testosterone in sport. *Journal of Bioethical Inquiry*, *15*(4), 579–587.

Kessler, S. J., & McKenna, W. (1978). *Gender: An ethnomethodological approach*. University of Chicago Press.

Kirkup, J. (2019, May). Women are being silenced from speaking about transgender rights. *The Spectator*. https://blogs.spectator.co.uk/2019/05/women-are-being-silenced-from-speaking-about-transgender-rights/ (accessed 24 May 2020).

Korolczuk, E., & Graff, A. (2018). Gender as 'ebola from Brussels': The anticolonial frame and the rise of illiberal populism. *Signs: Journal of Women in Culture and Society*, *43*(4), 797–821.

Kováts, E. (2018). Questioning consensuses: Right-wing populism, anti-populism, and the threat of 'gender ideology'. *Sociological Research Online*, *23*(2), 528–538.

Krutkowski, S., Taylor-Harman, S., & Gupta, K. (2019). De-biasing on university campuses in the age of misinformation. *Reference Services Review*. Advance online publication. https://doi.org/10.1108/RSR-10-2019-0075

Kuhar, R., & Paternotte, D. (2017). *Anti-gender campaigns in Europe: Mobilizing against equality*. Rowman & Littlefield.

Lambelet Coleman, D. (2019). *A victory for female athletes everywhere*. Quillette. https://quillette.com/2019/05/03/a-victory-for-female-athletes-everywhere/ (accessed 24 May 2020).

Laqueur, T. W. (1990). *Making sex: Body and gender from the Greeks to Freud*. Harvard University Press.

Lester, C. (2017). *Trans like me: A journey for all of us*. Virago Press.

Lewandowsky, S., Ecker, U. K., & Cook, J. (2017). Beyond misinformation: Understanding and coping with the 'post-truth' era. *Journal of Applied Research in Memory and Cognition*, *6*(4), 353–369.

Love, A. (2019). Media framing of transgender athletes: Contradictions and paradoxes in coverage of MMA Fighter Fallon Fox. In M. Rory (Ed.), *LGBT athletes in the sports media* (pp. 207–225). Palgrave Macmillan.

MacDonald, E. (1998). Critical identities: Rethinking feminism through transgender politics. *Atlantis: Critical Studies in Gender, Culture & Social Justice*, *23*(1), 3–12.

Marres, N. (2018). Why we can't have our facts back. *Engaging Science, Technology, and Society*, *4*, 423–443.

McClintock, A. (2013). *Imperial leather: Race, gender, and sexuality in the colonial contest*. Routledge.

Mog, A., & Swarr, A. L. (2008). Threads of commonality in transgender and disability studies. *Disability Studies Quarterly*, *28*(4).

Monro, S. (2007). Transmuting gender binaries: The theoretical challenge. *Sociological Research Online*, *12*(1), 1–15.

Moore, M. (2018). Standing up for girls and boys. In H. Brunskell-Evans & M. Moore (Eds.), *Transgender children and young people: Born in your own body* (pp. 218–232). Cambridge Scholars Publishing.

Moore, M. (2019). *Gender ideology? Up yours!* Freedom News. https://freedomnews.org.uk/gender-ideology-up-yours/ (accessed 24 May 2020).

Patel, N. (2017). Violent cistems: Trans experiences of bathroom space. *Agenda*, *31*(1), 51–63.

Pearce, R. (2018). *Understanding trans health: Discourse, power and possibility*. Policy Press.

Pearce, R. (2020). A methodology for the marginalised: Surviving oppression and traumatic fieldwork in the neoliberal academy. *Sociology*. Advance online publication. https://doi.org/10.1177/0038038520904918

Pearce, R., & Lohman, K. (2019). De/constructing DIY identities in a trans music scene. *Sexualities*, *22*(1–2), 97–113.

Pilgrim, D. (2018). Reclaiming reality and redefining realism: The challenging case of transgenderism. *Journal of Critical Realism*, *17*(3), 308–324.

Prince, V. (1973). Sex vs gender. In D. R. Laub & P. Gandy (Eds.), *Symposium on gender dysphoria syndrome*. Stanford University Medical Center.

Puar, J. K. (2014). Disability. *Transgender Studies Quarterly*, *1*(1–2), 77–81.

Raymond, J. G. (1979). *The transsexual empire: The making of the she-male*. Beacon Press.

Richardson, M., & Meyer, L. (2011). Preface. *Feminist Studies*, *37*(2), 247–253.

Riggs, D. W., Pearce, R., Pfeffer, C. A., Hines, S., White, F., & Ruspini, E. (2019). Transnormativity in the psy disciplines: Constructing pathology in the Diagnostic and Statistical Manual of Mental Disorders and Standards of Care. *American Psychologist*, *74*(8), 912.

Sandland, R. (2005). Feminism and the Gender Recognition Act 2004. *Feminist Legal Studies*, *13*(1), 43–66.

Serano, J. (2007). *Whipping girl: A transsexual woman on sexism and the scapegoating of femininity*. Seal Press.

Singleton, M. L. (2016). *Thinking differently conference*. http://womensliberationfront.org/thinking-differently-conference/ (accessed 24 May 2020).

Slater, J., & Liddiard, K. (2018). Why disability studies scholars must challenge transmisogyny and transphobia. *Canadian Journal of Disability Studies*, *7*(2), 83–93.

Smythe, V. (2018, November 29). I'm credited with having coined the word 'Terf'. Here's how it happened. *The Guardian*. www.theguardian.com/commentisfree/2018/nov/29/im-credited-with-having-coined-the-acronym-terf-heres-how-it-happened

Snorton, C. R. (2017). *Black on both sides: A racial history of trans identity*. University of Minnesota Press.

Spanier, B. (1995). *Im/partial science: Gender ideology in molecular biology*. Indiana University Press.

Stone, S. (2006). *The empire strikes back: A posttranssexual manifesto*. In S. Stryker & S. Whittle (Eds.), *The transgender studies reader* (pp. 221–235). Routledge.

Stryker, S., & Aizura, A. (2013). Introduction. In S. Stryker & A. Aizura (Eds.), *Transgender studies 2* (pp. 1–12). Routledge.

Stryker, S., & Whittle, S. (Eds.). (2006). *The transgender studies reader*. Routledge.

Trinko, K. (2019). *What it's like to lose your children to the 'transgender cult,' from a mom who knows*. Daily Signal. www.dailysignal.com/2019/10/30/what-its-like-to-lose-your-children-to-the-transgender-cult-from-a-mom-who-knows/ (accessed 24 May 2020).

Warren, C. (2017). Calling into being: Tranifestation, black trans, and the problem of ontology. *Transgender Studies Quarterly*, *4*(2), 266–274.

World Athletics. (2019). *Eligibility regulations for the female classification (athletes with differences of sex development). Version 2.0*. www.worldathletics.org/news/press-release/questions-answers-iaaf-female-eligibility-reg (accessed 24 May 2020).

Westbrook, L., & Schilt, K. (2014). Doing gender, determining gender: Transgender people, gender panics, and the maintenance of the sex/gender/sexuality system. *Gender & Society*, *28*(1), 32–57.

Author biographies

Ruth Pearce is a Visiting Researcher in the School of Sociology and Social Policy at the University of Leeds. Her work explores issues of inequality, marginalisation, power, and political struggle from a trans feminist perspective. Ruth is the author of *Understanding Trans Health* (Policy Press, 2018), and co-editor of *The Emergence of Trans* (Routledge, 2020). She blogs about her work and interests at http://ruthpearce.net.

Sonja Erikainen is a research fellow at the University of Edinburgh Centre for Biomedicine, Self and Society, where their interdisciplinary research focuses on social, historical and ethical issues around biomedicine and scientific knowledge production. Their research and publications cover areas including gender and sport science, hormones in scientific and popular cultures, and the promissory futures of science. They are the author of *Gender Verification and the Making of the Female Body on Sport: A History of the Present* (Routledge, 2020).

Ben Vincent (they/them) has a PhD in Sociology from the University of Leeds, which followed degrees in biological natural sciences and multidisciplinary gender studies, from the University of Cambridge. Their first book, *Transgender Health*, was highly commended at the BMA Medical Book Awards. They are the author of *Non-Binary Genders: Navigating Communities, Identities, and Healthcare*, and co-editor of the collection *Non-Binary Lives*. They are online via @gender-ben on Twitter.

Sex wars and (trans) gender panics: Identity and body politics in contemporary UK feminism

The Sociological Review Monographs
2020, Vol. 68(4) 25–43
© The Author(s) 2020
Article reuse guidelines:
sagepub.com/journals-permissions
DOI: 10.1177/0038026120934684
journals.sagepub.com/home/sor

Sally Hines
Department of Sociological Studies, University of Sheffield, UK

Abstract
This article considers how sex and gender – as conceptual categories and as a lived experience – are subject to contestation and renegotiation in the contemporary UK. Exploring gendered shifts through the lenses of identity and embodiment, the article captures key moments where certainties have been undone within feminist and transgender thought and activism. Yet such fissures resound with calls for a return to traditional understandings of the sexed body. The article pays particular attention to debates within feminism around transgender issues, and sketches out a climate of transgender moral panic whereby conservative thinkers and some feminist activists are joining forces with the aim of resurrecting gender binaries.

Keywords
body politics, feminism, sex/gender, trans feminism, womanhood

Introduction

In 2017 the UK government announced that it would undertake a review of the 2004 Gender Recognition Act (GRA). The GRA had been significant in enabling trans people to change their birth certificates to their acquired gender without the requirement of surgical interventions. The Act also made it possible for trans people to marry after doing so. These were key rights that, prior to 2004, had been denied. The GRA was, at the time, an important piece of legislation, although its limitations were always evident. First, the GRA did not recognise people who fell outside, or between, the binary categories of male or female. Second, it granted only heterosexual people the right to marry. Third, although the Act did not insist on surgery, the criterion for gender recognition involved a long and overly bureaucratic process that was dependent upon the consent of medical practitioners

Corresponding author:
Sally Hines, Department of Sociological Studies, University of Sheffield, 805 Ecclesall Road, Sheffield, S11 8TH, UK.
Email: sally.hines@sheffield.ac.uk

and psychologists. Many trans rights and allied groups argued that these restrictions and demands were outdated and should be revoked (see Hines, 2013).

On embarking on the legal review process in 2018, the UK government opened a public consultation on the law as it stood, wherein a key question concerned the right to self-identify when applying for gender recognition. Campaigning organisations argued that this would make the recognition process simpler, faster and would, importantly, untangle recognition from a problematic history of medical pathologisation whereby trans people had to accept a diagnosis of mental illness before being recognised in their acquired gender.

As this article will address, proposals for self-identification have proved highly contentious within some sections of feminism – serving to open old wounds in debates around feminism and trans people. Since the mid-2000s, deliberations within feminism around trans lives have intensified to the degree that such contestations currently represent polarised positions. This article speaks to, and seeks to go beyond, these fissures. At the heart of current debates lie divergent understandings of the ontology of the categories of 'sex' and 'gender' and conflicting understandings of their relationship. Accordingly, the article begins by considering the meanings of sex and gender within a historical context: exploring theories of sex variation and attending to the construction of a sex/gender binary within 19th century European thought.

Differing ontological frameworks have persisted and, as the article moves on to address, have deeply impacted upon the epistemology of 'woman' within feminist theory and politics. Further, as the article explores, questions around the definition of 'sex', both in relation to womanhood and more widely, are at the heart of these tensions. The article subsequently examines these issues within, and beyond, second wave feminist thought and activism. It then turns to examine recent social, cultural and legal change in the UK, which provides the backdrop to current feminist disputes. Here the article pays particular attention to the ways in which battle lines have been drawn – and shattered – around bodies and identities within what have become marked as 'gender critical' and 'trans inclusive' feminist positions.

With the aim of thinking beyond the current trenchant nature of UK debate, the last part of the article sets out issues of commonality between feminist and trans politics, paying particular attention to politics of the body. In conclusion I argue for a reconsideration of feminist understandings of sex and gender in order to fully unite trans and feminist projects.

Historicising sex and gender categories

The ways in which the categories of sex and gender have been understood have never been consistent. The work of sexual historians thus explores multiple ways in which the human body has been comprehended in the 'West' from the time of ancient Greece through to 19th century Europe (Foucault, 1976). Anthropological research also indicates great historical divergence in understandings of the constitution of 'male' and 'female' across time and culture (Dyble et al., 2015; Kuhn & Stiner, 2006). Others have applied a global and post-colonial perspective to trace the ways in which Western thought has long privileged biology as an explanatory framework for difference and power: 'the idea that biology is destiny – or, better still, destiny is biology has been a staple of Western thought for centuries' (Oyěwùmí, 1997, p. 1). Work on gender diversity within a global context, such as that by Kai Pyle (2018) on Two Spirit people or Poiva Junior Ashleigh Feu'u (2017) on Faʻafafine cultures is important too in moving beyond a Western-centric discourse of transgender (see also Kulick, 1998).

Drawing on these bodies of scholarship enables the argument to be forwarded that rather than biology, it is social, cultural, political and economic factors that bring into being distinct ways of understanding sex, gender and their relationship.

During the 19th century, sexology – the scientific study of sex – came to dominate European understandings of human behaviour. Sex difference was positioned as biologically driven and considered constitutive of human behaviour: bodily difference became absolute. From this perspective, the bodily differences of men and women not only set them apart physically, they determined disparities in personality trait, behavioural characteristic and social role. Uppermost to a model of sex dimorphism was reproduction. The capacity of a woman to gestate – and of a man to impregnate – became the foundation of 19th century formulations of what men and women *were*. Thus, the essence of gender – of being a man or a woman – was tied to reproductive function. Feminist writers have produced a huge body of work on the ways in which women were essentially tied to their bodies in 19th century scientific thought and have created rich and varied accounts of the damages wrought on women's lives by these biological models (Ahmed, 2000; Alcoff, 2006; Butler, 1990; de Beauvoir, 1953; Firestone, 1970; Grosz, 1994; Lorde, 1984; Rich, 1979; Scott, 1992; Young, 1980/2005). Additionally, masculinity theorists have written of the limitations this framework has placed on men's self-expectations, experiences and emotional lives (Connell, 2005; Kimell & Messner, 2010; Nayak, 2006; Pascoe, 2011). More recently, scholars are recognising the confines of binary gender categorisation, especially for those who live beyond or between the categories of male or female (Barker & Iantaffi, 2019; Bornstein, 1994; Richards et al., 2017).

Central to the formulation of sexed and gendered difference was a binary model wherein male and female were polarised. Commonalities between men and women were negated as dissimilarities were underscored. Further – and crucially – variations between the binaries of male and female became pathologised. Yet such pathologisation could not be possible without recognition of bodies – and experiences – that were beyond the binary. Thus, throughout the 19th century, bodies and identities that lay across or outside of the male/female binary became visible. Here we arrive at the work of sexologists Magnus Hirschfeld (1910) and Havelock Ellis (1915), who developed understandings of gender diversity in which gender and sexuality came to be seen as distinct.

Prior to this, gender diversity had been understood within European sexology through the same framework as homosexuality – as an inferior imitation of heterosexuality emerging from biological error. This shifted as cross-gender identification began to be articulated as a distinct 'condition' and incorporated in what Michel Foucault (1976) described as the medicalisation of the 'peculiar'. The term 'transvestite' developed out of Hirschfeld's study 'Tranvestites' in which he defined cross-dressing as 'the impulse to assume the external garb of a sex which is not apparently that of the subject as indicated by the sexual organ' (1910, p. 13). Here we see, for the first time in European sexological thought, the conceptualisation of gendered behaviour as separate from sexuality.

Moreover, the possibilities that gender identity could be distinct from genital appearance emerged. Similarly, Ellis (1915) wrote against the prevalence of collapsing same-sex desire and gender diverse practices.

What was termed 'cross-dressing' became separated from the desire to 'live' as the sex that was not ascribed at birth – most notably through American sexological work by Harry Benjamin (1966), Robert Stoller (1968) and John Money and Anke Ehrhardt (1972). The divergent terms 'transvestism' and 'transsexualism' were so coined. Central to these developments was the notion that transsexual people were born into the 'wrong body'. Surgical procedures, which had been developing throughout this time and were increasingly available, were positioned as the appropriate 'treatment' to the wrong body condition. What was then known as 'sex change' surgery was proffered to bring the body into alignment with identity (Hines, 2007). My point here is not to suggest that gender diversity became de-pathologised through this later sexological work; indeed, pathology was key. Rather, the source of pathology changed – from a defect of sexuality to one of sex. Moreover, during this time an understanding emerged of the possibility that the sexed body may be distinct from how a person presented, or felt, their gender.

Woman and the feminist subject

Conceptualisations of the differences between sex – as biological – and gender – as cultural – were crucial to second wave feminist thought. The sex/gender binary thus became principal. Through the 1960s and 1970s studies of gender – as separate from sex – materialised through feminist work. Gender, it was stressed, was a social category, which was imposed and internalised across multiple sites – the family, education, work, the media, politics, health and medicine, consumerism – with the effect of limiting women's experiences and reducing power. As Florence Binard reflects, through the British Women's Liberation Movement (BWLM): 'women became aware that their subordinate position to men was not determined by so-called natural traits but mostly due to conditioning through unequal social structures' (Binard, 2017, p. 3). She continues:

> They were realising that there are no fundamental differences between the sexes bar those concerned with reproduction and this growing awareness that the 'feminine destiny' was a myth led them to question their positions on both political and personal grounds. The BWLM was a national movement that gathered its strength from its grassroots at local level, through the creation and existence of thousands of women's groups throughout the country. It was characterised by a myriad different type of public actions led by women that ranged from demonstrations, protest marches, strikes to music festivals, artistic events or drama performances; from workshops to conferences, that were heavily publicised and analysed thanks to a flourishing multifaceted feminist press. (Binard, 2017, p. 3)

What became known as 'anti-essentialism' importantly untied gender from biological characteristics. Yet, although the biological basis of 'gender' was seriously disrupted through these interventions, the biological premise of 'sex' remained fixed within much feminist thought; as reflected in Anne Oakley's distinction of sex and gender at the time:

'Sex' is a word that refers to the biological differences between male and female: the visible difference in genitalia, the related difference in procreative function. 'Gender' however is a matter of culture: it refers to the social classification into 'masculine' and 'feminine.' (Oakley, 1972, pp. 21–22)

Indeed, the understanding of gender as culturally constructed appeared through a binary model wherein the biological basis of sex was reinforced. As subsequent discussions in this article will address, the argument that sex arrives from biology has haunted feminist politics around trans issues in the 21st century.

As 'woman' was untied from biology, she became rooted in culture; as Simone de Beauvoir (1953, p. 283) famously insisted: 'One is not born, but rather becomes a woman'. A woman, then, was someone who had been socialised from birth into the restrictive structures of patriarchy and had endured subsequent oppressive life-experience. Later, feminist scholar and anthropologist Gayle Rubin explicitly articulated a framework in which sex and gender were distinct. In Rubin's work, the 'sex/gender system' marked 'a set of arrangements by which the biological raw material of human sex and procreation is shaped by human, social intervention' (1975, p. 165).

Rubin's distinction between sex and gender became the cornerstone of second wave feminism, though that is not to say that sex remained de-politicised. American radical feminist writer Shulamith Firestone (1970), for example, argued that women's oppression arose from their reproductive capacity and positioned reproductive technologies as a feminist utopia that would free women from the burdens of pregnancy. While in the UK socialist feminism emerged as the dominant feminist framework, reproduction was also central. Here concerns about reproduction were around the medicalisation of childbirth, the lack of childcare provided by the state, and the unwillingness of male partners to carry out childcare and domestic labour. The inequalities brought by reproduction, a socialist feminist school of thought also maintained, were the remnant of unenlightened thought that tied women to their biology. Equality in social and intimate spheres, and the development of law and policy to better support women in the public sphere were stressed as the way forward. Yet feminist understanding that sex, as well as gender, was culturally shaped soon began to emerge. French feminist theorist Christine Delphy (1984) was a forerunner in a feminist rethinking of sex – and its relationship to gender. Delphy questioned what lay at the crux of the sex/gender binary – the presumption that gender arises from the natural essence that is sex:

> We have continued to think of gender in terms of sex: to see it as a social dichotomy determined by a natural dichotomy. We now see gender as the content with sex as the container. . . . the container is considered to be invariable because it is part of nature, and nature 'does not change'. (Delphy, 1984, p. 52)

For Delphy, this model represented upturned thought. Instead, Delphy theorised sex as coming from gender: sexed differences are read through gender, not the other way around. As Diane Richardson explains, 'without the concept of gender we could not make sense of bodies as differently sexed' (2015, p. 210). This, Delphy suggested, creates a paradox for feminism:

> Feminists seem to want to abolish hierarchy and even sex roles, but not difference itself. They want to abolish the contents but not the container. They all want to keep some elements of gender. Some want to keep more, others less, but at the very least they want to maintain the classification. Very few indeed are happy to contemplate there being simply anatomical sexual differences which are not given any social significance or symbolic value. (Delphy, 1984, p. 52)

As feminist theory entered the 1990s, more scholars joined Delphy in her task to eradicate the container as well as spilling its contents. Judith Butler's work thus explored sex, not just gender, as a socially constructed concept:

> When the constructed status of gender is theorized as radically independent of sex, gender itself becomes a free-floating artifice, with the consequence that man and masculine might just as easily signify a female body as a male one, and woman and feminine a male body as easily as a female one. (Butler, 1990, p. 6)

Subsequently – and critically – Western feminist understandings of the categories of gender and sex as distinct enabled the recognition that gender was not binary. As the sex/gender binary was disturbed so too was the binary of male/female, leading to the acknowledgement of gender as potentially plural and allowing for gender expressions that were non-binary. Gender*s* were thus made visible in feminist thought. Elsewhere in the world, though, the variation of sex was not a novel idea and there is, as discussed, much historical and anthropological work that indicates the variable characteristics of sex, which takes account of intersex conditions as well as the many distinct conceptualisations and practices of sex and gender in non-Western cultures. Foucault's work (1976), in particular, has been instrumental in exploring how bodies come into being through historical processes. His notion of 'bio-power', whereby bodies are subjugated and regulated by modern nation-states, was taken up by feminist scholars to theorise the social control of women's bodies (Butler, 1990; Grosz, 1994). In their work on intersex, scholars such as Katherine O'Donovan (1985), Alice Dreger (2000) and Anne Fausto-Sterling (2000) have provided an explicit illustration of bio-power; bringing to light the ways in which medical intervention on babies with ambiguously sexed bodies are *made* male or female. This body of work is also important in illustrating how medical discourse and practice has fluctuated with regard to characterising sex. Thus:

> . . . what biological 'facts' determine sex have been the subject of much debate. Chromosomes, hormones, gonads (ovaries/testes), internal reproductive structures and genitalia have variously been seen as the basis for defining a person's sex. For instance, studies of medical responses to 'doubtful sex' – people who in the past were often referred to as third sex or hermaphrodites or more commonly nowadays intersex – suggest that definitions of what constitutes the male and the female body have changed. (Richardson, 2015, p. 210)

Steven Rose's (1998) analysis of the development of the mind–body dichotomy as it emerged through Enlightenment thinking is relevant here. As the body became tied to biology, Rose suggests, biology became separated from the social. Accompanying the male/female binary, then, from this reading, the sex/gender binary is a product of a specific historical time and circumstance. In countering sex/gender as an eternal or natural fact was also the vibrant work of feminist socio-biologists such as Myra Hird (2002) and Joan Roughgarden (2004), who documented the sexed variation of the natural and animal world to insist on the naturalness of diversity itself – including that of the human. Moreover, much important work has pointed to the ways in which the sex/gender binary model was constructed as a part of a colonial project. Tom Boellstorff et al. (2014) thus argue for 'decolonising transgender' by centring the gendered histories, identities, languages and understandings of indigenous peoples and people of colour. From a decolonial perspective, the category of transgender itself is a product of white colonial rule in which local understandings and practices of gender diversity were disappeared. A project of trans decolonisation thus starts with a critique of Western and white gender theory and seeks to explore the impact that colonialism, racism and whiteness have had on the gendered understandings and practices of indigenous peoples and people of colour (see Binahohan, 2014).

None of this is to argue that the body – or sex – does not matter. As feminist thought and politics have undeniably argued, the gendering of bodies means that women are subject to discrimination because of, and through, their bodies in ways that men are not. The contention, then, is not around whether the sexed body is material. The question in point surrounds the material nuances of the sexed body: an issue that became more vital – and increasingly vexed – as feminism turned its attention to transgender matters.

Trans visibility and the ghost of sex

Much has been written about the strain of feminism that has become known as 'trans exclusionary radical feminism', by scholars such as Carol Riddell (1996), Sandy Stone (1991) and Julia Serano (2007, 2013). I also have written widely on the relationship between feminism and trans issues (Hines, 2005, 2007, 2019). Here I do not wish to return to a prolonged discussion of the arguments and political cultures of those second wave feminists who positioned trans perspectives as inherently un-feminist (Jeffreys, 1997; Raymond, 1979). Suffice to say, that this argument rests on a rigid reading of the sex/gender binary and an essentialist understanding of 'woman' (and man) as one who was identified as such at birth on the basis of genital observation. Hence in Raymond's inversion of de Beauvoir, one does not become, but is born a woman.

Trans writers lucidly articulated the harms and exclusions experienced through the tying of gender to an essentialist understanding of sex (Feinberg, 1996; Halberstam, 1998; Riddell, 1996; H. Rubin, 1996; Stone, 1991; Stryker, 1998), and both trans and gender studies scholars carefully troubled a reductive reading of sex, gender and sexuality (Butler, 1990; Grosz, 1994; Hollibaugh, 1989; Rubin, 1989; Vance, 1989). What is more, feminist writers and, later queer scholars, continued to write against a singular feminist ontological position of the sex/gender binary. Monique Wittig (1980/2003), for example, positioned the categories of man and woman as political, rather than distinct essentialist, categories. Jane Flax (1987) and Cressida Heyes (2000) articulated an increasingly plural feminism; enunciating the impossibilities of speaking for 'woman', as such a unified subject position does not exist. In thinking back to this feminist literature, the necessity of examining the conditions under which the sex/gender distinction has become fiercely reinstated in recent years in UK feminism becomes clear.

The new millennium instigated unprecedented awareness of trans people in social and cultural spheres in the UK (Hines, 2007). Cultural fascination with the lives and, above all, the bodies of trans people has continued unabated. Alongside a social and cultural turn to trans (Hines, 2007), trans rights were put on the legal and political agenda. Following prolonged lobbying from trans rights organisations, the 2004 Gender Recognition Act (GRA 2004) enabled trans people over the age of 18, who were not in a pre-transition marriage and who identified as male or female, to change their birth certificates to reflect their acquired gender. The Act was ground-breaking in that it was the first gender recognition law in the world that did not require sterilisation (see Honkasalo, 2018). Yet many trans people were excluded from this new framework of rights: notably non-binary people, young trans people and people who remained married to their partners from before their transition. Subsequent lobbying around these gaps led to a widespread government consultation on the GRA, which has indicated the ways in which the current law is unfit for purpose. In particular, the lengthy and complicated process currently required to register for a 'gender recognition certificate', which is needed before changes in documentation (gender recognition) can be processed, is untenable. Legal administrative changes to shorten and simplify the process have thus been proposed. A model of self-identification or self-declaration, which decentres the involvement of medical practitioners and psychiatrists, has been projected in order to streamline the recognition process. Such a move can be contextualised within international campaigns for self-determination law and will bring the UK legal process in accordance with processes in many other countries across Europe and the globe, including Argentina, Malta, Norway, Pakistan and Uruguay, all of which inscribe self-identity into gender identity law.

While finding favour with trans rights organisations and proving unproblematic for most feminists, over the past five years there has emerged a vehement backlash against the proposed changes to the GRA from a minority of feminist groups who argue that self-declaration of gender will reduce the safety and well-being of cis[1] women. At the hub of this battle is the sex/gender binary wherein 'sex' is reinstated as the primary source of women's oppression in order to agitate against trans rights. More so, reproductive function has gained primacy as the fundamental site of women's disadvantage.

Amidst the UK government's consultation on the GRA, the feminist organisation 'A Woman's Place UK' (WPUK) formed in 2017. The primary goal of WPUK is to agitate against self-declaration of gender within recognition processes. Such a move, it is argued, would open women's spaces, such as toilets, changing rooms and crisis centres, to men. Consequently, their guidance on the GRA consultation, states:

> We believe that a change to self-identification is likely to threaten the rights of women and girls, as well as those with other protected characteristics, and that the government must consider carefully the impact of these changes before attempting to bring them into law. (Women's Place UK, 2020)

WPUK and affiliated organisations have organised meetings across the UK at which speakers have directly positioned trans women as a potential threat to 'women'. A key rhetorical tactic here is the intentional mis-gendering of trans women. At one meeting, for example, a speaker's presentation consisted of slides of photographs of UK trans women whose appearances were mocked as they were talked of with male pronouns: the message being that these were not women, but men 'pretending' to be women. As I have previously suggested (Hines, 2019), the notion of 'deception' is central to feminist denouncements of transgender people. In turn, this links to media-propelled cases of 'gender fraud' where people have been tried and/or convicted of concealing their gender histories from their sexual partners (see Sharpe, 2018; Whittle, 2013). For Elisabeth Grosz, in such instances, the law does not seek 'to protect sexual autonomy against fraudulent solicitation of sex, but rather to protect gender norms and compulsory hetero-sexuality' (2010, p. 96). The gender fraud argument also fuels current provocations against lesbian trans women from some sections of lesbian and/or feminist groups. At London's 2018 Pride march, for example, a group of women positioned themselves at the front of the parade with banners calling for the 'T' (trans) to be removed from the LGBT acronym. Correspondingly, the group 'Get the L out' have organised a number of events at which the lesbian identities of trans women have been refuted. As journalist Gemma Stone (2019) has recently documented, their presence has become usual at Pride events across the UK and internationally.

Though small in number and with much opposition from the majority of members of feminist and LGBT communities, anti-trans feminist groups have had a high media profile in the UK and have linked with international organisations such as the US group 'Hands Across the Aisle'. Under the tagline 'gender is the problem not the solution', Hands Across the Aisle's website declares that:

> For the first time, women from across the political spectrum have come together to challenge the notion that gender is the same as sex. We are radical feminists, lesbians, Christians and conservatives that are tabling our ideological differences to stand in solidarity against gender identity legislation, which we have come to recognise as the erasure of our own hard-won civil rights. As the Hands Across the Aisle Coalition, we are committed to working together, rising above our differences, and leveraging our collective resources to oppose gender identity ideology. (Hands Across the Aisle, 2020)

The irony of feminist groups aligning themselves with the US Christian right who have activated so rigorously against women's reproductive rights is clearly astounding. It is important to reiterate that this is a minority feminist position, yet it is one that shows no sign of abating. At the time of writing, for example, a group led by academics Sheila Jeffreys and Heather Brunskell-Evans have produced a 'Declaration of Women's Sex-Based Rights', which seeks to:

> . . . re-affirm that women's human rights are based upon sex. It argues that these rights are being eroded by the promotion of 'gender identity', and that the inclusion of men who claim to be women in the category 'women' undermines the whole notion and practice of women's rights as human rights. (Womensgrid, 2020)

In recent years, then, UK organisations have sought to isolate sex from gender, placing it as the apex of what makes a woman. From this perspective, sex is tightly defined by genitals, reproductive organs, and chromosomal and hormonal make-up, while gender is characterised as identity. While the latter is (sometimes) granted the possibility of fluidity, sex, it is argued, is only ever binary – male/female. Though gender may be subject to change, sex is fixed: a trans woman may 'identify as' a woman but she will never *be* a woman since sex-as-natural-biology is the defining component of womanhood. Behind the superficiality of gender lies the substance of sex. We are, then, back to Raymond's (1979) argument that trans women are, essentially, men. The argument then follows that trans women are a potential danger to 'real' women, especially in the context of sex-segregated spaces: a man may appear as a woman in order to access women's toilets or changing rooms with the intention of committing sexually abusive acts. This claim is forwarded as a rallying cry against proposed changes to the GRA despite lack of evidence of such occurrences in countries where legal self-declaration of gender recognition is already in place.

Reducing womanhood to reproductive capacity and role undoes decades of feminist work that has sought to upturn conservative thought that relegates gender role to sex. Further, the positioning of sex as the source of oppression presumes a universal characteristic of womanhood in which all cis women are disadvantaged in the same way. Work by feminists of colour, disabled, lesbian and bisexual, working class and trans feminists has provided rich analysis of the intersecting facets of women's oppression, pointing to the ways in which minority women are discounted for within dominant feminist frameworks that offer a narrow definition of what a woman – and thus a feminist subject – is (white, able bodied, heterosexual, middle class and cisgender). Universal accounts of womanhood have thus been subject to important critique at political and conceptual levels.

There is, then, nothing new in the policing of 'woman' to limit feminist political membership – as acutely illustrated by black feminist activist Sojourner Truth's rhetorical question: 'Ain't I a woman?' in her speech to white suffrage campaigners at a women's rally in Ohio in 1851. As I have argued elsewhere (Hines, 2007), conflicts around the category woman have consistently beset feminist thought and activism. Current attempts to exclude trans women from feminism could be seen simply as the latest instance within a very long tradition wherein dominant women seek to, literally, construct feminism in their own image. Yet, as the article moves on to explore, the binary articulation of sex in order to serve an exclusionary agenda is scientifically, as well as politically, untenable.

The diversity of sex

There are clearly considerable variations in both the genitalia and the reproductive organs of people placed within the expansive categories of male and female: some men are born without testicles and some women without a uterus; some men do not produce sperm as some women do not produce eggs; genitalia and reproductive organs can change throughout a man or woman's life due to injury or surgery. There are also significant diversities in the hormonal and chromosomal make-up of men and women. In her book *Myths of Sex, Science and Society*, neuroscientist Cordelia Fine challenges understandings of sex that are based on hormonal difference: what she terms that 'familiar, plausible, pervasive and powerful story' (2017). In her narration of 'Testosterone Rex', Fine pays particular attention to myths around testosterone. Though 'Testosterone Rex' appears to be 'undefeatable', Fine shows how, to the contrary, the 'sexual natural order' is diverse and malleable (2017). There are, she argues, more similarities in the biological make-up of men and women than differences. Work on intersex by scholars such as Fausto-Sterling (1985, 1993, 2000, 2019) and Kessler (1998) also configures sex outside a binary – in this instance bringing to light the diversity of chromosomal make-up. As Morgan Carpenter argues:

> Intersex people and bodies have been considered incapable of integration into society. Medical interventions on often healthy bodies remain the norm, addressing perceived familial and cultural demands, despite concerns about necessity, outcomes, conduct and consent. (Carpenter, 2016, p. 74)

Though Western culture is, as Fausto-Sterling says, 'deeply committed to the idea that there are only two sexes' (1993, p. 23) there are many human chromosomal combinations other than XX (typically used to denote female) and XY (typically used to denote male): 'biologically speaking, there are many gradations running from female to male; and depending on how one calls the shots, one can argue that along that spectrum lie at least five sexes – and perhaps even more' (Fausto-Sterling, 1993, p. 23). Further, 'each of those categories is in itself complex; the percentage of male and female characteristics, for instance, can vary enormously among members of the same subgroup' (1993, p. 23). In her most recent work, Anne Fausto-Sterling thus proposes an orthogonal model, which 'intertwines sex, gender, orientation, bodies, and cultures without a demand to choose one over the other' (Fausto-Sterling, 2019, p. 529).

As gender verification in Olympic sports shows, attempts to fit biological, hormonal and chromosomal diversity into a binary model are frequently unsuccessful (see Erikainen, 2020). As bone researcher Alexandra Kralick has argued, many athletes are let down by attempts to 'draw a hard line between the sexes', a practice, which, for Kralick, 'represents a fundamental misunderstanding about the nature of biological sex. Science keeps showing us that sex also doesn't fit in a binary, whether it be determined by genitals, chromosomes, hormones, or bones' (2017). Attempts to define 'woman' on the bases of biology or genetics, then, raises a range of sticky questions for the rights of trans, cis, and/or intersex women; as Ruth Pearce asks:

> If we are to define womanhood on the basis of genetics, how can we account for intersex conditions such as androgen insensitivity syndrome, which mean that some people born with XY chromosomes have 'female' genitalia and secondary sexual characteristics? If we are to define womanhood on the basis of an ability to conceive, carry a pregnancy, give birth and breastfeed a child, how are we to account for hysterectomy, mastectomy, sterility, women born without wombs? How, moreover, are we to account for a woman's right *not* to be defined by her reproductive capacity? (Pearce, 2019, p. 22, emphasis in original)

There is, therefore, much evidence to counter binary readings of sex, which indicates the fault-lines of sexual dimorphism, or what Ruth Hubbard critiques as the 'astonishingly weak empirical foundations on which the medical orthodoxies of binary sex and gender are built' (1998, p. 198). The reduction of gender to sex within some strains of feminism is thus scientifically as well as politically problematic. To return to Pearce:

> This argument assumes that there is something essential and inherent about a 'woman's body', that can be shared by cis women (individuals assigned female at birth who do not reject this

assignation) but not trans women. It moreover posits that there is something universal about the shared social experiences of cis women that trans women cannot share, thereby positioning the 'social construction' of womanhood as a deterministic form of socialisation rather than evidence of gender's artifice and malleability. (Pearce, 2019, p. 21)

Further still, campaigns to exclude trans women from gender segregated spaces on the basis of natural difference rest upon an alarmingly simple premise that such bodily distinctions can be easily noted. Critical – and deeply ethical – questions also become apparent when considering how for example, through genital examination or chromosome tests – such sex monitoring may be conducted. Aside from the impossible task of simplifying the dynamism of human bodies, questions around how, and by whom, gendered bodies could be observed, certified and regulated in public spaces are starkly pertinent.

The paradoxes and problematics of using 'sex' to articulate bodies are thus profound. Almost 30 years ago Catherine MacKinnon (1991) pointed to the interchangeable use of sex and gender and, in following decades, the language of sex to denote bodily difference has become increasingly redundant. Thus, the terms sex and gender have become transposable in everyday speech as well as in the language of policy and law. As Sandland (2005) has indicated, the terms are used interchangeably in the GRA itself, while, ironically, the International Olympic Committee now speak of 'gender' and not 'sex' verification practices.

A concerted linguistic move from sex to gender would not only be significant in ironing out vernacular inconsistencies. More importantly, it would offer a more successful model through which to account for the complexities of bodies and identities; a project that must be uppermost for feminism if it is remain vital for current and future times. Key to this is the dual task of productively accounting for difference and articulating modes of commonality. With this in mind, the article moves on to explore key overlapping concerns within trans and feminist politics, paying particular attention to the issue of bodily autonomy.

Tracing common ground

The body has long been a key feminist issue. Within second wave feminism the body was central to the notion that the 'personal is political' and explicit in two of the eight demands of the Women's Liberation Movement in the 1970s: free contraception and abortion on demand, and an end to all discrimination against lesbians and a woman's right to define her own sexuality. These demands motivated a number of feminist rights-based claims surrounding, for example, reproductive choice and sexual agency, autonomy around childbirth and sexual health, the fostering of positive body image and improving cultural representations of women's bodies and sexualities. Feminist campaigns around these issues have led directly to changes in law, for example, around the availability of contraception and access to abortion, legislating against sexual harassment, and improving media standards; while improving women's control around how and where to give birth, and increasing input into issues concerning health and well-being. In each instance, self-determination around how the body is understood, portrayed and treated is held as a primary source of women's ability to lead better lives. The body, then, becomes a basis for liberation.

For trans women, too, the body is deeply political. Trans women, and especially trans women of colour, endure extremely high levels of sexual violence and domestic abuse, in addition to sexualisation and objectification in the media – represented as both a subject of fear and of fascination. Moreover, many countries across the globe still compel trans people to undergo surgical interventions prior to recognition, with 16 countries in Europe and Central Asia alone maintaining sterilisation requirements (Transgender Europe, 2019): a practice that the United Nations cite as a human rights violation. Thus, issues around the recognition of, and the rights afforded to, gendered bodies have remained constant campaigning issues for trans movements since their inception in the 1970s. Indeed, here, the right to embodiment is the political motivator. Concerns around medical practice and health care are paramount to trans rights movements (see Davy, 2011; Pearce, 2018; Vincent, 2018), and issues of gendered violence and sexual harassment remain increasingly important. Further, the representation of trans bodies, particularly in the media, is an important campaigning issue. Reflecting on how issues of bodily autonomy are crucial for both cis and trans women at the levels of the individual, social and political confirms the inclusive temperament of 'woman'; indicating further the errors of trans-exclusionary feminism. At this juncture it is important to turn to work that has explicitly addressed the interconnections of trans and feminist projects.

Jacob Hale's (1996) consideration of the potential for both distinct and connected characteristics of women is productive for the development of inclusive feminism. Hale points to the specific qualities that are taken to denote 'woman', including biological make-up and appearance, gender behaviour, gender role and gendered history. Of these, particular characteristics may, he suggests, have incompatible degrees of importance with others. A trans woman may, for example, have different genitals to someone who is assumed to be a cis woman though outwardly her appearance means that she experiences social (including sex) discrimination in the same way. Vaginal hypoplasia, for example, may result in an underdeveloped or entirely absent vagina in people who are assigned female at birth. Susan Kessler and Wendy McKenna (1978) accordingly use the concept of 'cultural genitals' rather than 'biological genitals'. What is important here are social perceptions of biological difference rather than biological characteristics themselves. As Jason Cromwell (1999) has argued, bodily materiality only emerges through social interaction.

Henry Rubin (1996) sought to conceive of a feminism that was able to take account of what he called 'differently located bodies which appear similar in form' (1996, p. 8). Rubin proposed an 'action paradigm', whereby political practice, rather than biology, is centred within feminism in order to enable an analysis of embodiment without essentialist connotations. Similarly, Julia Serano (2013) argues that feminism has to be large enough to account for the femininities of women who were not assigned female at birth. In Emi Koyama's 'trans feminism' 'no political, medical or religious authority shall violate the integrity of our bodies against our will or impede our decisions regarding what to do with them' (2003, p. 247). Trans feminism, Koyama suggests, believes in 'fostering an environment where women's individual choices are honoured, while scrutinising and challenging institutions that limit the range of choices available to them' (2003, p. 247). To my mind, Koyama's treaty articulates the essence of the slogan 'the personal is political'. Alongside bodily autonomy, Koyama identifies body image, violence and reproductive and health care as connecting issues of importance for all women.

Rachel Anne Williams (2019) maps three waves of trans feminism that echo the waves of feminism per se. As the first wave of Western feminism sought to recognise women at the levels of the political and public through suffrage campaigns, the first wave of trans feminism brought trans women to public attention in the 1950s through, for example, media reporting of Christine Jorgenson's hormonal transition. Central to second wave feminism were legal demands for equality, common also, Williams suggests, to second wave trans feminism's campaigns for improvements in health care, housing and employment. Key to feminism's third wave has been the question of difference. Here Williams addresses the turn to intersectionality within feminism as writers and activists homed in further on the ways in which race, class, sexuality and disability impact on gendered identity and experience. This concern is also reflected, according to Williams, in the increasing recognition of different ways of being gender diverse within trans communities.

Kimberlé Crenshaw's work on intersectionality has been significant to the development of trans feminism. Crenshaw argued that 'because the intersectional experience is greater than the sum of racism and sexism, any analysis that does not take intersectionality into account cannot sufficiently address the particular manner in which Black women are subordinated' (1989, p. 149). In their introduction to an issue of *Transgender Studies Quarterly* (TSQ) on trans/feminisms, Susan Stryker and Talia M. Bettcher (2016) similarly show how intersectionality motivates trans feminism, emphasising the alliances between trans women and women of colour, both of whom have represented groups excluded from the interests of white cis feminism. As the feminism issue of TSQ illustrates, in many parts of the world (Brazil, Ecuador, Spain, Russia, France and Italy) there exist strong alliances between feminist and trans communities. In writing about trans feminism in Ecuador, Claudia Sofía Garriga-López, for example, shows that the divisions between trans and feminism that are apparent in the UK are not evident in other parts of the globe where trans struggles are seen as an integral part of the fight against patriarchy and colonialism:

> Trans activists have been at the forefront of feminist and LGBT struggles for many decades, and the category of 'transfeminism' signals the articulation of these practices into a cohesive political standpoint. (Garriga-Lopez, 2016, p. 107)

Tracing feminist alliances is also important to enable a move beyond neoliberal goals of recognition and to hope for more than inclusion. Making visible the connections between different groups of subordinated women is therefore important if, as feminists, we are to ensure that our movement retains a political commitment. Strengthening the allegiances between women who are marginalised on the basis of class, sexuality, disability, faith, race and ethnicity is crucial for a feminist praxis of social justice.

Conclusions

This article has addressed the emergence in UK feminism of what has become known as a 'trans-exclusionary radical feminist' (TERF) perspective. This standpoint is positioned against proposed changes to the Gender Recognition Act, which are anticipated to introduce self-identification in order to make the administrative process of gender recognition more straightforward. Although this is a marginal feminist perspective, it has become increasingly vocal in recent years, buoyed by support from some feminists with high media profiles. The article has outlined, and critiqued, the ways in which an essentialist reading of sex has re-emerged within these debates.

The move to define the identity and experience of woman through a purely biological lens is, I have argued, problematic in several ways. First, the presumption that the category of woman denotes a universal experience, wherein reproductive function is central to women's oppression, negates individual, historical and cultural specificity. This reductive reading of sex is problematic for the distinct ways in which sex – and gender – have been understood in different times and places, and in relation to the varied sexed make-up of bodies themselves.

While not denying the materiality, or the material consequences, of the body in women's oppression, I suggest that it is perceived reproductive function that figures as a site of control, not reproductive capacity in and of itself. For who knows the body parts and genetic make-up of strangers? That it is common for trans-exclusionary feminists to assume that they are always able to recognise a trans woman makes this a substantial, rather than a rhetorical, question. In attempts to argue for the exclusion of trans women from competitive women's sport, trans-exclusionary feminists, for example, recently turned to social media to question the genders of a group of successful Chinese cis women athletes. Using the media photograph of the celebrating team members, three of the group were declared to be transgender – or in their nomenclature, male. Such moves highlight the white Western-centric lens through which gender is, literally, seen, and reinstated by misogynistic tropes of how women's bodies should appear in order to be recognised and valued.

The subsequent feminist trans-exclusionary argument that men may appear in public spaces as women in order to physically and sexually abuse women is also nonsensical through this line of questioning. For, how and by whom can the body parts and genetic make-up of strangers be observed and regulated? A trans-exclusionary politics of moral panic has, for example, recently led to cases where cis women have been asked to leave women's toilets because they have been assumed to be trans. In 2018, for example, police forcibly removed a cis woman from a women's toilet in North Carolina, US, after receiving calls that she was not feminine enough. The state had recently passed the 'bathroom bill', which made trans people use the toilet corresponding to that on their birth certificate rather than that with which they identified. In 2019 the Bill was repealed after campaigns by LGBT right groups (see Holpuch, 2019). Moreover, as has been explored, work on sex variation and natural diversity indicates the fault-lines in attempts to strictly define sexed bodies. What is at stake here are understandings of sex, not sex itself. The article has thus drawn on a range of work that locates the category of woman (and that of man) at the site of the cultural and the political. 'Woman', I suggest, becomes a productive category when it is freed from sex. I therefore argue for a linguistic move away from sex and towards gender in social, cultural, legal and medical discourse.

The category 'woman' also appears at its most politically effective when it is opened out to account for differently gendered bodies. As trans feminist work has shown, it is then possible to trace the common ground between the specific feminist projects of women and non-binary people who are differently located. Not only is this crucial for understanding the diversity of gendered bodies, it is key to accounting for the structural forces and power dynamics of class, race, disability and sexuality. Allegiances across these lines of difference are vital for a transformative political project that theorises and activates against patriarchal forces as they are constructed through varied systems of oppression. Sara Ahmed (2016) thinks of this as a politics that is built through an 'affinity of hammers', which work to chip away at the system. I suggest that it is only through securing a political framework that seeks to be respectfully mindful of difference and committed to alliance-building that feminism can retain its political purpose so as to be fit for current times.

Funding

The author received no financial support for the research, authorship, and/or publication of this article.

Note

1. Cis, or cisgender, is a term for someone whose identity is congruent with the sex that they were assigned at birth.

References

Ahmed, S. (2000). *Strange encounters: Embodied others in post-coloniality*. Routledge.
Ahmed, S. (2016). An affinity of hammers. *Transgender Studies Quarterly, 3*(1–2), 22–34.
Alcoff, L. M. (2006). *Visible identities: Race, gender, and the self*. Oxford University Press.
Barker, M. J., & Iantaffi, A. (2019). *Life isn't binary: On being both, beyond, and in-between*. Jessica Kingsley.
Benjamin, H. (1966). *The transsexual phenomenon*. The Julian Press.
Binahohan, B. (2014). *Decolonizing trans/gender 101*. Biyuti Publishing.
Binard, F. (2017). The British Women's Liberation Movement in the 1970s: Redefining the personal and the political. *The French Journal of British Studies, XXII* Hors série.
Boellstorff, T., Cabral, M., & Cardenas, M. (2014). Decolonizing transgender: A roundtable discussion. *Transgender Studies Quarterly, 1*(3), 419–439.
Bornstein, K. (1994). *Gender outlaw: On men, women and the rest of us*. Routledge.
Butler, J. (1990). *Gender trouble: Feminism and the subversion of identity*. Routledge.
Carpenter, M. (2016). The human rights of intersex people: Addressing harmful practices and rhetoric of change. *Reproduction Health Matters, 24*(47), 74–84.
Connell, R. (2005). *Masculinities*. Polity Press.
Crenshaw, K. (1989). Demarginalizing the intersection of race and sex: A black feminist critique of antidiscrimination doctrine, feminist theory, and antiracist politics. *University of Chicago Legal Forum, 1989*, 139–167.
Cromwell, J. (1999). *Tranmen and FTMs*. University of Illinois Press.
Davy, Z. (2011). *Recognizing transsexuals: Personal, political and medicolegal embodiment*. Ashgate.
de Beauvoir, S. (1953). *The second sex* (H. M. Parshley, Trans.). Jonathan Cape Publishers.
Delphy, C. (1984). *Close to home: A materialist analysis of women's oppression*. Verso.
Dreger, A. (2000). *Hermaphrodites and the medical invention of sex*. Harvard University Press.
Dyble, M., Salali, N., Chaudhary, G. D., Page, A., Smith, D., & Thompson, J. (2015). Sex equality can explain the unique social structure of hunter-gatherer bands. *Science, 348*(6236), 796–798.
Ellis, H. (1915). *Sexual inversion*. F. A. Davis.

Erikainen, S. (2020). *Policing the sex binary: Gender verification and the boundaries of female embodiment in elite sport*. Routledge.

Fausto-Sterling, A. (1985). The new research on women: How does it affect the natural sciences? *Women's Studies Quarterly, 13*(2), 30–32.

Fausto-Sterling, A. (1993). The five sexes: Why male and female are not enough. *The Sciences*, March/April, 20–25.

Fausto-Sterling, A. (2000). *Sexing the body: Gender politics and the construction of sexuality*. Basic Books.

Fausto-Sterling, A. (2019). Gender/sex, sexual orientation, and identity are in the body: How did they get there? *The Journal of Sex Research, 56*(4–5), 529–555.

Feinberg, L. (1996). *Transgender warriors: Making history from Joan of Arc to Dennis Rodman*. Beacon Press.

Feu'u, P. J. A. (2017). A comparative study of fa'afafine of Samoa and the whakawahine of Aotearoa New Zealand. In E. Hazenberg & M. Meyerhoff (Eds.), *Representing trans: Linguistic, legal and everyday perspectives* (pp. 171–203). Victoria University Press.

Fine, C. (2017). *Testosterone rex: Myths of sex, science, and society*. Icon Books.

Firestone, S. (1970). *The dialectic of sex: The case for feminist revolution*. William Morrow and Company.

Flax, J. (1987). Postmodernism and gender relations in feminist theory. *Signs: Journal of Women in Culture and Society, 12*(4), 621–643.

Foucault, M. (1976). *The history of sexuality*. Pantheon Books.

Garriga-Lopez, C. S. (2016). Transfeminist crossroads: Reimagining the Ecuadorian state. *Transgender Studies Quarterly, 3*(1–2), 104–119.

Grosz, E. (1994). *Volatile bodies: Toward a corporeal feminism*. Indiana University Press.

Grosz, E. (2010). Practice of feminist theory. *Difference, 21*(1), 94–108.

Halberstam, J. (1998). *Female masculinity*. Duke University Press.

Hale, J. (1996). Are lesbians women? *Hypatia, 11*(2), 94–121.

Hands Across the Aisle. (2020, March). *Who we are*. https://handsacrosstheaislewomen.com/home/ (last accessed 3 June 2020).

Heyes, C. J. (2000). Reading transgender, rethinking women's studies. *NWSA Journal, 12*(2), 170–180.

Hines, S. (2005). 'I am a feminist but. . .': Transgender men, women and feminism. In J. Reger (Ed.), *Different wavelengths: Studies of the contemporary women's movement* (pp. 57–79). Routledge.

Hines, S. (2007). *TransForming gender: Transgender practices of identity, intimacy and care*. Policy Press.

Hines, S. (2013). *Gender diversity, recognition and citizenship: Towards a politics of difference*. Palgrave Macmillan.

Hines, S. (2019). The feminist frontier: On trans and feminism. *Journal of Gender Studies, 28*(2), 145–157.

Hird, M. J. (2002). For a sociology of transsexualism. *Sociology, 36*(3), 577–595.

Hirschfeld, M. (1910). *The transvestites: The erotic drive to cross-dress*. Prometheus Books.

Hollibaugh, A. (1989). *My dangerous desires: A queer girl dreaming her way home*. Duke University Press.

Holpuch, A. (2019, July 23). North Carolina: Trans people given the right to use bathrooms matching identity. *The Guardian*. www.theguardian.com/society/2019/jul/23/north-carolina-bathroom-bill-transgender (last accessed 3 June 2020).

Honkasalo, J. (2018). When boys will not be boys: American eugenics and the formation of gender nonconformity as psychopathology. *NORMA: International Journal for Masculinity Studies, 11*(4), 270–286.

Hubbard, R. (1998). *The politics of women's biology*. Rutgers University Press.

Jeffreys, S. (1997). Transgender activism: A lesbian feminist perspective. *Journal of Lesbian Studies*, *1*(3–4), 55–74.

Kessler, S. (1998). *Lessons from the intersexed*. Rutgers University Press.

Kessler, S., & McKenna, W. (1978). *Gender: An ethnomethodological approach*. University of Chicago Press.

Kimmel, M. S., & Messner, M. A. (2010). *Men's lives*. Pearson.

Koyama, E. (2003). The transfeminist manifesto. In R. Dicker & A. Piepmeier (Eds.), *Catching a wave: Reclaiming feminism for the 21st century* (pp. 244–260). Northeastern Press.

Kralick, A. (2017). *We finally understand that gender isn't binary. Sex isn't, either*. Slate. https:// slate.com/technology/2018/11/sex-binary-gender-neither-exist.html (accessed 3 June 2020).

Kuhn, S. L., & Stiner, M. C. (2006). What's a mother to do? The division of labor among Neandertals and modern humans in Eurasia. *Current Anthropology*, *47*(6), 953–980.

Kulick, D. (1998). *Travesti: Sex, gender, and culture among Brazilian transgendered prostitutes*. University of Chicago Press.

Lorde, A. (1984). *Sister outsider: Essays and speeches*. The Crossing Press.

MacKinnon, C. (1991). Reflections on sex equality under law. *Yale Law Journal*, *100*(5), 1281–1328.

Money, J., & Ehrhardt, A. A. (1972). *Man and woman, boy and girl: Differentiation and dimorphism of gender identity from conception to maturity*. Johns Hopkins University Press.

Nayak, A. (2006). Displaced masculinities: Chavs, youth and class in the post-industrial city. *Sociology*, *40*(5), 813–831.

Oakley, A. (1972). *Sex, gender and society*. Maurice Temple Smith Ltd.

O'Donovan, K. (1985). *Sexual divisions in law*. Weidenfeld and Nicolson.

Oyěwùmí, O. (1997). *The invention of women: Making an African sense of western gender discourses* (new ed.). University of Minnesota Press.

Pascoe, C. J. (2011). *Dude, you're a fag: Masculinity and sexuality in high school*. University of California Press.

Pearce, R. (2018). *Understanding trans health: Discourse, power and possibility*. Policy Press.

Pearce, R. (2019). Moving through the world as a woman. In G. Crimmins (Ed.), *Strategies for resisting sexism in the academy: Higher education, gender and intersectionality* (pp. 17–34). Palgrave Macmillan.

Pyle, K. (2018). Naming and claiming: Recovering Ojibwe and Plains Cree two-spirit language. *Transgender Studies Quarterly*, *5*(4), 574–588.

Raymond, J. (1979). *The transsexual empire: The making of the she-male*. Beacon Press.

Rich, A. (1979). *Of women born, motherhood as experience and institution*. Virago.

Richards, C., Bouman, W., & Barker, M.-J. (2017). *Genderqueer and non-binary genders*. Palgrave Macmillan.

Richardson, D. (2015). Rethinking sexual citizenship. *Sociology*, *51*(2), 208–224.

Riddell, C. (1996). Divided sisterhood: A critical review of Janice Raymond's *The Transsexual Empire*. In R. Ekins & D. King (Eds.), *Blending genders: Social aspects of cross-dressing* (pp. 160–174). Routledge.

Rose, S. (1998). *Lifelines: Biology beyond determinism*. Oxford University Press.

Roughgarden, J. (2004). *Evolutions rainbow: Diversity, gender, and sexuality in nature and people*. University of California Press.

Rubin, G. (1975). The traffic in women: Notes on the 'political economy' of sex. In R. Reiter (Ed.), *Toward an anthropology of women* (pp. 157–210). Monthly Review Press.

Rubin, G. (1989). Thinking sex: Notes for a radical theory of the politics of sexuality. In C. Vance (Ed.), *Pleasure and danger: Exploring female sexuality* (pp. 267–293). Pandora.

Rubin, H. (1996). Do you believe in gender? *Sojourner*, *21*(6), 7–8.

Sandland, R. (2005). Feminism and the Gender Recognition Act 2004. *Feminist Legal Studies*, *13*(1), 43–66.

Scott, J. W. (1992). Multiculturalism and the politics of identity. *October*, *61*(Summer), 12–19.

Serano, J. (2007). *Whipping girl: A transsexual woman on sexism and the scapegoating of femininity*. Seal Press.

Serano, J. (2013). *Excluded: Making feminist and queer movements more inclusive*. Seal Press.

Sharpe, A. (2018). *Sexual intimacy and gender identity 'fraud'*. Routledge.

Stoller, R. (1968). *Sex and gender: On the development of masculinity and femininity*. Science House.

Stone, G. (2019, July). Anti-trans activists are taking the power out of pride. *The Independent*. www.independent.co.uk/voices/pride-anti-trans-activists-parade-march-london-a8991371. html (last accessed 3 June 2020).

Stone, S. (1991). The empire strikes back: A posttranssexual manifesto. In K. Straub & J. Epstein (Eds.), *Body guards: The cultural politics of sexual ambiguity* (pp. 248–279). Routledge.

Stryker, S. (1998). 'The transgender issues': An introduction. *GLQ*, *4*, 2.

Stryker, S., & Bettcher, (2016). Introduction/trans/feminisms. *Transgender Studies Quarterly*, *3*(1–2), 5–14.

Transgender Europe. (2020, March). *Trans Rights Europe & Central Asia map & index 2019*. Transgender Europe. https://tgeu.org/trans-rights-europe-central-asia-map-index-2019/ (last accessed 3 June 2020).

Vance, C. (1989). Social construction theory: Problems in the history of sexuality. In A. van Kooten Nierkerk & T. Van Der Meer (Eds.), *Homosexuality, which homosexuality?* (pp. 13–34). An Dekker.

Vincent, B. (2018). *Transgender health: A practitioner's guide to binary and non-binary trans patient care*. Jessica Kingsley.

Whittle, S. (2013). Where did we go wrong? Feminism and trans, two teams on the same side. In S. Stryker & S. Whittle (Eds.), *The transgender studies reader* (pp. 194–203). Routledge.

Williams, R. A. (2019). *Transgressive: A trans woman on gender, feminism and politics*. Jessica Kingsley.

Wittig, M. (2003). The straight mind. In A. Jones (Ed.), *The feminism and visual studies culture reader* (pp. 130–135). Routledge (Original work published 1980).

Womensgrid. (2020, March). *Womensgrid women's groups, news, issues, vacancies*. www.womensgrid.org.uk/ (last accessed 3 June 2020).

Women's Place UK. (2020, March). *WPUK guidance on GRA consultation*. womansplaceuk.org/ wpuk-guidance-on-gra-consultation (last accessed 3 June 2020).

Young, I. M. (2005). Throwing like a girl: A phenomenology of feminine body comportment, motility, and spatiality. *Human Studies*, *3*(2), 137–156 (Original work published 1980).

Author biography

Sally Hines is Chair of Sociology at the University of Sheffield, UK. She has published widely on issues around gender diversity, gender and sexuality, feminism, recognition and citizenship. Her latest book, *Is Gender Fluid?: A Primer for the 21st Century*, was published in 2020 by Thames and Hudson. Sally is currently working on two large projects, the first looking at trans/masculine pregnancy and the second addressing young people's understandings and experiences of gender.

The ontological woman: A history of deauthentication, dehumanization, and violence

The Sociological Review Monographs
2020, Vol. 68(4) 44–60
© The Author(s) 2020
Article reuse guidelines:
sagepub.com/journals-permissions
DOI: 10.1177/0038026120938292
journals.sagepub.com/home/sor

Cristan Williams
Transgender Archive, USA

Abstract

Trans-exclusionary radical feminists (TERFs) make use of an ethical, moralistic framework to support specific rhetoric and behavior. Taken together, these form a self-referential ideology that functions to protect an essentialist ontology, which reliably harms cisgender, transgender, and feminist communities. Through an examination of the historical record of US radical feminist and TERF discourses, including first-hand accounts, this article considers how the ontological framework that inspires TERF rhetoric and behavior has functioned as a cycle of moral fulfillment, even as it necessitates the eradication of trans bodies. The article analyzes how TERF morality, rhetoric, and action construct social forms through a sexed binary by relying on an appeal to the natural, which serves to objectify ontological embodiment. It also foregrounds the different historical and contemporary positionalities of trans-exclusionary and trans-inclusive radical feminisms, and concludes with a reminder of the complementary attributes of trans feminism and radical feminism that are evidenced by decades of cooperation.

Keywords

gender ontology, morality, radical feminism, rhetoric, trans exclusion

The ontological question

In the mid-1960s, around the time that the term 'transgender' was beginning to appear in medical discourses (Williams, 2014f), groups of feminists especially in Anglophone and European contexts began excluding certain women from feminist spaces. During this period, the excluded women in the 1960s were principally lesbians, as being a lesbian was considered akin to being an un-woman: someone who had left 'the Territory of Womanhood altogether' (Koedt, 1973, p. 247). This created a constituency of feminists split in two: authenticated women who enjoyed visibility and inclusion within feminist spaces, and deauthenticated women who endured shunning and had to fight for their

Corresponding author:
Cristan Williams, Transgender Archive, P.O. Box 542287 Houston, Texas 77254-2287, USA.
Email: cristan@transadvocate.com

inclusion. This type of constituency-policing would later significantly affect transgender women, and thus offers important context for the history of deauthentication, dehumanization, and violence directed at trans women.

In 1970, in response to their exclusion, some lesbians began promoting a notion of 'woman' that could be inclusive of their experiences, describing a 'women-identified woman' as one who obtained 'her internal sense of self' from 'ideals of nurturing, community, and cooperation that she defined as female' (Gianoulis, 2015) because she was not 'considered a "real woman"' (Radicalesbians, 1970). Reflecting upon the exclusion of lesbians in feminist spaces, Rita Mae Brown, a member of both the Radicalesbians and Furies Collective, framed the experience thusly: 'those [feminist] women, most of whom were rather privileged and very bright, treated lesbians the way men treated them . . . [Betty Friedan] tossed me out and said that I was the Lavender Menace' (Makers, 2012). The deauthentication of lesbian women's experiences of selfhood to compel them to assume a social context not representative of their truths, experience, or class realities was and is an enfeebled attempt to grasp at empowerment through a form of lateral violence; an animus directed against one's peers rather than one's oppressors. Such empowerment strategies have been disruptive and destructive to constituencies of women.

During a 1979 speech, Monique Wittig (1992, p. 12) described the following experience:

> Lesbians should always remember and acknowledge how unnatural, compelling, totally oppressive, and destructive being woman was for us in the old days before the women's liberation movement. It was a political constraint, and those who resisted it were accused of not being real women. But then we were proud of it, since in the accusation there was already something like a shadow of victory: the avowal by the oppressor that woman is not something that goes without saying, since to be one, one has to be a real one.

For radical feminists like Wittig, 'woman' was not a sexed class constructed with reference to an essential or reductive attribute. Rather, 'woman' was defined by material conditions within culture. As Andrea Dworkin (1983, p. 223) argued, it is a system of material oppression that keeps 'women women in an immovable system of sex hierarchy.' Significantly, for both Wittig and Dworkin, the move to root feminism in an inherent biological, psychological, or reified ontology was to endorse the very essentialism upon which patriarchy was built:

> [A]s Andrea Dworkin emphasizes, many lesbians recently 'have increasingly tried to transform the very ideology that has enslaved us into a, religious, psychologically compelling celebration of female biological potential.' . . . What the concept 'woman is wonderful' accomplishes is that it retains for defining women the best features (best according to whom?) which oppression has granted us, and it does not radically question the categories man and woman, which are political categories and not natural givens. It puts us in a position of fighting within the class 'women' not as the other classes do, for the disappearance of our class, but for the defense of 'woman' and its reinforcement. (Wittig, 1992, pp. 13–14)

Wittig (1992, p. 2) further argued that 'there is no sex. There is but sex that is oppressed and sex that oppresses. It is oppression that creates sex and not the contrary.'

Such analysis harkens back to the very foundations of radical feminism. Before Simone de Beauvoir (2009, p. 283) asserted that: 'One is not born, but rather becomes, woman,' early radical feminists such as Ruth Herschberger (1948, pp. 3–4) noted the cultural nature of the sexed body binary:

> As important as the differences in sex organs – the books imply – is that the mature male should possess broad squared shoulders, heavy brows, straight arms, narrow hips, cylindrical thighs, blunt toes and bulging calves. The mature female is chartered by soft sloping shoulders, a short neck, bent arms, wide hips, conical thighs, small feet and knock-knees. . . . For these representatives of the basic differences between the sexes appear to have been put together by calipers and glue rather than by the shakier hands of Mother Nature.

Most cisgender people within US and European culture will, at some point in their life, undertake body modifications to better embody their sexed persona and emulate what is, we are told, a natural sexed body binary. Billions are spent each year on hair care, removal, and maintenance; cosmetic surgeries; workouts; exogenous chemicals; and 'health' and 'lifestyle' products. Many of these are targeted to cisgender population's need to embody 'the True Male and the True Female, the average, the typical, and to judge by a look around us, [the] possibly extinct' (Herschberger, 1948, p. 3). In a world where most cisgender bodies have biological attributes of both 'the True Male and the True Female,' where one in 100 people are, to one degree or another, intersex (Ainsworth, 2015), and where transgender people transition their phenotype from one category to another, trans feminists are joining early radical feminists in questioning systems predicated upon discrete, natural, and unconstructed body binaries. Such ontological questions threaten the moral landscape that sex essentialists depend on.

It is ironic then that trans-exclusionary radical feminist activists (TERFs) have invested decades into promoting a central ideological position, namely that a 'woman' is defined by her Nature and/or God-given female body experience. This is an ontological claim; an argument about the nature of being. TERFs perceive a material conflict with their ideological position when they encounter trans people. As with any identarian movement based upon rooting out impurity of form, instead of interrogating their ideology, they attack that which questions it.

The morality

Any comprehensive analysis of TERF rhetoric, morality, or behavior must begin with the political dialectic popularized by early sex-essentialist activists such as Janice Raymond, Mary Daly, and Robin Morgan. The moral reasoning promoted by Raymond in her 1979 book, *The Transsexual Empire: The Making of the She-Male*, is found in nearly all sex-essentialist anti-trans interventions, from so-called 'bathroom bills' – laws forcing transgender and intersex people to use bathrooms corresponding to their sex assigned at birth – to TERF protests at Pride parades. At the heart of the ethical calculus Raymond popularized is an ad naturam fallacy – an argument which relies on an appeal to the natural – wherein cisgender bodies are natural, whole, and therefore good, while transgender bodies are unnatural, broken, and therefore bad. While such a natural/unnatural binary is useful for

Raymond's morality, it is nonetheless a moral trap distracting the cisgender reader from the ways in which they themselves work to construct their own bodies into a binary. As Susan Stryker argued in 1994,

> You are as constructed as me; the same anarchic Womb has birthed us both. I call upon you to investigate your nature as I have been compelled to confront mine. . . . Heed my words, and you may well discover the seams and sutures in yourself. (Stryker, 2006, p. 247)

Raymond (1979, p. 17) attempted to protect her moral framework from being critiqued as simply an appeal to the morality of the natural, asserting: 'I am not arguing that what is natural is good, I am not polarizing technology against nature.' This might withstand scrutiny if it were not immediately followed by the statement, 'I am making an appeal to the integrity or harmony of the whole' (Raymond, 1979, p. 17). Raymond is not appealing to the body's natural state but, rather, its whole state. Her equivocation seems exceptionally disingenuous as she consistently critiques trans people's implicitly non-natural states through terms such as 'male-to-constructed-female' (Raymond, 1979, p. 3). While Raymond claims that her 'whole' (i.e., unaltered) body ontology is not presented as a moral opposite to that which is unnatural (and therefore bad) she nevertheless appeals to the concept of 'natural-born' woman. For instance, she takes pains to detail that which is non-'genuine' (i.e., 'synthetic') about trans people: 'Instead of developing genuine integrity, the transsexual becomes a synthetic product. Synthetic parts, such as chemical hormones and surgical artifacts of false vaginas and breasts, produce a synthetic whole' (Raymond, 1979, p. 165). Raymond's usage of 'the harmony or integrity of the whole' and 'synthetic whole' implies moral polarities. Consider the following examples:

> As alchemy treated the qualitative as quantitative in its attempts to isolate vital forces of the universe within its laboratories of matter, transsexual treatment does the same by reducing the quest for the vital forces of selfhood to the artifacts of hormones and surgical appendages . . . [producing] a surgically constructed androgyne, and thus a synthetic hybrid. (Raymond, 1979, p. 155)

> [Transsexuals] purport to be the real thing. And our suspension of disbelief in their synthetic nature is required as a moral imperative. (Raymond, 1979, p. xxiii)

This is an ad naturam moral argument. Raymond's morality even privileges her in denying humanity to trans women. Trans women are, instead, represented as 'synthetic products.' When trans people are no longer human in the sense that Raymond is, the moral imperative to respect trans people's body autonomy, identity, selfhood, and life becomes less important: 'transsexualism itself is a deeply moral question rather than a medical-technical answer. I contend that the problem of transsexualism would best be served by morally mandating it out of existence' (Raymond, 1979, p. 120). While Raymond may claim that she is not appealing to the morality of the natural, it is precisely this morality that enables her, and all sex-essentialist activists who use her moral framework, to condemn that which must be viewed as unnatural: namely, trans bodies. Raymond's ad naturam morality deems transitioned phenotypes to be inherently synthetic, violating the untransitioned body's natural 'integrity.'

In *Gender Hurts*, Sheila Jeffreys, building on Raymond, acted to protect her own stake in the morality of the natural. She states that the word 'cisgender' should not be used because it impugns the nature of her own claim to a naturally sexed body binary: claiming that 'cis' is being applied 'to all those who are not unhappy with their "gender"', Jeffreys (2014, p. 50) argues that:

> . . . the term 'cis' creates two kinds of women, those with female bodies who are labeled 'cisgender', and those with male bodies who are 'transwomen'. Women, those born female and raised as women, thus suffer a loss of status as they are relegated to being just one kind of woman and their voices will have to compete on a level playing field with the other variety, men who transgender.

For Jeffreys, this is a moral issue, and it is upon this sense of morality that she constructs her rhetoric around bodies that are sexed rather than body attributes that are sexed:

> Another reason for adherence to pronouns that indicate biology is that, as a feminist, I consider the female pronoun to be an honorific, a term that conveys respect. Respect is due to women as members of a sex caste that have survived subordination and deserve to be addressed with honour. (Jeffreys, 2014, p. 9)

In explicitly appealing to the ad naturam morality within her sexed body, Jeffreys is pronouncing her attachment to and support of behavioral norms and taboos predicated upon a coercive binary cultural system. While we generally refer to such systems as 'gender,' Jeffreys' drive to lay claim to identity labels rooted in a body binary means that she has privileged herself to disregard another's identity precisely because, within her gender system, such behavior is honorable. With an ad naturam foundation, certain ways of speaking about trans people become honorable, and as history bears witness, those who claim such moral authority do not limit themselves to words alone.

The rhetoric

The foundation of sex-essentialist discourses is a rhetoric rigged to ensure authenticity is forever withheld from trans experiences. Such rhetorical posturing might be epitomized by the so-called 'woman-born woman' rubric. The book *A to Z of the Lesbian Liberation Movement* defines woman-born women as:

> . . . women who were born women [as] opposed to male to female transgendered persons who may have, and retain, male privilege. Identifying or declaring oneself woman-born woman helps to keep 'woman only' or lesbian-separatist space pure. (Myers, 2009, p. 245)

Within the 'woman-born woman' framework, there exists a discrete 'woman' that is authentic, and one that is not. This approach was institutionalized by a minority of activists at the Michigan Womyn's Music Festival (MichFest), a woman-only feminist event held from 1976 to 2015. When surveyed by cisgender radical lesbian feminists in 1992, 73.1% of respondents said they wanted MichFest to be inclusive of trans women (Burkholder, 1993). However, for many years the festival maintained a so-called 'womyn-born-womyn' policy. In 2014, a TERF group produced a MichFest zine booklet for 'radical feminists' that claimed to offer an 'opportunity to answer the following questions: what is radical feminism; where is it going and/or where should it go; and, why and how should women join the movement?' (Pettersen, 2014, p. 1). The zine answers these questions through assertions such as:

> There are and will be plenty of women (and of course, men) who do not put women first in their advocacy work, but instead, will fall for the lies and false promises of gender liberation for 'all women' – including men who claim to be women. The transactivist movement is like an invasion of the body snatchers, only worse, because not only does it harm our ability to organize authentic safe spaces for women, but it is harmful to those who practice transgenderism too. Synthetic hormones, puberty inhibitors and genital mutilation are not methods of human liberation and health. (Pettersen, 2014, pp. 2–3)

Within TERF discourses, trans people are rhetorically constructed as the opposite of cisgender: unnatural, monstrous, and dangerous to themselves and others. This reflects Raymond's representation of the trans experience: the opposite of cisgender body integrity and spirit is transgender body mutilation and violence. Consider Raymond's (1979, pp. 103–104) argument that

> Rape, of course, is a masculinist violation of bodily integrity. All transsexuals rape women's bodies by reducing the real female form to an artifact, appropriating this body for themselves. However, the transsexually constructed lesbian-feminist violates women's sexuality and spirit, as well.

Thirty-five years later, Raymond conceded that transsexual people do not, in fact, rape cisgender women by merely existing, and explained that the term 'rape' was used at that time as a euphemism for violation (Vigo, 2014). However, even with this revision, her meaning remains clear: the existence of trans bodies is a violation of authenticated women's bodies, sexuality, and spirit.

The way in which the trans experience is represented within contemporary TERF communities is merely a reflection of their own ideological histories. Themes of violation, inauthenticity, caricature, mutilation, and monstrosity continue to feature prominently as a foundational moral dialectic which is re-enacted daily on social media and within feminist spaces. Not only are the bodies of trans people mutilated; the bodies of trans people are 'smelly,' as Jeffreys contends (Williams, 2015a), or 'decaying,' as Raymond asserts (Raymond, 1979, p. 167).

The message TERF opinion leaders send is clear: trans women represent the wolf in sheep's clothing; an enemy that could be anywhere, especially in authenticated women's spaces. For Jeffreys (2014), when a trans woman urinates in a public restroom, it is a violation of an authenticated woman's human rights. Such moral contextualization of trans women contribute to a social climate wherein trans women are publicly beaten (Amusing, 2011) or sexually assaulted by cisgender women (Williams, 2019) when merely attempting to use the restroom (see also Jones and Slater, this issue).

1970s: The West Coast Lesbian Conference and Olivia Collective controversies

Perhaps the earliest known instance of TERF aggression causing a violent rift within a feminist community occurred after Beth Elliott, a trans woman, asked to join the San Francisco Daughters of Bilitis lesbian feminist organization in 1971. Elliott was 'honest about her transition and, after heated controversy and disagreements among the members, was accepted, even becoming vice president of the local chapter' (Gallo, 2006, p. 190). The 'heated controversy' concerning her presence in the Daughters of Bilitis landed on a national stage at the 1973 West Coast Lesbian Conference (WCLC): though Elliott had helped organize the event, a TERF group calling itself the Gutter Dykes demanded that the conference become a trans-exclusionary space. The coming TERF violence was foreshadowed by a preconference phone call to Elliott. The anonymous woman on the other line asked for 'Mr. Elliott,' instructed her to not attend the event she helped organize, and ended the call with a death threat. When Elliott dared to participate, the Gutter Dykes violently disrupted the event, physically attacked trans-supportive radical feminist performers Robin Tyler and Patty Harrison, who stopped the group from bashing Elliott (Williams, 2014d), and threatened to continue the disruption unless Elliott was removed.

Some of the controversial discourse was preserved by conference organizer and Lesbian Tide Collective member Barbara McLean (1973, pp. 36–37) in her diary, later reprinted in The Lesbian Tide:

> This woman is insisting that Beth Elliott not be permitted to perform because Beth is a transsexual. Beth was on the San Francisco steering committee for the conference, a part of the original group that gave birth to the idea. . . . No. We do not, cannot relate to her as a man. We have not known her as a man.
>
> 'He has a prick! That makes him a man.'
>
> That's bullshit! Anatomy is NOT destiny! There is a contradiction here. Do we or do we not believe that anatomy is destiny?
>
> '[This is] the most bizarre and dangerous co-optation of lesbian energy and emotion [we] can imagine.'

McLean's diary also recorded her thoughts on an infamously transmisogynistic keynote address by Robin Morgan:

> [Robin Morgan] said that rather than call for unity, she chooses to call for polarity. I'm confused. . . . Especially since the announced purpose for the conference is UNITY . . . I'm angry. I somehow feel betrayed . . . Now she's trashing us over the transsexual thing. Now she's trashing EVERYONE. I can't believe she ever wrote anything about 'sister-hood.'

For the first time on a US national stage, Morgan's speech introduced numerous tropes commonly found to this day in contemporary sex-essentialist radical feminist discourse:

[A]re we yet again going to defend the male supremacist yes obscenity of male transvestitism? How many of us will try to explain away – or permit into our organizations, even, men who deliberately reemphasize gender roles, and who parody female oppression and suffering as 'camp'? No. I will not call a male 'she': thirty-two years of suffering in the androcentric society, and of surviving, have earned me the name 'woman'; one walk down the street by a male transvestite, five minutes of his being hassled (which he may enjoy), and then he dares, he dares to think he understands our pain? No. In our mothers' names and in our own, we must not call him sister. We know what's at work when whites wear blackface; the same thing is at work when men wear drag. (Morgan, 1973, cited in Ridinger, 2004, p. 204)

Even in this early example, we can observe the clash between inclusionary and exclusionary radical feminist discourse. Note that the sex-essentialist gaze produces a 'dangerous' trans caricature who is taking away women's 'energy' and 'emotion.' Such moralistic rhetoric is commonplace in contemporary sex-essentialist discourse, and for sex-essentialist activists such as TERFs, it is a functional moral imperative. Trans people are constructed as monstrous, parasitic, or even embodied caricatures of murderers. Mary Daly (1978) insisted that trans people are 'Frankenstein' constructs, invaders bent on violating women's boundaries, while Germaine Greer (1999) compared trans people to horror movie serial killers who murder their own mothers.

While Robin Morgan's anthologized version of her keynote WCLC address includes many anti-trans tropes commonly featured in contemporary sex-essentialist discourses, her comments specifically concerning Elliott are often edited out. Missing from the commonly anthologized version is the following call to action, which precipitated TERF violence at the WCLC:

[Elliott], the same man *[sic]* who, when personally begged by women not to attend this Conference, replied that if he [*sic*] were kept out he [*sic*] would bring a Federal suit against these women on the charges of 'discrimination and criminal conspiracy to discriminate. . .' Where The Man is concerned, we must not be separate fingers but one fist. I charge [Elliott] as an opportunist, an infiltrator, and a destroyer – with the mentality of a rapist. And you women at this Conference know who he [*sic*] is. Now. You can let him [*sic*] into your workshops – or you can deal with him [*sic*]. (Blasius, 1997, p. 429)

The phone call Morgan references wherein Elliott was 'begged' not to attend was the same call that began by misgendering her and ended with a death threat (Nettick & Elliott, 1996, p. 256). After Morgan's speech, a Conference-wide vote was taken on whether the WCLC should become trans-exclusionary. In *Transgender History*, Stryker (2008, p. 105) recounts that 'more than two-thirds of those present voted to allow Elliott to remain, but the anti-transsexual faction refused to accept the popular results and promised to disrupt the conference if their demands were not met.' Having received permission to stay, Elliott took to the Conference stage to play a scheduled acoustic guitar set. It was at this point that the Gutter Dykes rushed the stage intent on bashing Elliott, while other radical feminists used their own bodies to shield her from the violence.

Conference organizer and Lesbian Tide Collective founder Jeanne Córdova[1] characterized the unrest as a seismic event: 'It was like an earthquake – at first, a little earthquake. Then an 8.5' (Faderman & Timmons, 2006, p. 191). Fearing further violence and disruption, Elliott left the event. This incident was later featured in *The Transsexual Empire* as evidence of the essentially 'destructive' nature of trans women (Raymond, 1979, p. 85). However, Raymond's account erases the TERF violence, Morgan's call to have Elliott 'dealt with' and the courage of the radical feminists who used their own bodies to shield a trans woman from a public bashing.

This was not the last time that cis radical feminists stood up against TERF groups claiming to represent authentic radical feminism, nor was it the last time that such events were publicly misrepresented. Trans-inclusive radical feminist groups such as Cell 16 were similarly targeted for their inclusion of trans women. The pioneering radical feminist lesbian separatist women's music collective Olivia Records was not only trans-inclusive, but trans-affirming, and even provided trans medical care (Williams, 2014b). When Raymond learned of what she apparently perceived to be Olivia's treachery, she set in motion a series of events that culminated in an organized terrorist action against the women of Olivia and specifically, collective member and out trans woman Sandy Stone. Stone has described how events turned potentially deadly after Raymond began sending letters to feminist groups about Olivia's approach to trans inclusion:

> [W]e were getting hate mail about me. After a while the hate mail got so vicious that the mail room made a decision to not pass that mail along to me. This was vile stuff. A lot of it included death threats. . . . The death threats were directed at me, but there were violent consequences proposed for the Collective if they didn't get rid of me. (Williams, 2014b)

While organizing a tour to 'provide women's music for women in major cities,' Stone recounted that Olivia received a letter warning them of a separatist paramilitary group of women called the Gorgons in Seattle, who carried live weapons:

> We were told that when we got to town, [the Gorgons] were going to kill me. . . . We did, in fact, go to Seattle, but we went as probably the only women's music tour that was ever done with serious muscle security. They were very alert for weapons and, in fact, Gorgons did come, and they did have guns taken away from them.

> I was pants-wetting scared at that event. I was terrified. During a break between a musical number someone shouted out 'GORGONS!' and I made it from my seat at the console to under the table the console was on at something like superluminal speed. I stayed under there until it was clear that I wasn't about to be shot . . . Not that it would have done me any good to be under there. (Williams, 2014b)

Raymond (1979, pp. 101–102) herself addressed Stone's involvement in Olivia Records in *The Transsexual Empire*:

> Stone is not only crucial to the Olivia enterprise but plays a very dominant role there . . . . This only serves to enhance his [*sic*] previously dominant role and to divide women, as men [*sic*] frequently do, when they make their presence necessary and vital to women. Having produced such divisiveness, one would think that if Stone's commitment to and identification with women were genuinely woman-centered, he [*sic*] would have removed himself from Olivia and assumed some responsibility for the divisiveness.

In Raymond's account, TERF violence is erased and, in its place, appears a perverse caricature of Stone which acts as the narrative source of 'divisiveness' – a profane euphemism for the violent threats this trans-inclusive radical feminist women's collective faced. Ginny Berson, a radical feminist and co-founder of both the Furies and Olivia collectives, responded to Raymond's description:

> The anti-trans activists created some problems for us, and we went through some ugly and hard times because of them. Not because of Sandy . . . It was horrible. It was ugly and destructive and mean-spirited and just stupid. How much easier it is to attack people close to you than to focus on the patriarchy! It was painful. It felt like everything we had done was invisible and irrelevant to those people. (Williams, 2016b)

Fearing for her safety, the safety of her fellow collective members, and the future of Olivia in the face of a threatened national TERF-led boycott, Stone left the collective. However, she went on to apply the radical-to-the-root feminist ethics she learned at Olivia to what became a foundational document for both trans feminism and transgender studies: 'The Empire Strikes Back: A Posttranssexual Manifesto' (Stone, 1992).

Raymond's eventual influence was far more devastating than any violent movement to crush trans-inclusive radical feminist spaces. It was her work that helped to precipitate the end of both public and private insurance coverage of trans medical care (Williams, 2014a) during a period when employment discrimination against trans people was ruled legal (*Ulane* v. *Eastern Airlines*, 1984). If we are to place any level of confidence in research linking the lack of medical care to the high mortality rate of trans people (Zaker-Shahrak et al., 2012), we must concede that the medical system Raymond helped to pioneer resulted in unnecessary deaths.

1990s: MichFest and Camp Trans

As Raymond's policy work began to affect trans people's ability to access affirmative healthcare in the US, the woman-born woman dialectic gained increasing cultural currency. In 1991, Nancy Burkholder, a trans woman, was thrown out of MichFest. Until that point, few – including Burkholder – knew there was a no-trans policy in place. When she was ejected, cisgender lesbian feminist Janis Walworth began organizing a response that would later become known as Camp Trans.

Walworth organized a letter-writing campaign, contacted queer media outlets to get the word out about what had happened to Burkholder, and returned to MichFest in 1992 and 1993 with friends. She began distributing educational leaflets titled 'Gender Myths,' but was told by MichFest security that they should leave because they were in physical danger:

> . . . the festival security stopped by and told us that the trans women in our group would have to leave, 'for their own safety.' Tensions were definitely rising, we were told. We had scheduled to do some workshops and some folks were definitely hostile. We were told that, for our own safety, the trans women would need to leave the festival as soon as possible. (Williams, 2016a)

While the MichFest Leather Dykes said they would provide bodyguard protection for Walworth's team, it was decided that avoiding violence was the best course of action.

Thus, an outside outreach camp was created in 1993, which later came to be called, 'Camp Trans'. As with Raymond's account of the threats against Olivia Records, much of this reality is erased from Sheila Jeffreys' historical account published in *Gender Hurts*:

> [T]he siege of the festival began in 1993 when some transgender activists set up 'Camp Trans' opposite the entrance to the festival to protest the policy of not admitting self-identified transgenders. (Jeffreys, 2014, p. 167)

Gone is the reality that cisgender lesbian women began what became Camp Trans. Hidden is the threat of violence that made Camp Trans necessary as an outside entity, and gone are the brave Leather Dykes who offered to physically protect Camp Trans activists.

Also missing from Jeffreys' account is the fact that by the late 1990s, Camp Trans was largely facilitated by the Lesbian Avengers, and that, as part of the group's activities in 1999, a group of young Avengers bought a 16-year-old trans girl entry to MichFest from the festival ticket booth. The Lesbian Avengers explicitly stated that everyone in the group was from Camp Trans and some of their group was trans. Everyone in the group was sold tickets, but the moment they entered the gates, a group began trailing them shouting, 'MAN ON THE LAND!' This continued until MichFest security moved everyone to a tent where the young woman was made to stand in front of the group while TERFs spent the next two hours berating her. One adult even openly threatened her life. What follows are the Lesbian Avengers' accounts of this harrowing experience:

S. [Lesbian Avenger]:	About 10 TERFs were waiting for us when we came in. The whole 'MAN ON THE LAND!' started as soon as we walked in. I mean, at the time, we're kids, we're teenagers and these are all adults. . . . [I]t was just so fucked up. We were trying to give out t-shirts and stickers about being inclusive. But it was getting bad.
K. [trans girl in the Lesbian Avenger group]:	A huge crowd of yelling people formed around us and I started crying at that point. It got so loud that Nomy Lamm, who was performing there as part of Sister Spit, came over and stood up for us . . . The crowd and me were walked over to a tent area. . . . [T]here was a queue of people who were going to get to say whatever they wanted to say. I remember, specifically, one woman looking right at me and telling me that I needed to leave the Land as soon as possible because she had a knife and didn't know if she would be able to control herself if I was around her. . . . [A]s soon as one person stopped speaking, another would start, so nobody said or did anything about the death threat. . . . I was sobbing and [B] was holding my face close to hers, telling me that it would be over soon, but then I just checked out.

S: The moderator did nothing. It was just a mudslinging, hatred pouring out. It was just like one by one by one being like, 'You're a rapist! You're raping the Land! You're destroying womanhood! I don't know what I'm going to do to you!' – it was just violent, hatred, and I know that most of it was geared at [K]. I was up there being attacked, but I wasn't getting the brunt of it. . . . At least 30 people were allowed to speak at us, but there were around 75 under the tent, and if you included the people around the tent who were watching and listening, well over 100. (Williams, 2014e)

In keeping with the decades-long tradition of erasing trans-inclusive radical feminists' voices and experience, MichFest organizer Lisa Vogel (1999) addressed what occurred to K thusly:

A number of spontaneous gatherings developed where participants discussed and debated the presence of the Son of Camp Trans activists and their actions. Volunteer facilitators helped to structure discussions so that various viewpoints, including those of the Son of Camp Trans, could be heard.

Instead of an unruly mob that set upon itself the task of stalking, harassing, and ultimately threatening the life of a teenage trans girl, MichFest claimed that both sides of the debate could be heard. Erased too was the experience of the MichFest performer, Nomy Lamm, who used her own body to protect the trans youth:

I think I just felt really protective. I was like, 'No way! Huh uh! You're not gonna fuck with this brave [kid] who put herself on the frontlines here!' I felt angry that people couldn't see that this was a person, a vulnerable young person . . . I can't imagine how traumatic that must have been for her.

When I was on stage I said, 'I just want to say that including trans women in this space is not going to take anything away, it's going to add to it. I've been in women-only spaces that include trans women and that's been my experience.' I was surprised that a bunch of people stood up and cheered. It made me feel hopeful. (Williams, 2014e)

Naming exclusion

When considering the practical effect of TERF ideology upon both trans and feminist communities, one must consider how much effort, time, and attention is wasted in acts of lateral violence. How many organizations were fundamentally disrupted or shuttered altogether? Where might trans and feminist communities be without the animus inflicted, for decades, upon these communities?

While TERF opinion leaders would have us believe that it is trans existence that is problematic, for both trans people and feminist spaces, the historical record reveals a very different story that is long overdue in the telling. It was for that very reason an online feminist space popularized the notion that inclusive radical feminists were different from a group that called themselves radical feminist, but who primarily worked to attack the equal existence of trans people, especially in feminist spaces.

While TERFs frequently claim that trans people coined 'TERF' as a slur; a term that is 'insulting, hyperbolic, misleading, and ultimately defamatory' (Hungerford, 2013), the reality is that the acronym was popularized by cisgender feminists who were part of a radical feminist community. Viv Smythe, an early promoter of the term (Smythe, 2018), recounts how and why 'TERF' arose within feminist discourse in 2008:

> [TERF] was not meant to be insulting. It was meant to be a deliberately technically neutral description of an activist grouping. . . . We wanted a way to distinguish TERFs from other radfems with whom we engaged who were trans*-positive/neutral, because we had several years of history of engaging productively/substantively with non-TERF radfems, and then suddenly TERF comments/posts seemed to be erupting in RadFem spaces where they threadjacked dozens of discussions, and there was a great deal of general frustration about that. It is possible that one of us picked it or something similar up from an IRC [internet relay chat] discussion elsewhere and then we both adopted/adapted it for ourselves, perhaps transforming it from some other initialism into an acronym, because we both appreciate the utility of acronyms in simplifying discourse . . . distinguishing between different arms of activism is what social activist movements do as they grow and develop and react to change within and without. (Williams, 2014c)

The emerging ability to describe a difference between TERFs and other radical feminists is a response to the decades-long appropriation of radical feminism itself by a group primarily concerned with the eradication of trans bodies within society. Even as traditional media platforms continue to conflate sex-essentialist activism with radical feminism (BBC, 2019), new media platforms routinely make this much needed distinction (Peltz, 2019). TERF, as an internet-born term, offers those concerned about the erasure of trans-inclusive radical feminist history the ability to concisely distinguish between radical feminists and sex-essentialist activists who claim their anti-trans activism represents radical feminism.

Whether we are speaking of heteronormative women excluding lesbian women for not being the right kind of woman, or TERFs excluding trans women for the same reason, these supposed strategies for women's empowerment are both painful and toxic. The now decades-old sex-essentialist movement continues to justify itself through a morality it constructs with a rhetoric of denaturalization and dehumanization. This, in turn, justifies lateral violence against trans and feminist communities. The history recounted in this article reveals that such empowerment strategies are inherently disruptive and destructive to constituencies of women. TERF rhetoric, morality, and behaviors are, at their core, an attempt to exact a gain from another woman's forced loss of both humanity and authenticity.

In 1977, Dworkin (1996, p. 60) called out what she termed an 'ideological rot' within a certain type of feminism:

> . . . women have increasingly tried to transform the very ideology that has enslaved us into a dynamic, religious, psychologically compelling celebration of female biological potential. This attempted transformation may have survival value – that is, the worship of our procreative capacity as power may temporarily stay the male-supremacist hand that cradles the test tube. But the price we pay is that we become carriers of the disease we must cure.

In Dworkin's analysis, some women have toxic strategies for attempting to access empowerment. Her words are echoed by Catherine MacKinnon's radical feminist perspective:

> My views on this have not changed one iota over time, although they have become more informed as more trans people have written, spoken out, and more discussion has been engaged, and as I have met more and more out trans people (mostly transwomen) all over the world. My basic feeling, with Simone de Beauvoir, is 'one is not born, one rather becomes a woman.' How one becomes a woman is not, I think, our job to police, even as everything about that process is worth inquiry and detailed understanding. (Williams, 2015b)

When one considers these analyses from some of the foundational radical feminist opinion leaders and organizations, we find a movement that in some significant ways begins to resemble the central analysis of what has become known as 'trans feminism.' It is difficult to read some of the most influential radical feminist thinkers and not notice how their ideas about a supposedly natural sexed body binary sound a lot like trans feminist critiques of body binaries.

Conclusion

TERF activism is founded upon a sex-essentialist ideology wherein 'woman' is reducible to any number of nature or God-given (non-cultural) essential biological attributes such as chromosomes, fecundity, and bone morphology. For TERFs, the presence or absence of these essential attributes defines one's material condition so that trans men are oppressed as women in society and trans women are not. When such an analytical framework is contrasted against the radical feminist analyses of thinkers such as Wittig and MacKinnon, the foundational differences between trans-exclusionary and trans-inclusive radical feminisms could not be more stark.

The complementary attributes of trans feminism and radical feminism are evidenced in decades of cooperation and community-building between cis and trans feminists. TERFs, aided by uninformed media platforms, have enjoyed the largely unquestioned position of representing 'radical feminist' and 'lesbian feminist' analysis within traditional news outlets. Therefore, TERF, as an addition to the feminist vocabulary, constructs a much-needed lexical firewall between a group primarily concerned with the eradication of trans bodies, and a group primarily concerned with the eradication of patriarchy.

It is the need to defend an ontological woman rooted in sex-essentialism that morally animates TERF rhetoric and behaviors. The fear that women are being 'erased' (O'Neil, 2018) provides an ethical lens through which serious and immediate action to police the category 'woman' becomes moral, leading TERFs to advocate against the Equality Act (The Heritage Foundation, 2019) and the Violence Against Women Act (House Judiciary, 116th Congress, 2019) in the US. It is through this lens that TERFs dehumanize trans people and it is through this process of dehumanization that aggressive action against the existence of trans bodies becomes a moral imperative.

While radical feminist, trans, and TERF approaches share foundational analyses regarding bodies and reproduction, TERF analysis diverges from radical and trans feminisms in that it often asserts that all aspects of gender are sexist and must therefore be abolished. Leaving aside the particulars of how individuals might cease contextualizing and communicating their subjective experience of phenotype, TERFs objectify trans people as the embodiment of gender and therefore sexism itself. Instead of focusing on the systemic architecture of sexism within society, as radical and trans feminists do, TERFs primarily focus upon the eradication of that which they believe has come to embody all that is oppressive about patriarchal culture: trans people.

Funding

The author received no financial support for the research, authorship, and/or publication of this article.

Note

1. It's worth noting that Córdova later self-identified as a 'trans-butch' lesbian (Córdova, 2011). The Lesbian Avengers interviewed requested that their identities be withheld because they feared how TERF activists might react to their history being disclosed.

References

Ainsworth, C. (2015). Sex redefined. *Nature, 518*(7539), 288–291.
Amusing. (2011, April 21). *Violence in another Mc Donalds almost kills customer*. LiveLeak. www.liveleak.com/view?i=ec0_1303444048 (last accessed 22 June 2020).
BBC. (2019, May 22). *Twitter-ban feminist defends transgender views ahead of Holyrood meeting*. BBC News. www.bbc.com/news/uk-scotland-48366184 (last accessed 22 June 2020).
Blasius, M. (1997). *We are everywhere: A historical sourcebook of gay and lesbian politics*. Routledge.
Burkholder, N. (1993, April 28). *MWMF Anti-TS Awareness: 1992 Gender Survey Results*. Google Groups: soc.motss. https://groups.google.com/forum/#!msg/soc.motss/lfAgstey_SY/7rlqMQ-8FAEJ (last accessed 22 June 2020).
Córdova, J. (2011, September 6). *Chaz, Larry, and Me*. This Lesbian World. http://thislesbian-world.blogspot.com/2011/09/chaz-larry-and-me.html (last accessed 22 June 2020).
Daly, M. (1978). *Gyn/ecology: The metaethics of radical feminism*. Beacon Press.
de Beauvoir, S. (2009). *The second sex*. A. A. Knoff.
Dworkin, A. (1983). *Right-wing women*. Perigee Books.
Dworkin, A. (1996). Biological superiority: The world's most dangerous and deadly idea. In S. Jackson & S. Scott (Eds.), *Feminism and sexuality: A reader* (pp. 57–61). Columbia University Press.
Faderman, L., & Timmons, S. (2006). *Gay L.A.: A history of sexual outlaws, power politics, and lipstick lesbians*. Basic Books.
Gallo, M. M. (2006). *Different daughters: A history of the Daughters of Bilitis and the rise of the lesbian rights movement*. Carroll & Graf Publishers.
Gianoulis, T. (2015). *Woman-identified woman*. glbtq Encyclopedia Project. www.glbtqarchive.com/ssh/woman_identified_woman_S.pdf (last accessed 22 June 2020).
Greer, G. (1999). *The whole woman*. A.A. Knopf.
Herschberger, R. (1948). *Adam's rib*. Pellegrini & Cudahy.
House Judiciary, 116th Congress. (2019, March 7). *Witness statement, Julia Beck*. Congress. gov. www.congress.gov/116/meeting/house/109021/witnesses/HHRG-116-JU08-Wstate-BeckJ-20190307.pdf (last accessed 22 June 2020).

Hungerford, E. (2013, August 2). *Sex is not gender.* CounterPunch. www.counterpunch.org/2013/08/02/sex-is-not-gender/ (last accessed 22 June 2020).

Jeffreys, S. (2014). *Gender hurts: A feminist analysis of the politics of transgenderism.* Routledge.

Koedt, A. (1973). Lesbianism and feminism. In A. Koedt, E. Levine, & A. Rapone (Eds.), *Radical feminism* (pp. 246–258). Quadrangle/New York Times Book Co.

Makers. (2012, December 3). *Rita Mae Brown, author & activist.* Makers. www.makers.com/profiles/591f2763bea17771623a7f2c (last accessed 22 June 2020).

McLean, B. (1973, May 1). *Diary of a mad organizer.* The Lesbian Tide. http://revolution.berkeley.edu/assets/Conference-Report-on-Beth-Elliot-full-1.png (last accessed 22 June 2020).

Myers, J. (2009). *The A to Z of the lesbian liberation movement still the rage.* Scarecrow Press.

Nettick, G., & Elliott, B. (1996). *Mirrors: Portrait of a lesbian transsexual.* Masquerade Books.

O'Neil, T. (2018, October 22). *Radical feminists eviscerate New York Times for warning that Trump would 'erase' transgender people.* PJ Media. https://pjmedia.com/trending/radical-feminists-eviscerate-new-york-times-for-warning-that-trump-would-erase-transgender-people/ (last accessed 22 June 2020).

Peltz, M. (2019, February 26). *Right-wing media and think tanks are aligning with fake feminists who dehumanize trans people.* Media Matters for America. www.mediamatters.org/tucker-carlson/right-wing-media-and-think-tanks-are-aligning-fake-feminists-who-dehumanize-trans (last accessed 22 June 2020).

Pettersen, T. (2014). *Sparks from the flame: Radical feminist greetings & messages for MichFest 2014.* we.riseup.net. https://we.riseup.net/assets/324706/Sparks-From-the-Flame-Thistle-Petterson.pdf (last accessed 22 June 2020).

Radicalesbians. (1970). *The woman-identified woman.* History is a weapon. www.historyisaweapon.com/defcon1/radicalesbianswoman.html (last accessed 22 June 2020).

Raymond, J. (1979). *The transsexual empire: The making of the she-male.* Beacon Press.

Ridinger, R. B. (2004). *Speaking for our lives: Historic speeches and rhetoric for gay and lesbian rights (1892–2000).* Harrington Park Press.

Smythe, V. (2018, November 28). I'm credited with having coined the word 'Terf'. Here's how it happened. *The Guardian.* www.theguardian.com/commentisfree/2018/nov/29/im-credited-with-having-coined-the-acronym-terf-heres-how-it-happened (last accessed 22 June 2020).

Stone, S. (1992). The empire strikes back: A posttranssexual manifesto. *Camera Obscura: Feminism, Culture, and Media Studies, 10*(2(29)), 150–176.

Stryker, S. (2006). My words to Victor Frankenstein above the village of Chamonix: Performing transgender rage. In S. Stryker & S. Whittle (Eds.), *The transgender studies reader* (pp. 244–256). Routledge.

Stryker, S. (2008). *Transgender history.* Seal Press.

Stryker, S. & Whittle, S. (Eds.). (2006). *The transgender studies reader.* Routledge.

The Heritage Foundation. (2019, January 28). *The inequality of the Equality Act: Concerns from the left.* www.heritage.org/event/the-inequality-the-equality-act-concerns-the-left (last accessed 22 June 2020).

Ulane v. *Eastern Airlines*, 84-1431. (1984, August 29). Transgender Law and Policy Institute. www.transgenderlaw.org/cases/ulane.htm (last accessed 22 June 2020).

Vigo, J. (2014, August 25). *Dispelling fictions and disrupting hashtags.* Counterpunch. www.counterpunch.org/2014/08/25/dispelling-fictions-and-disrupting-hashtags/ (last accessed 22 June 2020).

Vogel, L. (1999, August 24). *Festival reaffirms commitment to Womyn-Born space.* Michigan Womyn's Music Festival. http://eminism.org/michigan/19990824-vogel.txt (last accessed 22 June 2020).

Williams, C. (2014a, September 18). *Fact checking Janice Raymond: The NCHCT report.* The TransAdvocate. www.transadvocate.com/fact-checking-janice-raymond-the-nchct-report_n_14554.htm (last accessed 22 June 2020).

Williams, C. (2014b, August 16). *TERF hate and Sandy Stone.* The TransAdvocate. www.transadvocate.com/terf-violence-and-sandy-stone_n_14360.htm (last accessed 22 June 2020).

Williams, C. (2014c, March 15). *TERF: what it means and where it came from.* The TransAdvocate. www.transadvocate.com/terf-what-it-means-and-where-it-came-from_n_13066.htm (last accessed 22 June 2020).

Williams, C. (2014d, August 17). *That time TERFs beat RadFems for protecting a trans woman from their assault.* The TransAdvocate. www.transadvocate.com/that-time-terfs-beat-radfems-for-protecting-a-trans-woman-from-assault_n_14382.htm (last accessed 22 June 2020).

Williams, C. (2014e, September 2). *The Michigan Womyn's Music Festival: The historic RadFem vs TERF vs Trans fight.* The TERFs. http://theterfs.com/2014/09/02/the-michigan-womyns-music-festival-the-historic-radfem-vs-terf-vs-trans-fight/ (last accessed 22 June 2020).

Williams, C. (2014f). Transgender. *Transgender Studies Quarterly, 1*(1–2), 232–234.

Williams, C. (2015a, January 28). *Sex essentialism: TERF patriarchy and smelly vaginas.* The TransAdvocate. www.transadvocate.com/sex-essentialism-terfs-and-smelly-vaginas_n_14924.htm (last accessed 22 June 2020).

Williams, C. (2015b, April 7). *Sex, gender, and sexuality: The TransAdvocate interviews Catharine A. MacKinnon.* The TransAdvocate. www.transadvocate.com/sex-gender-and-sexuality-the-transadvocate-interviews-catharine-a-mackinnon_n_15037.htm (last accessed 22 June 2020).

Williams, C. (2016a, January 16). *Questioning sex essentialism as feminist practice: An interview with Janis Walworth.* The Conversations Project. http://radfem.transadvocate.com/questioning-sex-essentialism-as-feminist-practice-an-interview-with-janis-walworth/ (last accessed 22 June 2020).

Williams, C. (2016b, February 15). *Sex essentialist violence and radical inclusion: An interview with Sandy Stone.* The Conversations Project. http://radfem.transadvocate.com/sex-essentialist-violence-and-radical-inclusion-an-interview-with-sandy-stone/ (last accessed 22 June 2020).

Williams, C. (2019, January 9). *Two cis women sexually assault trans woman in public bathroom.* The TransAdvocate. www.transadvocate.com/two-cis-women-sexually-assault-trans-woman-in-public-bathroom_n_25820.htm (last accessed 22 June 2020).

Wittig, M. (1992). *The straight mind and other essays.* Beacon Press.

Zaker-Shahrak, A., Chi, L. W., Isaac, R., & Tescher, J. (2012, April 13). *Economic impact assessment gender nondiscrimination in health insurance.* State of California Department of Insurance. https://transgenderlawcenter.org/wp-content/uploads/2013/04/Economic-Impact-Assessment-Gender-Nondiscrimination-In-Health-Insurance.pdf (last accessed 22 June 2020).

Author biography

Cristan Williams has founded numerous social service programs, community centers, and the Transgender Archive in Houston, Texas. She is the author of short stories, academic papers, and numerous longform articles. She has served on numerous public health boards, received numerous awards for her advocacy, and presented at universities throughout the US.

Whose feminism is it anyway? The unspoken racism of the trans inclusion debate

The Sociological Review Monographs
2020, Vol. 68(4) 61–70
© The Author(s) 2020
Article reuse guidelines:
sagepub.com/journals-permissions
DOI: 10.1177/0038026120934685
journals.sagepub.com/home/sor

Emi Koyama
Independent scholar, USA

Abstract
This essay was first published on Emi Koyama's website eminism.org in 2000. Koyama examines how constructs of universal womanhood have operated to exclude many from feminist spaces. Much of the language surrounding trans identities and bodies has changed in the 20 years since its authorship. Yet, the central tensions, illustrated through a critical account of the Michigan Womyn's Music Festival's trans-exclusion policy, remain. Koyama's powerful argument that 'no-penis' policies are inherently racist and classist continues to offer an important challenge to white feminists, be they trans or cis.

Keywords
classism, feminism politics, Michigan Womyn's Music Festival, racism, trans inclusion

I

I have never been interested in getting myself into the mud wrestling of the whole 'Michigan' situation (i.e. the debate over the inclusion of trans people in Michigan Womyn's Music Festival). But I have become increasingly alarmed in the recent months by the pattern of 'debate' between white middle-class women who run 'women's communities' and white middle-class trans activists who run the trans movement. It is about time someone challenged the unspoken racism, which this whole discourse is founded upon.

The controversy publicly erupted in 1991, when organizers of the Michigan Womyn's Music Festival expelled a transsexual woman from the campground, or 'The Land,' announcing that the festival is open only to 'womyn-born-womyn.' Next year, a small group of transsexual activists gathered in front of the Festival entrance to protest the policy. According to Davina Anne Gabriel, then the editor of *TransSisters: the Journal of Transsexual Feminism*, the 'stated intent [of the protest] from the very beginning was to

Corresponding author:
Emi Koyama.
Email: emi@eminism.org

persuade the organizers to change the festival policy to allow postoperative – but not preoperative – male-to-female transsexuals to attend.'[1] Based on the survey Gabriel and others conducted in 1992, they argued that a majority of festival participants would support such a policy change, while the same majority would oppose inclusion of 'preoperative' transsexual women.[2]

If that was the case in 1992, the debate certainly expanded by 1994, when the protest came to be known as 'Camp Trans.' 'In the first Camp Trans, the argument wasn't just between us and the festival telling us we weren't really women. It was also between the post-ops in camp telling the pre-ops they weren't real women!' says Riki Anne Wilchins, the executive director of GenderPAC. According to an interview, Wilchins advocates the inclusion of 'anyone who lives, or has lived, their normal daily life as a woman' including FtM trans people and many 'pre-operative' transsexual women.[3] Or, as Gabriel alleged, Wilchins made a 'concerted effort' to 'put herself in charge' of the protest and to 'force us ["post-operative" transsexual women] to advocate for the admission of preoperative MtF transsexuals.' Gabriel reported that she 'dropped out of all involvement in the "transgender movement" in disgust' as she felt it was taking the 'hostile and belligerent direction,' as symbolized by Wilchins.[4]

For several years since its founding in 1994, GenderPAC and its executive director Wilchins were the dominant voice within the trans movement. 'Diverse and feuding factions of the transgender community were brought together and disagreements set aside for the common good,' JoAnn Roberts describes of the formation of the organization. But like Gabriel, many initial supporters of GenderPAC became critical of it as Wilchins shifted its focus from advocating for rights of transgender people to fighting all oppressions based on genders including sexism and heterosexism. Dissenters founded alternative political organizations specifically working for trans people's rights.[5]

Similarly, five transsexual women including Gabriel released a joint statement just a few days before the Michigan Womyn's Music Festival 2000 criticizing both festival organizers and Wilchins as 'untenable, anti-feminist, and ultimately oppressive of women, both transsexual and non-transsexual.' Wilchins' tactics were too adversarial, confrontational and disrespectful to women, they argued. Non-transsexual and 'post-op' transsexual women alike 'deserve the opportunity to gather together in a safe space, free of male genitals,' because 'male genitals can be so emblematic of male power and sexual dominance that their presence at a festival . . . is inappropriate.' They further stated that 'people with male genitals who enter the festival risk offending and oppressing other attendees' (Elliot et al., 2000).

'We acknowledge that a post-op/no-penis policy is not perfect,' admitted the writers of the statement. 'This policy cannot address issues of race and class: specifically, the exclusion of women, especially women of colour, who are not able to afford sex reassignment surgery.' But it nonetheless is 'the best and fairest policy possible,' they argue, because it 'balances inclusion of transsexual women with legitimate concerns for the integrity of women's culture and safe women's space' (Elliot et al., 2000). Their pretence of being concerned about racism and classism betrays itself when they used it as a preemptive shield against criticisms they knew they would encounter.

As for the gender liberation philosophy of Wilchins, they stated that they agreed with her position that 'freedom of gender expression for all people is important.' Yet, 'as feminists,' they 'resent anyone attempting to co-opt' the 'love and creativity of the sisterhood of women' for 'a competing purpose' such as Wilchins' (Elliot et al., 2000). The pattern is clear: when they say 'feminism' and 'sisterhood,' it requires that anything other than 'the celebration of femaleness' – i.e. racial equality, economic justice and freedom of gender expression – to be set aside.

Jessica Xavier, one of the statement signatories, once wrote: 'We too want the safe space to process and to heal our own hurting. We too want to seek solace in the arms of our other sisters, and to celebrate women's culture and women's music with other festi-goers' (Xavier, 1999). Has it never occurred to her that her working-class and/or non-white 'sisters' might need (and deserve) such 'space' at least as much as she does?

II

While it was Maxine Feldman who performed openly as a radical lesbian feminist musi-cian for the first time, it was the success of Alix Dobkin's 1973 album *Lavender Jane Loves Women* that proved that there 'was a wide audience for such entertainment' and helped launch the unique culture of 'women's music' (Faderman, 1991). 'My music comes from and belongs to women experiencing women. So does my life . . . Long live Dyke Nation! Power to the women!' declared Dobkin in the cover of her debut album.[6]

The history of the trans inclusion/exclusion debate within women's music culture is almost as old as the history of the women's music culture itself. Olivia Records, the 'leader in women's music,' was founded in 1973, which stimulated the nationwide pro-liferation of highly political large annual women's music festivals, modelled after the hippie be-ins of the 1960s (Faderman, 1991). It was only three years later that they came under heavy attack for refusing to fire the recording engineer who was found to be a male-to-female transsexual lesbian. The series of 'hate mail, threats of assault, and death threats' intensified especially after the publication in 1979 of Janice Raymond's *The Transsexual Empire: The Making of the She-Male*, which described the engineer as a dominating man, eventually forcing her to leave the collective (Califia, 1997).

Feminist resistances to the inclusion of transsexual women in the women-only space are, on the surface, rationalized on the basis that transsexual women are fundamentally different from all other women due to the fact they were raised with male privilege. Because of their past as boys or men, they are viewed as a liability for the physical and emotional safety for other women. When radical feminism viewed sexual violence against women not as isolated acts by a small number of criminals, but as a social enforcer of male dominance and heteronormativity, a woman's concern for her safety became almost unquestionable (Brownmiller, 1975). The effectiveness of Raymond's malicious argument that 'all transsexuals rape women's bodies by reducing the female form to an artifact' was no surprise, given the context of the building momentum for the feminist holy war against violence against women (Raymond, 1979, p. 104).

Defenders of the 'womyn-born-womyn' policy argue that transsexual women who truly value the women's movement and culture should respect the festival policies by refraining from entering the Land. 'Just as many Womyn of Colour express the need for "room to breathe" they gain in Womyn-of-Colour space away from the racism that inevi-tably appears in interactions with a white majority, womyn born womyn still need and value that same "room to breathe",' argued Lisa Vogel, the owner of the Michigan Womyn's Music Festival.[7] This exact pattern of argument is extremely common in lesbian and/or feminist publications – complete with the comment about how much they respect women of colour space and how transsexual women should do the same for 'womyn-born-womyn.' 'I've spent years educating other white festigoers about honouring the workshops and spaces that are planned for women of colour only . . . It grieves me to see "progressive" folks attacking an event that is sacred for women-born-women,' wrote a reader of *Lesbian Connection*, for example.[8]

However, another reader of *Lesbian Connection* disagrees with this logic: 'If women born with vaginas need their space, why can't Michigan provide "women-born-women" only space the way they provide women-of-colour only space' instead of excluding transsexual women from the entire festival?[9] Logically, it would not made any sense to exclude an entire subgroup of women from a women's festival unless, of course, the organizers are willing to state on the record that transsexual women are not women.

Another flaw of the 'respect' argument is that 'women of colour only' spaces generally welcome women of colour who happen to have skins that are pale enough to pass as white. If the inclusion of pale-skinned 'women of colour' who have a limited access to white privilege is not questioned, why should women who may have passed as boys or men?

Radical feminism, in its simplest form, believes that women's oppression is the most pervasive, extreme and fundamental of all social inequalities regardless of race, class, nationality, and other factors (Crow, 2000). It is only under this assumption that the privilege transsexual women are perceived to have (i.e. male privilege) can be viewed as far more dangerous to others than any other privileges (i.e. being white, middle-class, etc.)

But such ranking of oppressions and simplistic identity politics is inherently oppressive to people who are marginalized due to multiple identities (e.g. women of colour) or creolized identities (e.g. mixed-race people). Cherríe Moraga wrote: 'In this country, lesbianism is a poverty – as is being brown, as is being a woman, as is being just plain poor. The danger lies in ranking the oppressions. The danger lies in failing to acknowledge the specificity of the oppression' (Moraga, 1981). Susan Brownmiller's failure to acknowledge how rape charges are historically used as a political weapon against the black communities and Andrea Dworkin's uncritical acceptance of the popular stereotypes about Hispanic communities being characterized by 'the cult of machismo' and 'gang warfare' illustrate this danger well (Eisenstein, 1983).

Combahee River Collective, the collective of Black lesbians, discussed the problem with the feminist identity politics in its famous 1977 statement. They wrote 'Although we are feminists and lesbians, we feel solidarity with progressive Black men and do not advocate the fractionalization that white women who are separatists demand . . . We reject the stance of lesbian separatism because it is not a viable political analysis or strategy for us' (Combahee River Collective, 1977). It is not simply that white radical feminists happened to be racist; rather, the series of assumptions behind radical lesbian feminism (e.g. women's oppression is the most pervasive and fundamental) was faulty as it privileged 'those for whom that position is the primary or only marked identity' (Duggan, 1995, p. 184).

Decades of protests by women of colour failed to educate those who have vested interest in maintaining this racist feminist arrogance. Here is an example: Alix Dobkin wrote in 1998 'fresh scare tactics were essential to turn a generation of "Lesbians" and "Dykes" against each other . . . when that failed to wipe us out, they tried "racist"' (Dobkin, 1998).

In other words, Dobkin attributed the accusation of racism to the patriarchy's attempt to 'wipe' lesbians out and *not* to the legitimate concerns of women of colour, effectively accusing these women of colour of conspiring with the patriarchy. 'What is the theory behind racist feminism?' asked Audre Lorde (Lorde, 1984b, p. 112). She argued, 'many white women are heavily invested in ignoring the real differences' because 'to allow women of Colour to step out of stereotypes . . . threatens the complacency of those women who view oppression only in terms of sex' (Lorde, 1984c, p. 118).

III

I used to think that feminists' reluctance to accepting transsexual women was arising from their constant need to defend feminism against the patriarchy as well as from the plain old fear of the unknown. I confess that I have given transphobic feminists far greater benefit of the doubt than I would to any other group of people exercising oppressive and exclusionary behaviours, and I regret that my inaction and silent complacency contributed to the maintenance of the culture that is hostile to transsexual people.

This realization came to me, ironically, during a panel presentation in spring 2000 by Alix Dobkin and several other lesbian-feminists about sharing 'herstory' of lesbian feminism. The room was packed with women in their 40s and up, and nearly all of them appeared white and middle-class. I was already feeling intimidated by the time the presentation began because everyone seemed to know everyone else except for me, but my level of fear and frustration kept piling up as the evening progressed.

The presentation was all about how great the women's community was back in the 70s, when it was free from all those pesky transsexuals, S/M practitioners and sex radicals (or so they think). I heard the room full of white women applauding in agreement with the comment that 'everyone trusted each other' and 'felt so safe regardless of race,' clearly talking about how she as a white woman did not feel threatened by the presence of women of colour, and it nauseated me. Another woman talked about how great it was that a private women's bar she used to hang out at had a long stairway before the door to keep an eye on potential intruders, and I felt very excluded myself because of my disability. I had never felt so isolated and powerless in a feminist or lesbian gathering before.

The highlight was when the sole Black woman stood up and said that she felt like an outsider within the lesbian-feminist movement. The whole room went silent, as if they were waiting for this uncomfortable moment to simply pass without anyone having to take responsibility. Feeling the awkward pressure, the Black woman added 'but it was lesbians who kept the American discussions on racism and classism alive,' which subsequently was met with a huge applaud from the white women. I kept wanting to scream 'It was lesbians of colour and working class lesbians who kept them alive, and you white middle-class lesbians had less than nothing to do with it,' but I did not have the courage to do so and it deeply frustrated me.[10]

Obviously, many lesbian-feminists – the same people who continue to resist trans-sexual people's inclusion in 'women's' communities – have not learned anything from the vast contributions of women of colour, working class women, women with disabilities, etc. even though they had plenty of opportunities to do so in the past few decades. It is not that there was not enough information about women of colour; they simply did not care that they are acting out racism, because they have vested interest in maintaining such a dynamic. The racist feminist that Audre Lorde so eloquently denounced is still alive.

I no longer feel that continued education about trans issues within women's communities would change their oppressive behaviours in any significant degree, unless they are actually willing to change. It is not the lack of knowledge or information that keeps oppression going; it is the lack of feminist compassion, conscience and principle that is.

Speaking from the perspective and the tradition of lesbians of colour, most if not all rationales for excluding transsexual women is not only transphobic, but also racist. To argue that transsexual women should not enter the Land because their experiences are different would have to assume that all other women's experiences are the same, and this is a racist assumption. Even the argument that transsexual women have experienced some degree of male privilege should not bar them from our communities once we realize that not all women are equally privileged or oppressed. To suggest that the safety of the Land would be compromised overlooks, perhaps intentionally, ways in which women can act out violence and discrimination against each other. Even the argument that 'the presence of a penis would trigger the women' is flawed because it neglects the fact that white skin is just as much a reminder of violence as a penis. The racist history of lesbian-feminism has taught us that any white woman making these excuses for one oppression have made and will make the same excuse for other oppressions such as racism, classism, and ableism.

IV

As discussed earlier, many lesbian-feminists are eager to brag how much respect they have toward the needs of women of colour to hold 'women of colour only' spaces. But having a respect for such a space is very different from having a commitment to anti-racism. The former allows white women to displace the responsibility to fight racism onto women of colour, while the latter forces them to confront their own privileges and racist imprinting.

Do white feminists really understand why women of colour need their own space? They claim they do, but judging from the scarcity of good literature written by white feminists on racism, I have to wonder. 'It was obvious that you were dealing with non-european women, but only as victims' of the patriarchy, wrote Audre Lorde in her famous letter to Mary Daly. White women's writings about women of colour frequently lose 'sight of the many varied tools of patriarchy' and 'how those tools are used by women without awareness against each other' (Lorde, 1984a, p. 69). White feminists often happily acknowledge ways in which white men's racism hurt women of colour (through poverty, prostitution, pornography, etc.) to pretend that they are advocates of women of colour, but often use it to absolve their own responsibility for racism. It is, then, no wonder that those who claim to 'respect' the space for women of colour simultaneously employ racist rhetoric against transsexual people without having to face their own contradictions.

Similarly, the transsexual women who wrote the 'statement' did not see any contradiction in expressing concerns about racism and classism in one sentence and endorsing the racist and classist resolution in the next. Like white middle-class feminists, these transsexual women felt perfectly justified to absolve their responsibility to confront racism and classism and then call it feminist.

To make things more complicated, some trans activists who are politically more savvy support a 'womyn-born-womyn' policy or at least accept it as an acceptable feminist position. Kate Bornstein, for example, 'encourages everyone to engage in mutually respectful dialogue, without specifying what outcome might be desirable or possible,' because 'exclusion by lesbian separatists' cannot be considered oppressive when lesbians do not have very much 'economic and social resources' (Bornstein, 1994, p. 83). Another transsexual woman, in a private conversation, told me that she would rather be excluded from the Land altogether than risk the possibility of a male entry under the pretence of being transsexual. While I appreciate their supposedly feminist good intentions, I must remind them that their arguments support and reinforce the environment in which white middle-class women's oppression against women of colour and working class women are trivialized or tolerated. I must remind them it is never feminist when some women are silenced and sacrificed to make room for the more privileged women.

V

White middle-class transsexual activists are spending so much of their energy trying to convince white middle-class lesbians that they are just like other women, and thus are not a danger to other women on the Land. 'We are your sisters,' is their typical plea. Supporters of transsexual women repeat this same sentiment: 'As a lesbian who has interacted with the local trans community, I can assure you that womyn-born-womyn have nothing to fear from MtF transsexuals,' wrote one woman.[11] But it is time that we stop pretending that transsexual women are 'just like' other women or that their open inclusion will not threaten anybody or anything. The very existence of transsexual people, whether or not they are politically inclined, is highly threatening in a world that essentializes, polarizes and dichotomizes genders, and the Michigan Womyn's Music Festival and lesbian-feminism are not immune from it.

The kind of threat I am talking about is obviously not physical, but social, political, and psychological. It is the same kind of threat bisexual and pansexual politics present to gay identity politics and mixed-race people present to Black Nationalism. Much has been written about the transformative potential of transsexual existence – how it destabilizes the essentialist definitions of gender and exposes the constructedness of essentialism.[12]

In the 'women's communities,' transsexual existence is particularly threatening to white middle-class lesbian-feminists because it exposes the unreliableness of the body as a source of their identities and politics, and the fallacy of women's universal experiences and oppressions. These valid criticisms against feminist identity politics have been made by women of colour and working class women all along, and white middle-class women have traditionally dismissed them by arguing that they are patriarchal attempts to trivialize women's oppression and bring down feminism as Dobkin did. The question of transsexual inclusion has pushed them to the position of having to defend the reliableness of such absurd body elements as chromosomes as the source of political affiliation as well as the universal differences between transsexual women and non-transsexual women, a nonsensical position fraught with many bizarre contradictions.

It is my guess that transsexual women know this intrinsically, and that is why they feel it is necessary to repeatedly stress how non-threatening they really are. By pretending that they are 'just like' other women, however, they are leaving intact the flawed and unspoken lesbian-feminist assumption that *continuation of struggle against sexism requires silent compliance with all other oppressions*.

Like Gloria Anzaldúa's 'New Mestiza,' transsexual people occupy the borderland where notions of masculinity and femininity collide. 'It is not a comfortable territory to live in, this place of contradictions.' But speaking from the borderland, from its unique 'shifting and multiple identity and integrity,' is where transsexual activists can find the most authentic strength.

The borderland analogy is not meant to suggest that transsexual people are somewhere between male and female. Rather, the space they occupy is naturally and rightfully theirs, as the actual Texas–Mexico borderlands belong to Chicano/as, and I am calling attention to the unnaturalness of the boundary that was designed to keep them out. 'A borderland is a vague and undetermined place created by the emotional residue of an unnatural boundary,' Anzaldúa wrote, 'it is in a constant state of transition. The prohibited and forbidden are its inhabitants' (Anzaldúa, 1987). The fact that many transsexual women have experienced some form of male privilege is not a burden to their feminist consciousness and credibility, but an asset – that is, provided they have the integrity and conscience to recognize and confront this and other privileges they may have received.

In her piece about racism and feminist identity politics, Elliott Femyne bat Tzedek discusses how threatening boundary-crossings are to those in the position of power and privilege. 'Think about the phrase . . . "You people make me sick." Think of how the person screaming this phrase may commit physical violence against what so disturbs him/her . . . those in power do actually feel sick, feel their lives being threatened . . . Men protecting male power have a much clearer view than Feminists do of exactly how threatening crossing gender is' (bat Tzedek, 1999).[13]

By the same token, feminists who are vehemently anti-transsexual have a much better understanding of how threatening transsexual existence is to their flawed ideology than do transsexuals themselves. The power is in consciously recognizing this unique positionality and making connections to the contributions of women of colour and other groups of women who have been marginalized within the feminist movement. With this approach, I am confident that transsexual women, along with all other women who live complex lives, will be able to advance the feminist discussions about power, privilege and oppression.

Acknowledgement

A version of this article has been published in *The Transgender Studies Reader* (2006, Routledge, pp. 698–705), ed. by Susan Stryker and Stephen Whittle.

Funding

The author received no financial support for the research, authorship, and/or publication of this article.

Notes

1. Davina Anne Gabriel, from an open letter to *Lesbian Connection* dated 27 January 2000. Distributed online.
2. Phrases 'pre-operative' and 'post-operative' are put inside quotation marks (except where it is part of someone else's quote) because it is my belief that such distinction is irrelevant, classist and MtF-centric (i.e. disregards experiences of FtM trans people). I believe that such over-emphasis on genital shape is deeply oppressive to trans people and contributes to the suppression and erasure of intersex people.
3. *InYourFace* interview of Riki Anne Wilchins. Distributed as a press release from GenderPAC on 18 August 1999.
4. Gabriel, from the open letter.
5. JoAnn Roberts, 'The Next Wave: Post-Reform Transgender Activism' (2000), distributed online.
6. *Lavender Jane Loves Women* (1973), as reprinted in the re-mastered CD edition.
7. Michigan Womyn's Music Festival press release on 24 August 1999.
8. From *Lesbian Connection*, Jan./Feb. issue, 2000.
9. Ibid.
10. These comments were made at a 'herstory sharing session' hosted by Lesbian Community Project in Portland, Oregon, in early May.
11. From Lesbian Connection.
12. For example, see Garber, M. (1993). Spare parts: The surgical construction of gender. In H. Abelove, M. A. Barale, & D. M. Halperin (Eds.), *The lesbian and gay studies reader* (pp. 321–336). Routledge.
13. Personally, I was surprised to find this article in a radical feminist publication, especially since the same issue of *Rain and Thunder* also published a very hurtful column by Alix Dobkin that appears to endorse violence against transsexual women in women's restrooms.

References

Anzaldúa, G. (1987). *Borderlands/La frontera: The new mestiza*. Aunt Lute Books.
Bat Tzedek, E. F. (1999). Identity politics and racism: Some thoughts and questions. *Rain and Thunder: A Radical Feminist Journal of Discussion and Activism*, 5.
Bornstein, K. (1994). *Gender outlaws: On men, women, and the rest of us*. Routledge.
Brownmiller, S. (1975). *Against our will: Men, women and rape*. Simon & Schuster.
Califia, P. (1997). *Sex changes: The politics of transgenderism*. Cleis Press.
Combahee River Collective. (1977). *A black feminist statement*. https://americanstudies.yale.edu/sites/default/files/files/Keyword%20Coalition_Readings.pdf (accessed 11 November 2019).
Crow, B. (2000). Introduction. In B. Crow (Ed.), *Radical feminism: A documentary reader*. NYU Press.
Dobkin, A. (1998, April 15). *Passover revisited*. Chicago Outlines. www.feminist-reprise.org/docs/passoveralix.htm (accessed 6 May 2020).
Duggan, L. (1995). *Queering the state*. In L. Duggan & N. D. Hunter (Eds.), *Sex wars* (pp. 179–193). Routledge:
Eisenstein, H. (1983). *Contemporary feminist thought*. George Allen & Unwin.

Elliot, B., Gabriel, D. A., Lawrence, A., Smith, G. A., & Xavier, J. (2000). *The Michigan Women's Music Festival and transsexual women: A statement by transsexual women.* http://eminism. org/michigan/20000809-elliott.txt (accessed 6 May 2020).

Faderman, L. (1991). *Odd girls and twilight lovers: A history of lesbian life in twentieth-century America.* Colombia University Press.

Lorde, A. (1984a). An open letter to Mary Daly. *Sister outsider: Essays and speeches* (pp. 66–71). Crossing Press.

Lorde, A. (1984b). The master's tools will never dismantle the master's house. *Sister outsider: Essays and speeches* (pp. 110–113). Crossing Press.

Lorde, A. (1984c). Age, race, class, and sex: Women redefining difference. *Sister outsider: Essays and speeches* (pp. 114–123). Crossing Press.

Moraga, C. (1981). La güera. In C. Moraga & G. Anzaldúa (Eds.), *This bridge called my back* Persephone Press.

Raymond, J. (1979). *The transsexual empire: The making of the she-male.* Beacon Press.

Xavier, J. (1999). *Trans am: The phantom menace at Michigan.* https://groups.google.com/ forum/#!msg/alt.support.srs/xXtG_BxYrqU/yGiBNNb0kckJ (accessed 6 May 2020).

Author biography

Emi Koyama is a multi-issue social justice activist and writer synthesizing feminist, Asian, survivor, dyke, queer, sex worker, intersex, genderqueer, and crip politics, as these factors, while not a complete descriptor of who she is, all impacted her life. Emi is putting the emi back in feminism at www.eminism.org.

Feminism will be trans-inclusive or it will not be: Why do two cis-hetero woman educators support transfeminism?

The Sociological Review Monographs
2020, Vol. 68(4) 71–88
© The Author(s) 2020
Article reuse guidelines:
sagepub.com/journals-permissions
DOI: 10.1177/0038026120934686
journals.sagepub.com/home/sor

María Victoria Carrera-Fernández
Faculty of Educational Sciences, Universidade de Vigo, Spain

Renée DePalma
Faculty of Educational Sciences, Universidade da Coruña, Spain

Abstract

As two cis-hetero woman feminist educators, we provide an educator's perspective on trans-exclusionary radical feminist (TERF) discourses. We begin by discussing the heterosexual matrix and the gender violence that it produces in schools as well as other socializing institutions. The socially constructed sexual binary constrains identity production to adhere to the heteronormative, at the same time excluding those who transgress this normativity. We continue by reviewing how schools are particularly significant spaces for these early social interactions, but the social discourses enacted in educational contexts mirror those of broader society. We then critically analyse some of the increasingly belligerent popular discourses promoted by TERF groups since the 1970s, appropriating feminist discourses to produce arguments that contradict basic premises of feminism. We trace possibilities for a collaborative response by reinforcing alliances between transfeminism and other feminist movements. Finally, as teacher-educators, we highlight among these a critical (queer) pedagogy that incorporates trans* experience as part of a broader feminist educational agenda: to contribute to the creation of a more equitable society based on critical reflections on the gender normative. Such a pedagogy not only rejects trans-exclusionary discourses that serve to reinforce hierarchies and promote violence, but embraces trans* experience as a productive educational resource for understanding human diversity. Human experience that challenges the sexual binary can help educators to critically question the heteronormative and to broaden our understandings; in the words of Eric Rofes, drawing upon 'status queer' to 'rethink our efforts and our role in either maintaining or radically transforming the status quo'.

Corresponding author:
María Victoria Carrera-Fernández, Faculty of Educational Sciences, Universidade de Vigo, Vigo 32004, Spain.
Email: mavicarrera@uvigo.es

Keywords
critical pedagogy, heteronormative, queer pedagogy, TERF, transfeminism

Heteronormativity and gender violence

With second wave feminism, sexuality was no longer a personal matter; it was recognized as a political issue. Simone de Beauvoir's *The Second Sex*, published in France in 1949 and translated into English in 1953, was particularly influential. The celebrated phrase 'One is not born woman, one becomes one' (de Beauvoir, 1949/1987, p. 13) calls into question the immutability of gender, with important consequences for feminism: since both femininity and masculinity are constructed, so too is the inequality and inferiority of women in a patriarchal society. De Beauvoir does away with the anatomical basis for subordination: man being the norm and woman 'the Other' lacking in identity and seeking recognition via the (male) norm (Lameiras et al., 2013).

Nevertheless, as Judith Butler (1990) reminds us, de Beauvoir's 'becoming' a woman still leaves room to believe that there is something given and natural that pre-exists us (sex), as well as something cultural and constructed that constitutes men and women as hierarchically different (gender). The category of 'woman', presented as natural, immanent and pre-discursive, perpetuates problematic dualities – mind–body, nature–nurture. Nearly a half-century later, Butler takes de Beauvoir's ground-breaking declaration one step further, in recognizing that sex is also discursively constructed – one of the most significant and lucid premises of Queer Theory.

Butler does not simply destroy the body, as some have erroneously interpreted (Femenías, 2000), but rather situates corporeal reality in its sociocultural context and observes that it is impossible to access the body without drawing upon our available cultural meanings, since the observer is immersed in language and culture (Butler, 1993). In fact, this philosophical premise can be clearly illustrated by reviewing human biology, specifically the bodies of intersex people. Their anatomy is catalogued as double, ambiguous, erroneous, inconclusive, or incomplete, because it does not fit neatly into the culturally-constructed male–female binary (Nieto, 2003). Their very corporeal existence subverts the cultural proposition, viewed by many as scientific, that there are two and only two 'natural' sexes. Feminist biologist Anne Fausto-Sterling (2000) points out that the sex of a body is actually much more complex than that captured by fixed categories, existing as more of a continuum of differences. Science, then, supports Butler's theoretical analysis: the ways in which we *interpret* (male and female) sex are determined more by our cultural concepts of gender than by actual biological reality.

As a victim of so-called corrective genital surgery, intersex activist Cheryl Chase (1998) also argues that these medical practices produce what practitioners claim to simply observe. It is this often-denied cultural rather than essential nature of sex that constitutes the heterosexual or heteronormative matrix (Butler, 1990). Heteronormativity is firmly rooted in the unquestioned assumption of the 'natural' existence of two exclusive, opposed, hierarchical and complementarily heterosexual sexes (Berlant & Warner, 1998). Subjects are either excluded from intelligibility or expected to adjust to the parameters of this structure, some of whom are compelled to use what Fausto-Sterling (2000,

p. 8) refers to as the 'surgical shoehorn'. Despite the efforts of Chase and other intersex activists, unnecessary surgical interventions continue to be carried out to 'normalize' infants born with non-binary physiology (Human Rights Watch, 2017).

None of us are exempt from what Butler refers to as gender performativity (1990, 1993), adapting to (or not) the gestures and behaviours considered socially appropriate for the sex we are assigned at birth – for sex is normative, rather than simply descriptive. In *Gender Trouble* (1990) Butler demonstrates how sexuality also interacts with the supposedly binary constructs of sex and gender, so that expressions of masculinity and femininity are guided by notions of hegemonic heterosexuality. Thus, certain identities are constructed as natural in contrast to transgressive or unintelligible configurations of sex, gender and sexuality that, exceeding the homonormative, are susceptible to gender violence, both personal and institutional. Zengin's review of Turkish physically invasive gendered institutional practices (on gay men and towards trans women) suggests that 'state control and regulation can be invested in particular forms of violent touch that are imbued with culturally specific morals; values; norms; and relations about gender, sex, and sexuality' (2016a, p. 232).

On the one hand, gender, understood as a performance, consists of a series of reiterative acts which, constrained by a rigidly regulatory framework, accumulate and congeal over time to appear substantial and essential. Yet at the same time, this same performative process provides the possibility for failed reiteration, which can lead to change, resistance and subversion. In this way, the very freedom of the subject who is called upon to repeat and reinforce the gender normative, can open fissures that may eventually lead to a destabilization of power (Butler, 1990). The imperative to reproduce the norm is accompanied by another crucial mechanism of control – exclusion. We exercise exclusion throughout our lives: through self-exclusion of the aspects of our 'I' that fail to cohere with gender norms and/or our own self-concept, and through rejection of others who subvert these norms.

In this way, through repetition and exclusion, the full range of human reality is framed within the limits of heteronormativity, establishing two distinct, complementary and hierarchical models of intelligible gender: man/masculine/heterosexual and woman/female/heterosexual. Beyond the margins of this hegemony we find the unintelligible realities, which include intersex (which exceed the sexual binary), trans*[1] (which threatens the coherence between the corporeal body and experienced gender), and homo/bi/lesbian/pan/a- sexualities (which challenge obligatory heterosexuality).

The heteronormative not only essentializes sexual and gender difference by calling for constant repetition of the norms, but also supports gender inequality through mechanisms of exclusion and violence toward those who transgress these norms. Gender, sex and sexuality work together to produce a homophobic, transphobic and sexist society. Women, who occupy a subordinate position in the hierarchy, are subjected to gender violence and discrimination, as are those with intersecting (Burgos, 2007) or unintelligible (Butler, 1990, 1993) experiences. Intersex and trans* people are among those positioned at the outside of the margins. In García López's (2017, p. 146, our translation) historical account of societal responses to intersexuality, he concludes that 'The body that is punished (burnt at the stake, for example) eventually became the body policed and regulated by various institutions.' Platero Méndez's analysis of the murder of trans* man

Roberto Gonzalez Onrubia concludes that the loss of humanity he suffered for his sexual unintelligibility was the first step toward his violent death: 'It was this binary social norm that generated a profound alterity, a division between an "Us" that belongs to the cisgender majority and an "Other" – the subject who stands out for his distance from and rupture of the sex assigned at birth' (2016, p. 232, our translation).

In sum, heteronormativity is built on sexism, homophobia and transphobia (Sharma, 2009) in ways that render it impossible to overthrow gender-related violence, without taking into account these three pillars that uphold it. In other words, gender violence should be understood as going beyond the violence suffered by (cis) women. This is especially relevant in schools, which we consider to be spaces of especially intense social interactions at early ages where children and young people are learning about themselves and others, and therefore drawing upon dominant social understandings to define themselves and others as legitimate and intelligible (or not).

Schools as heteronormative spaces

Schools, as institutions of socialization, are places where social inequalities are reproduced and the Other is constructed as unintelligible (and therefore less human). From the moment we are assigned sex at birth, primary socialization agencies such as the school and the family respond with different expectations and treatment, based on this crucial social assignation. In this sense, the school serves to consolidate and legitimate identity categories that are positioned within the heterosexual matrix, and exclude those that exceed these limits (Carrera Fernández et al., 2011). Schools in particular serve to hierarchically differentiate gender into two distinct categories, provide gender normative behaviour models, promote a normative template for homosexual relationships, and exclude as beyond the limits of intelligibility experience that does not conform to these models.

These strategies are largely unconscious and form part of what is defined as the hidden curriculum – subtle practices that we take for granted and which are, therefore, difficult to define and uncover. These may include silences – simply not mentioning certain realities (such as 'uncomfortable' truths about historical or current figures that challenged the gender binary). This hidden curriculum also includes active representations that reinforce certain erroneous or incomplete knowledge – such as the simplification of biological reality in sex education classes. The ways in which teachers interact with children can also transmit a gender-normative curriculum – by transmitting different expectations based on perceived gender, or by intervening in some kinds of bullying incidents, but not others. Teachers may fill knowledge gaps, left by inadequate professional training, with their own misconceptions about gender diversity fuelled by the 'broader climate of misunderstanding and fear' (Bartholomaeus et al., 2016, p. 6). Backlash conservative activism has targeted educational practice aimed at addressing the hidden gender curriculum, as evidenced by recent protests in the UK ('The LGBT teaching row explained', 2019) and in Spain (Jones, 2020).

Perhaps the most troubling and insidious aspect of the hidden curriculum of gender in schools is that socially produced heteronormativity is presented as irrefutable truths that the school simply describes and transmits. Schooling is strongly attracted to simple truths and stable identities, leaving out messy complexities, which include well-established non-binary scientific understandings:

> A different reading of the data to that usually presented in school textbooks – but one more in line with the scientific evidence about the working of sex hormones – is that femaleness and maleness lie on a continuum. Such a model of the consequences of the actions of the sex hormones became common among endocrinologists in the 1940s. (Reiss, 2016, p. 203)

Beyond the curriculum, school is also a place where peer interactions reinforce heteronormative understandings in the daily practices of socialization. In practices of heteronormative control, a normative self is performed by producing and penalizing a non-normative Other (Carrera Fernández et al., 2011). In this way, violence toward those who do not conform to gender norms becomes a strategy for gaining peer status. Such heteronormative social interactions are not necessarily violent or exclusive; young people's friendship and bonding practices, as well as those deployed by teachers to establish rapport with their students, reinforce normative gender and sexuality (Krebbekx, 2018).

As teacher-educators, we are particularly concerned with how social discourses such as heteronormativity, cisgenderism and sexism are deployed in educational settings. Normalization and exclusion are two sides of the same coin, and schools contribute to the creation of social inequalities as they help to shape insider and outsider identities. Schools are never neutral; as agents of socialization, they may be sites for social reproduction or social transformation (Freire, 2004). Unless educators make a conscious effort to critique them, schools unquestioningly accept and therefore reproduce the oppressive discourses that circulate in broader society. As we will argue throughout the following sections, trans-exclusionary discourses not only oppress adult people who identify as trans*, but they also constrain children and young people who are learning how to *do* gender. As cisgender feminist educators, we see transfeminism as an emancipatory project that resonates with our own feminist agenda and supports a transformative pedagogy.

Trans-exclusionary feminism? The Others of the Other

Given our current understandings of gender, it would seem logical that the oppressed would join hands in defence against oppression, but this is not necessarily the case. Trans-exclusionary radical feminist (TERF) discourses are produced by simplifying and twisting basic feminist premises and deploying a language not so very far removed from that of the extreme right (Williams, 2014). In fact, some consider TERF to be a hate group disguised as feminism (Allen, 2013). Nevertheless, this relatively recently coined term provides a name for a phenomenon that dates back to second wave feminism. Janice Raymond's *The Transsexual Empire: The Making of the She-Male* (1979) is particularly paradigmatic of this early trend, while others such as Sheila Jeffreys and Germaine Greer have added their voices to the rejection of trans* in the name of feminism.

In this section we critically explore the basic arguments characterizing TERF ideology: (1) transsexuality reproduces gender roles and contributes to the domination of women, requiring the abolition of gender and transsexuality; (2) support for transsexuality constitutes part of a state conspiracy against women, feminism, and lesbianism; (3) trans* women are men attempting to forcibly steal female and lesbian identities; (4) trans* men are women who betray their fellow women, as well as feminism and lesbianism; (5) trans*inclusive feminists are not really feminists; and (6) there are valid models of womanhood and lesbianism that should be imposed, ranging from the rejection to the reproduction of traditional femininity. We draw on insights from transfeminist and queer understandings in order to respond to these TERF arguments.

Gender, and therefore 'transsexuality', must be abolished

Raymond (1979) and Jeffreys (throughout her work, and especially in *Gender Hurts: A Feminist Analysis of the Politics of Transgenderism* [2014]), both present gender as a conservative ideology that provides the pillar of women's subordination – a caste system created by men, a patriarchal construction designed to ensnare women so that men can exploit and abuse them. Transsexuality/transgenderism, they claim, is based on the reproduction of gender stereotypes and, by logical extension, gender itself. Therefore, they call for the abolition of gender, the elimination of the existence of trans* and its threat to women and feminism (Jeffreys, 2014; Raymond, 1979).

As gender educators, we consider the TERF reading of trans* as a phenomenon that reproduces gender roles to be a biased and partial understanding of broader and more complex realities. As human beings we are all complicit in 'doing gender' – processes that are not exclusive to trans* individuals. At the same time, these processes include gender transgressions as well as reproductions, which contribute to resistance and subversion (Burgos, 2007; Butler, 1993, 2004). Indeed, these transgressions of gender norms are especially pronounced in the case of trans* people, who open new possibilities for embodying gender, flexibilizing and disrupting conventional understandings (Butler, 2014). As Stone points out in 'The Empire Strikes Back: A Posttranssexual Manifesto' (1992) – a direct response to Raymond's Transsexual *Empire* – rather than divide women, transsexuals multiply binary gender discourses. Drawing upon Donna Haraway (1992), Stone (1992, p. 168) argues that transsexual people should be viewed as 'the promises of monsters', that is, as physical entities in a state of continual transformation that exceed the margins of culturally intelligible representations. Like Stone, we view the monstrous as a metaphor for productive unintelligibility.

TERF proponents, in their focused crusade to abolish gender, deny trans* realities, establishing a customized version of what they consider to be 'nature' which neither contemplates the desire to *be* man or woman, nor admits the possibility that, in some cases, one may wish to satisfy this desire through the use of hormonal or surgical techniques (Raymond, 1979). Sex, which is crucial, is clearly distinguished from gender, which is irrelevant (Raymond 1979, p. 20):

> The male-to-female transsexual is a 'fantastic woman', the incarnation of a male fantasy of feeling like a woman trapped in a man's body, the fantasy rendered flesh by a further male medical fantasy of surgically fashioning a male body into a female one. These fantasies are based in the male imagination, not in any female reality. It is this female reality that the

surgically-constructed woman does not possess, not because women innately carry some essence of femininity but because these men have not had to live in a female body with all the history that entails. It is that history that is basic to female reality, and yes, history is based to a certain extent on female biology.

This distinction between sex and gender is problematic, if we consider that it is not possible to understand the body without the language of culture, that is, that sex has always been gender (Butler, 1993; Chase, 1998; Fausto-Sterling, 2000). The sexual binary is cultural rather than essential, a reality that is quite literally embodied by intersex people. The TERF premise that gender is a social construction coincides with the transfeminist perspective, but their belief that this somehow denies materiality effectively erases trans* experience (Butler, 2014). As social justice educators, we support McQueen's (2016) argument that only through recognizing these experiences can we identity and comprehend, and ultimately overcome, oppression. As Butler points out (2004, 2014), it is just as necessary to defend people's right to access the gender they claim for themselves as it is to support those who reject gender altogether, since it is ethically reprehensible to deny individual agency in definition and recognition of the self.

TERF discourses not only exercise symbolic violence in silencing trans people through arguments to abolish gender, but they also direct verbal violence toward specific trans* individuals, by defending acts of misgendering and refusing to use people's own established pronouns. These acts are explained by invoking an immutable 'biological' sex (that assigned at birth) (Greer, 1999; Jeffreys, 2014; Raymond, 1979), thus reinforcing the notion of an essentialized sexual binary. This approach to naming trans* people contradicts important feminist premises (Minou, 2010). Feminism defends for women that sex is not the destiny of their gender, that gender is a social construct that can and should be challenged, and that self-determination of their own bodies is not negotiable. At the same time, TERF proponents, co-opting feminist spaces, make exactly the opposite claims for trans* people: that sex is the inevitable destiny of their gender, that their gender is irrevocably rooted in this (culturally recognized) biological configuration, and that they cannot exercise agency over the development and expression of their corporeal reality.

In the same way that TERF proponents argue that trans* people are bad for women and feminism, they extend this argument to include the theories and social movements that include them. Defining feminism as the political movement based on the experience of women who were born women and raised under the female sex caste system (Jeffreys, 2014), they see queer theory and politics as removed from women's experiences of oppression that silence and intimidate them – recognizing trans* people's experiences would relegate gender to performance and a form of individual expression (Daly, 1978; Raymond, 1979).

This negation, rejection, and violence toward trans* people can only lead to one possible solution to the problem of transsexualism – its elimination. As Raymond argues (1979, p. 180), 'nonsexist counselling is another direction for change that should be explored. The kind of counselling to "pass" successfully as masculine or feminine that now reigns in gender identity clinics only reinforces the problem of transsexualism.' This 'nonsexist counselling' means following the example of those feminists, lesbians and homosexuals who, despite experiencing the oppression of gender roles, did not resort to transsexualism (Jeffreys, 2014; Raymond, 1979) – a solution that erroneously reduces gender to a question of personal choice (McQueen, 2016).

'Transsexuality' is part of a state conspiracy against women, feminism and lesbianism

Like her predecessor Raymond (1979), Jeffreys considers transsexuality to be not only the individual reproduction of gender roles, but also a conspiracy or 'state project' that violates human rights: 'I have to say, so called progressive and left people are not recognizing the human rights violations of transgenderism or how crazy the legislation is' (2006, p. 15). She also views gender reassignment surgery as the response of the 'transsexual empire' to be harmful to not just transsexuals themselves but also, in a broader sense, to feminism (1993, 2003, 2014).

However, Jeffreys reserves her most hostile rejection for the UK Gender Recognition Act (2004), which allows trans* people to certify their experienced gender without necessarily submitting to hormone treatment or surgical intervention (Jeffreys, 2008, 2011). She compares the British government's support for a process by which trans* individuals may change their birth certificate to the Iranian government's legalization of genital sex reassignment surgery, which she sees as a government-sponsored technique to eliminate homosexuality and reproduce gender norms that subordinate women (Jeffreys, 2008, 2011). Another voice of the TERF movement, Julie Bindel (2009) argues that sex reassignment surgery is nothing more than a modern version of the aversion therapies used to convert LGB people into heterosexuals. In 2017, the UK government consulted on reforming the GRA, potentially eliminating the required diagnosis of gender dysphoria. Self-defined 'gender-critical' feminist groups resisted on the basis of similar claims that cast gender recognition as a threat to cis women's rights (Sharpe, 2020).

As for trans* children, Jeffreys (2012, 2014) considers practices such as hormonal blocking therapy to delay the onset of puberty to be a social engineering project designed to force children to conform to rigid gender categories. She compares such therapies to early 20th century eugenics campaigns – the forced sterilization of delinquents as well as the poor, homosexuals and the Roma. Nevertheless, as Honkasalo (2020) points out, the logic of eugenics continues to be applied directly to trans* people by state regulations that limit full gender recognition rights based on demonstrable infertility. In an astonishing denial of historical and continuing injustice, Jeffreys accuses trans* children themselves of perpetuating sexist social engineering practices, conveniently and negligently ignoring the suffering of these children and their right to self-determination and recognition (Moore, 2015). Cathy Brennan and Elizabeth Hungerford (2011), other TERF proponents, have gone so far as to prepare a written response to the United Nations Entity for Gender Equality and Empowerment of Women's *Call for Communications: Human Rights Violations Affecting the Status of Women*, arguing that the gender identity of trans* individuals should not be recognized or protected as a way to improve women's lives.

Trans* women are men who steal female and lesbian identities

Trans* women are especially targeted by TERF activists, who deny their existence as women and as lesbians (in the case of trans women who love women). They are therefore accused of forcibly co-opting feminine identities (Greer, 1999; Jeffreys, 2003, 2014). Raymond (1979, p. 183) argues that 'Transsexuals are not women. They are deviant males', and goes on to further characterize the trans woman as an inevitably flawed imposter:

> [I]t is precisely because the transsexually constructed lesbian-feminist is a man, and not a woman encumbered by the scars of patriarchy that are unique to a woman's personal and social history that he can play our parts so convincingly and apparently better than we can play them ourselves. . . . What is also typically masculine in the case of the transsexually constructed lesbian-feminist is the appropriation of women's minds, convictions of feminism, and sexuality. (Raymond, 1979, p. 103)

Along similar lines, Bindel (2004) proposes that trans* women, whom she describes as 'men in dresses', cannot claim the rights and public protection afforded to women, because they are not and never will be women. Greer (BBC, 2015) deploys a similar argument when she claims that, like herself, many cisgender women think that trans women (whom she calls male to female transgender people) do not look, sound, or act like women.

To explain the existence of trans* women, Jeffreys (2014) draws upon the controversial work of Blanchard (2005), who distinguishes between transsexual women – actually submissive gay men who want to sleep with other homosexual men – and those she defines as autogynephilic (see Serano, this collection) – those who experience sexual excitement over the image of themselves as women, or who might even enjoy masochistic satisfaction upon losing the social status of their male caste. Such notions have been strongly rejected by trans* women themselves (Serano, 2007) as well as professionals who work with them (Moser, 2010). Adopting a perspective similar to that of her contemporaries Raymond and Jeffreys, Germaine Greer (BBC, 2015) appeared on *BBC Newsnight* to make light of Caitlyn Jenner's transition, arguing that she had undergone sexual reassignment surgery to capture some of the limelight enjoyed by the other women in her family (the Kardashians). In *The Whole Woman* (1999), she attacks governments that recognize as women individuals she refers to as men who believe themselves to be women and who have gone to the trouble of self-castration to prove it. In such recognition, she accuses the state of viewing women not just as the other sex, but as a non-sex or as defective men. Intersex people are also prone to TERF rejection, as evident in Greer's commentary on the South African Olympic athlete Caster Semenya, who was submitted to sex verification testing and later cleared for competition in women's events in 2010:

> Supposing that the verdict of the sex police is that Semenya is mentally female and physically male, what would it mean for other women athletes if she was allowed to compete with such an unfair biological advantage? People who don't ovulate or menstruate will probably always physically outperform people who do. But then, doesn't all competitive sport canonise and glamorise the exploitation of genetic advantage? Who said life was fair? (Greer, 2009, p. 1)

Trans* men are women who betray their fellow women, as well as feminism and lesbianism

While TERF criticism is more strongly directed toward trans* women than trans* men, these men have also been cast as 'traitors' whose actions prove harmful to women, to feminism and to lesbian politics. They are described as a very minor phenomenon, numerically speaking, who nevertheless contribute to supporting a false claim that women (those assigned as such at birth) constitute part of the transsexual phenomenon (Raymond, 1979). They are presented as women who attempt to acquire male privilege on an individual level, and in so doing betray feminism by joining the caste of men (Jeffreys, 2014). The rejection of trans* men is also based on their pernicious effects on lesbian politics, because by changing their bodies and/or presenting themselves as men they replace lesbians, which supposedly may lead to the disappearance of lesbianism. Jeffreys (2014, p. 121) exemplifies this argument: 'Although there are some apparent benefits for individual women who transgender, the harms are considerable, in terms of not only their physical longterm health, but also what it does to their partners, to lesbian communities and to feminism.'

Trans*inclusive feminists are not really feminists

From the TERF perspective, it is not enough simply to denounce trans* women and men. It is also necessary to convince feminists and lesbians to take up these same discourses of denial and rejection and to denounce those feminists who do not follow these exclusionary principles. The argument is that feminists who accept a 'man's' transition when 'his' wife, children and mother are subjected to an 'under-recognised form of psychological violence towards women' are betraying not only the affected women, but also feminism itself (Jeffreys, 2014, p. 99). The same line of reasoning also insists that real feminists and lesbians, unlike trans*inclusive feminists such as Burgos (2007), Butler (1990, 1993), Elliot (2010) and Overall (2012), should join together in opposing the normalization of trans* men, in order to avoid the damage these 'women' inflict on themselves and in feminist and lesbian politics (Jeffreys, 2014).

Valid models of womanhood and lesbianism should be imposed

TERF politics attempt to patrol the frontiers of cis identity as well as those of so-called true lesbian identity, using strategies that mirror those deployed by the patriarchy in establishing and protecting normative heterosexuality. In 'Bisexual Politics' (1999) Jeffreys denounces bisexuality for reaffirming the heterosexual imperative that women should love men, therefore undermining lesbian feminism. Jeffreys sees bisexuality as a strategy for concealing gay and lesbian identities in order to maintain heterosexual privilege, while at the same time enjoying the pleasures and benefits of homosexuality and lesbianism.

These stances defending 'true' sexual identities and orientations are complemented by the imposition of ambivalent models of femininity. Some of these reject the reproduction of feminine stereotypes, while others seem to take the opposite approach. Jeffreys (2000, 2005) infantilizes, discredits and devalues women who modify their bodies in a range of different ways: those who apply makeup, wear high heels, or have tattoos. Women who undergo plastic surgery are seen as duped by men and the patriarchy, passively adopting the culture of male dominance, in the same way that transsexual men and women undergo reassignment surgery because they are supposedly compelled by the patriarchy to do so. She also argues that these and similar body modification practices are more common among groups with lower sociocultural status, such as women, lesbians, gay men, and people who have suffered sexual abuse (Jeffreys, 2000). Greer (2008) expresses a quite different view, although equally sexist and authoritarian, when she mockingly described the dress that Michelle Obama wore to the electoral ball in 2008 as a 'butcher's apron' and a 'travesty', while also criticizing Obama's daughters' attire as not 'girly' enough. Similar unfortunate comments were directed at the Australian Prime Minister Julia Gillard in 2012, whose style of dress Greer also found wanting, and went so far as to criticize her 'big arse' (Groer, 2012). TERF proponents set out a series of strict guidelines for feminism, lesbianism and womanhood that serve to limit the freedom of cis women, but are especially intended to police the identity and corporality of trans* people (Butler, 2014). These subjects are transformed into a homogeneous entity (Stone, 1992) and victimized, silenced and annihilated; at the same time they are cast as perpetrators and aggressors. Moore's reaction to Jeffreys' *Gender Hurts* might easily be applied to TERF arguments in general. She argues, '*Gender Hurts* feels like a sustained assault. Jeffreys simply does not regard us as fully human. To read her book as a trans woman is to stand in a wash of hate and to struggle to stay on your feet' (Moore, 2015, p. 767). Jeffreys' and other TERF voices invalidate trans* experience and promote a conspiracy theory around trans-being that justifies dehumanization and violence toward trans* people.

An educator's perspective on TERF discourses

As educators, we are committed to broadening understandings, promoting empathy and providing dialogic alternatives to violence – all goals that are impeded by TERF perspectives that render invisible the social injustices perpetrated by a heteronormative patriarchy.

TERF proponents deny the existence of cisgender privilege, described by Serano (2007) as the advantages enjoyed by women and men who identify with the sex they were assigned at birth. They also fail to recognize transphobia suffered by trans* people, arguing that men who transition don't lose their male privileges (see Camminga, this collection), but continue to exercise their authority over women in various social contexts (Jeffreys, 2014). Such a systematic denial of the violence enacted toward the trans* community in general, and trans* women in particular, is inconsistent with demonstrated social realities in public and private spheres (European Union Agency for Fundamental Rights 2014; Grant et al., 2011; Kann et al., 2016). A comprehensive gender equality education cannot simply ignore the impact of this violence because their victims do not fit preconceived notions of who counts as a 'real' woman.

In their rejection of both trans* men and women, TERF arguments fail to consider that most of these people have felt, lived, or been socialized in their acquired gender since an early age (McQueen, 2016), so that it is not only cis women who have been subjected to and moulded by a patriarchy that considers them 'the Other' (Serano 2007).

Furthermore, what it means to 'be socialized' varies hugely, and expectations of masculinity and maleness can be sources of stigma and vulnerability for those individuals assigned male at birth who 'fail'. It follows as well that for either case, regardless of the nature and origins of the sense of self, we have a moral imperative as equality educators to recognize the diversity of trajectories through which people become sexual beings, and to support their right to self-determination (Butler, 2014).

TERF perspectives fail to grasp an important implication of the patriarchy: in order to effectively respond to the violence it generates, it is necessary to recognize the shared oppression of women and all people who transgress the heteronormative matrix (Sharma, 2009) – that is, adopt a transfeminist perspective. These forms of patriarchal oppression make up two sides of the same coin, so that any conceptual basis that attempts to address one while ignoring the other is doomed to fail. As Sharpe (2020) points out, TERF arguments construct a false incompatibility between trans* and cis women's rights. We find these struggles to be profoundly interrelated and essential to a comprehensive gender education.

A call for transfeminist alliance

Trans* activism has traditionally been relegated to the practically silent 'T' tacked on to the end of initials meant to designate a collective movement to secure rights of sexual minorities. According to Susan Stryker (2008), some of these movements have been accused of homonormativity (Duggan, 2002), a term that emerged in US-based activist circles in the 1990s to describe (1) gay and lesbian people who saw trans* issues as irrelevant to their cause and viewed gender-normativity as a path to securing social privilege, (2) lesbians who developed subcultural norms based on biological determinism, and (3) anyone who constructs trans* as a different category of people altogether – either as a distinct (other) gender or a fetishized sexual orientation not related to gay, lesbian, bisexual, or straight: 'from the outset of the post-World War II gay rights movement, transgender practices and identities marked communal boundaries between the normative and the transgressive' (Stryker, 2008, p. 151). Such attempts to distance trans* activists from the political agenda, therefore, have not been limited to TERF proponents.

Yet like sexual dissidence movements, feminism is complex and multi-voiced, and cannot be defined exclusively by a particular ideology promoted as universal by a few devoted sectarian followers, no more than it can be reduced to the concerns of particular (White, Western) women. Sophie Lewis (2019) points out that such dialogues across diversity have formed the basis for more inclusive feminisms in America, where indigenous and Black feminists have raised productive debates on how gender interacts with other marginalizing factors such as race and social class.

According to Lucas Platero Méndez and Esther Ortega-Arjonilla (2016), trans experiences have formed a more integral part of Spanish feminism, with trans* women participating in key nationwide feminist conferences beginning in 1993. In contrast with the narrative of conflict and exclusion more typical of Anglo-European contexts, the concerns of trans* activists were represented in the development of a shared agenda through public debate and compromise. Based on their own experiences as well as interviews with women involved in these early movements, we identify several reasons for this history of collaboration: (1) in Spain's particular political context,[2] emerging trans* activists were excluded from the fledgling homosexual rights movement in the 1980s, which aimed for normativity in the face of the concurrent AIDS scare; (2) the trans* movement was largely led by women; (3) the prominence of lesbians in mainstream feminism facilitated the participation of trans* women; and (4) existing personal relationships among members of both groups helped these women understand each other's experiences. While these negotiations have not been, and never will be, without their points of contention, Spanish feminism has acquired a more nuanced and characteristic nature as a result, 'Transfeminism led to Spanish feminism in general becoming more queer, more decolonial, and intersectional' (Platero & Ortega-Arjonilla, 2016, p. 54).

In more recent years, however, TERF discourses have proliferated in Spain. In a conference on *Feminist Politics: Liberties and Identities* celebrated in July 2019 (Gijón), feminist academics, politicians, journalists and writers gathered to engage in debates that generated some troubling transphobic statements. Some of these included misgendering and attacks on transfeminism that provoked indignant responses via the Twitter hashtag #HastaElCoñoDeTransfobia ('Up to my cunt with transphobia'). On the political plane, Lidia Falcón, leader of the Feminist Party of Spain, has recently come out in opposition to trans* rights legislation: the controversy ignited by her transphobic discourse resulted in the party's exclusion from Spain's United Left coalition party ('United Left Leadership', 2020). In an unprecedented shifting of alliances, some feminist discourse is aligning with that of the radical right, with allegations of 'gender ideology' and the 'gay lobby' (see Pearce et al., this collection). At the same time, a long history of productive collaboration between trans* and cis feminist activists is being undermined by the emergence of transphobic sectors within Spanish feminism.

Asli Zengin, who defines herself as a Turkish cisgender feminist activist and trans ally, finds an unfortunate point of commonality between cis women's and trans women's experiences – the constant threat of violence. This violence is rooted in sexist expectations of the perpetrators and the systematic sexism that allows the state to reduce the punishment in both cases due to pleas of undue provocation. Perpetrators of the murder of cis women may claim, for example, that the victim flirted with another man or failed to perform expected sexual (or other) duties. Those who kill trans women often cry deception and claim they were enraged by the prospect of what they considered homosexual relations, clearly a threat to their self-concept of hegemonic masculinity. According to Zengin (2016b), the lives of women and trans* people are considered less valuable in a patriarchal society, a shared suffering that results in a shared claim to feminism. In the face of this shared oppression, we argue that forging alliances is a far more effective political strategy than fomenting divisions and creating false debates about who 'really' gets to be considered a woman, and therefore share in feminist movements.

Toward transfeminism as part of queer (critical) educational practice

As cis women educators, we heed Zengin's call for cis women and trans* activists to unite to achieve common feminist goals. We see a particular relevance for this collaboration in the institution of schooling, where reducing gender violence of all kinds through quality education must be a priority. In critical pedagogy, education is seen as a vehicle for social justice, and thus a potential ally of (trans)feminist activism. Paulo Freire, in his well-known work, *Pedagogy of the Oppressed* (1986), defended a literacy of the people in which we become aware of our own reality, a raising of consciousness that goes beyond simply learning to read text – we learn to read the world we inhabit. Questioning assumed truths and dialogue with others are principal pedagogical tools for critical understanding: we shift from being passive spectators to actively participating in our world.

Queer educational practice (Britzman, 1995) situates this Freirean approach within a more specific approach to queer pedagogy – reading the world beyond rigid binary and hierarchical concepts of intelligible sex–gender–sexuality that underpin violence toward and exclusion of experiences existing beyond the margins of coherence (Butler, 1993). A critical (queer) pedagogy directly confronts heteronormativity by revealing the discourses (about sex, gender and sexuality) that support it. Such educational practice draws upon feminist and trans* understandings to operationalize transfeminism as an educational tool.

What can transfeminism contribute to this queer pedagogical project? By challenging an unscientific and oppressive gender regime, trans* experiences expose the fragility of the heteronormative. This gender regime is supported by trans-exclusionary discourses that must be dismantled, and transfeminism is an important tool for such a paradigm change. A critical queer pedagogy informed by transfeminism might include the following elements:

1. Understand the range of human diversity – prioritizing human experience and scientific understandings over social constructions
2. Recognize the synergies between cis women's and trans* oppressions, and how these affect all those who transgress normative sex–gender–sexuality
3. Identify the conscious and unconscious ways in which cisgenderism and sexism, along with obligatory heterosexuality, form part of a hidden school curriculum
4. Design pedagogies that invite children and young people to critically reflect on oppressive social constructions of sex, gender and sexuality

Critically interrogating the normative provides a basis for valuing the other possibilities and positionings inherent in human diversity. This may include a cisgender heterosexual woman who fails/refuses to meet the patriarchal expectations imposed upon her (for dress, for submission. . .), or it may include a trans* person whose physicality and/ or history threaten to weaken boundaries between the very categories that uphold the patriarchy. A trans-inclusive feminism would support schools in providing the kind of education that we all need; trans-exclusionary voices within feminist circles only serve to divide us and support a heteronormative and oppressive status quo.

Funding

The authors received no financial support for the research, authorship, and/or publication of this article.

Notes

1. We follow the Spanish tradition of using the term trans*, with the asterisk to remind us that this notion includes a spectrum of identities and experiences that challenge gender normativity (Platero Méndez, 2014). In referencing the work of others, we tend to use their terms (such as transgender or transsexual), as these encode their understandings.
2. The Franco dictatorship, which ended in 1975, delayed the progress of interest-group activism that contested the conservative Catholic regime.

References

Allen, E. (2013, August 9). *Unpacking transphobia in feminism.* TransAdvocate. www.transadvocate.com/unpacking-transphobia-in-feminism_n_9964.htm (last accessed 31 May 2020).

Bartholomaeus, C., Riggs, D. W., & Yarrow, A. (2016). *Exploring trans and gender diverse issues in primary education in South Australia.* Flinders University.

BBC News. (2015, October 24). *Germaine Greer: Transgender women are 'not women'.* BBC. www.bbc.com/news/av/uk-34625512/germaine-greer-transgender-women-are-not-women (last accessed 30 May 2020).

Berlant, L., & Warner, M. (1998). Sex in public. *Critical Inquiry, 24*(2), 547–566.

Bindel, J. (2004, January 31). Gender benders, beware. *The Guardian.* www.theguardian.com/world/2004/jan/31/gender.weekend7 (last accessed 31 May 2020).

Bindel, J. (2009, November). *The operation that can ruin your life.* standpointmag. https://standpointmag.co.uk/issues/november-2009/the-operation-that-can-ruin-your-life-features-november-09-julie-bindel-transsexuals/ (last accessed 31 May 2020).

Blanchard, R. (2005). Early history of the concept of autogynephilia. *Archives of Sexual Behaviour, 34*(4), 235–251.

Brennan, C., & Hungerford, E. (2011). *2011 Letter to the UN on 'gender identity' legislation.* Sex Matters. https://sexnotgender.com/gender-identity-legislation-and-the-erosion-of-sex-based-legal-protections-for-females/ (last accessed 31 May 2020).

Britzman, D. (1995). Is there a queer pedagogy? Or stop reading straight. *Educational Theory, 45*(2), 151-165.

Burgos, E. (2007). Identidades entrecruzadas. *Thémata. Revista de Filosofía, 39,* 245–253.

Butler, J. (1990). *Gender trouble: Feminism and the subversion of identity.* Routledge.

Butler, J. (1993). *Bodies that matter: On the discursive limits of 'sex'.* Routledge.

Butler, J. (2004). *Undoing gender.* Routledge.

Butler, J. (2014, May 1). *Judith Butler addresses TERFs and the work of Sheila Jeffreys and Janice Raymond.* The TERFs. http://theterfs.com/2014/05/01/judith-butler-addresses-terfs-and-the-work-of-sheila-jeffreys-and-janice-raymond/ (last accessed 31 May 2020).

Carrera Fernández, M. V., DePalma, R., & Lameiras Fernández, M. (2011). Toward a more comprehensive understanding of bullying in school settings. *Educational Psychology Review, 23*(4), 479–499.

Chase, C. (1998). Hermaphrodites with attitude: Mapping the emergence of intersex political activism. *GLQ: A Journal of Lesbian and Gay Studies, 4*(2), 189–211.

Daly, M. (1978). *Gyn/Ecology: The metaethics of radical feminism.* Beacon Press.

de Beauvoir, S. (1987). *El segundo sexo* (Vol. I). Cátedra (Original work published 1949).

Duggan, L. (2002). The new homonormativity: The sexual politics of neoliberalism. In R. Castronovo & D. D. Nelson (Eds.), *Materializing democracy: Toward a revitalized cultural politics* (pp. 175–194). Duke University Press.

Elliot, P. (2010). *Debates in transgender, queer and feminist theory: Contested sites.* Ashgate.

European Union Agency for Fundamental Rights. (2014). *Being trans in the European Union. Comparative analysis of EU LGBT survey data*. Publications Office of the European Union.

Fausto-Sterling, A. (2000). *Sexing the body: Gender politics and the construction of sexuality*. Basic Books.

Femenías, M. (2000). *Sobre sujeto y género. Lecturas feministas desde Beauvoir a Butler*. Catálogos.

Freire, P. (1986). *Pedagogy of the oppressed*. Continuum.

Freire, P. (2004). *Pedagogy of indignation*. Paradigm Publishers.

García López, D. J. (2017). Politización de la vida y medicalización de la política: la producción del cuerpo intersexual. *Eikasia, Revista de Filosofía, 75*, 141–157.

Gender Recognition Act. (2004). *UK Government*. www.legislation.gov.uk/ukpga/2004/7/contents (last accessed 31 May 2020)

Grant, J. M., Mottet, L. A., Tanis, J., Harrison, J., Herman, J. L., & Keisling, M. (2011). *Injustice at every turn: A report of the national transgender discrimination survey*. National Center for Transgender Equality and National Gay and Lesbian Task Force.

Greer, G. (1999). *The whole woman*. A. A. Knopf.

Greer, G. (2008, November 17). Germaine Greer: If Michelle Obama's such a great dresser, what was she doing in this red butcher's apron? *The Guardian*. www.theguardian.com/world/2008/nov/17/michelleobama-fashion (last accessed 31 May 2020).

Greer, G. (2009, August 20). Caster Semenya sex row: What makes a woman? *The Guardian*. www.theguardian.com/sport/2009/aug/20/germaine-greer-caster-semenya (last accessed 31 May 2020).

Groer, A. (2012, May 16). Feminist icon Germaine Greer: Aussie PM Julia Gillard has 'big arse' and bad jackets. *Washington Post*. www.washingtonpost.com/blogs/she-the-people/post/feminist-icon-germaine-greer-aussie-pm-julia-gillard-has-big-arse-and-bad-jackets/2012/05/16/gIQAakiVTU_blog.html (last accessed 31 May 2020).

Haraway, D. (1992). The promises of monsters: A regenerative politics for inapropriate/d others. In: L. Grossberg, C. Nelson & P. A. Treichler (Eds.), *Cultural studies* (pp. 295–337). Routledge.

Honkasalo, J. (2020). In the shadow of eugenics: Transgender sterilization legislation and the struggle for self-determination. In R. Pearce, I. Moon, K. Gupta & D. L. Steinberg (Eds.), *The emergence of trans: Cultures, politics and everyday lives* (pp. 17–33). Routledge.

Human Rights Watch. (2017, July 25). *'I want to be like nature made me'. Medically unnecessary surgeries on intersex children in the US*. www.hrw.org/report/2017/07/25/i-want-be-nature-made-me/medically-unnecessary-surgeries-intersex-children-us (last accessed 31 May 2020).

Jeffreys, S. (1993). *The lesbian heresy: A feminist perspective on the lesbian sexual revolution*. Spinifex.

Jeffreys, S. (1999). Bisexual politics. *Women's Studies International Forum, 22*(3), 273–285.

Jeffreys, S. (2000). 'Body art' and social status: Cutting, tattooing and piercing from a feminist perspective. *Feminism & Psychology, 10*(4), 409–429.

Jeffreys, S. (2003). *Unpacking queer politics: A lesbian feminist perspective*. Blackwell.

Jeffreys, S. (2005). *Beauty and misogyny: Harmful cultural practices in the West*. Routledge.

Jeffreys, S. (2006, April 7). *Not just about pornography: The radical politics of Andrea Dworkin*. Comments at Andrea Dworkin Commemorative Conference. www.feministes-radicales.org/wp-content/uploads/2012/05/Sheila-Jeffreys-speaks-on-Woman-Hating-Andrea-Dworkin-commemorative-conference-2006.pdf (last accessed 31 May 2020).

Jeffreys, S. (2008). They know it when they see it: The UK Gender Recognition Act 2004. *British Journal of Politics & International Relations, 10*(2), 328–345.

Jeffreys, S. (2011, April 11). The McCarthyism of transgender and the sterilization of transgender children. www.feministes-radicales.org/wp-content/uploads/2012/05/Sheila-Jeffreys-The-McCarthysm-of-Transgender-Sterilization-of-Transgender-Children.pdf (last accessed 31 May 2020).

Jeffreys, S. (2012). The transgendering of children: Gender eugenics. *Women's Studies International Forum*, *35*(5), 384–393.

Jeffreys, S. (2014). *Gender hurts: A feminist analysis of the politics of transgenderism*. Routledge.

Jones, S. (2020, January 20). Row in Spain over far-right party's parental veto policy for classes. *The Guardian*. www.theguardian.com/world/2020/jan/20/spains-government-vows-to-over-turn-parental-pin-initiative (last accessed 31 May 2020).

Kann, L., Olsen, E. O., & McManus, T., et al. (2016). *Sexual identity, sex of sexual contacts, and health-related behaviors among students in grades 9-12 -United States and selected sites, 2015*. Centers for Disease Control and Prevention. www.cdc.gov/mmwr/volumes/65/ss/ ss6509a1.htm (last accessed 31 May 2020).

Krebbekx, W. (2018). Watching six-packs, chilling together, spreading rumours: Enacting heteronormativity through secondary school friendships and teaching practices. *Gender and Education*. Advance online publication. https://doi.org/10.1080/09540253.2018.1538496

Lameiras, M., Carrera, M. V., & Rodríguez, Y. (2013). *Sexualidad y salud: El estudio de la sexualidad humana desde una perspectiva de género*. Universidade de Vigo.

Lewis, S. (2019, February 8). Opinion | How British feminism became anti-trans. *The New York Times*. www.nytimes.com/2019/02/07/opinion/terf-trans-women-britain.html (last accessed 31 May 2020).

McQueen, P. (2016). Feminist and trans perspectives on identity and the UK Gender Recognition Act. *The British Journal of Politics and International Relations*, *18*(3), 671–687.

Minou, C. L. (2010, February 1). Julie Bindel's dangerous transphobia. *The Guardian*. www. theguardian.com/commentisfree/2010/feb/01/julie-bindel-transphobia (last accessed 31 May 2020).

Moore, B. (2015). Book Review. Sheila Jeffreys, Gender Hurts: A Feminist Analysis of the Politics of Transgenderism. *Sexualities*, *18*(5–6), 765–768.

Moser, C. (2010). Blanchard's autogynephilia theory: A critique. *Journal of Homosexuality*, *57*(6), 790–809.

Nieto, J. A. (2003). La intersexualidad y los límites del modelo 'dos sexos/dos géneros'. In O. Guash & O. Viñuales (Eds.), *Sexualidades. Diversidad y control social* (pp. 69–104). Ballaterra.

Overall, C. (2012). Trans persons, cisgender persons, and gender identities. In N. Power, R. Halwani & A. Soble (Eds.), *Philosophy of sex: Contemporary readings* (pp. 251–267). Rowman & Littlefield.

Platero Méndez, L. (2014). *Trans*sexualidades: Acompañamiento, factores de salud y recursos educativos*. Bellaterra.

Platero Méndez, R. L. (2016). ¿Dónde está la ira trans*? El asasinato de Roberto González Onrubia. In R. M. Mérida Jiménez (Ed.), *Masculinidades disidentes* (pp. 229–250). Icaria.

Platero Méndez, R. L., & Ortega-Arjonilla, E. (2016). Building coalitions: The interconnections between feminism and trans* activism in Spain. *Journal of Lesbian Studies*, *20*(1), 46–64.

Raymond, J. (1979). *The transsexual empire: The making of the she-male*. Beacon Press.

Reiss, M. J. (2016). Education and sexualities: The next generation. In P. Aggleton (Ed.), *Education and sexualities: Major themes in education* (pp. 195–210). Routledge.

Rofes, E. E. (2005). *A radical rethinking of sexuality and schooling: Status quo or status queer?* Rowman & Littlefield.

Serano, J. (2007) *Whipping girl: A transsexual woman on sexism and the scapegoating of feminin-ity*. Seal Press.

Sharma, J. (2009). Reflections on the construction of heteronormativity. *Development*, *52*(1), 52–55.

Sharpe, A. (2020). Will gender self-declaration undermine women's rights and lead to an increase in harms? *The Modern Law Review*. Advance online publication. https://doi.org/10.1111/1468-2230.12507

Stone, S. (1992). The empire strikes back. A posttranssexual manifesto. *Camera Obscura*, *10*(2 (29)), 150–176.

Stryker, S. (2008). Transgender history, homonormativity, and disciplinarity. *Radical History Review*, *2008*(100), 145–157.

The LGBT teaching row explained. (2019, May 22). BBC News. www.bbc.com/news/uk-eng-land-48351401 (last accessed 31 May 2020).

The United Left leadership approves the expulsion of the Feminist Party. (2020, February 22). Web 24 News. www.web24.news/a/2020/02/the-united-left-leadership-approves-the-expul-sion-of-the-feminist-party.html (last accessed 2 June 2020).

Williams, C. (2014, March 15). *TERF: What it means and where it came from*. TransAdvocate. www.transadvocate.com/terf-what-it-means-and-where-it-came-from_n_13066.htm (last accessed 31 May 2020).

Zengin, A. (2016a). Violent intimacies, tactile state power, sex/gender transgression, and the politics of touch in contemporary Turkey. *Journal of Middle East Women's Studies*, *12*(2), 225–245.

Zengin, A. (2016b). Mortal life of trans/feminism: Notes on 'gender killings' in Turkey. *Transgender Studies Quarterly*, *3*(1–2), 266–271.

Author biographies

María Victoria Carrera-Fernández teaches at the University of Vigo (Spain). Her research focuses on bullying from a socioecological perspective, gender, heteronormativity and ethnicity. Recent publications include 'Me and us versus the others: Troubling the bullying phenomenon' (*Youth & Society*, 2019) and 'Patrolling the boundaries of gender' (*International Journal of Sexual Health*, 2020).

Renée DePalma teaches at the University of A Coruña (Spain). She was Senior Researcher on the UK-based No Outsiders project, investigating approaches to address sexualities equality in primary schools (2006–2009). Recent publications include the chapter 'Sexual diversity at the early childhood education level' in *Schools as Queer Transformative Spaces* (Eds. Kjaran & Sauntson, 2019).

Autogynephilia: A scientific review, feminist analysis, and alternative 'embodiment fantasies' model

The Sociological Review Monographs
2020, Vol. 68(4) 89–104
© The Author(s) 2020
Article reuse guidelines:
sagepub.com/journals-permissions
DOI: 10.1177/0038026120934690
journals.sagepub.com/home/sor

Julia Serano
Independent scholar, USA

Abstract

It is generally accepted within psychology and among trans health providers that transgender people who transition do so because they have a gender identity that is incongruent with their birth-assigned sex, and distinct from their sexual orientation. In contradiction to this standard model, the theory of autogynephilia posits that transgender women's female gender identities and transitions are merely a by-product of their sexual orientations. While subsequent research has yielded numerous lines of evidence that, taken together, disprove the theory, autogynephilia is still often touted by anti-transgender groups, including trans-exclusionary feminists. Here, I provide an updated overview of the scientific case against autogynephilia. Following that, I will forward an alternative 'embodiment fantasies' model that explains all the available findings better than autogynephilia theory, and which is more consistent with contemporary thinking regarding gender and sexual diversity. I will also demonstrate how autogynephilia theory relies on essentialist, heteronormative, and male-centric presumptions about women and LGBTQ+ people, and as such, it is inconsistent with basic tenets of feminism.

Keywords

autoandrophilia, autogynephilia, sexual fantasies, transgender, transsexual

Introduction

Over the last decade, psychologist Ray Blanchard's autogynephilia theory has been increasingly cited within trans-exclusionary radical feminism. The concept appears to have first entered trans-exclusionary radical feminist (TERF) discourses through Sheila Jeffreys' writings (Jeffreys, 2005, 2014). It has since become a recurring talking point on 'gender critical' websites such as 4thWaveNow, r/GenderCritical (a subsection of the

Corresponding author:
Julia Serano, Independent Scholar
Email: hi@juliaserano.com

website Reddit), Mumsnet, and others, where it is usually invoked to insinuate that trans women are merely 'sexually deviant men'. In such settings, autogynephilia is typically presented as though it were well-established scientific dogma, when in reality the theory has never been widely accepted within sexology and psychology, and numerous follow-up studies have disproven its primary claims. Furthermore, trans-exclusionary feminists' uncritical embrace of autogynephilia contradicts the long history of feminist scholarship critiquing the ways in which scientific research and theories are often overly reduction-ist, and riddled with androcentric and heteronormative biases (reviewed in Crasnow et al., 2018; Fehr, 2004).

In this article, I will review the scientific case against autogynephilia theory, and pro-vide an alternate model that is far more consistent with all the available evidence and contemporary thinking in the fields of sexology and psychology. Additionally, I will demonstrate how autogynephilia theory is steeped in gender-essentialist and male-cen-tric views of gender and sexuality, and thus is inconsistent with feminist thought.

Autogynephilia: Historical context and the scientific evidence

Today, it is widely accepted that gender identity, gender expression, sexual orientation and physical sex characteristics may vary from one another within any given individual, and that gender dysphoria (incongruence between one's gender identity and assigned sex/gender) may first arise during childhood, adolescence, or adulthood (American Psychological Association, 2015; Coleman et al., 2011; Hidalgo et al., 2013). There has also been a growing recognition that many sexual fantasies and patterns of arousal that have historically been categorised as 'sexual deviations' or 'paraphilias' (i.e. pathologi-cal sexual interests) are not especially rare, nor are they inherently unhealthy (Joyal et al., 2015; Moser and Kleinplatz, 2006). As a result, researchers have gradually moved away from viewing solitary and consensual expressions of sexuality as manifestations of psychopathology (Giami, 2015). For all of these reasons, there is now a general consen-sus amongst contemporary trans health professionals that transgender people are diverse with regard to their gender expressions, sexual orientations, sexual fantasies and life trajectories (just as cisgender people also vary in these aspects of their lives).

But this was not always the case. For most of the twentieth century, research into these matters was steeped in gender essentialism and reductionism. Women and men were believed to be naturally distinct from one another in their genders and sexualities, and individuals who did not neatly fit into this strict binary (i.e. LGBTQ+ people) were categorised into subtypes based upon superficial similarities and presumed underlying pathologies. During this time period, assigned male at birth (AMAB) transgender-spec-trum people were often classified into one of two subgroups: transsexuals or transves-tites. *Transsexuals* – those who socially and/or physically transition; more commonly called *trans women* and *trans men* today – were simplistically imagined as 'males with feminised brains' and 'females with masculinised brains', respectively. Given this con-ceptualisation, researchers presumed that trans women would not only identify as women, but should also be feminine in gender expression throughout their lives and exclusively sexually oriented toward men; this archetype was sometimes called the 'classical transsexual'. Notably, researchers who subscribed to this 'sexual inversion' narrative often described gay men in a similar fashion (i.e. feminised brain, therefore feminine in gender expression and exclusively attracted to men) and believed that homosexuality and transsexuality merely represent different outcomes for the same 'type' of person. In contrast, *transvestites* (often called *crossdressers* today) were envisioned as otherwise 'normal' (read: heterosexual and masculine) men, except for the fact that they (1) occasionally wore female-typical clothing, usually in secret, and (2) sometimes experienced sexual arousal associated with dressing femininely and/or imagining themselves as having sex characteristics associated with women (e.g. breasts, vulva). For reasons that will become clear, I will collectively refer to these latter sexual experiences as *female/feminine embodiment fantasies (FEFs)* (Serano, 2010, 2016).

Throughout the 1970s and 1980s, this transsexual/transvestite dichotomy was called into question, as increasing numbers of trans women did not fit the 'classical transsexual' archetype, either because they were not outwardly feminine during childhood, and/or did not experience gender dysphoria until adolescence or adulthood, and/or were asexual, bisexual, or lesbian in sexual orientation, and/or had a previous history of identifying as crossdressers and/or experiencing FEFs. Here, I will collectively refer to such individuals as 'non-classical' trans women, but not because I believe them to be distinct from, or less authentic than, their 'classical' counterparts. Rather, they are 'non-classical' in the sense that they challenged the 'classical transsexual' standard that most researchers and medical gatekeepers enforced at the time. Today, all of these differing outcomes ('classical' and 'non-classical' alike) are readily explained in terms of gender and sexual diversity, as I outlined earlier.

But in 1989, as practitioners were still trying to make sense of these exceptions to the 'classical transsexual' and 'transvestite' categories, Blanchard forwarded a new theory of transgender taxonomy and aetiology: autogynephilia (Blanchard, 1989a, 1989b). The theory proposed that there were two fundamentally different types of trans women, each characterised by different 'erotic anomalies' (Blanchard, 1989a, p. 322). According to Blanchard, 'homosexual transsexuals' are trans women who fit the 'classical transsexual' archetype. The label suggests that Blanchard imagined these individuals as akin to feminine gay men, and other proponents of the theory, such as J. Michael Bailey, have suggested that they transition in order to attract heterosexual men (Bailey, 2003, p. 146). Blanchard grouped asexual, bisexual and lesbian (i.e. 'non-classical') trans women, along with male crossdressers, under the label 'autogynephiles', on the basis that (according to his theory) they were all primarily motivated by 'autogynephilia' (literally 'love of oneself as a woman'). While some people today inappropriately use the term autogynephilia in a manner similar to how I use FEFs – i.e. to refer to a particular type of sexual fantasy or pattern of arousal that some people happen to experience – Blanchard conceptualised autogynephilia very differently. Blanchard insisted that autogynephilia was a paraphilia that arises as a result of a 'misdirected heterosexual sex drive'. That is, rather than being exclusively attracted to women (as most AMAB individuals are), something goes 'awry' in 'autogynephiles' (Blanchard refers to this as an 'erotic target location error' – see Serano, 2010). As a result, they become primarily attracted to the thought or image of *themselves* as women. Blanchard also claimed that autogynephilia was both a sexual orientation that competes with attraction to other people, and that it is the cause of any gender dysphoria and desire to transition experienced by 'non-classical' trans women (reviewed in Serano, 2010).

In other words, autogynephilia is not simply a theory positing the existence of FEFs. Researchers were already well aware of this phenomenon, having previously called it by various names (e.g. automonosexualism, transvestic fetishism, cross-gender fetishism). Rather, what makes autogynephilia unique is that it asserts that there are two fundamentally different types of trans women, each having a distinct sexual cause for their transsexuality (i.e. either homosexuality, or autogynephilia). Thus, the theory should be judged, not by whether or not FEFs exist, but rather by whether its taxonomical and aetiological claims hold true. Or as Bailey put it, classifying trans women into distinct types 'diagnostically makes sense only if the different types have fundamentally different causes. Otherwise, why not distinguish "tall," "medium-sized," and "short" transsexuals, or "blonde" and "brunette" subtypes?' (Bailey, 2003, p. 162).

Blanchard elaborated on autogynephilia theory over a series of papers published between 1989 and 1993. This work received little attention at first, until the early 2000s, when it was promoted by Anne Lawrence and in Bailey's pop-science book *The Man Who Would Be Queen*, at which point it came under intense scrutiny (Serano, 2020). Amongst the most prevalent objections to the theory were: (1) a general sense that trans women are fairly diverse and do not neatly fall into two discrete subtypes; (2) Blanchard's own research showed that significant numbers of 'autogynephilic transsexuals' (e.g. trans woman attracted to women) did not experience FEFs, while significant numbers of 'homosexual transsexuals' (i.e. trans women attracted to men) did; (3) Blanchard's studies also showed that many (if not most) 'non-classical' trans women report experiencing gender dysphoria or a desire to be female before they ever experienced FEFs, therefore FEFs could not possibly be causative of gender dysphoria; (4) both 'non-classical' trans women and male crossdressers often report a sharp decline (and sometimes complete absence) in FEFs over time, indicating that such fantasies are not central to these individuals' identities or sexualities; (5) Blanchard and others often dismissed all the aforementioned exceptions to the theory as being due to lying or misreporting on the part of 'autogynephiles', which essentially rendered the theory unfalsifiable (and therefore unscientific); (6) Blanchard did not use any controls in his experiments – e.g. he never administered his autogynephilia-related surveys to cisgender women; (7) Blanchard's original rationale for the theory relied heavily on the presumption that 'non-classical' trans men did not exist, but it has since become clear that they are actually quite common. All these lines of reasoning are discussed in greater detail in critical reviews by Moser (2010) and Serano (2010). Thus, even without any follow-up studies, it appeared that Blanchard's proposed taxonomy ('homosexual' versus 'autogynephilic') and aetiology (that FEFs are the cause of transsexuality in 'non-classical' trans women) were not supported by his own evidence.

In subsequent years, several independent research groups have tested autogynephilia theory, and their results further disprove its taxonomical and aetiological claims. For starters, every single follow-up study has shown that, while the correlations that Blanchard and other researchers prior to him described generally hold true (i.e. that FEFs are more common in 'non-classical' trans women than 'classical' ones), counter to

Blanchard's theory there are always substantial numbers of 'classical' trans women who report experiencing FEFs and 'non-classical' trans women who report never experiencing them (Nuttbrock et al., 2011a; Smith et al., 2005; Veale et al., 2008). These studies also challenge several additional claims necessary for autogynephilia theory to be substantiated, such as the idea that FEFs compete with sexual attraction toward other people, that asexual trans women are predominantly 'autogynephilic' and that bisexual trans women are merely 'pseudobisexuals' (Nuttbrock et al., 2011a; Veale et al., 2008).

A longstanding critique of Blanchard's theory had been that his subtypes were not empirically derived, but rather stemmed from his initial grouping of individuals based on their sexual orientation, thus 'begging the question' that trans women fall into subtypes based on sexual orientation. In contrast to this approach, Veale (2014) performed taxometric analyses on her subjects' responses to questions regarding sexual orientation, FEFs, and other aspects of sexuality, and found that the results were dimensional rather than categorical (i.e. trans women fell along a spectrum rather than into distinct subtypes). In an earlier study using the same dataset, Veale et al. (2008) found that when trans women were grouped according to their experiences with FEFs, they did not differ significantly on measures of sexual orientation.

The possibility that factors other than sexual orientation may be responsible for FEFs is further supported by Nuttbrock et al. (2011a, 2011b), who found that FEFs varied considerably among trans women depending upon age and race (with the highest levels observed in older and white subjects), and that these outcomes were mediated by a history of dressing femininely in private. This finding strongly supports alternative theories that have posited that FEFs arise from, or are exacerbated by, social factors such as secretive crossdressing and/or having to hide or repress female/feminine inclinations (Serano, 2007, 2016; Veale et al., 2010); I will discuss such theories more in the following section.

As previously mentioned, Blanchard never used any cisgender controls in his studies, presumably because he assumed that FEFs were unique to trans female/feminine-spectrum people. Two research groups have since administered autogynephilia scales (similar or nearly identical to Blanchard's) to cisgender women. Moser (2009) found that 93% of his cisgender female subjects had experienced FEFs in some capacity, with 28% experiencing them frequently. Veale et al. (2008) also found that cisgender women frequently report FEFs, with 52% experiencing them at levels comparable to Blanchard's 'autogynephilic' group (see also Moser, 2010). When roughly 65% of cisgender women respond affirmatively to questions like 'I have been erotically aroused by contemplating myself in the nude', or 'I have been erotically aroused by contemplating myself wearing lingerie, underwear, or foundation garments' (Moser, 2009), it seems both illogical and needlessly stigmatising to single out trans women as supposedly being 'autogynephiles' for having similar erotic experiences (unless, of course, the label is primarily intended to pathologise trans women's sexualities even when they are female-typical).

In addition to cisgender women experiencing FEFs, subsequent studies have shown that many cisgender people experience cross-sex/gender sexual fantasies as well. In a recent study of 4175 Americans' sexual fantasies, Lehmiller (2018) found that nearly a third of his subjects reported having sexual fantasies that involved being the 'other sex', and a quarter had fantasised about crossdressing. Blanchard has insisted that the counterpart to

FEFs – sometimes called 'autoandrophilia', but which I will refer to as *male/masculine embodiment fantasies (MEFs)* – does not exist (Cameron, 2013), but Lehmiller found that 11% of the women in his study had experienced such fantasies. In a separate study of women's sexual fantasies, Dubberley (2013) devotes an entire chapter to fantasies wherein her subjects imagined themselves possessing a penis and/or being a man, and there is plenty of additional anecdotal evidence (much of it online) detailing cisgender women (as well as transgender men) experiencing MEFs (Serano, 2016, and references therein).

Taking all this together, two things seem clear. First, *embodiment fantasies* (i.e. sexual arousal in response to one's real or imagined body and/or expressions of gender) seem to be fairly common and exist in a variety of permutations. (In the following section, I will discuss why they may occur more frequently or intensely in certain subpopulations.) Thus, it would be disingenuous to assert or insinuate that they are a trans female/feminine-specific phenomenon (as autogynephilia theory does). Second, the notion that FEFs have the potential to cause transsexuality is specious and not supported by the evidence (Serano, 2010, 2020). After all, almost a third of Lehmiller's subjects experienced cross-sex/gender sexual fantasies (Lehmiller, 2018, p. 66), yet the vast majority of these people will never develop gender dysphoria or desire to transition. Furthermore, most 'non-classical' trans women either never experience FEFs, or experience FEFs only *after* they have experienced gender dysphoria, thus ruling out the possibly that FEFs caused them to become transgender (Serano, 2010). The most reasonable conclusion is that gender dysphoria develops independently in a small percentage of AMAB people, and a subset of those individuals (along with a subset of cisgender women and men) will subsequently develop FEFs for other reasons, which I will explore in the next section.

To summarise, numerous independent lines of research have shown that autogynephilia theory's major tenets – its taxonomy and aetiological claims – are false. Therefore, the concept of autogynephilia must be rejected. Admittedly, a few researchers still vociferously promote the theory, most notably Lawrence and Bailey, whose reviews and research (along with Blanchard's) account for almost all of the unwaveringly pro-autogynephilia academic literature; elsewhere, I refute many of their attempts to handwave away the counter-evidence I have presented here (Serano, 2010, 2020). Others researchers still tacitly support autogynephilia (by citing the theory, or portraying it as a 'controversial yet viable' model) perhaps due to their unfamiliarity with the research that I have reviewed here, out of respect for Blanchard's and Bailey's stature within the field, and/or because they view the theory as consistent with other beliefs or biases that they hold (detailed in the final section). Finally, some researchers have taken to using the term 'autogynephilia' as shorthand to describe FEFs; this should be avoided, as 'autogynephilia' inaccurately portrays these fantasies as paraphilic, trans female/feminine-specific, a sexual orientation unto itself, and the cause of gender dysphoria in trans women who experience them.

Embodiment fantasies, and transgender, queer and female subjectivities

Thus far, we have reviewed the scientific case against autogynephilia. But if we step back and consider other fields of enquiry (e.g. phenomenology, sociology, gender studies), the theory appears even more suspect. Perhaps its most glaring omission is that autogynephilia entirely ignores embodiment – the well-accepted notion in philosophy and cognitive studies that our thoughts, perceptions and desires do not happen in a vacuum, but rather occur within, and are shaped by, our bodies.

Virtually all sexual fantasies and activities involve bodies – not just the bodies of our real or imagined partners, but our own bodies as well. While sexual fantasies are not limited to bodies (they may also involve certain settings, situations, positions, behaviours, other objects, and even intricate narratives), they do often feature our own bodies interacting in various ways with other people's bodies (Bettcher, 2014; Dubberley, 2013; Lehmiller, 2018; Leitenberg & Henning, 1995). Sometimes our attention might be focused more on another person's body: appreciating their physical attributes; imagining things we wish to do to, or with, their body. Other times we might be focused more on our own body: imagining other people finding us desirable; imagining them doing things to, or with, our body, and the sensations we might physically experience as a result. Often, both of these aspects (along with other elements) will be in play simultaneously during our sexual fantasies and experiences. But in other cases, one aspect may be more prevalent or even predominate. And just as we may sometimes fantasise about imaginary sex partners, it is not uncommon for individuals to imagine being entirely different people in their fantasies, or 'having a different body shape, genital appearance, or personality' (Lehmiller, 2018, p. xviii).

This is why I favour 'embodiment fantasies' as a non-pathologising umbrella term for those sexual fantasies and patterns of arousal wherein the focus is mostly (or in some cases, solely) placed on our own embodiment (Serano, 2010, 2016). Bettcher (2014) has since expanded upon this concept of embodiment eroticism, providing numerous examples that illustrate the complexity of erotic content (which may involve our actual or imagined body, attraction toward real or imagined others, interactions between these bodies, additional elements or scenarios, plus the sexual meanings that we attribute to all of these things). Bettcher's work demonstrates how autogynephilia theory reduces this rich content down to mere 'attraction to' people and objects. This is what allows Blanchard to misrepresent trans women's embodiment fantasies as 'misdirected heterosexual sex drives' and 'erotic target location errors' (Bettcher, 2014).

In an earlier critique of autogynephilia (Serano, 2007, pp. 268–269), I facetiously coined the term 'autophallophilia' to describe the seemingly common fantasy that men sometimes have of receiving oral sex from a nondescript or faceless partner. My intention in forwarding the term was not to pathologise such fantasies, but rather to illustrate that cisgender men experience embodiment fantasies as well, even if they may not think of them in this way. Part of the reason why these individuals (and most researchers who might study them) would be disinclined to view such fantasies in terms of 'autophallophilia' or MEFs is precisely because they are cisgender, and thus able to take their physical sex attributes for granted. Having a penis would likely be the unquestioned backdrop of most sexual fantasies that they experience, so its presence within the fantasy would not be seen as notable. In contrast, many transgender people (especially non- and pre-transition individuals) cannot take such attributes for granted, and are therefore likely to focus more on their own embodiment during both fantasies and real-life sexual experiences – e.g. imagining themselves inhabiting the 'right body' or having the 'appropriate parts' (i.e. those congruent with their identified gender). Critics of autogynephilia have long pointed out how MEFs and FEFs are an obvious coping mechanism to mitigate gender dysphoria, and the fact that trans women typically experience a sharp decrease in FEFs upon transitioning lends further credence to this notion (reviewed in Serano, 2010).

Another reason why many cisgender men are able to take their bodies for granted is because they are men. Gender theorists have chronicled how male bodies and perspectives tend to be viewed as neutral and the default standpoint in our culture, whereas female bodies and perspectives are marked and viewed as 'other' (Bem, 1993; de Beauvoir, 1989). Having been socialised in a heterosexual-male-centric culture, we all (to varying degrees) have internalised what feminists call 'the male gaze' – a mindset wherein men are viewed as sexual subjects who act upon their own desires, whereas women are viewed as passive sexual objects of other people's desires (Fredrickson & Roberts, 1997; Mulvey, 1975). While the male gaze is most often discussed with regard to media representations, it can also inform our own self-conceptualisations and desires. For instance, it is relatively easy for many men (who regard themselves primarily as sexual subjects) to think about sex strictly in terms of whom they are 'attracted to'. But for many women, in addition to their own physical attractions toward other people, they will also be highly cognisant of the ways in which they are being sexually evaluated, appreciated, or objectified by other people (whether strangers, potential partners, or lovers), and this is bound to influence their subjectivity on sexual matters (Fredrickson & Roberts, 1997). Indeed, in their review of the research on sexual fantasies, Leitenberg and Henning (1995, p. 484) reported that, as a general rule, 'Men's fantasies are more active and focus more on the woman's body and on what he wants to do to it, whereas women's fantasies are more passive and focus more on men's interest in their bodies'; Lehmiller (2018) found that this trend still largely holds true today. This disparity provides a relatively straightforward explanation for why FEFs are frequently experienced by women (whether cisgender or transgender, as both have to navigate the male gaze), whereas men are less likely to experience analogous MEFs.

Furthermore, given that we live in a culture where men are deemed sexual subjects and women objects of desire, it should not be surprising that female-specific clothing (and feminine gender expression more generally) is sometimes imbued with sexual meanings, whereas reciprocal items of masculine clothing and expression are typically viewed as utilitarian and devoid of sexual connotations (Serano, 2007). This helps explain why the phenomenon historically known as 'transvestic fetishism' (i.e. sexual arousal experienced in response to crossdressing) has been found to be rather commonplace in trans female/ feminine-spectrum individuals, but is reported far less frequently in trans male/masculine-spectrum individuals. Unfortunately, this fairly obvious connection has remained obscured, as the researchers who studied the phenomenon classified it as a paraphilia and presumed that something must be inherently wrong with individuals who exhibited it. If, instead of studying this phenomenon as a psychopathology unto itself, these researchers had carried out controlled studies (à la Moser, 2009; Veale et al., 2008) they would have found that many cisgender women also experience sexual arousal in response to wearing (or contemplating wearing) certain items of feminine clothing, at least in certain contexts. As further evidence that the concept of transvestic fetishism has been largely shaped by researchers' heteronormative and male-centric biases, psychologist Robert Stoller once argued that trans men cannot possibly experience transvestic fetishism on the basis that, 'Men's clothes have no erotic value whatsoever; these people have no clothing fetish' (Stoller, 1968, p. 195). Of course, some people *are* attracted to maleness and masculinity, and a subset of such individuals *do* experience sexual arousal in response to masculine clothing, as Bockting et al. (2009) found for many of their gay and bisexual male subjects.

A third factor that may influence embodiment fantasies is sexual orientation, albeit not in the way that Blanchard envisioned. Specifically, if an individual is attracted to femaleness and femininity in a more general sense (e.g. they find such qualities erotic in their partners), then these same attributes might also be sexually salient with regard to their own embodiment, leading to more frequent or intense FEFs. (A similar correlation between attraction to maleness and masculinity, and MEFs, might also be expected.) Or to phrase this conversely: If an individual is *not* attracted to female or feminine attributes more generally, then they may be less likely to find FEFs arousing or compelling. This fairly simple explanation (which Blanchard never explored) is consistent with the correlations researchers have found between sexual orientation and embodiment fantasies, but without invoking direct causality.

While sexual orientation may partially explain the correlations Blanchard and others have reported, I do not believe it to be the primary factor. Rather, I argue that the frequent or intense FEFs experienced by many pre-transition 'non-classical' trans women stem largely from the fact that they passed through a 'crossdresser stage'.[1]

In the essay 'Crossdressing: Demystifying Femininity and Rethinking Male Privilege' (Serano, 2007), I detailed the social forces that distinguish this transgender trajectory from others; here I will highlight the most pertinent points. First, it is well established that transgender people may experience the onset of gender dysphoria at various ages (Coleman et al., 2011). Individuals who become aware of their gender dysphoria early in childhood are likely to never fully identify with their birth-assigned gender – in fact, they often assert that they are, or should be, the 'other' (binary) gender from an early age. In contrast, individuals who become aware of their gender dysphoria later in childhood may have already come to accept their birth-assigned gender, as well as 'gender constancy' (the belief that one's gender can never change). As a result, these 'late-onset' trans people may initially self-conceptualise themselves as 'a boy who wants to be a girl' (or vice versa) for a period of time before fully embracing their gender-variant identities. This transitional stage can be especially perilous for trans female/feminine-spectrum children, given that feminine boys are stigmatised to a far greater extent than masculine girls in our culture (Kane, 2006; Sandnabba & Ahlberg, 1999; Sullivan et al., 2018). This strict gender-policing essentially coerces these individuals into concealing or repressing any female/feminine inclinations they may have (if they are able to), particularly in public settings, and to only ever indulge them in private, either though daydreaming and fantasy, or secretive crossdressing – hence, the 'crossdresser stage'. Notably, there does not seem to be an analogous crossdresser stage for trans male/masculine individuals, presumably because their public explorations of gender will be tolerated to a greater degree (i.e. others will perceive them as simply 'tomboys'). Veale et al. (2010) have forwarded a similar model of crossdresser development.

During the pre-Internet era (when Blanchard conducted his research), there was little-to-no public awareness or accessible resources regarding transgender people, and trans children and teenagers were often left to their own devices to make sense of their situations. For trans individuals in the crossdresser stage, this meant grappling with one's gender dysphoria in a milieu where (1) male-centrism ensures that girls'/women's experiences and perspectives are 'othered' (and thus may seem 'alien' or 'exotic'); (2) the male gaze encourages the general objectification of femaleness and femininity; and (3) these individuals may also be experiencing sexual attraction toward girls/women (independent of their gender dysphoria) for the first time. Given this set of circumstances, it is understandable why trans individuals in the crossdresser stage might experience FEFs (to varying degrees, and in some cases very intensely) in association with their early explorations of female gender identity and feminine gender expression.

As I have discussed throughout this section, embodiment fantasies may come in various forms. Some embodiment fantasies centre on the self: we are the same person that we are in everyday life, it is just that the focus of erotic attention is placed on our own body. Other embodiment fantasies revolve around us being or becoming someone else. Perhaps we share some qualities with this 'someone else' – e.g. they may be mostly like us, but only more attractive. In other cases, we might imagine ourselves as someone whom we believe (or were taught to believe) is entirely unlike us. If we cannot readily relate to this 'someone else', we may draw heavily upon stereotypes. And in cases where we are not supposed to be (let alone *want* to be) this 'someone else', these embodiment fantasies may feel forbidden and taboo. Obviously, FEFs and MEFs may fall into this 'other'-embodiment fantasy category, albeit to varying degrees. Given that male experiences and perspectives are centred across Anglo-American culture, it might not be much of a stretch for a cisgender woman to imagine herself as a man in her fantasies. But because women's experiences and perspectives are 'othered', cisgender men might find FEFs to be especially exotic (what feminists and postcolonial theorists often call 'exoticisation of the Other'). Furthermore, because femaleness/femininity are valued less than maleness/masculinity in our society, cisgender men may feel a sense of shame or 'moral incongruence' if they find FEFs particularly enjoyable or erotic, leading them to feel distressed about their own behaviours (Grubbs & Perry, 2019; Serano, 2020).

Some trans women's experiences with FEFs may overlap somewhat with those of cisgender men, particularly if they are in the crossdresser stage (wherein they are forced to publicly identify as male and repress any female/feminine inclinations). In other words, their FEFs during this phase may be predominantly 'other'-embodiment fantasies, characterised by exoticisation, stereotypes and feelings of shame. In the case of cisgender men, this dynamic might never change. But as I chronicle in my aforementioned 'Crossdressing' essay, this dynamic does gradually change for trans women (as well as many crossdressers), as their gender dysphoria will lead them to explore and experiment with gender in real life, rather than exclusively within fantasies (Serano, 2007, 2010). Over time, femaleness and femininity will become 'demystified' to them, and they will begin to integrate their 'boy-mode' and 'girl-mode' into one whole person. They will stop feeling ashamed of their transgender, queer, female and/or feminine identities, and may begin openly expressing them in public. As they do, they will come to relate to women's experiences and perspectives, especially once they begin moving through the world as women themselves. As this happens, FEFs may still occur on some level (as they do for cisgender women), but they will not be the sensationalised 'other'-embodiment fantasies of the past. Instead, they will largely be 'self'-embodiment fantasies, rooted in their own bodies and self-understandings. Blanchard was never able to adequately explain the sharp reduction in FEF prevalence that many trans women eventually experience – he actually proposed that it must be because these individuals have formed a 'pair-bond' with their female selves (reviewed and critiqued in Serano, 2010). But human sexuality is not a static thing, and trans people's self-conceptualisations, subjectivities and desires may evolve over time.

Contemporary proponents of autogynephilia seem to believe that, just because Blanchard identified 'two subtypes' of trans women in a Canadian gender identity clinic in the 1980s, that these same two subtypes must still exist in the same form today, and presumably for perpetuity. This ignores the large body of research demonstrating that, while gender and sexual minorities exist in all cultures, their specific identities and behaviours are often shaped by local norms and social pressures, and that even within a given culture, different generational cohorts of LGBTQ+ people often display dramatically different self-understandings, life trajectories and sexual histories (Hammack, 2005). In the 30-plus years since Blanchard conducted his original research, there have been massive shifts in transgender awareness, visibility, legal recognition and access to healthcare and resources. Today, 'late-onset' trans women are not necessarily forced into a crossdresser stage, as they can readily access information about transgender lives via the Internet or trans peers. Instead of engaging in secretive crossdressing and fantasy, many of these individuals come out as nonbinary, genderfluid, trans dykes, or queer women, and they often begin presenting femininely and/or socially transitioning as teenagers or young adults. And this lack of a secretive 'crossdresser stage' largely explains why these younger trans women experience far fewer FEFs than their counterparts from previous generations (Nuttbrock et al., 2011a, 2011b).

Sexologists today have moved away from viewing people who share the same sexual orientation, or experience similar sexual fantasies, as being the same 'type' of person, or suffering from the same 'paraphilia'. Embodiment fantasies come in many different permutations, and people may experience them for a variety of reasons. Like all sexual fantasies, embodiment fantasies are not a permanent condition – they may appear, disappear, reappear, intensify, de-intensify, evolve, or shift over time. Any future research into embodiment fantasies should acknowledge the full breadth of this phenomenon, rather than misrepresenting them as some kind of transgender-specific psychopathology.

Autogynephilia promotes male-centrism, gender essentialism and sexualises trans women

Thus far, I have reviewed the scientific case against autogynephilia, and forwarded an alternative 'embodiment fantasy' model that is consistent with all the available data and contemporary thinking on gender and sexual diversity. However, it is doubtful that the case I have made here (no matter how sound) will convince the theory's staunchest defenders. In my experience, people who embrace autogynephilia often do so not because it best fits the evidence, but rather for ideological or sociological reasons. In this final section, I want to review these rationales, as they provide a better understanding of auto-gynephilia-related discourses.

Many people harbour gender-essentialist beliefs – for instance, that femininity and attraction to men is intrinsically female, and masculinity and attraction to women intrinsically male (Budge et al., 2018). When confronted with exceptions to this 'rule', gender-essentialists' go-to explanation is to presume these individuals must be 'feminised men' or 'masculinised women' – an assumption that invariably conflates gender expression with sexual orientation (Budge et al., 2018). Autogynephilia is a gender-essentialist theory, as it pathologises all transgender people for failing to conform to (cis)gender expectations. But of its two subtypes, Blanchard's 'homosexual' group neatly fits a simplistic 'feminised brain' narrative, and as such, they receive relatively little consideration or scrutiny in his studies. In contrast, trans women who are not exclusively attracted to men, and/or not especially feminine as children, seemed to Blanchard to require some kind of extraordinary explanation, for which he invented autogynephilia. Tellingly, Bailey and Blanchard (2017) have recently expanded Blanchard's typology to include *five* transgender subtypes, two of which are designed to explain the existence of 'non-classical' trans men (whose existence Blanchard initially dismissed, see Blanchard, 1989a). It seems both inefficient and scientifically dubious to invent new transgender subtypes (each with their own aetiology) any time a new demographic emerges that does not fit gender-essentialist stereotypes. It is far more parsimonious to acknowledge (as many contemporary researchers now do) that gender identity, gender expression and sexual orientation can diverge from one another (and from one's birth-assigned sex) within any given individual.

Speaking of stereotypes, according to autogynephilia lore, Blanchard 'discovered' that there are 'two types' of trans women, each with differing sexual motivations. In reality, these two types predate Blanchard's work, as they are common stereotypes that have existed in the cisgender imagination for quite some time. In a review of a half-century's worth of transgender-themed media depictions – the vast majority of which were produced without any knowledge or information about actual trans people or Blanchard's theory – I identified two recurring trans woman stereotypes: the 'deceiver' and the 'pathetic' transsexual (Serano, 2007). In an independent analysis of laypeople's reactions to trans women, Bettcher (2007) described these same stereotypes as 'deceivers' and 'pretenders'. These stereotypes differ from one another primarily with regard to trans women's ability to 'pass' as cisgender women, and the motivations that are ascribed to each group reflect naive cisgender assumptions about why a 'man' might want to 'become' a woman. Perhaps because they are visibly feminine (which is also a common stereotype of gay men), 'deceivers' are typically presumed to be gay men who become women in order to sexually attract heterosexual men. The 'pathetic'/'pretender' stereotype is applied to trans women who do not 'pass' (and thus are incapable of 'deceiving' men), and the most common ulterior motive projected onto them is that they become women in order to fulfil some kind of bizarre sexual fantasy. These stereotypes share an obvious resemblance to Blanchard's 'homosexual' and 'autogynephile' subtypes, respectively. Given that these stereotypes have consistently appeared in the media since the 1960s (Serano, 2007, 2009), it seems likely that they may have influenced Blanchard's taxonomy. And perhaps the reason why people today still find autogynephilia theory compelling, despite the overwhelming evidence against it, is because it confirms their previously held stereotypes regarding trans women.

While the media (and cisgender laypeople's imaginations) consistently reproduce these two sexually motivated trans woman stereotypes, they also repeatedly overlook the existence of trans men. In rare cases where trans men *are* represented, it is usually not done in a sexually titillating manner (as it is with trans women), nor are trans men's transitions generally depicted as sexually motivated. It is hard not to draw parallels here with Stoller's claim that 'men's clothes have no erotic value whatsoever', or Blanchard's insistence that 'autoandrophilia'/MEFs do not exist. I have argued that these discrepancies – i.e. that trans women's motivations *must* be sexual, whereas trans men's *cannot possibly* be sexual – stem from the differing values that we (as a society) place on women versus men (Serano, 2007, 2009). In a male-centric society, the idea that someone might want to become a man seems somewhat understandable, whereas the reciprocal gender transition strikes most people as confounding. Thus, people tend to presume that trans women transition in order to obtain the one type of 'power' that women are commonly viewed as having: the ability to be objects of heterosexual male desire. In other words, the pervasive assumption that trans women transition for sexual reasons is rooted in the misogynistic belief that women, as a whole, have no worth beyond their ability to be sexualised (Serano, 2007, 2009).

Finally, in addition to male-centrism and gender essentialism, some people embrace autogynephilia theory (despite all the counter-evidence) because they are suspicious of, or ideologically opposed to, transgender people. Autogynephilia is a particularly useful tool in this regard, as it not only invalidates trans women's gender identities (by misrepresenting them as 'men' who suffer from psychopathologies), but because it *sexualises* them – it reduces trans women to their presumed sexual behaviours and motivations, to the exclusion of other characteristics (Serano, 2009). There is a large body of evidence demonstrating that women who are sexualised (often via 'slut-shaming') are viewed as less than human, are not taken seriously, are not treated with empathy, and face stigmatisation and social isolation as a result (American Psychological Association Task Force, 2007; Armstrong et al., 2014; Vrangalova et al., 2013). Similarly, other marginalised groups – including people of colour, immigrants and LGBTQ+ communities – are also routinely depicted as hypersexual or sexually deviant, and thus potential threats to non-minority women and children (Casares, 2018; Collins, 2000; Fejes, 2008; Frank, 2015; Stone, 2018).

Given that sexualisation is a tried-and-true tactic to dehumanise and socially exclude marginalised groups, it is unsurprising that social and religious conservatives – who routinely condemn women and LGBTQ+ people for their failure to conform to gender and sexual norms – increasingly invoke autogynephilia in their attempts to disparage transgender people (cf. Fitzgibbons et al., 2009). Feminists, on the other hand, have historically opposed male-centrism, heteronormativity and gender essentialism. Given the long history of women being slut-shamed, and gender and sexual minorities (e.g. lesbians) being falsely accused of being sexual deviants and predators, it is hypocritical for any self-identified feminist to resort to these same tactics (via invoking Blanchard's autogynephilia theory) in their attempts to exclude transgender people.

Funding

The author received no financial support for the research, authorship, and/or publication of this article.

Note

1. To be clear, some people are lifelong crossdressers (for whom it is not a 'stage'), and gender dysphoria is not the only reason why people crossdress. My analysis of the 'crossdresser stage' here specifically refers to eventually self-defined trans women, and is informed by many personal communications I have had with trans women about this particular stage of their lives.

References

American Psychological Association. (2015). Guidelines for psychological practice with transgender and gender nonconforming people. *American Psychologist, 70*(9), 832–864.

American Psychological Association Task Force on the Sexualization of Girls. (2007). *Report of the APA Task Force on the sexualization of girls.*

Armstrong, E. A., Hamilton, L. T., Armstrong, E. M., & Seeley, J. L. (2014). 'Good girls': Gender, social class, and slut discourse on campus. *Social Psychology Quarterly, 77*(2), 100–122.

Bailey, J. M. (2003). *The man who would be queen: The science of gender-bending and transsexualism.* Joseph Henry Press.

Bailey, J. M., & Blanchard, R. (2017). *Gender dysphoria is not one thing.* 4thWaveNow. https://4thwavenow.com/2017/12/07/gender-dysphoria-is-not-one-thing (accessed 20 August 2018).

Bem, S. L. (1993). *The lenses of gender: Transforming the debate on sexual inequality.* Yale University Press.

Bettcher, T. M. (2007). Evil deceivers and make-believers: On transphobic violence and the politics of illusion. *Hypatia, 22*(3), 43–65.

Bettcher, T. M. (2014). When selves have sex: What the phenomenology of trans sexuality can teach about sexual orientation. *Journal of Homosexuality, 61*(5), 605–620.

Blanchard, R. (1989a). The classification and labeling of nonhomosexual gender dysphorias. *Archives of Sexual Behavior, 18*(4), 315–334.

Blanchard, R. (1989b). The concept of autogynephilia and the typology of male gender dysphoria. *Journal of Nervous and Mental Disease, 177*(10), 616–623.

Bockting, W., Benner, A., & Coleman, E. (2009). Gay and bisexual identity development among female-to-male transsexuals in North America: Emergence of a transgender sexuality. *Archives of Sexual Behavior, 38*(5), 688–701.

Budge, S. L., Orovecz, J. J., Owen, J. J., & Sherry, A. R. (2018). The relationship between conformity to gender norms, sexual orientation, and gender identity for sexual minorities. *Counselling Psychology Quarterly, 31*(1), 79–97.

Cameron, L. (2013). *How the psychiatrist who co-wrote the manual on sex talks about sex.* Motherboard. https://motherboard.vice.com/en_us/article/ypp93m/heres-how-the-guy-who-wrote-the-manual-on-sex-talks-about-sex (last accessed 8 June 2020).

Casares, C. (2018). *Trump's repeated use of the Mexican rapist trope is as old (and as racist) as colonialism.* NBCNews.com. www.nbcnews.com/think/opinion/trump-s-repeated-use-mexican-rapist-trope-old-racist-colonialism-ncna863451 (accessed 3 November 2018).

Coleman, E., Bockting, W., Botzer, M., Cohen-Kettenis, P., DeCuypere, G., Feldman, J., . . . Zucker, K. (2011). Standards of care for the health of transsexual, transgender, and gender-nonconforming people, version 7. *International Journal of Transgenderism, 13*(4), 165–232.

Collins, P. H. (2000). *Black feminist thought: Knowledge, consciousness and the politics of empowerment.* Routledge.

Crasnow, S., Wylie, A., Bauchspies, W. K., & Potter, E. (2018). *Feminist perspectives on science.* The Stanford Encyclopedia of Philosophy. https://plato.stanford.edu/archives/spr2018/entries/feminist-science (last accessed 8 June 2020).

de Beauvoir, S. (1989). *The second sex.* Vintage Books.

Dubberley, E. (2013). *Garden of desires: The evolution of women's sexual fantasies.* Black Lace.

Fehr, C. (2004). Feminism and science: Mechanism without reductionism. *NWSA Journal, 16*(1), 136–156.

Fejes, F. (2008). *Gay rights and moral panic: The origins of America's debate on homosexuality.* Palgrave Macmillan.

Fitzgibbons, R. P., Sutton, P. M., & O'Leary, D. (2009). The psychopathology of 'sex reassignment' surgery. *National Catholic Bioethics Quarterly, 9*(1), 97–125.

Frank, G. (2015). *The anti-trans bathroom nightmare has its roots in racial segregation.* Slate. https://slate.com/human-interest/2015/11/anti-trans-bathroom-propaganda-has-roots-in-racial-segregation.html (accessed 3 January 2019).

Fredrickson, B. L., & Roberts, T.-A. (1997). Objectification theory: Toward understanding women's lived experiences and mental health risks. *Psychology of Women Quarterly, 21*(2), 173–206.

Giami, A. (2015). Between DSM and ICD: Paraphilias and the transformation of sexual norms. *Archives of Sexual Behavior, 44*(5), 1127–1138.

Grubbs, J. B., & Perry, S. L. (2019). Moral incongruence and pornography use: A critical review and integration. *The Journal of Sex Research, 56*(1), 29–37.

Hammack, P. L. (2005). The life course development of human sexual orientation: An integrative paradigm. *Human Development, 48*(5), 267–290.

Hidalgo, M. A., Ehrensaft, D., Tishelman, A. C., Clark, L. F., Garofalo, R., Rosenthal, S. M., Spack, N. P., & Olson, J. (2013). The gender affirmative model: What we know and what we aim to learn. *Human Development, 56*(5), 285–290.

Jeffreys, S. (2005). *Beauty and misogyny: Harmful cultural practices in the West.* Routledge.

Jeffreys, S. (2014). *Gender hurts: A feminist analysis of the politics of transgenderism.* Routledge.

Joyal, C. C., Cossette, A., & Lapierre, V. (2015). What exactly is an unusual sexual fantasy? *The Journal of Sexual Medicine, 12*(2), 328–340.

Kane, E. (2006). 'No way my boys are going to be like that!' Parents' responses to children's gender nonconformity. *Gender and Society, 20*(2), 149–176.

Lehmiller, J. J. (2018). *Tell me what you want.* De Capo Press.

Leitenberg, H., & Henning, K. (1995). Sexual fantasy. *Psychological Bulletin, 117*(3), 469–496.

Moser, C. (2009). Autogynephilia in women. *Journal of Homosexuality, 56*(5), 539–547.

Moser, C. (2010). Blanchard's autogynephilia theory: A critique. *Journal of Homosexuality, 57*(6), 790–809.

Moser, C., & Kleinplatz, P. J. (2006). DSM-IV-TR and the paraphilias: An argument for removal. *Journal of Psychology & Human Sexuality, 17*(3–4), 91–109.

Mulvey, L. (1975). Visual pleasure and narrative cinema. *Screen, 16*(3), 6–18.

Nuttbrock, L., Bockting, W., Mason, M., Hwahng, S., Rosenblum, A., Macri, M., & Becker, J. (2011a). A further assessment of Blanchard's typology of homosexual versus non-homosexual or autogynephilic gender dysphoria. *Archives of Sexual Behavior, 40*(2), 247–257.

Nuttbrock, L., Bockting, W., Rosenblum, A., Mason, M., & Hwahng, S. (2011b). Sexual arousal associated with private as compared to public feminine dressing among male-to-female transgender persons: A further response to Lawrence (2011). *Archives of Sexual Behavior*, *40*(6), 1093–1096.

Sandnabba, N. K., & Ahlberg, C. (1999). Parents' attitudes and expectations about children's cross-gender behavior. *Sex Roles*, *40*(3–4), 249–263.

Serano, J. (2007). *Whipping girl: A transsexual woman on sexism and the scapegoating of femininity*. Seal Press.

Serano, J. (2009). *Psychology, sexualization and trans-invalidations*. Keynote lecture presented at the 8th Annual Philadelphia Trans-Health Conference. www.juliaserano.com/av/Serano-TransInvalidations.pdf (last accessed 8 June 2020).

Serano, J. M. (2010). The case against autogynephilia. *International Journal of Transgenderism*, *12*(3), 176–187.

Serano, J. (2016). Reconceptualizing 'autogynephilia' as female/feminine embodiment fantasies. In Serano, J., *Outspoken: A decade of transgender activism and trans feminism* (pp. 151–155). Switch Hitter Press.

Serano, J. (2020). *Autogynephilia, ad hoc hypotheses, and handwaving*. Medium. https://medium.com/@juliaserano/autogynephilia-ad-hoc-hypotheses-and-handwaving-cecca4f6563d (last accessed 8 June 2020).

Smith, Y. L. S., van Goozen, S., Kuiper, A., & Cohen-Kettenis, P. T. (2005). Transsexual subtypes: Clinical and theoretical significance. *Psychiatry Research*, *137*(3), 151–160.

Stoller, R. J. (1968). *Sex and gender: On the development of masculinity and femininity*. Science House.

Stone, A. L. (2018). Frame variation in child protectionist claims: Constructions of gay men and transgender women as strangers. *Social Forces*, *97*(3), 1155–1176.

Sullivan, J., Moss-Racusin, C., Lopez, M., & Williams, K. (2018). Backlash against gender stereotype-violating preschool children. *PLoS ONE*, *13*(4), e0195503.

Veale, J. F. (2014). Evidence against a typology: A taxometric analysis of the sexuality of male-to-female transsexuals. *Archives of Sexual Behavior*, *43*(6), 1177–1186.

Veale, J. F., Clarke, D. E., & Lomax, T. C. (2008). Sexuality of male-to-female transsexuals. *Archives of Sexual Behavior*, *37*(4), 586–597.

Veale, J. F., Lomax, T. C., & Clarke, D. E. (2010). The identity-defence model of gender-variant development. *International Journal of Transgenderism*, *12*(3), 125–138.

Vrangalova, Z., Bukberg, R. E., & Rieger, G. (2013). Birds of a feather? Not when it comes to sexual permissiveness. *Journal of Social and Personal Relationships*, *31*(1), 93–113.

Author biography

Julia Serano is the author of four books, including *Whipping Girl: A Transsexual Woman on Sexism and the Scapegoating of Femininity*, and *Excluded: Making Feminist and Queer Movements More Inclusive*. She has a PhD in Biochemistry and Molecular Biophysics from Columbia University, and researched evolution and developmental biology at UC Berkeley.

The
Sociological
Review
Monographs

The Sociological Review Monographs
2020, Vol. 68(4) 105–125
© The Author(s) 2020
Article reuse guidelines:
sagepub.com/journals-permissions
DOI: 10.1177/0038026120934693
journals.sagepub.com/home/sor

A critical commentary on 'rapid-onset gender dysphoria'

Florence Ashley
McGill University, Canada

Abstract

The term 'rapid-onset gender dysphoria' (ROGD) was coined in 2016 to describe an alleged epidemic of youth coming out as trans 'out of the blue' due to social contagion and mental illness. The term reflects a deliberate attempt to weaponise scientific-sounding language to dismiss mounting empirical evidence of the benefits of transition. This article offers an introduction to the theory of ROGD and its history, presents a detailed critique of the empirical and theoretical claims associated with the theory, and highlights structural concerns with the ROGD discourse. The article argues that claims associated with ROGD, including assertions of declining mental health and degrading familial relationships following coming out, are best explained by the leading ROGD study's recruitment of parents from transantagonistic websites against a background of growing visibility and social acceptance of trans people. ROGD theory is best understood as an attempt to circumvent existing research demonstrating the importance of gender affirmation, relying on scientific-sounding language to achieve respectability.

Keywords

gender affirmation, gender identity, rapid-onset gender dysphoria, social contagion, trans youth

The notion of transgender youth coming out 'out of the blue' following exposure to trans communities is not new, but only recently coalesced into the politicised pseudo-diagnostic category of rapid-onset gender dysphoria (ROGD). Introduced in 2016, the term reflects a deliberate attempt to weaponise scientific-sounding language to dismiss mounting empirical evidence of the benefits of transition for youth (see e.g. Durwood et al., 2017; Lopez et al., 2017; Olson et al., 2016; Telfer et al., 2018; Turban et al., 2020; What We Know, n.d.). By offering a critical account of the social process by which the concept of ROGD was created and propagated and by drawing parallels to the political mobilisation of the scientific-sounding language of Parental Alienation Syndrome and False Memory Syndrome, this article contributes to wider sociological debates on the nature of scientific discourse.

Corresponding author:
Florence Ashley, McGill University, Montreal, QC H3A 0G4, Canada.
Email: Florence.pare@mail.mcgill.ca

ROGD is alleged as distinct from traditional presentations of gender dysphoria such as early-onset (onset prior to puberty) and late-onset gender dysphoria (onset at or after puberty). According to ROGD theory, young persons who have shown no prior indication of gender dysphoria would suddenly begin to mistakenly believe that they are transgender. ROGD would be attributable to social contagion (the spreading of behaviour from one person to another through imitation), and especially through exposure to trans internet communities in youth predisposed to false beliefs (Bailey & Blanchard, 2017). Theorists of ROGD have argued that medical transition is unlikely to benefit members of this subgroup and may even harm them due to the causal relationship to social contagion and psychological vulnerability (Littman, 2018; Marchiano, 2017a). In the discourse surrounding ROGD, the desire to transition is frequently attributed to the devaluation of womanhood and sexualisation of women's bodies. The voices of trans teenagers alleged to have ROGD are conveniently absent from writings promoting the theory.

ROGD has seen an uptake among clinicians associated with the corrective approach, which aims at reducing the likelihood of youth growing up trans and has been likened to conversion therapy (Pediatric and Adolescent Gender Dysphoria Working Group, n.d.; Temple Newhook et al., 2018, p. 220; Zucker et al., 2012). While the corrective approach long focused on pre-pubescent children whose gender identity is claimed to be malleable, ROGD theory offers an excuse to extend the corrective approach to teenagers and young adults. Attempts to change gender identity and/or promote identification with sex assigned at birth has been widely opposed by professional associations (Ashley, n.d.; Coleman et al., 2012; UKCP et al., 2017).

This article aims to introduce readers to the construct of ROGD and its methodological and interpretive flaws. Despite professing to be scientific, observations associated with ROGD are best explained without positing a new clinical subgroup with pathological roots. ROGD theory is best understood as an attempt to circumvent existing research that demonstrates the importance of gender affirmation, relying on scientific-sounding language to achieve respectability. In the first section, I provide a short overview of the history of ROGD theory. In the second section, I evaluate the plausibility of empirical and theoretical claims made by proponents of ROGD theory. In the third section, I make three structural remarks about the broader social discourse underpinning ROGD.

A short history of ROGD theory

The first recorded use of 'rapid-onset gender dysphoria' was 2 July 2016 in a post on the blog 4thWaveNow, which is dedicated to opposing gender-affirmative care for trans youth. The post invited parents of children who evidenced 'a sudden or rapid development of gender dysphoria beginning between the ages of 10 and 21' to participate in a study by Lisa Littman, then an adjunct assistant professor of preventive medicine at the Icahn School of Medicine at Mount Sinai, New York (4thWaveNow, 2016). The study also recruited participants via Transgender Trend and Youth Trans Critical Professionals, organisations dedicated to opposing 'trans ideology', giving rise to serious concerns about sampling bias (Restar, 2020). The study, based exclusively on parent reports, was first published as a poster abstract in the *Journal of Adolescent Health* (Littman, 2017) and subsequently as an article in *PLoS ONE* in August 2018 (Littman, 2019).[1] The study described ROGD as a new presentation of gender dysphoria, grounded in social contagion.

While a few articles suggesting a link between youth coming out as trans and social media were published before the study's poster abstract (4thWaveNow, 2016; Marchiano, 2016), references to social contagion drastically increased after it was published. Most noteworthy in the early phase between publication of the abstract and full study are essays by Lisa Marchiano (2017a), and Bailey and Blanchard (2017). Marchiano provided feedback to Littman throughout the drafting and submission process of the full study, while Bailey and Blanchard's work has long been criticised for perpetuating stereotypes and prejudices against trans women, notably suggesting that LGBQ trans women's primary motivation for transitioning is sexual arousal (Armstrong, 2004; Serano, 2010; see also Serano, this collection). Shortly after Bailey and Blanchard's article was published on 4thWaveNow, Barbara Kay (2017) wrote about ROGD in the *National Post*, Canada's leading conservative newspaper. Articles in newspapers such as the Canadian *Globe and Mail* (Soh, 2018), *The Times* in the UK (Turner, 2018) and *The Australian* (Lane, 2019) later followed, both before and after the full study was published.

Later in 2017, ROGD begun being mentioned in academic publications. Controversial Canadian psychologist Kenneth Zucker, whose clinic was closed in 2015 amidst allegations of engaging in conversion practices, referred to Littman's poster presentation in two publications (Zucker, 2017, 2018), whereas Marchiano has published a peer-reviewed article on the theory (2017b), largely based on a previous online essay. Littman's full study has since been cited in dozens of articles, commentaries and letters to the editor. The study has also influenced policy, with the conservative South Dakota house of representatives passing a Bill that would prohibit teaching students about gender dysphoria out of fear of social contagion (Lang, 2019). The Bill was later blocked at the state senate.

Although ROGD was rapidly adopted in circles that were critical of (and often hostile to) gender-affirmative care, it was also subject to strong criticism from trans health researchers and trans communities. Less than two weeks after publication, the journal announced that it would conduct a post-publication review. The review led the journal to publish a correction (Littman, 2019), a formal comment (Brandelli Costa, 2019), and an apology to trans communities (Heber, 2019). The corrected version of the paper better highlighted that the study does little more than generate new hypotheses for future testing and cannot be claimed to establish or validate the existence of ROGD. Despite this acknowledgement, opponents of gender-affirmative care continue to cite the study as evidence of ROGD's existence, and Lisa Littman herself has recently claimed that the study supports the ROGD hypothesis (Kay, 2019).

Empirical and theoretical claims associated with ROGD

Proponents of the theory view it as a new phenomenon that is distinct from traditional late-onset gender dysphoria, involving the spread of false belief caused by underlying mental illness, sexism and internalised homophobia. A degradation in mental health and parent–child relationship is said to follow coming out, as ROGD youth aren't 'really' trans and their underlying psychosocial problems are not attended to. Because of these beliefs, proponents of ROGD theory believe that gender-affirmative care is tantamount to abuse and that trans identities should instead be actively discouraged among these youth (Rosario Sánchez et al., 2019). In this section, I critically assess the empirical and theoretical claims associated with ROGD theory and argue that they are either unsubstantiated or banal.

Distinguishing ROGD from traditional late-onset gender dysphoria

According to proponents of ROGD, recent years have been the stage of an explosion of youth 'presenting with dysphoria "out of the blue" without ever having expressed any gender variance before', a phenomenon that 'was virtually unheard of until a few years ago' (Marchiano, 2017b, p. 348). In Lisa Littman's study, parents reported their children coming out as trans at 15.2 years old on average (2018, p. 2). Contradicting this proclaimed novelty, available data suggest that as many as 40% of trans adults begin to feel like they may not be cisgender at or after 11 years old, and 19% report beginning feeling that way after 15 years old (James et al., 2016). An average coming out age of 15.2 years old is far from unusual, especially given the common lag between realising or privately processing one might be trans and coming out.

Accounts of ROGD often fail to provide a viable clinical rationale for excluding the classification of late-onset gender dysphoria, a well-documented clinical presentation. According to the DSM-5 (American Psychiatric Association, 2013, pp. 455–456):

> Late-onset gender dysphoria occurs around puberty or much later in life. Some of these individuals report having had a desire to be of the other gender in childhood that was not expressed verbally to others. Others do not recall any signs of childhood gender dysphoria. For adolescent males [*sic*] with late-onset gender dysphoria, parents often report surprise because they did not see signs of gender dysphoria during childhood. . . . Parents of natal adolescent females [*sic*] with the late-onset form also report surprise, as no signs of childhood gender dysphoria were evident.

Take the example of Noah, a 'strikingly good looking' trans adolescent whom clinicians Marina Bonfatto and Eva Crasnow (2018) present as an example of ROGD. Without clear reasons, they hypothesise that Noah's gender dysphoria is caused by premature sexualisation of his changing 'female' body and by his mother's hostility towards femininity. Yet nothing in Noah's clinical presentation was unusual from the perspective of late-onset gender dysphoria, including disagreement between Noah and his parents regarding early childhood gender non-conformity.

Bailey and Blanchard (2017) have explained their motivation for viewing ROGD as a new clinical presentation by associating traditional late-onset gender dysphoria with autogynephilia (see Serano, this collection), a discredited theory which only applies to people assigned male at birth and which posits fetishistic underpinnings to gender dysphoria (Bettcher, 2014; Moser, 2009, 2010; Serano, 2010). Since 'traditional' late-onset gender dysphoria is nearly exclusively transfeminine, this means trans youth who are assigned female at birth must fall into a new category, hence ROGD.

The corrected version of Littman's study acknowledges that ROGD and late-onset gender dysphoria are not mutually exclusive, but nevertheless posits ROGD as a distinct phenomenon by pointing to historically low rates of late-onset gender dysphoria among youth assigned female at birth at gender identity clinics. However, that explanation is unsatisfactory insofar as clinic populations may not reflect overall trans populations: adults assigned male at birth have long been much more common at gender identity clinics despite roughly equal proportions in the overall population (James et al., 2016).

Despite Marchiano's descriptor 'out of the blue', there is nothing particularly significant or novel about the absence of pre-pubertal gender dysphoria. The DSM-5's description of late-onset gender dysphoria acknowledges that individuals may present with or without recalled childhood gender dysphoria. Puberty is known for its role in intensifying or unearthing gender dysphoria in part due to changes and development in secondary sexual characteristics (Steensma et al., 2011). Given what we know, there is no compelling reason to view suggested cases of ROGD as anything but commonplace late-onset gender dysphoria.

Trans as a psychic epidemic

The thesis of social contagion is allegedly supported by the stark rise in teenagers referred to gender identity clinics, as well as patterns of LGBT+ friend groups, internet usage and social isolation. However, none of these corroborate the existence of social contagion or psychic epidemic.

The stark rise in referrals is most likely attributable to more trans people seeking transition-related care in a context of increased trans visibility. The intensity of gender dysphoria and prevalence of mental health issues have remained stable at gender identity clinics in recent years (Arnoldussen et al., 2019), suggesting that the clinical population has not substantially changed. On the other hand, cultural determinants of access to transition-related care such as mainstream visibility are likely to have outsized effects on referral rates since the gender identity clinic population is exceedingly small compared to the overall number of trans people (Ashley, 2019c).

Lisa Littman's parent respondents reported that on average, 3.5 individuals in their child's friend group came out as trans and 63.5% of the children increased their internet and social media usage immediately prior to coming out (Littman, 2018, pp. 17, 20), leading proponents of the theory to claim that the armchair-diagnosed children were 'strongly influenced by their peers and by the media, who are promoting the transgender lifestyle as popular, desirable and the solution to all of their problems' (Parents of ROGD Kids, n.d.). The theory was said to be confirmed by how many of them increased in popularity after coming out and belonged to friend groups that 'poked fun' at cisgender, heterosexual people.

Despite the claims put forward by proponents of ROGD, these numbers are unsurprising. While Littman's figure of 3.5 trans friends per group may appear large given the relative rarity of trans people, the variables are not independent and trans youth will frequently seek out friend groups or online content that reflects their gender questioning. In one example given by Littman (2018, p. 17), the friend group of the trans teenager was known for regularly discussing gender and sexuality. Youth are not dropped into a sea of trans-affirming content, but actively seek it out. Given that relatively few people seriously question their gender, it is unsurprising that trans people would be overrepresented among those who questioned their gender and navigated cyberspace and meatspace – the physical world outside of cyberspace – accordingly. The importance of the internet as a source of support and information for trans people has long been known and was already being observed in the 1990s (Whittle, 1998). Moreover, many queer and trans people tend to be fascinated by queer and trans folk prior to understanding their own identity, often leading them to orbit and form groups around one or two individuals who are out to other young people, but maybe not to their parents. These groups are often critical to the development of positive self-understanding, emboldening youth to admit their gender identity and/or sexual orientation to themselves and, later, to others (Kuper et al., 2018).

Vulnerability and mental illness

For the hypothesis of social contagion to be plausible, being trans must hold a promise strong enough to overcome stigma and the pull of one's true gender identity – otherwise, youth would be unlikely to mistakenly believe they are trans. Under ROGD theory, the appeal of transition lies in offering a quick solution for an underlying psychological distress rooted in mental illness, and trans identities are depicted as 'a symptom of severe psychological pain or dysfunction' (Parents of ROGD Kids, n.d.) or as an attempt to resolve 'all unhappiness, anxiety, and life problems' (Bailey & Blanchard, 2017).

These remarks are supported by reference to allegedly abnormally high reported mental illness rates of 75% (Kaltiala-Heino et al., 2015, p. 5) and 62.5% (Littman, 2018, p. 14) among trans teenagers and especially trans teenagers assigned female at birth. The reported mental illnesses consisted predominantly of depression and anxiety. Contrary to assumption, the rates of mental health issues reported in both studies were in no way abnormal given what is known of trans mental health (Dhejne et al., 2016; James et al., 2016; Reisner et al., 2015). It is well-known that trans people suffer from high rates of anxiety and depression due to transphobia (Bauer et al., 2015) and that puberty exacerbates gender dysphoria (Steensma et al., 2011), leading to higher levels of distress among post-pubescent populations as compared to children. While mental health issues are common among trans people, rates of mental health issues in gender identity clinic referrals have remained substantially the same since 2000 (Arnoldussen et al., 2019), contradicting the claim of novelty underpinning ROGD theory.

That trans identity is pushed onto teenagers as a solution to all their problems also purportedly finds support in the Littman (2018, p. 21) study's claim that 28.7% of youth received online advice that they would never be happy if they didn't transition. The inverse statistic is more telling, however: a strong 71.3% majority of teens purported to have ROGD were never told that they needed to transition in order to be happy. With regard to the remaining 28.7% minority, the context and frequency of the advice was not reported, and so included youth who were only advised to transition after they extensively described their gender histories and experiences of dysphoria, together with youth who only received this advice once or twice, a far cry from peer pressure.

Transitioning as a flight from womanhood

In her 1994 introduction to second edition of *The Transsexual Empire*, Janice Raymond explained that the putative rarity of transmasculine individuals is due to the presence of feminism as a political outlet for frustration with rigid gender roles among women. According to her, trans men aren't as common as trans women because they can funnel their frustrations with gender into feminism. ROGD is instead being depicted as a flight from womanhood motivated by rigid gender roles and the sexual objectification of cis female bodies. Turning to why a trans teenager had a male gender identity, Bonfatto and Crasnow speculated that it was due to 'objectification and premature sexualisation' and his mother's alleged belief 'that being male is preferable to the embracing and celebration of femininity' (2018, p. 43). As is typical of public accounts of ROGD, links to internalised misogyny were purely speculative and not rooted in the teenager's own words. Sexual trauma is another oft-posited source of trans identities. Littman (2018, pp. 2, 14) reported sex or gender-related trauma in 30.1% of teens, 82.8% of whom were assigned female at birth. The absence of control groups and an overbroad definition of sex or gender-related trauma, which included sexual harassment, relationship issues, and break ups, undermine the statistic's utility. Additionally, Littman doesn't account for the fact that trans and gender non-conforming people are at a higher risk of being targeted by sexual harassment and violence (James et al., 2016).

These explanations are presented argumentatively and validated by the stark, 'unexplained' rise in clinical referrals of teenagers assigned female at birth (Aitken et al., 2015). However, the fact that it remains unexplained doesn't relieve ROGD theorists from adequately supporting their preferred explanation. What has changed since 1994 that made feminism no longer a viable political outlet, despite the proliferation of body acceptance movements? Are they suggesting that feminist movements have not only ceased, but regressed significantly?

As previously mentioned, gender identity clinic populations are not representative of the overall trans population. The stark size difference (in the order of magnitude of 20:1) between overall trans populations and clinic populations makes cultural factors impacting referral patterns the most plausible explanation for shift in assigned sex ratios (Ashley, 2019c). If the trans population is 20 times larger than the clinic population, 5% additional trans people seeking referrals corresponds to a 100% increase in clinical referrals. As Arnoldussen et al. (2019) have reported, the intensity of gender dysphoria and prevalence of mental health issues in gender identity clinics have remained stable despite the changing picture of referrals.

Given the various factors which are expected to play a role in shifting gender ratios in gender identity clinics, insufficient support exists for the claim that there is an unexplained and unexpected rise in transgender teenagers assigned female at birth. The attribution of this rise to internalised misogyny and responses to sexual trauma is unsubstantiated, and cultural factors impacting referral rates are more likely culprits than changes in the overall trans population.

Where are the butches?

Hand in hand with the claim that transmasculinities are a 'flight from womanhood' comes the claim that they are rooted in lesbophobia. Butch women – and, to a lesser extent, feminine gay men – are said to be pushed into transition by a society that is more tolerant of straight transgender identities than of cisgender LGBQ people.

One might wonder which society is more tolerating of trans people. Trans psychology has a long history of promoting cisgender gay outcomes over transgender ones (Zucker et al., 2012). Psychiatrist Richard Green, the former head the UCLA Gender Identity Research Clinic, stated as recently as 2017 that he is 'convinced that it is a helluva lot easier negotiating life as a gay man or lesbian woman than as a transwoman or transman' (Green, 2017, p. 82), a position that is reflected in the attitudes of parents of trans children found in case reports. On nearly all metrics, trans people are less accepted than cis LGBQ people (Ashley, 2019d). Most tellingly, 64% of trans and non-binary youth in the United States report that their families make them feel bad about their identity, compared to 34% of cisgender LGBQ youth (Human Rights Campaign, 2018, p. 8). Considering how few trans youth are straight – between 5% and 16.8% (Ashley, 2019d; Human Rights Campaign, 2018, p. 38) – it is difficult to suggest that transition is motivated by the desire to be straight, at least in the global North. Despite these figures and their own acknowledgement that it is harder being trans, trans health theorists have long posited that trans identities are an attempt to avoid being gay, leading to sexual orientation featuring prominently in early typologies. Those theories have since been largely abandoned by researchers in part due to more serious engagement by mental health professionals with trans accounts, which radically contradict this early work (see e.g. Bettcher, 2014; Serano, 2010).

Studies on the proportion of pre-pubertal youth referred to gender clinics who grow up trans have been used in support of the view that trans affirmation is homophobic, since most children at those clinics grow up to be cisgender and LGBQ (Temple Newhook et al., 2018). These studies have been intensely criticised for failing to distinguish gender non-conformity from being transgender, impugning their conclusions. As many as 90% of the subjects already identified with the sex they were assigned at birth (Olson, 2016, p. 156). Because these studies are concerned with pre-pubertal youth rather than adolescents and adults, which are the focus of ROGD theory, their relevance to ROGD was already tenuous. A study by DeLay et al. (2018) titled 'The Influence of Peers During Adolescence: Does Homophobic Name Calling by Peers Change Gender Identity?' has also been used to support the claim that transgender identities develop due to homophobia. However, this relied on a grave misinterpretation: what the study found was that gay boys attacked for their gender non-conformity felt less affinity with boys than girls, a somewhat unsurprising conclusion given that most of them were targeted precisely because they were effeminate. The study used the term 'gender identity' completely differently from how it is used in trans contexts.

Anecdotal references to worries among lesbians are also presented as evidence of gender transition's lesbophobic underpinnings: 'Lesbians are particularly worried about the teen trans trend, as most girls coming out as transgender are same-sex attracted. Many in the lesbian community are distraught to notice that butch lesbians are quickly disappearing' (Marchiano, 2017b, p. 350). Claims that butches are disappearing and becoming trans men are far from new. Much ink has been spilled over the 'FTM/Butch Border Wars' of the 1990s and early 2000s, even making it to *The New York Times* (Vitello, 2006). Despite purporting to be a new phenomenon, ROGD theory largely falls in line with rhetoric from the 1990s and 2000s. While many people who identified as butch women in the past are now transgender men or non-binary, it may have more to do with the growing availability and intelligibility of transgender identities than lesbophobia (Lee, 2001). Some trans men and non-binary folk continue to wear the butch label with pride and some of those who have abandoned it did so only because it is seen as a women-only label. Trans people's relationship to gender and sexuality labels is more complicated and messier than anti-trans activists suggest. Anecdotal worries do not provide evidence of lesbophobia.

The degradation of parent–child relationships and mental health

One of ROGD theory's central claims is that transition and gender affirmation makes teenagers purported to have ROGD worse off. The main evidence offered is found in Littman's (2018) parental reports of degrading mental wellbeing and familial relationships after coming out. In the study, parent respondents reported that their parent–child relationships had degraded in 57.3% of cases and that their child's mental wellbeing had deteriorated in 47.2% of cases (p. 22). This is unusual according to her, as 'existing research' on trans adults evidenced 'improved family relationships after coming out' in 61% of cases (Littman, 2017, p. S96) and is contrary to 'the narrative of discovering one's authentic self and then thriving' (Littman, 2018, p. 21). She does not provide a reference for the 61% figure.

Despite having come out an average of 15 months prior to their parents participating in the study, only 14 youth (5.5%) no longer identified as trans to their parents (p. 30). Of those 14, only 3 (1.2%) had begun transitioning and were counted as having detransitioned, in line with reported regret rates among trans adults (Dhejne et al., 2014; Wiepjes et al., 2018). It is worth noting, however, that detransition does not necessarily indicate regret (see Hildebrand-Chupp, this collection) and many youths who detransition are grateful for having had the opportunity to explore their gender identity (Ashley, 2019b; Turban & Keuroghlian, 2018; Turban et al., 2018).

While transition is strongly associated with improved mental health (What We Know, n.d.), the statistics must be reported in light of the Littman study's sampling from overtly transantagonistic groups (Restar, 2020). The difference is important because parental rejection of youth gender identity is causally related to deterioration of the parent–child relationship, as with any rejection of a component of youths' core sense of self. Given the context of dependency which structures teenager–parent dynamics, it is unsurprising that lack of acceptance leads to poor mental health, as was confirmed by at least one youth represented by the Littman study (Tannehill, 2018). It is well-known that poor parental acceptance of gender identity is one of the strongest predictors of suicidality among transgender people (Bauer et al., 2015).

While the phenomenon is undertheorised, coming out is anecdotally associated with temporary spikes in body and social gender dysphoria (MacKinnon, 2018; Price, 2019). Cultural meaning mediates experiences of body dysphoria. Much like how misgendering can feel more invalidating when you're actively trying to be read as a given gender, body dysphoria can also be magnified by social context. This distress, however, seems to decrease over time. Littman's observations may thus partly reflect an ephemeral phenomenon. Alongside access to affirmation, social and medical transition are associated with better mental health in the long term (What We Know, n.d.).

The Littman (2018) study's reported degradation in mental health and familial relationships can readily be explained by the oppositional attitudes of its parental participants, coupled with the social and psychological difficulties that are unfortunately associated with coming out in a world that remains unwelcoming of trans people. The reported trend would, in all likelihood, be radically different were the respondents accepting of their children (Olson et al., 2016).

Opposition to gender affirmation and support for conversion practices

Giving away their political hand, many proponents of ROGD theory advocate for discouraging teenagers' gender identities and accuse affirming clinicians of being negligent, making thinly veiled threats of legal action (PADad, 2018). Despite a legal obligation to maintain patient confidentiality, professionals' unwillingness to discuss teenagers' cases with parents was cast as further evidence of negligence (Littman, 2018). Littman suggests that professionals could gather information from parents despite youths, some of whom were adults, asking that the clinician maintain confidentiality vis-a-vis their parents. Her perspective seems to underestimate the scope of the duty of confidentiality, which goes so far as to preclude doctors from acknowledging that a person is their patient without permission, let alone the content and context of their discussions (e.g. contemplating medical transition, discussing childhood gender history, etc.). Despite over 67.2% of the youth in the study expressing a desire for hormone replacement therapy, only 11.3% of them had accessed hormones (Littman, 2018, pp. 15, 30). This low rate, despite youths having come out on average 15 months prior is plausibly attributable to the combination of parental opposition and the commonly long delays in transition-related care.

Sources promoting ROGD theory routinely generalise opposition to transition regardless of whether individuals fall under its proposed developmental pathway. The website Parents of ROGD Kids, for instance, claims that '[p]rofessionals who accept an individual's self-diagnosis and propose medical interventions are negligent' and that '[m]edical intervention for gender dysphoria should be a last resort' (n.d.). Controversial clinicians Bailey and Blanchard recommend 'against hiring gender clinicians who are hostile to our typology', a typology which includes autogynephilia and ROGD (2017). An open-letter posted to 4thWaveNow goes in a similar direction, stating (PADad, 2018):

> At a minimum, you should be raising the bar and making selection criteria considerably more stringent before prescribing 'puberty blockers,' HRT and surgeries. Because these treatments have permanent effects on patients' bodies and minds, you should be first requiring alternatives to these treatments which are more reversible.

This newfound support for conversion practices, which aim at changing or discouraging the gender identities of trans individuals, is worrisome. In recent times, such approaches had been theoretically narrowed to pre-pubertal youth under the belief that adolescents and adults' gender identities are no longer malleable (Zucker et al., 2012). However, these same practitioners seem to be welcoming ROGD theory (Pediatric and Adolescent

Gender Dysphoria Working Group, n.d.) and have endorsed the return of conversion practices for adults (Zucker et al., 2016). Unsurprisingly, ROGD has also been mobilised by conservative groups who oppose laws banning conversion practices (e.g. National Task Force for Therapy Equality, 2018).

ROGD notwithstanding, conversion practices are deemed unethical by the World Professional Association for Transgender Health (WPATH) Standards of Care (Coleman et al., 2012) and opposed by many leading professional associations (Ashley, n.d.). They are associated with severe psychological distress and suicidality, including a 2.27-fold increase in lifetime suicide attempts (Turban et al., 2020). Gender affirmation and access to transition remain the dominant and most empirically supported approach to trans youth care (Ashley, 2019b; Lopez et al., 2017; Rafferty, 2018; Telfer et al., 2018).

Structural remarks on ROGD discourse

Testimonial injustice and the absence of adolescent trans voices

The voices of trans youth are noticeably absent from the ROGD literature. Littman's study was based on parental reports sampled from transantagonistic websites, a significant limitation which was severely downplayed prior to post-publication review. While parent reports are not unusual in social science research, the decision to rely solely on parental reports is puzzling given the heavy sample bias and the unreliability of parent reports in the context of poor familial relationships. The chronology of ROGD theory and the choice to advertise solely on transantagonistic websites have led some to suspect that Littman's exclusion of trans voices was informed by prejudice or ideological alignment. Denying trans people's epistemic agency and credibility is one of the ways in which transantagonistic attitudes are operationalised (Ashley, 2019a; Bettcher, 2009; McKinnon, 2017).

The rare times trans voices can be found in the ROGD literature, they are inescapably contradicted. To claims of being transgender from trans youth, the retort is that they are not qualified to self-assess (Littman, 2018) even though gender identity is not a medical diagnosis and is indeed something of which trans people have privileged knowledge (Ashley, 2019a; Richards et al., 2015). Despite disavowing the validity of self-diagnosis, Littman ironically relies on parental responses as a proxy for diagnosing both childhood and adolescent gender dysphoria (Restar, 2020). To the 63.8% of teens in the study who were reported as accusing their parents of transphobia, Littman points to parents' support of same-sex marriage and equal rights for trans people as evidence to the contrary. Yet, support for trans equal rights does not equate to social acceptance or substantive rights, nor acceptance of trans people in their immediate family. Political claims made by trans groups are regularly described as 'asking for special rights' by opponents (Radcliffe, 2013), enabling parents to maintain a facade of progressivism while remaining deeply transantagonistic.

To support the hypothesis of ROGD, it would have been essential to obtain youths' own perspectives as to their mental wellbeing and the perceived reasons for improvement or decline. Furthermore, if these youths' belief of being trans is an unhealthy coping mechanism, we would expect a significant rate of detransition. Yet despite having come out on average 15 months ago, only 5.5% were reported to have re-identified with the sex they were assigned at birth and, of those, 78.6% had not taken steps towards social, legal, or medical transition (Littman, 2018). A common feature of reports of ROGD is that despite reporting bias and strong parental pressures against transition, most youth do not detransition, shedding serious doubt on ROGD's sweeping claims of a false belief epidemic.

Aetiology isn't destiny

Let us assume, for a moment, that there is indeed a new subgroup of youth who, having experienced trauma and mental illness, come to believe themselves to be trans as a maladaptive coping mechanism. It would not follow that social and/or medical transition is unethical or harmful. As Tey Meadow elegantly puts it (2018, p. 90):

> [I]t's not a huge leap to imagine that some forms of gender could be made of scar tissue, produced as much by trauma as by tenderness. But it's a quick and dangerous slide from thinking about gender deviance as compensatory and thinking it pathological.

Not all coping mechanisms are unhealthy. Even if it were the case that for some people believing oneself transgender is a coping mechanism brought on by trauma, transition may still be indicated. If the rise in transgender identities evidences social contagion – a claim I have shown to be unsubstantiated – it may yet be a healthy contagion. Rather than escapism, working from this premise, youth may simply be using available tools to deal with their problems, remaking themselves in the process. The overwhelming majority of youths mentioned in Littman's (2018) study continue to identify as trans. Describing Noah's alleged ROGD, Bonfatto and Crasnow go on to mention that he ended up taking puberty blockers and moving on to hormone replacement therapy, flourishing into a healthy trans adult: 'As his adolescence has drawn on he is functioning well and has moved on to university' (Bonfatto and Crasnow, 2018, p. 43). If identifying as trans could be described as a coping mechanism, none of the available evidence would suggest it being an unhealthy one.

Pathologising accounts of aetiology (the cause(s) of being trans) are as old as trans health itself (Pyne, 2014). Besides biological causes, mental illness and parental behaviour have commonly been posited. Even in recent years, proposed causes have included separation anxiety, autism-spectrum 'disorder', and parental transference of 'unresolved conflict and trauma-related experiences' (Zucker et al., 2012, pp. 378, 380). ROGD's proposal of mental illness and trauma as roots of trans identity is a familiar one.

Contrary to the assumption that aetiology is uniquely relevant to clinical ethics, many clinicians deem it unimportant (Vrouenraets et al., 2015). The primary focus should instead be on how to best support the individual. If we are concerned primarily for the wellbeing of adolescents, the cause of gender identity takes on a secondary or tertiary importance. The question we should ask is whether those said to have ROGD are harmed by gender-affirmative care. So far, all evidence points to the opposite conclusion: supporting trans people's gender identities and facilitating access to transition-related care makes them better off (Bauer et al., 2015; Turban et al., 2020; What We Know, n.d.).

Positing a traumatic and pathological aetiology does not overturn existing evidence in favour of gender affirmation. Aetiology isn't destiny.

Circumventing science through pseudoscience

Built on unsound empirical bases and shaky theoretical foundations, ROGD exhibits features of a discursive strategy that mobilises scientific language to circumvent evidence that challenges the status quo. Parallels may be drawn between ROGD, Parental Alienation Syndrome and False Memory Syndrome (Dallam, 2001; Meier, 2009; Schuman & Galvez, 1996).

In 1985, Richard Gardner proposed Parental Alienation Syndrome to refute accusations of child abuse in custody litigation. Suggesting that as many as 90% of children in custody litigation suffered from the syndrome (Meier, 2009), Gardner suggested that vengeful mothers had enlisted and brainwashed their children into believing, repeating and fabricating untrue claims of abuse. The proposed syndrome was based on claimed clinical experience rather than scientific evidence (Meier, 2009), and has been extensively mobilised in custody cases to disclaim abusive behaviour.

Similarly, the False Memory Syndrome construct did not emerge from disinterested research. Instead, it was coined by the False Memory Syndrome Foundation, an organisation of parents accused of child sexual violence, in 1992 (Dallam, 2001). The foundation was created by Peter and Pamela Freyd after their daughter Jennifer Freyd, a respected specialist in memory research, accused Peter of sexual assault. Although false and distorted memories are known to be possible, FMS was predicated on false memories of child sexual violence having reached epidemic proportions due to recovered memory therapies. Without epidemiological evidence or viable means of distinguishing between false memories and recovered memories, the foundation's advocacy and research lent scientific credibility to numerous individuals accused of child sexual violence. Neither proposed syndrome was ever included in the DSM.

The three theories share important features: (1) an extant phenomenon, (2) new scientific language, (3) claims of an epidemic primarily based on anecdotal evidence, and (4) a reactionary party concerned by a challenge to the status quo. The strength of the rhetorical strategy lies in its simultaneous appeal to common sense phenomena and the authority of science. Memories can be defective or distorted. Children can develop unwarranted hostility toward a parent during divorce. People can transition for the wrong reasons. Yet in each case, the further claim of an epidemic that is added to these extant phenomena fails to attract credible evidence and conflicts with known data. Scientific language discursively bridges this evidentiary gap by profiting from the public's shortcomings in distinguishing good from bad (and pseudo-) science. In so doing, proponents of ROGD elevate anecdotal cases to scientific truth, rationalising opposition to social and medical transition. Even if, as with the now-flourishing Noah, it was evidently the right decision.

Epistemological violence and burden of proof

One way of understanding the fundamental problem with ROGD theory is through the notion of epistemological violence. Epistemological violence occurs when data interpretations that have negative consequences for marginalised groups are selected despite the existence of alternative, equally (or more) plausible interpretations (Teo, 2010). From an ethical and epistemological standpoint, interpretations of data that do not perpetuate or reinforce marginalisation should be favoured over those that do.

The anecdotal and scientific data underpinning ROGD theory is best explained by the operative context of transantagonistic parenting against a background of growing visibility and social acceptance of trans people. Despite being presented as evidence of a new developmental pathway, studies such as Littman's (2018) are readily explainable using established knowledge, without relying on a host of unsupported and pathologising assumptions. As such, ROGD theory offers a conspicuous example of epistemological violence, relying on longstanding tropes of trans people as confused and mentally ill to legitimate opposition to social and medical transition.

Despite attempts to shift it onto proponents of gender-affirmative care, the burden of proof lies squarely on proponents of ROGD since they are seeking to displace the empirically backed consensus approach. Evidence only counts as supporting the existence of ROGD if it excludes the possibility of non-pathological, non-epidemic explanations – something that has yet to be offered. Unsurprisingly given the dearth of supporting evidence, many leading experts have rejected ROGD as lacking empirical support (Ashley & Baril, 2018; AusPATH, 2019; Gender Dysphoria Affirmative Working Group, 2018; WPATH, 2018). The post-publication clarification that Littman's article is merely hypothesis-generation rather than hypothesis-testing (Littman, 2019), besides its various flaws, further confirms this conclusion.

Conclusion

More panic than epidemic, proponents of ROGD paint themselves as a marginal group speaking truth to power. In sharp contrast, the theory has spread like wildfire since being coined a few years ago, making its way into national newspapers and being cited by writers, scholars and interest groups with a long history of hostility towards transgender people. As I hope to have shown, ROGD's concerning claims hide a barren empirical wasteland. Instead of a legitimate scientific hypothesis, ROGD is best understood as an attempt to mobilise scientific language to circumvent mounting evidence in favour of gender affirmation (Durwood et al., 2017; Lopez et al., 2017; Olson et al., 2016; Telfer et al., 2018; Turban et al., 2020; What We Know, n.d.) by positing a new clinical subgroup to whom the existing data do not apply. Since gathering new data takes years, this discursive strategy can in turn be used to justify opposing gender affirmation and pressuring youth to identify with the gender they were assigned at birth, a practice akin to conversion therapy.

Despite the facial neutrality of scientific language, the transantagonistic roots of ROGD are easily unearthed. Interposed between claims like '[i]dentifying as the opposite gender is NOT normal', 'she was female, and would never be otherwise' (Parents of ROGD Kids, n.d.), and 'I mean, you can't change your sex, right? It's scientifically impossible' (MacDonald, 2017), proponents of ROGD's self-narratives as accepting-but-concerned individuals cannot but be suspect.

Reports of an epidemic have been greatly exaggerated. Upon closer examination, ROGD reveals itself to be a construct mired in unfounded and prejudiced assumptions. It should be enthusiastically rejected.

Acknowledgements

Florence would like to thank Cáel M. Keegan for his help regarding the history and literature on the FTM/Butch Border Wars, to Jess de Santi for their editing help, and to the peer reviewers for their insightful comments. I would also like to extend an immense thanks to the editors of the collection Ben Vincent, Ruth Pearce and Sonja Erikainen for their amazing and tireless work.

Funding

The author received no financial support for the research, authorship, and/or publication of this article.

Note

1. The original version of the study was replaced by a corrected version and is now available as a supplementary file to the correction notice.

References

4thWaveNow. (2016). *Rapid-onset gender dysphoria: New study recruiting parents.* 4thWaveNow. https://4thwavenow.com/2016/07/02/rapid-onset-gender-dysphoria-new-study-recruiting-parents/ (last accessed 2 June 2020).

Aitken, M., Steensma, T. D., Blanchard, R., VanderLaan, D. P., Wood, H., Fuentes, A., Spegg, C., Wasserman, L., Ames, M., Fitzsimmons, C. L., Leef, J. H., Lishak, V., Reim, E., Takagi, A., Vinik, J., Wreford, J., Cohen-Kettenis, P. T., de Vries, A. L. C., Kreukels, B. P. C., & Zucker, K.J. (2015). Evidence for an altered sex ratio in clinic-referred adolescents with gender dysphoria. *Journal of Sexual Medicine, 12,* 756–763. https://doi.org/10.1111/jsm.12817

American Psychiatric Association. (2013). *Diagnostic and statistical manual of mental disorders, fifth edition (DSM-5).* https://doi.org/10.1176/appi.books.9780890425596

Armstrong, J. (2004). The body within: the body without. *The Globe and Mail.* www.theglobeandmail.com/incoming/the-body-within-the-body-without/article1000111/ (last accessed 2 June 2020).

Arnoldussen, M., Steensma, T. D., Popma, A., van der Miesen, A. I. R., Twisk, J. W. R., & de Vries, A. L. C. (2019). Re-evaluation of the Dutch approach: Are recently referred transgender youth different compared to earlier referrals? *European Child and Adolescent Psychiatry.* Advance online publication. https://doi.org/10.1007/s00787-019-01394-6

Ashley, F. (2019a). Gatekeeping hormone replacement therapy for transgender patients is dehumanising. *Journal of Medical Ethics, 45*(7), 480–482. http://dx.doi.org/10.1136/medethics-2018-105293

Ashley, F. (2019b). Thinking an ethics of gender exploration: Against delaying transition for transgender and gender creative youth. *Clinical Child Psychology and Psychiatry, 24*(2), 223–236. https://doi.org/10.1177/1359104519836462

Ashley, F. (2019c). Shifts in assigned sex ratios at gender identity clinics likely reflect change in referral patterns. *Journal of Sexual Medicine, 16,* 948–949. https://doi.org/10.1016/j.jsxm.2019.03.407

Ashley, F. (2019d). Homophobia, conversion therapy, and care models for trans youth: Defending the gender-affirmative approach. *Journal of LGBT Youth*. Advance online publication. https://doi.org/10.1080/19361653.2019.1665610

Ashley, F. (n.d.). *List of professional organisations opposing conversion practices targeting gender identity*. Florence Ashley. www.florenceashley.com/resources.html (last accessed 2 June 2020).

Ashley, F., & Baril, A. (2018). *Why 'rapid-onset gender dysphoria' is bad science*. The Conversation. https://theconversation.com/why-rapid-onset-gender-dysphoria-is-bad-science-92742 (last accessed 2 June 2020).

AusPATH. (2019). *AusPATH position statement on 'rapid-onset gender dysphoria (ROGD)'*. https://auspath.org/advocacy/ (last accessed 2 June 2020).

Bailey, J. M., & Blanchard, R. (2017). *Gender dysphoria is not one thing*. 4thWaveNow. https://4thwavenow.com/2017/12/07/gender-dysphoria-is-not-one-thing/ (last accessed 2 June 2020).

Bauer, G., Scheim, A. I., Pyne, J., Travers, R., & Hammond, R. (2015). Intervenable factors associated with suicide risk in transgender persons: A respondent driven sampling study in Ontario, Canada. *BMC Public Health*, *15*(525), 1–9. https://doi.org/10.1186/s12889-015-1867-2

Bettcher, T. M. (2009). Trans identities and first-person authority. In L. Shrage (Ed.), *You've changed: Sex reassignment and personal identity* (pp. 98–120). Oxford University Press.

Bettcher, T. M. (2014). When selves have sex: What the phenomenology of trans sexuality can teach about sexual orientation. *Journal of Homosexuality*, *61*, 605–620. https://doi.org/10.1080/00918369.2014.865472

Bonfatto, M., & Crasnow, E. (2018). Gender/ed identities: An overview of our current work as child psychotherapists in the Gender Identity Development Service. *Journal of Child Psychotherapy*, *44*(1), 29–46. https://doi.org/10.1080/0075417X.2018.1443150

Brandelli Costa, A. (2019). Formal comment on: Parent reports of adolescents and young adults perceived to show signs of a rapid onset of gender dysphoria. *PLoS ONE*, *14*(3), e0212578. https://doi.org/10.1371/journal.pone.0212578

Bryant, K. (2006). Making gender identity disorder of childhood: Historical lessons for contemporary debates. *Sexuality Research & Social Policy*, *3*(3), 23–39. https://doi.org/10.1525/srsp.2006.3.3.23

Coleman, E., Bockting, W., Botzer, M., Cohen-Kettenis, P., DeCuypere, G., Feldman, J., Fraser, L., Green, J., Knudson, G., Meyer, W. J., Monstray, S., Adler, R. K., Brown, G. R., Devor, A. H., Ehrbar, R., Ettner, R., Eyler, E., Garofalo, R., Karasic, D., . . . Zucker, K. (2012). Standards of care for the health of transsexual, transgender, and gender-nonconforming people. *International Journal of Transgenderism*, *13*(4), 165–232. https://doi.org/10.1080/15532739.2011.700873

Dallam, S. J. (2001). Crisis or creation? A systematic examination of false memory syndrome. *Journal of Child Sexual Abuse*, *9*(3–4), 9–36. https://doi.org/10.1300/J070v09n03_02

DeLay, D., Martin, C., Cook, R., & Hanish, L. (2018). The influence of peers during adolescence: Does homophobic name calling by peers change gender identity? *Journal of Youth and Adolescence*, *47*(3), 636–649. https://doi.org/10.1007/s10964-017-0749-6

Dhejne, C., Öberg, K., Arver, S., & Landén, M. (2014). An analysis of all applications for sex reassignment surgery in Sweden, 1960–2010: Prevalence, incidence, and regrets. *Archives of Sexual Behavior*, *43*(8), 1535–1545. https://doi.org/10.1007/s10508-014-0300-8

Dhejne, C., Vlerken, R. V., Heylens, G., & Arcelus, J. (2016). Mental health and gender dysphoria: A review of the literature. *International Review of Psychiatry*, *28*(1), 44–57. https://doi.org/10.3109/09540261.2015.1115753

Durwood, L., McLaughlin, K. A., & Olson, K. R. (2017). Mental health and self-worth in socially transitioned transgender youth. *Journal of the American Academy of Child & Adolescent Psychiatry*, *56*(2), 116–123. https://doi.org/10.1016/j.jaac.2016.10.016

Gender Dysphoria Affirmative Working Group. (2018). *Psychology Today response.* . www.gda-workinggroup.com/letter-to-psychology-today (last accessed 2 June 2020).

Green, R. (2017). To transition or not to transition? That is the question. *Current Sexual Health Reports*, *9*, 79–83. https://doi.org/10.1007/s11930-017-0106-5

Heber, J. (2019). *Correcting the scientific record on gender incongruence – and an apology.* EveryONE. https://blogs.plos.org/everyone/2019/03/19/correcting-the-scientific-record-and-an-apology/ (last accessed 2 June 2020).

Human Rights Campaign. (2018). *Gender-expansive youth report.* https://assets2.hrc.org/files/assets/resources/GEreport1.pdf (last accessed 2 June 2020).

James, S. E., Herman, J. L., Rankin, S., Keisling, M., Mottet, L., & Anafi, M. (2016). *The report of the 2015 U.S. transgender survey.* National Center for Transgender Equality. https://transequality.org/sites/default/files/docs/usts/USTS-Full-Report-Dec17.pdf (last accessed 2 June 2020).

Kaltiala-Heino, R., Sumia, M., Työläjärvi, M., & Lindberg, N. (2015). Two years of gender identity service for minors: Overrepresentation of natal girls with severe problems in adolescent development. *Child and Adolescent Psychiatry and Mental Health*, *9*(9), 1–9. https://doi.org/10.1186/s13034-015-0042-y

Kay, B. (2017, December 13). Barbara Kay: Parents face scorn for worrying about letting their children change genders. *The National Post.* https://nationalpost.com/opinion/barbara-kay-parents-victimized-in-the-identity-vs-mental-health-battle-over-transgendered-children (last accessed 2 June 2020).

Kay, J. (2019). *An interview with Lisa Littman, who coined the term 'rapid onset gender dysphoria'.* Quillette. https://quillette.com/2019/03/19/an-interview-with-lisa-littman-who-coined-the-term-rapid-onset-gender-dysphoria/ (last accessed 2 June 2020).

Kuper, L. E., Wright, L., & Mutanski, B. (2018). Gender identity development among transgender and gender nonconforming emerging adults: An intersectional approach. *International Journal of Transgenderism*, *19*(4), 436–455. https://doi.org/10.1080/15532739.2018.1443869

Lane, B. (2019). Cookie-cutter gender clinics for troubled teens. *The Australian.* www.theaustralian.com.au/inquirer/affirm-and-medicate-cookiecutter-gender-clinics-for-troubled-teens/news-story/9e8222edc2b22516e8c488ed3d5c199b/ (last accessed 2 June 2020).

Lang, N. (2019). *South Dakota's house just passed an anti-trans bill. It could be coming to your state next.* Rewire.News. https://rewire.news/article/2019/02/15/south-dakotas-house-just-passed-an-anti-trans-bill-it-could-be-coming-to-your-state-next/ (last accessed 2 June 2020).

Lee, T. (2001). Trans(re)lations: Lesbian and female to male transsexual accounts of identity. *Women's Studies International Forum*, *24*(3–4), 347–357. https://doi.org/10.1016/S0277-5395(01)00182-0

Littman, L. (2017). Rapid onset gender dysphoria in adolescents and young adults: A descriptive study. *Journal of Adolescent Health*, *60*, S95–S96. 10.1371/journal.pone.0202330

Littman, L. (2018). Parent reports of adolescents and young adults perceived to show signs of a rapid onset of gender dysphoria. *PLoS One*, *13*(8), e0202330. https://doi.org/10.1371/journal.pone.0202330

Littman, L. (2019). Correction: Parent reports of adolescents and young adults perceived to show signs of a rapid onset of gender dysphoria. *PLoS ONE*, *14*(3), e0214157. https://doi.org/10.1371/journal.pone.0214157

Lopez, X., Marinkovic, M., Eimicke, T., Rosenthal, S. M., & Olshan, J. S. (2017). Statement on gender-affirmative approach to care from the pediatric endocrine society special interest group on transgender health. *Current Opinion in Pediatrics*, *29*(4), 475–480. https://doi.org/10.1097/MOP.0000000000000516

MacDonald, L. (2017). *Call the police! Mom questions transgender treatment model, gets banned from support group*. 4thWaveNow. https://4thwavenow.com/2017/12/01/call-the-police-mom-questions-transgender-treatment-model-gets-banned-from-support-group/ (last accessed 2 June 2020).

MacKinnon, S. (2018). *Why I had to give up swimming to accept my trans identity*. Them.us. www.them.us/story/swimming-nonbinary-trans (last accessed 2 June 2020).

Marchiano, L. (2016). *Layers of meaning: A Jungian analyst questions the identity model for trans-identified youth*. 4thWaveNow. https://4thwavenow.com/2016/09/25/layers-of-meaning-a-jungian-analyst-questions-the-identity-model-for-trans-identified-youth/ (last accessed 2 June 2020).

Marchiano, L. (2017a). *Misunderstanding a new kind of gender dysphoria*. Quillette. https://quillette.com/2017/10/06/misunderstanding-new-kind-gender-dysphoria/ (last accessed 2 June 2020).

Marchiano, L. (2017b). Outbreak: On transgender teens and psychic epidemics. *Psychological Perspectives: A Quarterly Journal of Jungian Thought*, *60*(3), 345–366. https://doi.org/10.1080/00332925.2017.1350804

McKinnon, R. (2017). Allies behaving badly: Gaslighting as epistemic injustice. In I. Kidd, J. Medina & G. Polhaus (Eds.), *The Routledge handbook of epistemic injustice* (pp. 167–174). Routledge.

Meadow, T. (2018). *Trans kids: Being gendered in the twenty-first century*. University of California Press.

Meier, J. S. (2009). A historical perspective on parental alienation syndrome and parental alienation. *Journal of Child Custody*, *6*(3-4), 232–257. https://doi.org/10.1080/15379410903084681

Moser, C. (2009) Autogynephilia in women. *Journal of Homosexuality*, *56*, 539–547. https://doi.org/10.1080/00918360903005212

Moser, C. (2010). Blanchard's autogynephilia theory: A critique. *Journal of Homosexuality*, *57*, 790–809. https://doi.org/10.1080/00918369.2010.486241

National Task Force for Therapy Equality. (2018). *What happens when therapy is banned?* www.therapyequality.org/factsheet (last accessed 2 June 2020).

Olson, K. R. (2016). Prepubescent transgender children: What we do and do not know. *Journal of the American Academy of Child & Adolescent Psychiatry*, *55*(3), 155–156. https://doi.org/10.1016/j.jaac.2015.11.015

Olson, K. R., Durwood, L., DeMeules, M., & McLaughlin, K. A. (2016). Mental health of transgender children supported in their identities. *Pediatrics*, *137*(3), e20153223. https://doi.org/10.1542/peds.2015-3223

PADad. (2018). *Letter to a gender clinic: A parent's call to action*. 4thWaveNow. https://4thwavenow.com/2018/04/08/letter-to-a-gender-clinic-a-parents-call-to-action/ (last accessed 2 June 2020).

Parents of ROGD Kids. (n.d.) *We are the parents of ROGD kids*. Parents of ROGD Kids. www.parentsofrogdkids.com/ (last accessed 2 June 2020).

Pediatric and Adolescent Gender Dysphoria Working Group. (n.d.). *Who we are*. https://gdworkinggroup.org/who-we-are/ (last accessed 2 June 2020).

Price, D. (2019). *The dysphoria paradox*. Slate. https://slate.com/human-interest/2019/01/gender-dysphoria-treatment-transition-process.html (last accessed 2 June 2020).

Pyne, J. (2014). The governance of gender non-conforming children: A dangerous enclosure. *Annual Review of Critical Psychology*, *11*, 79–96.

Radcliffe, C. (2013). *Do we care about trans rights?* Huffington Post. www.huffingtonpost.com/charles-radcliffe/do-we-care-about-trans-rights_b_4293300.html (last accessed 2 June 2020).

Rafferty, J. (2018). Ensuring comprehensive care and support for transgender and gender-diverse children and adolescents. *Pediatrics*, *142*(4), e20182162. https://doi.org/10.1542/peds.2018-2162

Reisner, S. L., Vetters, R., Leclerc, M., Zaslow, S., Wolfrum, S., Shumer, D., & Mimiaga, M. J. (2015). Mental health of transgender youth in care at an adolescent urban community health center: A matched retrospective cohort study. *Journal of Adolescent Health*, *56*(3), 274–279. https://doi.org/10.1016/j.jadohealth.2014.10.264

Restar, A. J. (2020). Methodological critique of Littman's (2018) Parental-respondents accounts of 'rapid-onset gender dysphoria'. *Archives of Sexual Behavior*, *49*, 61–66. https://doi.org/10.1007/s10508-019-1453-2

Richards, C., Arcelus, J., Barrett, J., Bouman, W. P., Lenihan, P., Lorimer, S., Murjan, S., & Seal, L. (2015). Trans is not a disorder – but should still receive funding. *Sexual and Relationship Therapy*, *30*(3), 309–313. https://doi.org/10.1080/14681994.2015.1054110

Rosario Sánchez, R. (2019). *'No child is born in the wrong body' with Michelle Moore & Heather Brunskell-Evans*. Woman's Place UK. https://womansplaceuk.org/2019/10/14/no-child-is-born-in-the-wrong-body-with-michele-moore-heather-brunskell-evans/ (last accessed 2 June 2020).

Schuman, J., & Galvez, M. (1996). A meta/multi-discursive reading of 'false memory syndrome'. *Feminism & Psychology*, *6*(1), 7–29. https://doi.org/10.1177/0959353596061002

Serano, J. (2010). The case against autogynephilia. *International Journal of Transgenderism*, *12*, 176–187. https://doi.org/10.1080/15532739.2010.514223

Soh, D. (2018). Don't treat all cases of gender dysphoria the same way. *The Globe and Mail*. www.theglobeandmail.com/opinion/dont-treat-all-cases-of-gender-dysphoria-the-same-way/article37711831/ (last accessed 2 June 2020).

Steensma, T., Biemond, R., de Boer, F., & Cohen-Kettenis, P. (2011). Desisting and persisting gender dysphoria after childhood: A qualitative follow-up study. *Clinical Child Psychology and Psychiatry*, *16*(4), 499–516. https://doi.org/10.1177/1359104510378303

Tannehill, B. (2018). *'Rapid onset gender dysphoria' is biased junk science*. The Advocate. www.advocate.com/commentary/2018/2/20/rapid-onset-gender-dysphoria-biased-junk-science (last accessed 2 June 2020).

Telfer, M. M., Tollit, M. A., Pace, C. C., & Pang, K. C. (2018). *Australian standards of care and treatment guidelines for trans and gender diverse children and adolescents version 1.1*. The Royal Children's Hospital Melbourne. www.rch.org.au/uploadedFiles/Main/Content/adolescent-medicine/australian-standards-of-care-and-treatment-guidelines-for-trans-and-gender-diverse-children-and-adolescents.pdf (last accessed 2 June 2020).

Temple Newhook, J., Pyne, J., Winters, K., Feder, S., Holmes, C., Tosh, J., Sinnott, M.-L., Jamieson, A., & Pickett, S. (2018). A critical commentary on follow-up studies and 'desistance' theories about transgender and gender-nonconforming children. *International Journal of Transgenderism*, *19*(2), 212–224. https://doi.org/10.1080/15532739.2018.1456390

Teo, T. (2010). What is epistemological violence in the empirical social sciences? *Social and Personality Psychology Compass*, *4*(5), 295–303. https://doi.org/10.1111/j.1751-9004.2010.00265.x

Turban, J. L., Beckwith, N., Reisner, S. L., & Keuroghlian, A. S. (2020). Association between recalled exposure to gender identity conversion efforts and psychological distress and suicide

attempts among transgender adults. *JAMA Psychiatry*, *77*(1), 68–76. https://doi.org/10.1001/
jamapsychiatry.2019.2285

Turban, J. L., Carswell, J., & Keuroghlian, A. S. (2018). Understanding pediatric patients who
discontinue gender-affirming hormonal interventions. *JAMA Pediatrics*, *172*(10), 903–904.
https://doi.org/10.1001/jamapediatrics.2018.1817

Turban, J. L., & Keuroghlian, A. S. (2018). Dynamic gender presentations: Understanding transition and 'de-transition' among transgender youth. *Journal of the American Academy of Child
& Adolescent Psychiatry*, *57*(7), 451–453. https://doi.org/10.1016/j.jaac.2018.03.016

Turner, J. (2018). Trans teenagers have become an experiment. *The Times*. https://www.thetimes.
co.uk/article/trans-teenagers-have-become-an-experiment-87vn5m8fw (last accessed 2 June
2020).

UKCP, BACP, British Psychoanalytic Council, GLADD, The National Counselling Society,
ACC, Pink Therapy, COSRT, The British Psychological Society, BABCP, Royal College of
General Practitioners, NHS England, & NHS Scotland. (2017). *Memorandum of understanding on conversion therapy in the UK, Version 2*. www.bacp.co.uk/media/6526/memorandum-
of-understanding-v2-reva-jul19.pdf (last accessed 2 June 2020).

Vitello, P. (2006, August 20). The trouble when Jane becomes Jack. *New York Times*. https://www.
nytimes.com/2006/08/20/fashion/20gender.html (last accessed 2 June 2020).

Vrouenraets, L., Fredriks, A. M., Hannema, S., Cohen-Kettenis, P., & de Vries, M. (2015).
Early medical treatment of children and adolescents with gender dysphoria: An empirical
ethical study. *Journal of Adolescent Health*, *57*, 367–373. https://doi.org/10.1016/j.jado-
health.2015.04.004

What We Know. (n.d.). *What does the scholarly research say about the effect of gender transition on transgender well-being?* What We Know: The Public Policy Research Portal. https://
whatweknow.inequality.cornell.edu/topics/lgbt-equality/%20what-does-the-scholarly-
research-say-about-the-well-being-of-transgender-people%20/ (last accessed 2 June 2020).

Whittle, S. (1998). The trans-cyberian mail way. *Social and Legal Studies*, *7*(3), 389–408. https://
doi.org/10.1177/096466399800700304

Wiepjes, C. M., Nota, N. M., Blok, C. J., Klaver, M., Vries, A. L., Wensing-Kruger, S. A., . . .
Heijer, M. D. (2018). The Amsterdam Cohort of Gender Dysphoria Study (1972–2015):
Trends in prevalence, treatment, and regrets. *The Journal of Sexual Medicine*, *15*(4), 582–
590. https://doi.org/10.1016/j.jsxm.2018.01.016

World Professional Association for Transgender Health (WPATH). (2018). *WPATH statement
on 'rapid-onset gender dysphoria'*. WPATH. www.wpath.org/policies (last accessed 2 June
2020).

Zucker, K. (2017). Epidemiology of gender dysphoria and transgender identity. *Sexual Health*, *14*,
404–411. https://doi.org/10.1071/SH17067

Zucker, K. (2018). The myth of persistence: Response to 'A critical commentary on follow-up
studies and "desistance" theories about transgender and gender nonconforming children' by
Temple Newhook et al. (2018). *International Journal of Transgenderism*, *19*(2), 231–245.
https://doi.org/10.1080/15532739.2018.1468293

Zucker, K., Lawrence, A. A., & Kreukels, B. P. C. (2016). Gender dysphoria in adults.
Annual Review of Clinical Psychology, *12*, 217–247. https://doi.org/10.1146/annurev-
clinpsy-021815-093034

Zucker, K., Wood, H., Singh, D., & Bradley, S. (2012). A developmental, biopsychosocial model
for the treatment of children with gender identity disorder. *Journal of Homosexuality*, *59*(3),
369–397. https://doi.org/10.1080/00918369.2012.653309

Author biography

Florence Ashley (they/them) is a scholar specialising in trans law and bioethics, with a focus on clinical approaches to trans health. Their writing can be found in the *Journal of Medical Ethics, Journal of LGBT Youth, Clinical Child Psychology and Psychiatry, University of Toronto Law Journal*, and *NYU Review of Law & Social Change*.

Article

More than 'canaries in the gender coal mine': A transfeminist approach to research on detransition

The Sociological Review Monographs
2020, Vol. 68(4) 126–142
© The Author(s) 2020
Article reuse guidelines:
sagepub.com/journals-permissions
DOI: 10.1177/0038026120934694
journals.sagepub.com/home/sor

Rowan Hildebrand-Chupp

Department of Sociology, University of California-San Diego, USA

Abstract

Detransition is tied to three related but distinct concepts – the act of detransitioning, the 'detransitioner' identity, and the negative transition experience – which I refer to collectively using the umbrella term 'detrans'. Detrans research is inevitably political and value-laden, but different methodologies and research questions lend themselves to divergent goals. Drawing on work in the feminist philosophy of science and transfeminist scholarship, I draw a conceptual distinction between research aligned with the goals of 'preventing detrans' vs. 'supporting detrans'. Existing research has constructed detransition as a negative clinical outcome to be prevented because it has been focused on the causes of detrans and the detrans rate. Research associated with the goal of supporting detrans is defined by its focus on the experience and process of detrans itself. Research on preventing detrans constructs detrans as a divisive issue of zero-sum clinical risk, and it is not oriented toward helping people who detransition or who have a negative transition experience. Research on supporting detrans, in contrast, constructs detrans as an issue of inclusion and can be used to improve the medical and mental health care that detrans people receive. I argue that there is an urgent need for qualitative sociological research involving detrans people. I conclude with some broad guidelines for researchers studying detrans.

Keywords

detransition, feminist science studies, transfeminism, transgender, transition regret

What detransitioned Women actually want:

1. Study into the safest way to stop T[estosterone].
2. Clothes that fit.
3. People believing the first answer when we get asked about pronouns. . .

Corresponding author:

Rowan Hildebrand-Chupp, Department of Sociology, University of California, San Diego, CA 92093, USA.
Email: rhhildeb@ucsd.edu

4. Better peer support networks. . .
5. The Trans community to be a safe place. . .
6. Universal Health Care. Free therapy. Free surgery. Free recovery. Free meds. Free ambulances. Free and accessible and for everybody.
7. Student Loan Forgiveness. (Freack, 2019)

Donating because free speech and biological sex matters. Detransitioners are the canary in the gender coal mine – we must listen to them. (anonymous comment left on Caspian, 2019)

The epigraphs above express two very different approaches to research on detransition and detransition communities. The first is a blog post written by a detransitioned woman laying out her own tentative wish list. It is accompanied by the following note: 'notice how NONE of this is more gatekeeping' (i.e. restricting access to medical transition). Her desire for research on detransition is part of a broader agenda focused on providing material and social support to detransitioned women. The second epigraph is a note attached to an anonymous donation to James Caspian, a master's student at Bath Spa University whose thesis project studying detransition was blocked by the university's ethics review board.[1] By positioning detransitioners as the 'canary in the gender coal mine', the donor implies that the testimonies of detransitioners are valuable insofar as they signal a broader risk within the entire system of transition-related care, or perhaps within society as a whole. In the former approach, detransition research is important because it will help detransitioners; in the latter approach, detransition research is important because it documents a broader set of harms that must be prevented.

In this article, I explicate the distinction between these two goals, preventing vs. supporting detransition, in order to think through the possible futures of research on detransition. I begin by distinguishing between 'detransition' as an act, 'detransitioner' as an identity and the 'negative transition experience'. Drawing on feminist philosophy of science and transfeminist scholarship, I argue that research on detransition is inevitably value-laden and political, and I sketch out what a transfeminist approach to detransition research might look like. I then review some of the relevant literature, including both clinical scholarship on transition regret and lay research on the online detransitioned women's community carried out by detransitioned women themselves. In the second half of the article, I elaborate on the conceptual distinction between research on preventing detransition and research on supporting detransition, outlining the values, methodologies and consequences associated with each type. I conclude by providing some specific recommendations for future research on detransition, emphasising the importance of qualitative sociological research as well as other methodological approaches that focus on the experience and process of detransition itself in order to generate findings that might be used to help people who detransition.

Conceptualising detransition

Detransition can be broken down into three related but meaningfully distinct concepts: *detransitioning, detransitioner* and *negative transition experience*. The first refers to an observable act or process, the second refers to a specific identity or label that assigns a particular meaning to detransitioning, and the third refers to a subjective experience that can be associated with detransitioning. *Detransition* is, in one sense, a descriptive verb that refers to the act of returning in some way to a pre-transition state. Detransition can have both medical and social components. Medically, someone who is detransitioning may stop taking hormones, or they may begin taking different hormones that are meant to return their hormone levels to a pre-transition state and prevent further change or reverse certain changes to secondary sexual characteristics. It may also involve surgical reversal. Socially, someone who is detransitioning may return to using the pronouns and/ or name they used before transitioning, and they might change their gender presentation. Alternatively, someone who is detransitioning might keep their post-transition name, gender presentation and/or pronouns. Just as transition is an individual process that varies considerably, there are many ways to go through a process of detransition. The term *retransition* is sometimes used to refer to the act or process of transitioning again after having detransitioned at some previous point.

Detransitioner or *detransitioned woman/man* are terms used to refer to a specific way of understanding the experience of detransition, as an identity and community who share this identity. Because these are identities, any definition involves pinning down a set of loosely shared meanings that exist in a particular space and time. 'Detransitioned women' are women who identify as 'detransitioned', which generally means that they were (a) designated female at birth, (b) identified as transgender men, non-binary, genderqueer and/or transmasculine at some later point, and (c) subsequently stopped identifying as transgender and came to identify as detransitioned women. Some use the term 'detransitioned female' because they do not 'identify' as women; rather, they 'accept' or 'embrace' themselves, or at least their bodies, as female (see Hailey, 2017; Stella, 2016). In contrast, while a transgender woman might choose to detransition temporarily by stopping hormones for a limited period of time (see Kanner, 2018), she would almost certainly not refer to herself as a 'detransitioned woman', even if she is technically a 'woman who has detransitioned'. That is a result of the distinction between detransition as act and detransition as identity; becoming a detransitioner involves a fundamental shift in one's subjective understanding of oneself, an understanding that is constructed within these communities. Knowing a person's medical history would give no insight into whether that person had detransitioned in this sense, because it refers to a specific way of making meaning out of the experience of detransition.

Some detransitioners draw a distinction between being 'detransitioned' and being 'reidentified'. The former can refer to someone who medically transitioned and then medically detransitioned, while the latter can refer to someone who may only have socially transitioned, or who only ever identified as transgender but did not change their name, pronouns, or presentation. As a result, sometimes the term 'detransitioned/reidentified' is used to include both groups, but the term 'detransitioned' is also sometimes used as an umbrella term (see Hailey, 2017; Stella, 2016). The terms 'desister' or 'desisted' overlap with the term 'reidentified', in that they are sometimes used within detransition communities to refer to people who identified as transgender as some point as children or adolescents and then stopped. However, the term 'desister' comes from clinical research (e.g. Steensma et al., 2013), and it is relatively uncommon as a term of self-identification.

Rather than using the most conceptually precise terminology that strictly maintains this act/identity distinction (i.e. using the phrase 'medically detransitioned detransitioner' to refer to the intersection of detransition as act and detransition as identity), in this piece I use the term 'detransitioner' to refer to someone who both (a) transitioned and detransitioned medically and (b) identifies as a detransitioner or detransitioned man/woman/male/female. I recognise that the term detransitioner is not always used in this way, and that its meaning continues to be hashed out by these communities. To refer to the broader category of individuals who are or have been in the process of detransition, whether they adopt a detransitioner identity or not, I use the (admittedly awkward) phrase 'people who have detransitioned'. For example, the category 'people who have medically detransitioned' could include someone who has stopped taking hormones (a) because of medical complications, (b) because they only desired the longer-lasting effects from being on hormones for a few months, (c) because they want to become pregnant, (d) because they decided binary transition was not for them and now identify as non-binary, (e) because they now identify as a detransitioner, (f) because of a temporary lack of access to transition-related care, and so on.

I use the broad term *negative transition experience* (NTE) to capture a range of negative subjective evaluations of one's own transition or some aspect of it. The term NTE does not refer to the experiences of some third party. Though research on NTEs has often used narrower terms, like 'regret' and 'dissatisfaction' (see Dhejne et al., 2014; Lawrence, 2003), it seems likely that many NTEs do not fit within these concepts. For example, a number of detransitioners have described grief as a crucial aspect of their detransition experience (e.g. crashchaoscats, 2016). NTEs can be associated with a variety of aspects of transition: physical, psychological, economic and social (see Callahan, 2018). NTEs can shift over time, emerging, subsiding, or changing form. The decision to detransition is not defined by any particular subjective experience. Thus, no one concept, including 'regret', should be the a priori term used to describe transition. It is imperative for researchers to recognise that negative transition experiences are not synonymous with the act of detransition or with identifying as a detransitioner (see Stella, 2016). Though distinguishing between these three concepts (detransitioning, detransitioner and negative transition experience) is incredibly important, my main argument here applies to research involving all three. Rather than continuously restating all three concepts, I use the term '*detrans*' to refer to this constellation of concepts. While I have generally tried to avoid using existing terms in ways that stray too far from their common usage, I am using the term 'detrans' in an idiosyncratic, analytic way for the sake of concision. Nevertheless, I believe that the distinction between these aspects of detrans is crucial. Researchers must be very precise, both conceptually and methodologically, regarding which of these concepts they are studying.

Theoretical background

There is no value-neutral, apolitical way to study detrans. Different forms of detrans research are each entangled with different goals, in a way that is constitutive of knowledge production more broadly and cannot be simply reduced to bias. Researchers have a limited amount of time and resources to spend pursuing grants and carrying out research; constructing a research question necessarily involves deciding not to study others. Within institutional constraints, researchers make value-laden decisions about what topics they should study, what problems are most important, and what questions are most likely to yield compelling findings (Elliott, 2017). Because the existing body of detrans research is quite small, the importance of these decisions is magnified. Moreover, value-laden decisions made now can influence which questions researchers pursue in the future. Furthermore, the particular design of any given study provides empirical support for a limited set of interventions. Taken collectively, these decisions about what questions to ask (and how) constrain, at least to some extent, the types of interventions that can become seen as effective or necessary in the future. Even if these constraining effects diminish in the long-term as a wider range of possible approaches are explored, these decisions can have substantial impacts in the near-term. Feminist philosophers of science have gone even further, arguing that the practical goals of a body of research are deeply embedded in the way that research is conceived, carried out and evaluated (Douglas, 2000; Longino, 2013). In the words of Helen Longino, 'Research cannot be separated from conceptions of what we want the resulting knowledge for' (2013, p. 143).

Emi Koyama's transfeminist manifesto provides a valuable starting point for imagining a transfeminist approach to detrans research. She writes, '[E]ach individual has the right to define her or his own identities and to expect society to respect them' (Koyama, 2003, p. 245). This principle of gender self-determination has important methodological implications for studying detrans. Determining the past and present identity of a person who has detransitioned requires asking them. Therefore, we cannot and should not attempt to deny that detransitioners (a) ever identified as transgender in the first place or (b) truly stopped identifying as transgender (or a gender different from their assignment at birth). Koyama's second principle states, '[W]e hold that we have the sole right to make decisions regarding our own bodies, and that no political, medical, or religious authority shall violate the integrity of our bodies against our will or impede our decisions regarding what we do with them' (Koyama, 2003, p. 245). In the context of detrans research, this principle urges researchers to be sceptical of research that seeks to justify external constraints on decisions about transition *or* detransition. Instead, this principle implies that detrans research should be oriented toward enabling a wider range of options.

I also draw on Finn Enke's analysis of the term 'cis' to insist that we allow detransitioners to exist in the irreconcilable gap between our concepts of trans and cis. Enke writes, 'Despite their binary opposition, cis and trans are not functionally equivalent or parallel figures' (2012, p. 76). Detransitioners build community in the asymmetrical gap between these nonparallel figures. Unless we violate the principle of gender self-determination and ascribe some kind of false consciousness to them, detransitioned women and men are clearly not transgender. Describing them as cisgender is misleading, because it erases their history and experiences with transition and detransition. They often continue to deal with gender dysphoria (Stella, 2016), and many continue to experience what Heath Fogg Davis (2017) would describe as 'sex-identity discrimination'. By constructing a shared set of understandings about their experiences which overlaps with but is distinct from that of many trans communities, detransitioners refuse to 'preserve the stasis of cis as non-trans' (Enke, 2012, p. 74).

Cameron Awkward-Rich's (2017) essay, 'Trans, Feminism: *Or*, Reading like a Depressed Transsexual', suggests one way of imagining the relationship between transfeminism and detransition communities. He asks:

> [W]hat might our expectations for trans/feminist thought oriented to social justice be if we took pain – in this case the psychic pain produced in the encounter between competing theories of gender that seem aimed at each other's annihilation – as a given, not necessarily loaded with moral weight? (Awkward-Rich, 2017, p. 836)

He imagines the figure of the 'depressed transsexual' encountering conflicts between 'trans' and 'feminism'. He writes, 'The depressed transsexual, then, might assess this situation and determine that the problem is not so much that (some) feminists would like him gone. Rather, the problem is that he is here, and now we all have to figure out how to live with that' (Awkward-Rich, 2017, p. 832). I want to apply this same approach: detransitioners are here, and now we all have to figure out how to live with that.

The detransition literature

To date, very little research has been done on detransition. Existing research has almost exclusively studied questions related to the rate of detransition or NTEs. That research has generally centred around the constructs of 'surgical regret' and 'desistance', but these constructs do not neatly map onto the conceptual framework I have put forth. For example, some studies on 'surgical regret' have measured the rate of what I call negative transition experiences (i.e. 'regret' of a specific surgical procedure), while other studies on 'surgical regret' have measured the rate of medical detransition (i.e. 'regret' of medical transition altogether). Overall, this body of research suggests that the rate of medical detransition after gender-affirming surgery is low (e.g. Dhejne et al., 2014), and medical detransition is basically non-existent in desistance research. However, there is almost no research on the rate of detransition or NTEs among those who are taking hormones and have not undergone surgery. Similarly, the only research currently available on the online communities of detransitioners is from informal community surveys carried out internally. In general, existing research on detransition has primarily studied detrans as a negative clinical outcome to be avoided.

Transition regret

Most people who want to describe the detransition rate cite research on the rate of medical detransition after gender-affirming surgery (or 'surgical regret'). The most complete study available used Swedish government data regarding applications for gender-affirming surgery and 'regret applications' for a medical reversal of its effects (Dhejne et al., 2014). These applications were intertwined with the bureaucratic process for changing one's legal sex, and all costs were covered by national health insurance. Out of the 681 successful applicants for surgery in Sweden over the past 50 years, only 15 (2.2%) submitted regret applications. By accessing the complete records of applications to the Swedish government, Dhejne et al. provided a more complete picture than other studies that focused on a single clinic. The rate of regret applications among people who underwent gender-affirming surgery between 2001 and 2010 was only 0.3%. However, among those who did submit a regret application, the median length of time between surgery and regret application was about 8 years. Therefore, if half of the people who submitted a regret application did so 8 or more years after surgery, and the data on regret applications from the 2001–2010 cohort were collected in 2013 or 2014, this more recent 0.3% rate may be an artefact. Nevertheless, if one excludes the people who underwent surgery between 2001 and 2010, there were still only 14 regret applications out of 321 surgery applications (4.4%). Most studies of surgical regret have found rates below 5% (e.g. Hess et al., 2014; Krege et al., 2001; Lawrence, 2003; Nelson et al., 2009; Smith et al., 2005).

The existing body of research on surgical regret is limited in several ways. First, the research does not address the rate of transition regret for those who do not access surgery, or negative experiences with non-surgical aspects of transition. Second, the rigid clinical protocol and other features of the system for providing transition-related care in these European countries may not generalise to some other countries, like the United States. Third, it is possible that some people detransitioned without applying for a medical and legal reversal. While it seems likely that those who submitted 'regret applications' did detransition and stop identifying as transgender, it is still only a proxy for the act of detransition or for a shift in identity, and these statistics do not capture the particular motivations for detransition.

One study has assessed 'known cases of regret' after accessing hormones through informed consent clinics (Deutsch, 2012). Deutsch surveyed health professionals at 12 informed consent clinics in the United States that collectively treated 1944 patients and searched academic, legal and news databases for any cases involving a malpractice lawsuit regarding the provision of hormones. The sites surveyed reported 17 known cases of 'regret', with only three instances 'leading to reversal of gender transition', for a 'prevalence' of 0.1% (Deutsch, 2012, p. 141). She summarises these results as having 'revealed a low regret rate and an absence of any malpractice claims relating to regret' (Deutsch, 2012, p. 146).

Insofar as this study is an attempt to 'reveal' the 'regret rate', it is significantly flawed. Anecdotally, many detransitioners who have NTEs report that they did not confront their previous doctors; they simply stopped showing up at the clinic they previously received services from (e.g. crashchaoscats, 2018). In fact, when a well-funded socially conservative legal organisation began approaching detransitioners looking for potential plaintiffs for lawsuits against professionals providing transition-related care, prominent members of the detransitioned women's community circulated a statement online urging other members not to get involved (Callahan et al., 2017). Thus, any methodological design that relies on adding up all the complaints lodged or lawsuits filed is profoundly limited. Treating the prevalence of lawsuits as an empirically valid indicator of the rate of NTEs might even *encourage* those who experience NTEs to file lawsuits against medical and mental health professionals involved in providing transition-related care. Some people who have an NTE might, upon learning about research using this measure, come to view filing a lawsuit as the best way to make themselves heard.

Desistance

While surgical regret research has been used to suggest the detransition rate is low, desistance research has been used to imply that the detransition rate is much higher than generally recognised. Longitudinal research involving gender non-conforming and/or gender dysphoric children and adolescents suggests that most 'desist', i.e. come to identify with the gender they were designated at birth (e.g. Steensma et al., 2013; Wallien & Cohen-Kettenis, 2008). A number of scholars have criticised this research (e.g. Temple Newhook et al., 2018; Vincent, 2018b), and it does have a number of serious methodological limitations. Rather than wade into the complex debate over desistance research, however, I simply want to note that these studies do not report an overlap between desistance and medical detransition. There certainly are detransitioners who, if they had been enrolled in one of these longitudinal studies as a teenager, would have eventually been classified as a desister who also medically detransitioned (see e.g. McCann, 2017). Absence of evidence is not evidence of absence, but the available desistance research does not provide evidence for a substantial overlap between desistance and medical transition per se. More generally, my discussion here deals with the possibilities for research involving adults, not children or adolescents.[2]

Internal surveys of the online communities

Despite lacking formal research training, detransitioned women have carried out two online surveys of their communities to address the dearth of such research (Hailey, 2017; Stella, 2016). Summaries of these survey results have been posted online, including responses to the open-ended survey questions, but these data have not been formally published in any academic journal. Cari Stella's 2016 survey recruited 203 participants from Tumblr and private detransitioner Facebook groups. Participants included 'anyone female/AFAB [assigned female at birth] who formerly self-described as transgender', including 'women who transitioned, whether socially and/or medically, and have subsequently detransitioned, as well as individuals who still identify as nonbinary or genderfluid, but have desisted from medical or social transition'. The average age at which participants decided to 'come out as trans and/or start transitioning' was 17, and the average age at which participants decided to 'stop' was 21. Twelve per cent of participants experienced only 'social dysphoria', 14% experienced only 'physical sex dysphoria', and 74% experienced both. When asked, 'How has stopping transition impacted your dysphoria?', 11% said it was 'completely gone', 64.5% said that it was better, 17% said it was the same, and 7.5% said it was worse. Participants were asked, 'What led you to stop your transition?', given 14 options, and told to check all options that applied. Fifty-nine per cent of participants reported they 'found alternative ways to cope with dysphoria' and 63% selected 'political/ideological concerns'. These were the two most frequently selected options by around 30 percentage points. When participants were asked, 'Do you believe you were given adequate counselling and accurate information about transition?', 68% said no, 26% said 'somewhat', and 6% said yes. More broadly, 61% of participants had negative feelings 'toward transition in general', 8% had positive feelings, 17% had neutral feelings, and 14% had mixed feelings or were not sure. Stella's survey did not ask participants whether they had medically transitioned. More broadly, the design of the survey's questions does limit the interpretation of some of the findings; the lack of questions about medical transition, as well as the 'double-barrelled' question that merged coming out and beginning transition, make it impossible to tell what percentage of these participants are 'detransitioners' vs. 'reidentified'.

Hailey's 2017 survey focuses primarily on co-morbid mental health conditions. She recruited 211 detransitioned females through social media, defined as 'any natal females who had in some way desisted from transition or trans identity'. Hailey states that 22% had taken testosterone or hormone blockers, and 8% had undergone surgery. She asked participants what mental illnesses they had been diagnosed with, if any, following up with an open-ended question: 'Do you feel that any of the conditions listed above contributed to your trans identification and/or transition? If so, how?' She reports that a number of participants did draw connections between their gender dysphoria and their experiences with a range of mental health conditions and provides examples from the open-ended responses for each condition.

Though these are informal surveys, they do suggest a few key features of these communities. As noted above, the two most common reasons cited for detransition were that participants 'found alternative ways to cope with dysphoria' and 'political/ideological concerns'. This suggests that within detransitioned women's communities, detransition is both a strategy for managing dysphoric symptoms and a political act. Although many participants reported that detransition reduced their feelings of gender dysphoria, most participants continued to report some amount of gender dysphoria. One survey suggested that most participants from these communities did not medically transition. Overall, this literature review shows that detrans has been studied almost exclusively as a clinical outcome, and, outside of community surveys, not as an experience or process worthy of investigating itself.

Preventing detrans, supporting detrans

To think through the possibilities for research involving detrans people, I draw a conceptual distinction between research centred around two potential goals: preventing detrans and supporting detrans. Each type is characterised by an interrelated set of research questions, prototypical methodologies, embedded value judgements, and range of interventions. Research with the goal of preventing detrans involves studying what generalisable factors cause or predict detrans; research with the goal of supporting detrans involves studying the experience and process of detrans itself. As a result, there is an asymmetry between the two types: research on preventing detrans facilitates only interventions designed to reduce the detrans rate, while research on supporting detrans enables a wide range of interventions to help people during or after detrans in various ways. The values entailed by each type of research also reflect this distinction. Research on preventing detrans is entangled with negative value judgements about detrans ('Detrans is harmful in and of itself', 'Detrans is a clinical failure', 'Detrans is an outcome to be avoided'), while research on supporting detrans entails positive value judgements about detrans ('Detrans is a viable option', 'Post-detrans life can be liveable', 'Detrans experiences are important in and of themselves'). My argument is not that every researcher engaged in each of these types of research necessarily has these goals and value judgements; rather, this conceptual distinction is a way to describe how the research itself is, in a deeper sense, intertwined with certain goals and values.

Before delving into the methodologies and potential consequences associated with these two types of research, I want to address some potential objections to this conceptual distinction. First, isn't there some 'neutral ground' between these two options where we simply try to 'understand detrans'? Studying detrans will, in some way or another, inevitably affect the world. Even the most detached sociological study of detrans experiences will increase awareness of detransition as an option and as an experience, and therefore support detrans in an indirect way. Therefore, even this kind of study isn't truly 'neutral', because it will change the world.

Second, why should we group together research on the causes of detransition per se with research on the causes of NTEs? I categorise both of them under 'preventing detrans' because they share methodological features and implicit value judgements and enable similar types of interventions. Research on preventing detrans will generally not help people who have already detransitioned, who already identify as detransitioners, or who already have had NTEs. Conversely, research on supporting detrans will be of limited usefulness in making the causal claims needed to justify interventions focused on reducing the 'detrans rate' (e.g. restricting access to transition-related care).

Finally, are these two types even meaningfully distinct? One can frame this question methodologically: is it possible to investigate the causes of detrans by studying detrans experiences? This question raises complex issues regarding causal inference in qualitative sociological research. For example, imagine a qualitative interviewer carries out a study of the way that detrans people make meaning about their experiences through narratives. Some sociologists would argue that such data can only generate hypotheses for future research into the causes of detrans; others would argue that these data could provide explanations regarding 'local causality' in those specific cases (see Maxwell, 2004, 2013). Alternatively, some sociologists might reject the goal of developing generalisable causal theories using qualitative methods entirely. But even researchers who argue that qualitative research can be used to make causal claims acknowledge the limited utility of qualitative methods for providing straightforwardly generalisable answers to 'variance questions' about correlations (e.g. Maxwell, 2004, 2013). More broadly, it is possible to imagine a study that combines methodological designs associated with both goals, or that exists in some middle ground between them, but these possibilities do not negate the usefulness of the preventing/supporting distinction.

Methodologies

Rather than provide an in-depth analysis of different methodologies, my goal here is to sketch out a range of possible research designs for studying detrans and their associated methodological issues. In general, research on preventing detrans attends to the range of causes that lead to one outcome; in contrast, research on supporting detrans has a shared starting point, but it can go in many directions. Because of the difficulties with detrans research carried out in clinical contexts, I argue that a sociological approach is, in some ways, more feasible and useful. However, both clinical and sociological approaches are represented within each type of detrans research.

The prototypical methodological approach for clinical research on preventing detrans is the observational longitudinal study. A sample of trans participants are recruited from clinics that provide transition-related care. When a participant enters the study, research-ers gather data on the factors that they hypothesise cause or predict detrans: demograph-ics, psychological variables, environmental factors, etc. In prospective studies, participants are followed for many years and periodically surveyed or interviewed. In retrospective studies, researchers rely on official records (medical, legal, etc.) to gather data about participants' trajectories. Participants classified as detrans are compared to the rest of the cohort. The end result is a set of evidence that supports claims about which people who access transition-related care are most likely to become detrans, however defined. Such evidence could clearly be used to argue for changing clinical protocols, especially attempts to restrict access to transition-related care in order to lower the detrans rate. Alternatively, this methodological design could be used to test other hypoth-eses about what predicts detrans (e.g. internalised cissexism, job discrimination), which might enable a different form of surveillance and intervention into the lives of people who access transition-related care.

Studying the causes of detrans using an observational longitudinal design creates three sets of problems: getting enough data, getting meaningful data, and collecting data in a clinical context.[3] The research reviewed above suggests that medical detransition after gender-affirming surgery happens years later and is quite rare ($<5\%$), which causes statistical problems that can only be fully mitigated by increasing the size of the study. Accumulating a sample of people with NTEs who have detransitioned through a pro-spective longitudinal study is likely difficult because of participant drop out. Anecdotally, some detransitioners have reported feeling betrayed by, or at least suspicious of, the medical and mental health professionals that they previously sought services from, choosing to stop showing up for appointments instead of confronting those professionals (e.g. crashchaoscats, 2018). Therefore, the key participants might be the ones least likely to be available for follow-up. Retrospective designs using medical records can make it easier to collect data regarding a larger sample over a long period of time, but this design cannot capture the fundamentally subjective dimensions of detrans because it relies on medical detransition as an indicator of NTEs or identity shifts. Furthermore, even if the rate of medical detransition is higher among participants who are taking hormones and have not undergone surgery, the motivations for stopping hormone replacement therapy vary widely (see earlier section 'Conceptualising detransition'). Therefore, clinical researchers must ask participants about their decision in order to gain meaningful infor-mation about such an outcome. Finally, there are ethical issues involved with recruiting research participants in contexts that provide transition-related care, especially longitu-dinal research that seeks to recruit participants as they are starting their medical transi-tion, because potential participants may feel implicitly pressured to consent to a study in order to access care (Adams et al., 2017).

A prototypical methodological approach for research on supporting detrans would be the in-depth qualitative interview, which can shed light on detrans people's experiences and the way they navigate their lives. A study of people who have detransitioned could investigate the diverse range of meanings associated with detransition. A study involving detransitioners or people with NTEs could delve into their narratives, the kinds of struggles they have encountered when interacting with medical/mental health systems, their experiences of gender dysphoria, the ways they have found to manage that dysphoria, their experiences with detransition communities, and so on. Other useful qualitative design methods include focus groups, qualitative diary research and ethnography. Detransitioners have discussed their experiences extensively on social media (see Callahan, 2018), but qualitative research with detransition communities provides a way for researchers to, with participants' informed consent, systematically bring these experiences into the academic literature. Researchers could also use qualitative methods to learn more about the experiences of people who detransition and then retransition. Regardless, sociological research using qualitative methods is not only more feasible than the aforementioned longitudinal quantitative designs, but can provide practically useful research in a much shorter time frame.

Because research on supporting detrans starts with detrans people's lives, rather than attempting to reduce the number of detrans people in the world, it encompasses a wider range of clinical and sociological methodologies. A mental health researcher could gather information from online detransition communities about alternative strategies for reducing gender dysphoria in order to design and test the efficacy of a novel psychotherapeutic approach to gender dysphoria among detrans people. A sociologist could use discourse analysis to study how detrans people interact with representations of detrans on social media and in journalistic media coverage. A medical researcher could closely study the timeline of physical effects of medical detransition, both the near-term direct effects and the long-term health effects. These are just a few examples, but they point to the myriad possibilities that are enabled when we shift away from a narrow focus on measuring the 'detrans rate' and investigating the causes of detrans.

Consequences

The future of detrans research will have consequences for both the types of interventions that are enabled and the broader sociopolitical dynamics within and between trans communities, detransition communities, researchers, anti-trans political groups, and so on. Research on preventing detrans will almost certainly be used to argue for restricting access to transition-related care or for other interventions designed to reduce the likelihood of detrans. If, for example, millions of dollars were poured into years of research on the causes of NTEs, we *might*, 20 years from now, generate enough evidence to construct controversial interventions to reduce the rate of NTEs. These interventions, in turn, might take many years to have the intended effect, if ever. If they involve creating additional barriers for trans people to access health care, the harm done could vastly outweigh whatever marginal effect they might have on preventing detrans. All the time and money spent on such research would have done absolutely nothing to help detrans people in the meantime. Alternatively, researchers who believe strongly in the goal of preventing detransition might respond to the methodological difficulties of such an approach by producing poor quality research. For example, they might elide the distinction between different kinds of detransition in order to inflate sample sizes.

Research on supporting detrans could enable a variety of interventions designed to help detrans people. Currently, there is no clinical protocol for detransition, and there is no explicit place for detransition within the present model of gender-affirming care (Turban & Keuroghlian, 2018). Sociological research on supporting detrans would provide a valuable starting point for creating such a clinical protocol, with clear guidelines for medical and mental health professionals about how to provide competent, supportive care for detrans people. Research could also provide the basis for other therapeutic options for detrans people who continue to experience gender dysphoria (e.g. psychotherapy tailored to the needs of detrans people).

To put it differently, research on preventing detrans constructs detrans as a matter of risk, whereas research on supporting detrans constructs detrans as a matter of inclusion. In the former, detrans is an issue of zero-sum clinical risk that pits detrans and trans communities against each other: the risk of NTEs vs. the risk of harm from strategies to prevent NTEs. In the latter, detrans is an issue of clinical inclusion, a subpopulation with their own particular medical and mental health needs. Both types of research increase awareness of detrans, but in very different ways: as a problem to be mitigated vs. as a set of experiences to be included.

Neither type of research is uncontroversial, nor will either type of research lead to a stable political equilibrium. Research on preventing detrans will almost certainly be weaponised against trans communities and/or detrans communities, exacerbating tensions between these communities for decades to come. Research on supporting detrans will almost certainly increase the perception that detrans is a viable option, accelerating the construction of identities related to detransition and heightening the salience of detrans communities. This might, ironically, increase the number of people who identify as detransitioners, and they could push for research on the causes of detrans. Considering the stigmatising and invalidating historical associations with psychotherapeutic approaches to gender dysphoria (see e.g. Byne et al., 2012, p. 778; Meyerowitz, 2004), research on such interventions involving detrans people might be seen as dangerous or pathologising. But providing evidence that detrans people can live happy, satisfying lives, and designing interventions toward that end, actually undermines anti-trans rhetoric that uses the stories of detransitioners to claim that transitioning ruins lives. Certainly, the sociopolitical consequences of research into effective, non-medical interventions for managing gender dysphoria could be incredibly volatile, even if the only participants in such research were detransitioners. Regardless, research on supporting detrans is more likely to legitimise a pluralistic approach to detrans issues, whereas research on preventing detrans is more likely to legitimise a polarising zero-sum dynamic.

Recommendations

The conceptual framework I have put forward has clear implications for how future detrans research should be conducted. Broadly, it is crucial that researchers are thoughtful and precise about what aspect of detrans they are studying, the relationship between their construct and their methodology, and the way their object of study is communicated to potential participants. Depending on the context, detrans might be defined in a purely medical way, e.g. as referring merely to the process of stopping hormone replacement therapy for any reason, or it might be defined in a purely subjective way, as referring to a particular identity label. Similarly, although using respectful terminology is important, a set of terms that is affirming to participants from transgender communities could be offputting to participants from detransition communities, and vice versa. Some guidelines for research involving transgender participants do also apply to detrans research (Adams et al., 2017; Vincent, 2018a); after all, some detrans research involves recruiting both detransitioned and transgender participants! The best way to navigate these complexities is to be transparent (Vincent, 2018a) and to elicit feedback from potential participants before, during and after the process of designing and carrying out a study (Adams et al., 2017).

In particular, I believe qualitative interview-based sociological research involving participants from online detransition communities is feasible and urgently needed, regardless of whether the rate of detransition is increasing or decreasing. There is no need to use rhetoric about a 'rising epidemic' or 'contagion' in order to argue for the importance of studying detransitioners because their experiences are valuable in and of themselves. My impression is that detransition communities are eager to be involved with respectful research, including studies of the diverse range of experiences and narratives within detransition communities across gender, sexual orientation, class and race. As seen in the first epigraph, detransitioners have also expressed interest in medical research that could be used to refine clinical protocols for stopping hormone replacement therapy, which would benefit trans people who medically detransition for any reason as well. Regardless, researchers must not use qualitative research involving detransitioners to make tenuous, generalised claims about the causes of detransition more broadly; there are plenty of other valuable insights that such evidence can actually provide.

I began this piece by applying the distinction between preventing and supporting detrans to two quotes that imagine, in divergent ways, what it would mean to 'listen to detransitioners'. Although I did not delve into the complex discourses around detransition, I suspect the preventing/supporting distinction is conceptually useful outside of the context of detrans research. Yet some important ideas are excluded from this duality. For example, the call for broader economic justice made in the first epigraph shows how the political concerns of detransitioners can transcend detrans-specific issues. Similarly, the alignment between the goal of supporting detrans and the idea of clinical inclusion downplays the deeply ideological meaning of detransition for some detransitioners (see Stella, 2016). Nevertheless, the conceptual framework I have presented here highlights the importance of considering detransitioners as more than canaries, as more than ill-fated indicators of some broader risk to be prevented. Respecting the struggles of people who detransition, who identify as detransitioners, and who have negative transition experiences necessitates considering their experiences as real, distinct, and worthy of study in their own right.

Funding

The author received no financial support for the research, authorship, and/or publication of this article.

Notes

1. A sufficiently detailed account of this messy conflict is too convoluted to recount here. My attempts to obtain independent verification of important details by contacting Caspian for access to his study materials have been unsuccessful.
2. As the age of the respondents in the internal online surveys of the detransitioned women's community suggest, drawing a sharp distinction between these two sets of possibilities undoubtedly oversimplifies the issues involved.
3. Researchers could also use a cross-sectional design to study the clinical or social determinants of detrans. For example, a researcher could recruit samples of trans and detrans participants from online communities, using an online survey to test hypotheses about how certain variables correlate with detrans. Such a study is much more feasible than longitudinal research, but from the perspective of most quantitative researchers, it is considered significantly weaker causal evidence.

References

Adams, N., Pearce, R., Veale, J., Radix, A., Castro, D., Sarkar, A., & Thom, K. C. (2017). Guidance and ethical considerations for undertaking transgender health research and institutional review boards adjudicating this research. *Transgender Health*, *2*(1), 165–175. https://doi.org/10.1089/trgh.2017.0012

Awkward-Rich, C. (2017). Trans, feminism: *Or*, reading like a depressed transsexual. *Signs*, *42*(4), 819–841. https://doi.org/10.1086/690914

Byne, W., Bradley, S. J., Coleman, E., Eyler, A. E., Green, R., Menvielle, E. J., Meyer-Bahlburg, H. F., Pleak, R. R., & Tompkins, D. A. (2012). Report of the American Psychiatric Association Task Force on treatment of gender identity disorder. *Archives of Sexual Behavior*, *41*(4), 759–796. https://doi.org/10.1007/s10508-012-9975-x

Callahan, C. (2018). Unheard voices of detransitioners. In H. Brunskell-Evans & M. Moore (Eds.), *Transgender children and young people: Born in your own body* (pp. 166–180). Cambridge Scholars Publishing.

Callahan, C., Crash Robinson, M., Rosch, E., Mangelsdorf, H., Schroeder, A., . . ., K. L. R. (2017). *Statement against the ADF*. Detransitioned Women Resist the ADF website. https://detransitionedwomenresistadf.wordpress.com/ (accessed 13 October 2018).

Caspian, J. (2019). *Free speech matters*. CrowdJustice. www.crowdjustice.com/case/free-speech-matters-round2/ (accessed 8 July 2019).

crashchaoscats. (2016, August 8). *An open letter to Julia Serano from one of the detransitioned people you claim to 'support'*. crashchaoscats. https://crashchaoscats.wordpress.com/2016/08/08/an-open-letter-to-julia-serano-from-one-of-the%e2%80%ad-%e2%80%acdetransitioned-people-you%e2%80%ad-%e2%80%acclaim-to%e2%80%ad-%e2%80%acsupport%e2%80%ad/ (accessed 8 August 2019).

crashchaoscats. (2018, February 8). *Follow-up to 'Lost to follow-up'*. crashchaoscats. https://crashchaoscats.wordpress.com/2018/02/08/follow-up-to-lost-to-follow-up/ (accessed 8 July 2019).

Davis, H. F. (2017). *Beyond trans: Does gender matter?* NYU Press.

Deutsch, M. B. (2012). Use of the informed consent model in the provision of cross-sex hormone therapy: A survey of the practices of selected clinics. *International Journal of Transgenderism*, *13*(3), 140–146. https://doi.org/10.1080/15532739.2011.675233

Dhejne, C., Öberg, K., Arver, S., & Landén, M. (2014). An analysis of all applications for sex reassignment surgery in Sweden, 1960–2010: Prevalence, incidence, and regrets. *Archives of Sexual Behavior*, *43*(8), 1535–1545. https://doi.org/10.1007/s10508-014-0300-8

Douglas, H. (2000). Inductive risk and values in science. *Philosophy of Science, 67*(4), 559–579. https://doi.org/10.1086/392855

Elliott, K. C. (2017). *A tapestry of values: An introduction to values in science*. Oxford University Press.

Enke, A. F. (2012). The education of little cis: Cisgender and the discipline of opposing bodies. In A. F. Enke (Ed.), *Transfeminist perspectives in and beyond transgender and gender studies* (pp. 60–77). Temple University Press.

Freack. (2019). *What detransitioned women actually want*. Gosh Tumblr is Awful. https://questioningsideblog.tumblr.com/post/182713822523/what-detransitioned-women-actually-want (accessed 8 July 2019).

Hailey. (2017). *Survey of co-morbid mental health in detransitioned females: Analysis and results*. Re-sister. https://desisterresister.wordpress.com/2017/01/11/survey-of-co-morbid-mental-health-in-detransitioned-females-analysis-and-results/ (accessed 2 October 2018).

Hess, J., Neto, R. R., Panic, L., Rübben, H., & Senf, W. (2014). Satisfaction with male-to-female gender reassignment surgery. *Deutsches Ärzteblatt International, 111*, 795–801. https://doi.org/10.3238/arztebl.2014.0795

Kanner, R. (2018, June 22). *I detransitioned. But not because I wasn't trans*. The Atlantic. www.theatlantic.com/family/archive/2018/06/i-detransitioned-but-not-because-i-wasnt-trans/563396/ (accessed 5 May 2019).

Koyama, E. (2003). The transfeminist manifesto. In R. Dicker & A. Piepmeier (Eds.), *Catching a wave: Reclaiming feminism for the twenty-first century* (pp. 224–259). Northern University Press.

Krege, S., Bex, A., Lümmen, G., & Rübben, H. (2001). Male-to-female transsexualism: A technique, results and long-term follow-up in 66 patients. *BJU International, 88*(4), 396–402. https://doi.org/10.1046/j.1464-410X.2001.02323.x

Lawrence, A. A. (2003). Factors associated with satisfaction or regret following male-to-female sex reassignment surgery. *Archives of Sexual Behavior, 32*(4), 299–315. https://doi.org/10.1023/A:1024086814364

Longino, H. E. (2013). *Studying human behavior: How scientists investigate aggression and sexuality*. University of Chicago Press.

Maxwell, J. A. (2004). Using qualitative methods for causal explanation. *Field Methods, 16*(3), 243–264. https://doi.org/10.1177/1525822X04266831

Maxwell, J. A. (2013). *Qualitative research design: An interactive approach* (3rd ed.). Sage.

McCann, C. (2017). When girls won't be girls. *1843* (October/November 2017). www.1843magazine.com/features/when-girls-wont-be-girls

Meyerowitz, J. (2004). *How sex changed: A history of transsexuality in the United States*. Harvard University Press.

Nelson, L., Whallett, E. J., & McGregor, J. C. (2009). Transgender patient satisfaction following reduction mammaplasty. *Journal of Plastic, Reconstructive & Aesthetic Surgery, 62*(3), 331–334. https://doi.org/10.1016/j.bjps.2007.10.049

Smith, Y. L. S., Van Goozen, S. H. M., Kuiper, A. J., & Cohen-Kettenis, P. T. (2005). Sex reassignment: Outcomes and predictors of treatment for adolescent and adult transsexuals. *Psychological Medicine, 35*(1), 89–99. https://doi.org/10.1017/S0033291704002776

Steensma, T. D., McGuire, J. K., Kreukels, B. P. C., Beekman, A. J., & Cohen-Kettenis, P. T. (2013). Factors associated with desistence and persistence of childhood gender dysphoria: A quantitative follow-up study. *Journal of the American Academy of Child & Adolescent Psychiatry, 52*(6), 582–590. https://doi.org/10.1016/j.jaac.2013.03.016

Stella, C. (2016). *Female detransition and reidentification: Survey results and interpretation*. Guide on Raging Stars. http://guideonragingstars.tumblr.com/post/149877706175/female-detransition-and-reidentification-survey (accessed 26 September 2018).

Temple Newhook, J., Pyne, J., Winters, K., Feder, S., Holmes, C., Tosh, J., Sinnott, M. L., Jamieson, A., & Pickett, S. (2018). A critical commentary on follow-up studies and 'desistance' theories about transgender and gender-nonconforming children. *International Journal of Transgenderism, 19*(2), 212–224. https://doi.org/10.1080/15532739.2018.1456390

Turban, J. L., & Keuroghlian, A. S. (2018). Dynamic gender presentations: Understanding transition and 'de-transition' among transgender youth. *Journal of the American Academy of Child & Adolescent Psychiatry, 57*(7), 451–453. https://doi.org/10.1016/j.jaac.2018.03.016

Vincent, B. (2018a). Studying trans: Recommendations for ethical recruitment and collaboration with transgender participants in academic research. *Psychology & Sexuality, 9*(2), 102–116. https://doi.org/10.1080/19419899.2018.1434558

Vincent, B. (2018b). *Transgender health: A practitioner's guide to binary and non-binary trans patient care.* Jessica Kingsley.

Wallien, M. S. C., & Cohen-Kettenis, P. T. (2008). Psychosexual outcome of gender-dysphoric children. *Journal of the American Academy of Child & Adolescent Psychiatry, 47*(12), 1413–1423. https://doi.org/10.1097/CHI.0b013e31818956b9

Author biography

Rowan Hildebrand-Chupp is a doctoral student in Sociology and Science Studies at the University of California, San Diego. Rowan has a BA in Psychology from Reed College. Rowan's research focuses on how moral and cultural values shape the way experts define and use concepts, especially in historical and contemporary psychiatry.

Disregard and danger: Chimamanda Ngozi Adichie and the voices of trans (and cis) African feminists

The Sociological Review Monographs
2020, Vol. 68(4) 143–159
© The Author(s) 2020
Article reuse guidelines:
sagepub.com/journals-permissions
DOI: 10.1177/0038026120934695
journals.sagepub.com/home/sor

B Camminga
African Centre for Migration and Society, University of the Witwatersrand, South Africa

Abstract

In March of 2017, best-selling Nigerian author and feminist Chimamanda Ngozi Adichie, in an interview with Britain's Channel 4, was asked whether being a trans woman makes one any less of a 'real woman?' In the clip, which went viral shortly thereafter, Adichie responded by saying 'When people talk about, "Are trans women women?" my feeling is trans women are trans women.' Echoing the essentialist, predominantly white Global Northern, feminist politics of trans-exclusionary feminists (TERFs), by implying that trans women are not 'real' women because, as she assumes, they benefited from male privilege, Adichie set off a social media maelstrom. The publicised responses to her comments largely came from feminists and trans women in the Global North, and though many trans people from the African continent responded, with hashtags such as #ChimamandaKilledME, very few of these received any attention. As the hashtag suggests, for trans people living on the African continent, given the general lack of recourse to rights, Adichie's words as an African writer carry considerable weight. Given this, the absence of media attention is curious. This article offers a recentring, by focusing on those voices, maligned in the broader debate – trans people from the African continent. I argue that while Adichie might be stumbling over the questions that lie at the heart of TERF politics (what does it mean to be a woman? and does it matter how a person arrives at being a woman?), trans women on the African continent have been busy reconstituting the terms of the terrain.

Keywords
African feminism, Chimamanda Ngozi Adichie, male privilege, socialisation, transgender Africa

Come Fetch Your Fave[1]

> Single stories . . . facilitate ignorance, they make it impossible to see the full spectrum of others, they allow one to project notions onto another while solidifying position of superiority for no possibility of connection as human equals. (Adichie, 2009)

Corresponding author:
B Camminga, African Centre for Migration and Society, University of the Witwatersrand, Johannesburg, 2000, South Africa.
Email: cammingab@gmail.com

On the 10 March 2017 acclaimed Nigerian feminist and author Chimamanda Ngozi Adichie, promoting her new book *Dear Ijeawele, or A Feminist Manifesto in Fifteen Suggestions*, was asked the following in an interview on the UK television network Channel 4 News (2017):

> Does it matter how you've arrived at being a woman? I mean, for example, if you're a trans woman who grew up identifying as a man, who grew up enjoying the privileges of being a man, does that take away from becoming a woman? Are you any less of a real woman?

She responded by saying that her 'feeling' was that 'trans women are trans women'. She continued,

> It's not about how we wear our hair or whether we have a vagina or a penis. It's about the way the world treats us, and I think if you've lived in the world as a man with the privileges the world accords to men, and then switched gender, it's difficult for me to accept that then we can equate your experience with the experience of a woman who has lived from the beginning in the world as a woman, and who has not been accorded those privileges that men are. . . . And so I think there has to be – and this is not, of course, to say, I'm saying this with a certainty that transgender should be allowed to be. But I don't think it's a good thing to conflate everything into one. I don't think it's a good thing to talk about women's issues being exactly the same as the issues of trans women, because I don't think that's true. (Channel 4 News, 2017)

Described as a 'global feminist icon', a 'public thinker' (Brown, 2017) and 'one of the most vital and original novelists of her generation' (MacFarquhar, 2018), Adichie is perhaps most well known as author of award-winning and best-selling novel *Americanah* and her TED Talk *We Should All Be Feminists*, sampled by Beyoncé on her 2013 track 'Flawless' (Brown, 2017). As a 'self-professed card-carrying feminist', a self-identified 'African woman' (Adichie et al., 2017) and a vocal campaigner for LGBT rights in Nigeria, Adichie's work is deeply linked to her experiences and life on the African continent. In her work, she has spoken widely, and not uncontroversially, on issues of race, gender and the power and importance of language. Given this, the global response to her controversial comments was almost instant. In the following few days headlines such as 'Chimamanda Ngozi Adichie has sparked outrage for her comments about transgender women' (Oppenheim, 2017), 'Chimamanda Ngozi Adichie clarifies transgender comments as backlash grows' (Kean, 2017) and 'Women's issues are different from trans women's issues, feminist author says, sparking criticism' (Schmidt, 2017) appeared on English news websites across the Global North. African news site AllAfrica went with 'Africa: Trans-women are trans-women and women are women says Chimamanda Adichie' (Mbamalu, 2017).

While both cis and trans women in the Global North had their responses to Adichie's comments amplified over several media platforms, trans women from the African continent, those arguably with the highest stakes in the conversation, were ignored even when using provocative hashtags like *#ChimamandaKilledME*. In the almost overwhelming moment of what Adichie would later call 'trans noise' (Adichie, 2018), one common framing of her response, emanating largely from the Global North, has been an accusation that Adichie is in fact practising trans-exclusionary radical feminism. In other words, participating in a strand of white Western feminism which, at its most basic, does not deem trans women to be women, and at its most extreme understands trans women to be interlopers and a direct threat to (cis) women's rights. Increasingly, trans-exclusionary radical feminism has come to stand in for or represent what is perhaps at present the most visible form of popular feminism in the Global North. It is an understanding of feminist politics, as I will argue, that has very little, if anything, to do with the various strands of African feminism.

In this article, I read Adichie's past work, and the accounts of African trans and cis women who responded to Adichie's statements, against her arguments on womanhood. This is done in an effort to unpack the taken for granted assumptions that underpin Adichie's perceptions of trans women as they pertain to trans identity and women on the African continent. I use this article to focus on how these assumptions are constructed in relation to the lived realities of trans women from the African continent and current African feminist politics, in particular with regard to perceptions about gender, male privilege, the notion of 'womanhood' and language. I aim to provide an alternate African-based feminist analysis to the currently overwhelming centring of trans-exclusionary radical feminist (TERF) arguments from the Global North, and in doing so amplify voices that for various political reasons were not brought into circulation during the initial furore. Given Adichie's visibility as a feminist and a Nigerian, I explore why, in the moment of her pronouncements about trans women, not a single trans woman from the African continent was asked to respond. I argue that while Adichie might be stumbling over the question that lies at the heart of TERF politics: What does it mean to be a woman (and who gets to decide that)? Women trans and cis from the African continent, echoing the critique and heritage of generations of African feminists before them, have been resisting single stories, Anglocentric and colonising perceptions of gender, and by extension Anglocentric (and colonising) understandings of trans identity. Indeed they, trans and cis women, have long been reconstituting the terms of this already historically fraught terrain. Drawing on transnational feminism, I suggest that in the seemingly ongoing TERF media frenzy, the voices of trans and cis women from the African continent continue to be disregarded for the converse reason Adichie's is elevated: it represents a single story.

Spelling danger: Colonial gender and disruptions of bio-logic

Shocked by the mounting public outcry to her comments and calls to burn her books, in the days following the TV interview, Adichie shared two Facebook posts as a form of response. The second, titled 'Clarifying' (2017b), stated:

> I said, in an interview, that trans women are trans women, that they are people who, having been born male, benefited from the privileges that the world affords men, and that we should not say that the experience of women born female is the same as the experience of trans women. . . . I think the impulse to say that trans women are women just like women born female are women comes from a need to make trans issues mainstream. Because by making them mainstream, we might reduce the many oppressions they experience. . . . Perhaps I should have said trans women are trans women and cis women are cis women and all are women. Except that 'cis' is

not an organic part of my vocabulary. And would probably not be understood by a majority of people. Because saying 'trans' and 'cis' acknowledges that there is a distinction between women born female and women who transition, without elevating one or the other, which was my point. . . . I have and will continue to stand up for the rights of transgender people. Not merely because of the violence they experience but because they are equal human beings deserving to be what they are.

When Thabiso Ratalane (Collison, 2017), a 25-year-old South African 'woman of transgender experience' heard Adichie's words, she heard 'transgender women do not count as women'. Respondents from the African continent did not only hear that trans women were not women but that to be a woman, by Adichie's reading, has specific, presumably universal contours and expectations. In the vein of what has been called TERF politics, Adichie invoked a narrative which ties bodies to biology, gender, socialisation and ownership of space. At the outset, Adichie defines womanhood through the experiences of those 'born female' and raised as girls – (cis) women. She considers the ways in which they are raised to be constitutive elements of womanhood: sexualised, treated as secondary citizens and often exploited, social conditioning – undermining their sense of themselves, as girls and women. That is, a universal womanhood. Concomitantly, transgender women, according to Adichie, having been 'born male', cannot know what it is to experience girlhood, with its accompanying dangers, because those 'born male' are raised as men and experience 'male privilege'. Echoing the core tenets of TERF approaches to feminism – a biology-based/sex essentialist understanding – Adichie takes up what she presents as a universalist biological position.[2] A political alignment which contends that it is seemingly impossible to separate sex and gender. Sex is determined at birth, onto which a specific gender maps, and based on this, certain privileges are accrued (Hines, 2007). This essentialist understanding, she adds, does not dismiss the 'pain of gender confusion' or complexities trans women experience 'living in bodies not their own' but is instead a 'conception of gender' which is 'more honest and true to the real world' (Adichie, 2017b).

As with Adichie's universal 'woman', there also exists the singular universal 'transgender woman'. This is someone who 'switch[es]', at some point in her life, a seemingly simple linear migration, from being a man to a *trans* woman. The prefix 'trans', here, acts not as an adjective but as a qualifier, signalling the biological difference (and privilege) of being 'born male'. The particular construction of transgender existence Adichie alludes to, not only involves a type of clear transition from point A to point B, 'a switch', but also invokes the 'wrong body narrative' (Bettcher, 2013a) – an expression, critical to Global Northern constructions of transgender existence, intimated by the suggestion that trans women exist in 'bodies not their own'. The crux of her argument, and indeed its trans-exclusionary underpinnings, is seen when she expresses sympathy for trans women who she acknowledges must 'undergo difficulties as boys' (Adichie, 2017b). That is to say, difficulties not as people who are misgendered as boys, or as girls being perceived or raised as boys but as that which their biology, supposedly, dictates – boys. The place of trans people within feminist politics has long been disputed, but in the new millennium, this tension has seemingly escalated to hitherto unthought-of proportions. At the heart of TERF beliefs, which we see in Adichie's sentiments, is the idea, as noted, that gender and sex are somehow locked to one another. To be a trans woman, then, is read, at least in Global Northern perceptions of this particular strand of feminism, as 'a male practice, devised by a patriarchal medical system in order to construct subservient women' (Hines, 2019, p. 146). By extension, trans women are not and can never become women. As Sally Hines notes, this particular feminist perspective on trans existence 'has been extremely difficult to dispel in both feminist writing and activism' (Hines, 2019, p. 146). Authenticity has been the critical pivot point to these conflicts – 'of who is, or can be, considered to be a "woman"' (Hines, 2019, p. 146).

This question 'of who is, or can be, considered to be a "woman"' is not new. Indeed, it has particular cultural and political resonances for critical thinking from the Global South. Crucially it is tied to a longer history of gender as a critical tool of colonial imposition or, what Maria Lugones (2016) refers to as 'the coloniality of gender'. African feminist scholar Oyèrónkẹ́ Oyěwùmí (1997, p. 16), in her book *The Invention of Women: Making African Sense of Western Gender Discourses*, asks 'Women? What women? Who qualifies to be a woman in this cultural setting, and on what basis are they identified?' The exclusion of particular kinds of women, from the definition of what it might mean to be a woman, has historical precedence, for the African continent (Roy, 2016). As Oyèrónkẹ́ Oyěwùmí (1997), Obioma Nnaemeka (2004), Raewyn Connell (2014), Maria Lugones (2016), have argued, feminism from the Global North has long erased or outright denied the womanhood of various women in the Global South. Oyěwùmí argues that 'woman' as a concept 'is derived from Western experience and history, a history rooted in philosophical discourses about the distinction among body, mind, and soul and in ideas about biological determinism and the linkages between the body and the "social"' (2017, p. xiii). She calls this understanding, which echoes both Adichie's and TERF political sentiments, 'the Western bio-logic'. For Oyěwùmí, biology is itself socially constructed, and, is, by extension, inseparable from the social. Inseparable then from the space – nation, communal or societal – in which a body is situated.[3] Highlighting this linkage, Ratalane notes that as a South African 'woman of trans experience' she was not raised as 'typically male or female' (Collison, 2017), very clearly linking her trans identity to her geopolitical locale.

Ricki Kgositau (2017), a trans woman and activist from Botswana, pointed to a host of women who would fall short of Adichie's 'perfect definition of women'. She warned that for trans women like her, those from the African continent, 'this', that is Adichie's universality and her imposition of very Global Northern perceptions of womanhood, 'spells danger for me'. The danger here is two-fold. Firstly, for those living on the African continent, Adichie's words as a Nigerian icon carry substantial weight. 'Transgender' as a term is not widely used (Camminga, 2018a). In light of this, as Ugandan transgender activist Victor Mukasa (Mukasa & Balzer, 2009, p. 124) explains, 'generally, all gender non-conforming people are "automatically" branded homosexuals as in most of our communities, a man who looks or has tendencies of a woman is the proper picture of a gay man'. Accusations of homosexuality (given its widespread criminalisation) often carry the threat of violence, exploitation and in some cases even death. To have one's womanhood denied, to suggest that trans-ness is an indicator of maleness by virtue of having accrued perceived male privilege, in such an environment, is to suggest that trans women are, in fact, always already men. That is, deceptive men, but men nonetheless. Second, it is to perpetuate the colonial legacy of (violently) imposing particular ideas, of gender, sex and sexuality (and some would argue even feminism itself) vested in the Global North. It was not only trans women from the African continent that responded to Adichie highlighting these dangers. Kenyan poet and activist Shailja Patel (2017), a cis person, asked Adichie through a series of tweets what or how we might define 'a real woman'. Like Kgositau, she listed several examples of those who might have at one time or another been barred from the category, including those who could read and write. Women like Adichie.

Perceptions of privilege and feminism

For Kgositau, aside from questioning Adichie's biologically based definition of woman-hood, the real problem lies with Adichie's perception that all trans women are raised in the gender they are assigned at birth – in essence as boys – and forcibly so. Adichie's reliance on the accusation of male privilege for Kgositau is a clear indicator that for Adichie, trans women can never be or are never 'real' women, a category defined by the lack of male privilege. To put it another way, although she vehemently denied this, Adichie implied that trans women are not 'real' women in the same way that women, who are cis, are. This is because cis women – a term she does not use due to it 'not being an organic part of her vocabulary' – do not experience male privilege. Kgositau, similarly to Ratalane, disputes this. She notes that although there were several attempts to raise her as boy, these failed and that she was actually raised as a girl. For Kgositau, this directly disrupts the understanding that trans women universally experience male privilege. As Kgositau (2017) explains:

> . . . for having been assumed to be male but expressing and identifying as a feminine being I did not benefit from any male privilege at any point for my expressions an identity as a girl made it impossible to fit into this privilege nor assume it in a way that could be positively reinforced.

In a similar vein to Kgositau, Miss Sahhara (2017), a trans woman, model and Nigerian refugee living in the UK who runs the online support community transvalid.org, argued that Adichie's assertions about the definite accumulation of male privilege were a contentious accusation to make given the patriarchal nature of Nigerian society. She was the only respondent to call Adichie herself a 'TERF' outright. Pointing to their shared heritage, and the danger Kgositau alluded to, Miss Sahhara noted how people assigned male who express femininity in Nigerian society are often treated as an aberration, and that this is usually followed by violence. Speaking as a trans woman who grew up in Nigeria, Miss Sahhara disrupts even Adichie's bio-logic, in stating that she feels that her gender, that of being a woman from the African continent, is in fact rooted or 'influenced' by her biology, being assigned male, that which Adichie would dismiss as inherently privileged.

> My gender and self identification comes from my brain. I was not influenced by my environment or society . . . if I was influenced by society, then the beatings, abuse, bullying, Church deliverance/prayers and harassment I got for being womanly in Nigeria should have realigned

my brain to act/dress/look like a male. I rebelled growing up by looking and presenting as the female I am. My gender is obviously influenced by biology and not by environment, I was discouraged from all things feminine growing up, but it never stopped me from being fabulously girly, will you and Chimamanda call that 'MALE PRIVILEGE'? (Miss Sahhara, 2017)

One of the critical issues raised by Miss Sahhara and Kgositau is the assumption that they were ever men, rather than *misgendered* as men in societies which do not privilege those assigned male who express any form of femininity. Similarly to Miss Sahhara, a South African trans activist for rural trans women, Seoketsi Mooketsi (2017), tweeted:

As a Trans womxn I'm hypersexualised . . . exploited for my body, not paid, denied education, employment & told I'm not 'Womxn Enough'.

Challenging Adichie's ideas regarding a 'harmful sense of self' as the defining burden of 'female born women' who experience their bodies as 'repositories of shame' while having to 'to cater to the egos of men' (2017b), Mooketsi highlights the very real experiences of shame and harm which leave trans women exploited and catering to those self-same egos. Indeed, whereas Adichie suggests trans women, by virtue of being 'born male' and therefore always already being men, are spared the socialisation and problematic self value issues experienced by (cis) women, Mooketsi makes clear that her day-to-day experiences, as a woman, are comprised of exactly that. The difference being, that in the case of Mooketsi, these experiences, rather than functioning as an affirmation of her womanhood are often accompanied by its direct denial. Reflecting Mooketsi's arguments, trans women from the African continent who responded to Adichie underlined how their experience of being misgendered as boys, if they were not raised as girls as Kgositau was, still did not mean they experienced the stereotypical male privilege Adichie intends. As Kgositau (2017) offers:

We need to interrogate the under-privilege that comes with renouncing and divorcing oneself from this male assignment from birth; transwomen [*sic*] are harshly punished by society for actually refusing this male assignment and privilege that comes with it. They are labelled, insulted, raped and even murdered for refusing this privilege by virtue of being women in bodies categorised as male; that is the many blindspots to Ms. Adichie's simplification of male privilege to simply being attained just by the sex one is assigned at birth. For transwomen [*sic*] given that many's [*sic*] feminine expressions manifest very early on in life, they never get to benefit any male privilege for they are an irritation to masculine maleness.

Philosopher Talia Mae Bettcher (2013b), in her article 'Trans Woman and the Meaning of "Woman", refers to the denial of trans women's authenticity as women as a form of transphobia through which a type of 'identity enforcement' takes place. She goes on to suggest that when a person is defined by their trans-ness in relation to their woman-ness, in Adichie's case as 'a trans woman is a trans woman', what it really infers 'in dominant cultural contexts . . . is understood to mean "a man who lives as a woman"' (Bettcher, 2013b, p. 235). Marking some of Oyěwùmí's critique, Bettcher calls this 'the taken-for-granted assumption' of the dominant cultural view of transgender identity as it functions in the Global North. For Bettcher (2013b, p. 242), and as several trans women from the

African continent point out, 'this conflict over meaning is deeply bound up with the distribution of power and the capacity to enforce a way of life, regardless of the emotional and physical damage done to the individual'.

Given Adichie's status, this type of identity enforcement can have genuine material effects on the lives of women already struggling to survive. Mooketsi's hashtag *ChimamandaKilledME*, which remained part of her twitter handle for several weeks after Adichie's public statements, is a testament to this. As Ratalane contends, 'we are at this critical stage where transgender women are highly marginalised and face high levels of violence. So any insensitive comment that denigrates trans women – or discounts their experiences . . . justifies such violence' (Collison, 2017). Phumelele Nkomozake (2017), the author of the blog mytransrevolution.wordpress.com, echoed Ratalane in slamming Adichie for the 'abuse' of her power and her misrepresentations of trans women, stating: 'You do not know me. I was never a man. I have always been a woman.' By 'me', as with Miss Sahhara, Ratalane, Kgositau and Mooketsi, she means women of trans experience from the African continent.

Sins and semantics

Language matters. (Adichie, 2017a)

Following the Channel 4 interview, Adichie, at an event in Paris, told *The Atlantic*'s national correspondent Ta-Nehisi Coates and editor in chief Jeffrey Goldberg that she understood the ensuing furore as a kind of growing intolerance to dissent. She framed this as an expectation around conforming to language 'orthodoxy . . . and if you don't, you become a bad, evil person, and it doesn't matter what you've done in the past or what you stand for' (Adichie et al., 2017). For Adichie, her 'major sin' since the initial interview had been to refuse to abide by this language orthodoxy (Allardice, 2018). Yet, in the past language has been a profoundly feminist concern for Adichie.[4] We might want to say, as Adichie has, that the issues raised by her critics are simply semantics, and perhaps this would be possible if she were not someone whose entire career has been built around constructing and exacting ideas from language. This is not merely about the use of the term 'cis' which, as noted, Adichie understands as 'foreign to her' (whereas a term like 'trans' is seemingly not). It is about what Kgositau (2017) has called her 'reckless' use of language, the kind of language that is dangerous, and the kind of language that perpetuates violence. For Kgositau, this is seen in the way in which Adichie refers to trans women as 'they' – a separate group. Also, perhaps seen in her statement that trans women should be allowed to be 'what' they are. Not who, but what. In light of these, possibly more minor examples, it is critical to consider Adichie's words.

Firstly, as noted, she constructs gender as both binary and something trans people 'switch' between, a position that echoes TERF perceptions of trans identity. Secondly, the use of this specific term 'switch' reifies a particular understanding of trans identity grounded in the Global North. Indeed, switching suggests access to hormones and affirming healthcare that is not available across the African continent and therefore, in many senses, is simply not part of the trans imaginary. It, therefore, fails to account for and invalidates the existence of trans identities prior to (or regardless of) affirming healthcare

(Iranti-Org, 2017). Miss Sahhara (2017) goes so far as to reject medicalisation. As a trans woman from Africa, she argues that she did not 'switch' or 'transition' rather 'my brain and sense of self has always been female, my self-definition may not be synonymous with most trans women, *but it is my definition.* I grew up thinking, looking and acting like the female I thought I was [emphasis added]' (Miss Sahhara, 2017). This point is critical in the assumption of what it might mean to be transgender within the presently dominant Global Northern models of transgender identity and the reality of being transgender in the Global South. The very same models that TERF politics, invested in particular bio-logics and Western models of gender identity, are constructed in relation too. As Miss Sahhara clarifies:

> The way I look/dress and present myself as a human being is a choice, but the way I feel is not a choice. I did not choose to have the feelings I have. Who will choose to be hated, misunderstood and rejected? We all want to be loved, accepted and respected for who we are. Please don't confuse my struggles as a choice. (Miss Sahhara, 2017)

Returning to Oyěwùmí (1997, p. 10): if, as Adichie argues, gender is socially constructed, then 'gender cannot behave in the same ways across time and space'. Writers and feminists from the Global South, as noted by Desiree Lewis (2001, p. 6), have long argued that 'women's socially inscribed identities in Africa take very different forms from women's acquisition of gender identities in the West'. Why would this be any different for trans women?

Susan Stryker (2006, p.12) explains that 'transgender is without a doubt, a category of first world origin that is being exported for third world consumption'. It is invested with particular ideas of gender and hails a particular person when used – as with the term feminist – usually, someone who is white. Trans scholar Viviane K. Namaste (2005, p. xi) is deeply critical of what she calls the anglocentric bias of the term transgender. Namaste stresses that it is necessary for feminism in particular to be aware of the how specific language and concepts 'are marked by specific nationalist and colonialist traditions . . . institutional mechanisms through which imperialism is achieved, denying rights to some humans, according them to others'. As Jesse Shipley and Chika Unigwe (2018) note in their article 'Naming as Righting and Regulating', location matters. How African sexualities and gender identities are framed and by whom has crucial and at times deeply political impacts.

To uncritically apply names and concepts invested and 'constructed by people with colonising and nationalising agendas' (Shipley & Unigwe, 2018) runs the risk of turning the specificity of experiences that are, to use decolonial terms, geo- and corpo-politically situated into a broader monolithic narrative with no nuance – a single story. Naming and language, for instance, the terms 'women' or 'transgender', must expand and transform to fit experiences and actualities. In a press release addressing Adichie's comments, South African transgender, intersex and queer media rights organisation Iranti-Org (2017) noted that in her approach to a very narrow definition of womanhood, Adichie was perpetuating the very thing she has built a platform on working against. The organisation, which works with and for transgender people across the African continent, addressed Adichie directly. They asked her, in their response article, to consider how 'she is now silencing and speaking over the many trans voices who have also been colonised and misrepresented for far too long, and to not let Western definitions and stereotypes be her sole source of knowledge on trans identities' (Iranti-Org, 2017).

What perhaps lies at the heart of the language issue is the term 'cis'. Adichie suggests that it is both foreign to her and represents a 'type of language orthodoxy'. To suggest as such is actually to highlight the asymmetry that exists between trans and cis. It also brings the power relations of language and the ways in which trans people are consistently separated as 'Other' into full visibility (Bettcher, 2013a). Trans women have always had to justify who they are, while cis women, like Adichie, more generally do not or have not had to. It is this continuous creation of 'Other', to say 'trans women are trans women', a negative recognition, that situates trans women outside the category of 'woman' as defined and policed by a cis woman. It is this exclusion that so easily echoes, and to a certain extent is co-opted, as trans-exclusionary. Not only does Adichie define the category, but also she refuses to see her privilege in the very fact that she assumes she can do so. In her response, cis Zimbabwean novelist Panashe Chigumadzi (2017) called on cis feminists 'to recognise that this is an issue beyond semantics'. For Chigumadzi, the creation of a fixed category of womanhood defined by cis women, something which lies at the heart of TERF perceptions, necessarily implies boundaries, which need policing 'in ways that often have violent consequences for those who do not fit neatly into the category'.

Are there trans women in Africa?[5]

> The single story creates stereotypes, and the problem with stereotypes is not that they are untrue, but that they are incomplete. They make one story become the only story. (Adichie, 2009)

In her TED Talk *The Danger of a Single Story*, Adichie explains how, as a child exposed to particular perceptions of the world, perceptions already explicitly invested in whiteness and Western ideals shaped her expectations of the world around her. Since she was living in Nigeria at the time, this was a world which was not commensurate with the one she read about. In the talk, she goes on to explain how this single story, one that is anglocentric, lacks nuance and represents groups as homogeneous, has historically often worked to the detriment of those that are not white and Western. For Adichie, stereotypes silence nuance and the only way to redress this is to elevate a diversity of voices. In this moment, for critics like Mia Fischer, the response from Adichie brought to the fore a kind of single-story feminism, one which resonates in the Global North. A feminism that has long privileged the views of particular women or presented these views as universalising: claiming to speak for all women everywhere. Feminism today, or at least popular feminism for Fischer, continually 'emphasises cisgender perspectives and experiences, replicating a cis-hegemonic feminism' (2017, p. 897). A feminism labelled by Adichie's critics in the Global North as 'TERF'. For Cameron Awkward-Rich (2017, p. 828) it is utterly surprising given the breadth of feminism today that trans-exclusionary radical feminism continues to 'so frequently stand in for what feminism *is*'. Regardless of how TERFs are dismissed or written off as perpetuating bad science or pure hatefulness, 'they persist and continue to structure mainstream representations of trans lives. For this reason, it seems to me that we too must take them seriously in order to properly understand the appeal' (Awkward-Rich, 2017, p. 828). What then, is the appeal here? Put another way, why the focus on Adichie?

The circulation of feminist thought globally is complex and largely uneven. There are, as noted, particular historical, institutional, social and political structures 'allowing for differential scales of power and powerlessness' (Roy, 2016, p. 292). Srila Roy refers to these as enduring 'circuits of marginalisation' (Roy, 2016, p. 292). Transnational feminist writing by authors such as Roy (2016), Tambe (2010) and Amanda Lock Swarr and Richa Nagar (2010) remind us that this flow of feminisms is never one-sided or unidirectional. It is never just from the Global North to the Global South, but rather, there is a circulation of feminist ideas and principles that happen within realms of difference and inequality. It cannot be forgotten that these circuits have, in part, been fostered by ongoing Northern epistemological domination which often privileges 'the voices of a few hand-picked Southern scholars' (Roy, 2016, p. 292). Acclaimed South African author Sisonke Msimang notes that in recent years Adichie has 'been used as an expert' on issues of race, gender and African politics. For Msimang (2017), Adichie has become a spokesperson for the West, a household name who has 'used her voice to galvanise the urgency of diverse voices and perspectives. A worthy cause, for sure, but one that has been manipulated to foment divisions within the women's movement worldwide' (Sanchez, 2017). Kgositau (2017) underlines these points when she notes that although the original interviewer, in asking Adichie about trans women, placed her in a difficult situation, a question which Adichie herself acknowledged verged on 'anti-feminist', she chose to answer as she did. This was, for Kgositau, a trivial use of trans people's lives on a global platform aimed at feeding already existing tensions and creating discordance – tensions which she continued to feed in her Facebook clarifications following the original incident.

The responses of cis women like Msimang (2017), Chigumadzi (2017) and Patel (2017), cis women in the Global South, point to a type of politics far more closely aligned to understanding trans women as women. The kind of politics which in global 'circuits of marginalisation' offers a direct challenge to TERF approaches to trans bodies which seemingly dominate popular perceptions of feminism. As Chigumadzi (2017) explains:

> . . . when black, African cisgender women (that is, women who identify with the gender they were assigned with at birth) such as feminist icon Chimamanda Ngozi Adichie, insist that because of the difference of their experience of womanhood 'transwomen are transwomen' [*sic*] and therefore not part of the category 'woman,' it becomes a deep dishonour to the centuries-old traditions of black and African feminisms seeking to disrupt white and Western women's exclusionary definitions of womanhood. . . . Black and African feminists have long taught us that, indeed, anatomy is not destiny. As a cisgender black feminist, I believe that it is an indictment on our contemporary activism that it purports to 'support' transwomen [*sic*], only to exclude them in the very same ways that we have historically been excluded from the category of 'Woman'.

This is not to say that there is a homogeneous African feminism which sits in direct contradiction to popular versions of feminism in the Global North. Instead, as African feminists such as Filomena Chioma Steady (1996), Josephine Ahikire (2014), Nana Darkoa

Sekyiamah (2014), Danai Mupotsa (2014) and many others have pointed out, feminism on the African continent is comprised of 'myriad heterogeneous experiences and points of departure' (Ahikire, 2014, p. 8). African feminism combines the very many dimensions of oppression across the continent to produce 'a more inclusive brand of feminism through which women are viewed first and foremost as human, rather than sexual, beings' (Steady, 1996). These debates of radical feminism, as Gwendolyn Mikell (1997) noted in the 1990s, are not the ways characteristic of African feminism.

To return to Patel's (2017) tweets, she ends by asking 'Who gets to unwoman women? Who profits from the policing of women? What is threatened by transgressive women and gender variance?' Kgositau (2017), from her perspective as a trans woman from Botswana, calls Adichie's approaches and, indeed, Adichie's feminism, 'long dead and buried'. The kind of feminism which, as a trans woman from the African continent, does not resonate with her, and with the trans and indeed cis women who responded. The kind of Western bio-logic feminism which, she points out, operates on the premise of 'who has a vagina and who does not'. Kgositau (2017), in a moment of acerbic pity for the seemingly foreign and out of touch ideas in which she perceives Adichie to be invested, calls out Adichie's 'vagina politics' as 'fossils of feminism'. The kind of feminism that might be labelled 'TERF' in the Global North, but as Kgositau seems to suggest, holds no currency for her and indeed many of the feminist writers and activist of non-trans experience like Patel who did respond. What might we infer from the vocal support of cis feminists such as Msimang, Chigumadzi, Patel and others? Perhaps, that the kind of feminism attempting to dominate transnational circulation currently, a feminism presenting itself as universally applicable, is in fact not. Rather, on the African continent, at least visibly and vocally, concerning trans women is a feminism which, in the lineage of other feminisms from the South, refuses to 'speak about the whole world . . . in a conceptual language derived from the most powerful part of it' (Connell, 2014, p. 521).

An entirely different story

> Stories matter. Many stories matter. Stories have been used to dispossess and to malign, but stories can also be used to empower and to humanise. Stories can break the dignity of a people, but stories can also repair that broken dignity. (Adichie, 2009)

The Danger of a Single Story is perhaps one of Adichie's most-watched TED Talks. In it she challenges humanity to acknowledge and listen to each other's complexity. Yet, in the instance of the Channel 4 interview, Adichie, quite peculiarly, presents a single narrative. One which sees 'trans women as trans women', not as people who are often misgendered or coercively assigned in a particular way at birth. A position that perhaps, though not intentionally meant as such, echoes and therefore very easily opened itself up to accusations of TERF intention. Adichie, in her own confounding single story of trans existence, invested in very particular Global Northern narratives of gender and perceived perceptions regarding the body, conveniently overlooks her own privilege and power. That is the power and privilege cis people have in being correctly gendered from birth. Moreover, the assumptions she makes as a cis woman are constitutive of this – for example, that she supposedly had the right to answer a question on whether trans women are women.

Feminists from the African continent have for the most part responded, at least on public platforms, in support of transgender women, questioning Adichie and her stance. It is notable too that responses from authors such as Msimang and Chigumadzi suggest the possibility of a different space for feminism and trans women within South Africa in particular. My own, albeit anecdotal, experience of writing for the South African collection *Feminism Is* (Camminga, 2018b) as a trans person who identifies as a feminist, has been exceptionally positive, inclusive and welcoming. At the same time, although publicly feminist spaces and feminists on the African continent seem to be more open, it does not negate the physical danger that trans people across the African continent experience daily. What I am suggesting though is that the narrative of trans-exclusionary feminism in the Global North, which currently seems to be dominant at least in a popular cultural sense, is seemingly not an issue in the same way on the African continent. The voices of those I have centred in this essay have provided an outright and explicit rejection of both the kind of feminism and gender politics that Adichie espouses. Critically, it is not just trans women doing so but cis women too. Perhaps Chigumadzi (2017) says it best:

> When our trans sisters have to look at us, and ask as our feminist foremother Sojourner Truth did a century and half ago, 'Ain't I A Woman?', it tells us that our visions of freedom from the oppressions that we face as black women are not only unimaginative, exclusionary, and violent, but historically regressive.

For Oyěwùmí (1997, p. 13), these debates, about the differences between women and the 'preoccupation with gender bending/blending that have characterised feminism', are culturally specific concerns invested in the social hierarchies of the West. She adds that what seems to be truly fascinating is how feminism has become so deeply imbricated in the 'ethnocentric and imperialistic characteristics of the Western discourse it sought to subvert' (Oyěwùmí, 1997, p. 13). This is because the concerns that have informed this feminism are Western and have continued to be so in a self-perpetuating colonialist sense. Oyěwùmí (1997, p. 13) also notes then that feminism, as seemingly is the case for Adichie, remains 'enflamed by the tunnel vision of the bio-logic' of Western discourse. A discourse structured on historical power. It is this power that is crucial here, as Adichie herself notes:

> It is impossible to talk about the single story without talking about power. There is a word, an Igbo word, that I think about whenever I think about the power structures of the world, and it is 'nkali.' It's a noun that loosely translates to 'to be greater than another.' Like our economic and political worlds, stories too are defined by the principle of nkali: How they are told, who tells them, when they're told, how many stories are told, are really dependent on power. Power is the ability not just to tell the story of another person, but to make it the definitive story of that person. The Palestinian poet Mourid Barghouti writes that if you want to dispossess a people, the simplest way to do it is to tell their story and to start with, 'secondly.' Start the story with the arrows of the Native Americans, and not with the arrival of the British, and you have an entirely different story. (Adichie, 2009)

Start the story, as Ratalane, Miss Sahhara, Mooketsi, Kgositau, Chigumadzi, Msimang and Patel have, by acknowledging history, geo- and corpo-political difference, along with colonial impositions of language and gender and how terms travel and have imperialist tendencies but can and do transform, and you have an entirely different story.

Funding

The author received no financial support for the research, authorship, and/or publication of this article.

Notes

1. These are the words of a Twitter-user, @Seoketsi_M, who tweeted this under the hashtag #ChimamandaKilledme in 2017. The account no longer exists.
2. Trans-inclusive feminism in the Global North is also highly critical of these bio-logics.
3. Nigel Patel (2019) does similar work linking the gendered colonisation of trans people of colour in South Africa to the violent legacy of sex segregated bathroom spaces. Patel suggests that the difficulties trans people in South Africa experience accessing bathrooms safely cannot simply be understood as an issue of gender but is intertwined with the particular history of racism and colonialism in South Africa. For more on bathrooms, see Slater and Jones, this collection.
4. For example, Adichie has taken public issue with terms like 'baby bump' which she has argued obfuscates the more serious issues of maternity leave and the gender pay gap (Allardice, 2018).
5. This a riff on a statement Elaine Salo made to Amina Mama (2001) regarding the suggestion that there are no feminists in Africa.

References

Adichie, C. N. (2009). *The danger of a single story*. Ted.com. www.ted.com/talks/chimamanda_ adichie_the_danger_of_a_single_story (accessed 28 December 2018).

Adichie, C. N. (2017a). *Dear Ijeawele, or a feminist manifesto in fifteen suggestions*. Penguin.

Adichie, C. N. (2017b, March 12). Chimamanda Ngozi Adichie – Clarifying. *Facebook*. www. facebook.com/chimamandaaadichie/photos/a.469824145943/10154893542340944/?type=3& theater (accessed 28 December 2018).

Adichie, C. N. (2018). *Chimamanda Ngozi Adichie responds to the 'trans noise' at Abantu Book Festival*. Abantu Book Festival Soweto Johannesburg. https://soundcloud.com/matshela-nemamabolo/chimamanda-ngozi-adichie (accessed 11 December 2018).

Adichie, C. N., Coates, T.-N., & Goldberg, J. (2017, November 14). *The intolerant left*. https:// www.theatlantic.com/entertainment/archive/2017/11/the-intolerant-left/545783/ (accessed 11 December 2018).

Ahikire, J. (2014). African feminism in context: Reflections on the legitimation battles, victories and reversals. *Feminist Africa*, *19*, 7–21.

Allardice, L. (2018, April 28). Chimamanda Ngozi Adichie: 'This could be the beginning of a revolution'. *The Guardian*. www.theguardian.com/books/2018/apr/28/chimamanda-ngozi-adichie-feminism-racism-sexism-gender-metoo (accessed 28 December 2018).

Awkward-Rich, C. (2017). Trans, feminism: Or, reading like a depressed transsexual: Winner of the 2017 Catharine Stimpson Prize for Outstanding Feminist Scholarship. *Signs*, *42*(4), 819–841.

Bettcher, T. (2013a). Trapped in the wrong theory: Rethinking trans oppression and resistance. *Signs*, *39*(2), 383–406.

Bettcher, T. M. (2013b). Trans woman and the meaning of 'woman'. In N. Power, R. Halwani & A. Soble (Eds.), *The philosophy of sex* (pp. 233–250). Rowan & Littlefield.

Brown, L. A. (2017, December 11). *Chimamanda Ngozi Adichie: 'Sometimes it feels like the universe is conspiring against me'*. qz.com. https://qz.com/quartzy/1133732/chimamanda-ngozi-adichie-talks-about-feminism-and-raising-her-daughter-in-a-gendered-world/ (accessed 28 December 2018).

Camminga, B. (2018a). *Transgender refugees and the imagined South Africa: Bodies over borders and borders over bodies*. Palgrave Macmillan.

Camminga, B. (2018b). Feminism is. . .for every single body. In J. Thorpe (Ed.), *Feminism is* (pp. 121–135). Kwela.

Channel 4 News (2017). *Chimamanda Ngozi Adichie interview*. YouTube. www.youtube.com/watch?v=KP1C7VXUfZQ&feature=youtu.be (accessed 17 March 2017).

Chigumadzi, P. (2017, March 17). *'Ain't I a woman?' On the irony of trans-exclusion by black and African feminists*. AFROPUNK. www.afropunk.com/m/blogpost?id=2059274%3ABlogPost%3A1460067 (accessed 24 March 2017).

Collison, C. (2017, March 31). *Slice of life: Only I can define myself*. mg.co.za. https://mg.co.za/article/2017-03-31-00-slice-of-life-only-i-can-define-myself/ (accessed 31 March 2017).

Connell, R. (2014). Rethinking gender from the South. *Feminist Studies*, *40*(3), 518–539.

Fischer, M. (2017). Trans responses to Adichie: Challenging cis privilege in popular feminism. *Feminist Media Studies*, *17*(5), 896–899.

Hines, S. (2007). Feminist theories. In D. Richardson & V. Robinson (Eds.), *Introducing gender and women's studies* (pp. 23–37). Red Globe Press.

Hines, S. (2019). The feminist frontier: On trans and feminism. *Journal of Gender Studies*, *28*(2), 145–157.

Iranti-Org. (2017, March 13). *PRESS RELEASE: A response to Chimamanda Ngozi Adichie*. Iranti. www.iranti-org.co.za/content/Press_Releases/2017/Chimamanda-Adichie.html (accessed 18 March 2017).

Kean, D. (2017, March 13). Chimamanda Ngozi Adichie clarifies transgender comments as backlash grows. *The Guardian*. www.theguardian.com/books/2017/mar/13/chimamanda-ngozi-adichie-clarifies-transgender-comments?CMP=share_btn_fb (accessed 17 March 2017).

Kgositau, T. R. (2017). *Ricki Kgositau – Open letter to Ms.Chimamanda Adichie*. Facebook. www.facebook.com/ricki.kgositau/posts/10154461876673861?comment_id=10154467228193861&ref=notif&notif_t=feed_comment_reply&notif_id=1489565207004629 (accessed 18 March 2017).

Lewis, D. (2001). Introduction: African feminisms. *Agenda*, *16*(50), 4–10.

Lugones, M. (2016). The coloniality of gender. In W. Harcourt (Ed.), *The Palgrave handbook of gender and development: Critical engagements in feminist theory and practice* (pp. 13–33). Palgrave Macmillan.

MacFarquhar, L. (2018, May 28). Chimamanda Ngozi Adichie comes to terms with global fame. *The New Yorker*. www.newyorker.com/magazine/2018/06/04/chimamanda-ngozi-adichie-comes-to-terms-with-global-fame (accessed 28 December 2018).

Mbamalu, S. (2017, March 13). *Africa: Trans-women are trans-women and women are women says Chimamanda Adichie*. All Africa. http://allafrica.com/stories/201703130562.html (accessed 18 March 2017).

Mikell, G. (1997). Introduction. In G. Mikell (Ed.), *African feminism: The politics of survival in Sub-Saharan Africa* (pp. 1–53). University of Pennsylvania Press.

Miss Sahhara. (2017, March 17). *Miss saHHara – Timeline*. Facebook. www.facebook.com/sahhara/posts/600263683506918:0 (accessed 17 March 2017).

Mooketsi, S. (2017, March 16). *#ChimamandaKilledME (@Seoketsi_M) | Twitter*. https://twitter.com/Seoketsi_M (accessed 17 March 2017).

Msimang, S. (2017, April 10). *All your faves are problematic: A brief history of Chimamanda Ngozi Adichie, stanning and the trap of #blackgirlmagic*. Africasacountry.com. http://africasacountry.com/2017/04/all-your-faves-are-problematic-a-brief-history-of-chimamanda-ngozi-adichie-stanning-and-the-trap-of-blackgirlmagic/ (accessed 14 April 2017).

Mukasa, V., & Balzer, C. (2009). 'People have realized the need for an African trans movement'. Interview with Victor Mukasa, African trans activist representing IGLHRC (International Gay and Lesbian Human Rights Commission) and TITs Uganda (Transgenders Intersex Transsexuals Uganda). *Liminalis, 3*, 122–127.

Mupotsa, D. (2014). Review: Queer African Reader. Edited by Sokari Ekine and Hakima Abbas. Nairobi and Oxford: Pambazuka Press, 2013. *Feminist Africa, 19*, 113–120.

Namaste, V. K. (2005). *Sex change, social change*. Women's Press Toronto.

Nkomozake, P. (2017, March 31). *Are trans rights part of these human rights?* Queerstion. www.queerstion.org/2017/03/31/are-trans-rights-part-of-these-human-rights/ (accessed 31 March 2017).

Nnaemeka, O. (2004). Nego feminism: Theorizing, practicing, and pruning Africa's way. *Signs, 29*(2), 357–385.

Oppenheim, M. (2017, March 12). Chimamanda Ngozi Adichie has sparked outrage for her comments about transgender women. *The Independent*. www.independent.co.uk/arts-entertainment/books/news/chimamanda-ngozi-adichie-transgender-women-channel-four-a7625481.html (accessed 18 March 2017).

Oyěwùmí, O. (1997). *The invention of women: Making an African sense of western gender discourses*. University of Minnesota Press.

Patel, S. (2017). *Thread. Women deemed 'not real women' in many times and places: Black women Colonized African, Asian, Indigenous women Unmarried women*. Twitter. https://twitter.com/shailjapatel/status/841556703023898624 (accessed 18 March 2017).

Patel, N. (2019). Violent cistems: Trans experiences of bathroom spaces. In Z. Matebeni & B. Camminga (Eds.), *Beyond the mountain: Queer life in Africa's 'gay capital'* (pp. 38–54). Unisa Press.

Roy, S. (2016) Women's movements in the Global South: towards a scalar analysis. *International Journal of Politics, Culture and Society, 29*(3), 289–306.

Salo, E., & Mama, A. (2001). Talking about feminism in Africa. *Agenda, 16*(50), 58–63.

Sanchez, R. R. (2017, March 20). *The third wave's tokenization of Chimamanda Ngozi Adichie is anything but intersectional*. Feministcurrent. www.feministcurrent.com/2017/03/20/third-waves-tokenization-chimamanda-ngozi-adichie-anything-intersectional/ (accessed 22 March 2017).

Schmidt, S. (2017, March 13). Women's issues are different from trans women's issues, feminist author says, sparking criticism. *The Washington Post*. www.washingtonpost.com/news/morning-mix/wp/2017/03/13/womens-issues-are-different-from-trans-womens-issues-feminist-author-says-sparking-criticism/?utm_term=.a03acd4a3d54 (accessed 17 March 2017).

Sekyiamah, N. D. (2014). Review: Women, Sexuality and the Political Power of Pleasure. Edited by Andrea Cornwall, Susie Jolly, and Kate Hawkins. London and New York: Zed Books, 2013. *Feminist Africa, 19*, 109–112.

Shipley, J. W., & Unigwe, C. (2018, January 8). *Naming as righting and regulating: Recent work on gender and sexuality in Africa*. Brittlepaper. https://brittlepaper.com/2018/01/naming-righting-regulating-reflections-work-gender-sexuality-africa-jesse-weaver-shipley-chika-unigwe/ (accessed 28 December 2018).

Smith, D. (2017, March 21). Chimamanda Ngozi Adichie on transgender row: 'I have nothing to apologise for'. *The Guardian*. www.theguardian.com/books/2017/mar/21/chimamanda-ngozi-adichie-nothing-to-apologise-for-transgender-women (accessed 21 March 2017).

Stryker, S. (2006). (De)subjugated knowledges: An introduction to transgender studies. In S. Stryker & S. Whittle (Eds.), *The transgender studies reader* (pp. 1–17). Routledge.

Steady, F. C. (1996). African feminism: A worldwide perspective. In R. Terborg-Penn & A. Benton-Rushing (Eds.), *Women in Africa and the African diaspora* (pp. 3–21). Howard University Press.

Swarr, A. L., & Nagar, R. (Eds.). (2010). *Critical transnational feminist praxis*. SUNY Press.

Tambe, A. (2010) Transnational feminist studies: A brief sketch. *New Global Studies*, *4*(1), 1–7.

Uwujaren, J. (2017, March 14). *Why Chimamanda Ngozi Adichie's comments on trans women are wrong and dangerous*. Coalition. http://coalition.org.mk/zoshto-komentarite-na-chimamanda-ngozi-adichie-za-trans-zhenite-se-pogreshni-i-opasni/?lang=en (accessed 5 December 2018).

Author biography

B Camminga (they/them) is the co-convenor of the African LGBTQI+ Migration Research Network (ALMN). Their work considers the interrelationship between the conceptual journeying of the term 'transgender' from the Global North and the physical embodied journeying of transgender refugees from the African continent. Their first monograph *Transgender Refugees & the Imagined South Africa* (Palgrave, 2019) was awarded the 2019 Sylvia Rivera Award in Transgender Studies.

The toilet debate: Stalling trans possibilities and defending 'women's protected spaces'[1]

The Sociological Review Monographs
2020, Vol. 68(4) 160–177
© The Author(s) 2020

Article reuse guidelines:
sagepub.com/journals-permissions
DOI: 10.1177/0038026120934697
journals.sagepub.com/home/sor

Charlotte Jones
Wellcome Centre for Cultures and Environments of Health, University of Exeter, UK

Jen Slater
Department of Education, Childhood and Inclusion, Sheffield Hallam University, UK

Abstract
As one of the few explicitly gender-separated spaces, the toilet has become a prominent site of conflict and a focal point for 'gender-critical' feminism. In this article we draw upon an AHRC-funded project, Around the Toilet, to reflect upon and critique trans-exclusionary and trans-hostile narratives of toilet spaces. Such narratives include ciscentric, heteronormative and gender essentialist positions within toilet research and activism which, for example, equate certain actions and bodily functions (such as menstruation) to a particular gender, decry the need for all-gender toilets, and cast suspicion upon the intentions of trans women in public toilet spaces. These include explicitly transmisogynist discourses perpetuated largely by those calling themselves 'gender-critical' feminists, but also extend to national media, right-wing populist discourses and beyond. We use Around the Toilet data to argue that access to safe and comfortable toilets plays a fundamental role in making trans lives possible. Furthermore, we contend that – whether naive, ignorant or explicitly transphobic – trans-exclusionary positions do little to improve toilet access for the majority, instead putting trans people, and others with visible markers of gender difference, at a greater risk of violence, and participating in the dangerous homogenisation of womanhood.

Keywords
bathroom, feminism, gender critical, TERF, transphobia

Corresponding author:
Charlotte Jones, Wellcome Centre for Cultures and Environments of Health, University of Exeter, Exeter, EX4 4PY, UK.
Email: charlotte.jones@exeter.ac.uk

Introduction

The Sunday Times published an article in 2018, announcing that women's toilets at London landmarks may – in 'the most radical move yet' – soon be opened to 'self-identifying' transgender women, regardless of 'whether or not they have transitioned' (Gilligan, 2018). One person, described in the article as a feminist, called the premise 'mind-blowing. It effectively abolishes women's protected spaces . . . It is dangerous for women and girls' (Gilligan, 2018). In fact, there was nothing radical or novel about this motion: under the Equality Act 2010, trans people are authorised to use gender-separated[2] spaces that align with their identity, and many have always been doing so across the United Kingdom, often without being questioned or noticed. Following a complaint over its accuracy, *The Sunday Times* was forced to withdraw the article a year later and print a clarification. By this time, however, the misleading claims had already contributed to a simmering dispute over toilet access and proprietorship.

This article considers how the toilet has become an unexpected focal point for dissensus in contemporary feminism in the UK, spotlighting divisions over trans bodies, identities and freedoms. Over the last decade, hostility directed towards trans people from some factions within feminism has monopolised public discourse around the movement (as outlined by Ahmed, 2016; Hines, 2019; Phipps, 2016). Access to the toilet has thus become a symbol overloaded with significance. For many 'gender-critical' feminists, the walls of women-only facilities have come to symbolise the boundaries of womanhood: a 'safe' space where the terms of inclusion are vehemently regulated and protected. Feminists taking this position are widely referred to as 'trans-exclusionary radical feminists' (TERFs) by their adversaries. However, 'TERF' has been rejected as pejorative by those it describes, who instead often call themselves 'gender-critical'. The meaning and beliefs of 'gender-critical' feminists are detailed later in the article. Whilst epistemologies and ontologies of gender and sex are not confined to the toilet, this location offers an especially productive space for gatekeeping. The complex, abstract and nebulous concepts of gender and sex are solidified and made visible and communicable through the toilet's infrastructure: its walls, its facilities, the signs on its doors, and the surveillance of the space. Toilets also present an unavoidable point of social confluence: the rules and composition of the toilet affect us all, and prohibition against some occupants could have far-reaching consequences. Access to suitable toilets facilitates all our movements away from home.

We open this article with a contextual overview of 'gender-critical' arguments around trans people's access to toilets in the UK. We do this as there is little in the way of extensive academic engagement with 'gender-critical' arguments on toilets from a trans-inclusive perspective. Trans people have been cast as the 'subjects' of these debates, often without invitation to comment or share their viewpoints or experiences. Despite the considerable attention the issue has been given, access to toilets is one of many matters to withstand for trans people, alongside concerns about access to education, healthcare and employment, as well as rates of violence and homelessness (Bachmann & Gooch, 2018). Nevertheless, the ability to use toilets comfortably and safely has significance (Slater & Jones, 2018). This article therefore provides necessary data centring the stories of trans people. Moving forwards, we hope this will offer a means to discuss the issue without the misrepresentation or disregard of trans experiences.

The data from which this article draws were collected for the Around the Toilet project, to explore potential points of coalition by centring disabled, trans and queer people, whose use of toilets may be obstructed in a number of different ways (see also Slater & Jones, 2018; Slater et al., 2018, 2019). We use 'trans' as a term to describe anyone who does not wholly identify as the gender that they were assigned at birth, including non-binary people. We are cautious here to avoid 'prescriptive' conceptions of trans, queer and disabled identities or labels, and instead seek to recognise their multiplicity, intricacy and fluidity. We draw on the project's pursuit to understand the complexity of '(in)accessibility' in toilet spaces in order to illustrate how access, comfort and safety can produce contexts of 'possibility' (Pearce et al., 2020; see also Cox, 2017). This research also facilitated other modes of coalition: our project team, composed of early-career researchers and community partners, reflected a range of disciplinary backgrounds and research interests, but also sought to consolidate commitments to feminist, queer, trans and disability politics. There was an intuitive and necessary connection between these movements for many of us, who – in some cases – had personal experience of multiple marginalisation across these axes. However, the frequently combative relationship between these movements, as this article does some work towards illustrating, shows that sites of friction must also be investigated within our projects of collaboration and allegiance.

A feminist concern: Protecting women's spaces

The feminist history of public toilets in the UK has been documented (Penner, 2001; Walkowitz, 1992) and located within Western women's ongoing struggles for access to, and safety within, the built environment (Banks, 1991). Whilst London's first public toilets for men were installed in 1851, it was over 40 years later that provisions for women were finally introduced (Penner, 2001), and campaigns for women to have better toilet access continue to this day in the UK and elsewhere. It has been highlighted that decisions regarding the presence or absence, size and location of women's toilets are made within culturally and historically specific gendered power structures. For instance, Penner (2001, p. 37) indicates that resistance shown in response to early-twentieth-century campaigns to install women's toilets in Camden Town in London rested upon wider unstated concerns about the 'powerful message' women would be given 'about their right to occupy and move through the streets' if amenities were built there for their benefit. The deficit of facilities 'was no oversight but part of a systematic restriction of women's access to the city of man' (Greed, 2010, p. 117), grounded in the presumption that a woman's 'proper place' was the home, 'tending the hearth fire, and rearing children' (Kogan, 2007, p. 5).

The significance of current women-only provisions is often positioned within this history. Today's toilet is therefore recognised by some feminist scholars as a 'hard-won' radical occupation of public space (Greed & Bichard, 2012). Jeffreys (2014a, p. 46), for example, describes women's public toilets as 'essential to women's equality', and Greed (2010, p. 121) shares concerns that without these facilities 'women's [public] presence [would be] threatened' as 'the "bladder's leash" [would tether] women to [the] home'. Yet, these accounts rarely acknowledge that early women's toilets were not designed for all women (Patel, 2017; Penner, 2001, 2013). Victorian toilets were regularly segregated not only by gender but also by class (Penner, 2001) and, as Patel (2017, p. 52) notes, 'the creation of a sex-segregated bathroom space to enclose and protect the feminine was formed exclusively in relation to white femininities'. Indeed, until the 1960s in the American South, and the 1990s in South Africa, toilets would be not only gender-separated, but divided upon racial lines (Penner, 2013). Neither were disabled women considered within women's toilet provision: it was 1970 before (all-gender) accessible toilets were legislated in the UK (Ramster et al., 2018). The histories of women's toilets, therefore, were never a fight for *all* women's liberation; rather, they are a reminder that 'woman' was (and often continues to be) used as shorthand for white, wealthy, non-disabled, cisgender and heterosexual women. Such histories illustrate 'how misleading it is to speak of "women's needs" as a unified entity' (Penner, 2001, p. 41).

Whilst public facilities for women have been celebrated as a feminist victory (Greed & Bichard, 2012; Jeffreys, 2014a), toilet scholarship also highlights how gender inequalities persist. Queues are most often found for women's toilets, in part due to greater provision and a better variety of facilities for men[3] (Greed, 2010; Hanson et al., 2007; Ramster et al., 2018), but also because women are reported to spend longer in toilets, and visit them more frequently (Greed, 2010; Knight & Bichard, 2011; Ramster et al., 2018). This could be for a variety of socio-cultural reasons, including imbalances in caring responsibilities, gendered clothing, and the tendency to sit rather than stand. Ciscentric, biological explanations pertaining to 'the anatomy of the female-sexed [*sic*[4]] body' (Ramster et al., 2018, p. 60) are also often highlighted, emphasising experiences such as menstruation, pregnancy, miscarriage and higher levels of incontinence (Fair Play For Women [FPFW], 2017; Greed, 2010; Jeffreys, 2014a). Further, shortcomings in toilets are understood to affect women disproportionately: 'hard scratchy' toilet paper in public toilets (Greed, 2010, p. 138), for example, and pay-to-use toilets, which cost more cumulatively for those who use toilets most frequently (Greed, 2010, p. 140). Some have shared their frustration about the failure to foreground gender in public toilet design and provision, despite long-standing attempts to highlight its significance (Greed, 2010, Ramster et al., 2018). Thus, toilet provision is viewed as still not adequately meeting women's needs, and those wishing to maintain a gender-separated space argue for improved and expanded women-only provisions (Greed, 2019).

The toilet is also an area of interest within broader feminist discussions of safety and the need for 'women-only' spaces. Women's toilets are widely espoused in popular discourse and scholarship as a rare and valuable location for unity and solidarity (Greed, 2010; Jeffreys, 2014a; Ramster et al., 2018). They are understood to provide a fundamental location for gendered learning: 'how to do their hair, hold their bodies, use menstrual products, and adjust their clothes' (Molotch, 2010, p. 7), as well as a space to escape the scrutiny of wider society (or those positioned outside of womanhood), and perform covert personal upkeep (Barcan, 2010; Greed, 2010; Ramster et al., 2018). As such, women-only toilets are described as a 'safe space' (Jeffreys, 2014a, p. 50), a refuge for women 'in a male-oriented public sphere' (Ramster et al., 2018, p. 62), and especially necessary due to women's oppression (Jeffreys, 2014a). For some, the need to highlight the indispensability of women's toilets aligns with a broader concern that all women-only spaces are under question (Lewis et al., 2015). In 'safe space' literature, the threat of sexual violence – by men, against women – is foregrounded: a secluded, gender-specific setting grants protection from potential harm (Barcan, 2010; Jeffreys, 2014a; Ramster et al., 2018). However, the security of women's toilets is also recognised as precarious due to their potential misuse, wherein 'people are undressed, vulnerable and engaged in a private act' (Ramster et al., 2018, p. 69). Women's toilets are therefore positioned as both especially safe and (potentially) especially dangerous.

We have illustrated how toilets are positioned as a women's issue in multiple ways: (1) due to the campaigns for women's facilities historically and their late introduction and instalment, they are considered a symbol of progress for women's liberation; (2) ongoing inequalities in access and the lower quality of women's provisions illustrate a need for continued gender-specific campaigning; and (3) public toilets are perceived to offer a rare opportunity for a sense of community amongst women and a 'safe space' away from men. As we will explore, there is a growing concern that women-only toilets are endangered. This perceived threat to women's facilities is represented as a threat to women's rights and progress, as well as jeopardising the solidarity and security found in single-gender spaces. However, whilst we agree that *all* women need access to toilets, we will argue that such assertions continue to rely on a very narrow definition of womanhood, excluding not only trans women, but also some cisgender women.

A fight for territory

Questions of access, safety and inclusion in gender-separated toilets became an international talking point in 2016 when North Carolina in the United States passed a law prohibiting trans people's use of public toilets that do not match the sex listed on their birth certificates. Commonly known as 'bathroom bills', these laws were then proposed in at least 15 other states, although none were enacted. There have been no similar threats in the UK, and trans people's right to access the toilet of their choosing is covered by the Equality Act 2010. Nevertheless, due to hearsay, misinformation, and an increasingly visible movement of 'gender-critical' feminists, trans people's freedom has also been debated locally. This was aggravated in 2018 during the UK government's consultation on the Gender Recognition Act 2004 (GRA). The GRA currently allows trans people to change their legal gender (including their birth certificate) if ratified by medical and legal professionals. During the consultation, trans people and their allies argued that the current process is intrusive, inaccessible, daunting and expensive, and that it should be replaced with a system based on trusting trans people's knowledge of their own gender (Gendered Intelligence, 2019). Although the GRA has no direct impact on trans people's entitlement to gender-separated spaces, it nevertheless emboldened opponents to trans inclusion (FPFW, 2018a; Woman's Place UK, 2018; see also Hines, 2019).

Contention surrounding trans people's – largely trans women's – use of public toilets that correspond to their gender has been claimed as an issue of (cisgender) women's rights, with manifest opposition to trans-inclusive toilets from some feminist campaigning groups and academics with a 'gender-critical' standpoint. 'Gender-critical' feminists oppose 'identity' or gender-based rights, instead arguing that women are oppressed as a biological class and deserve rights based on binary and essentialist understandings of male/female sex categories. These perspectives either elide or actively dispute the conceivability of trans identities. Whilst branches of feminism with an antagonistic relationship to trans people have a long history (Heyes, 2013; Hines, 2019), trans-hostile feminists are currently especially conspicuous, attempting to counteract ongoing progress made to the legal rights, social visibility and medical treatment received by trans people in the UK. Although 'gender-critical' feminists may be in a minority, they nevertheless 'have a high level of social, cultural and economic capital' (Hines, 2019, p. 154).

The primary focus of debates about toilet-use in the UK has been directed towards a perceived increase in all-gender[5] toilets (which are understood to be replacing gender-separated provision), and trans people's – primarily trans women's – use of separated facilities that align with their gender.[6] These concerns coalesce at the *possibility* that cisgender women will be required to share communal toilet space with anyone else, particularly – as Jeffreys (2014a, p. 42) revealingly puts it – 'male-bodied transgenders [*sic*] who seek to access women's toilets'. Jeffreys' derogatory emphasis on the presumed physiology of trans women is deliberate. As Ahmed (2016, p. 25) observes, intentional and 'violent misgendering enables trans women to be positioned as imposters' within feminist or women-only contexts and 'as perpetrators rather than victims of male violence'. The supposed revolution in trans-inclusive toilet legislation and design is portrayed as part of a 'new' liberation movement led by trans activists and supported by 'queer and purportedly progressive theorists' (Jeffreys, 2014a, p. 42). The toilet has become a focal point for trans rights, particularly for those who contest those rights.

The framing of women-only toilets as a fundamental concern for feminism has meant that the potential ramifications of changing toilet design are subsumed within broader principles of women's safety and rarely substantiated. One transphobic campaign group, Fair Play For Women, claim that 'female toilets and changing rooms are being turned mixed-sex around the country, leading to a huge rise in crimes against females, including sexual assault and rape' (FPFW, 2018b). These safety risks are not evidenced; research into the safety of trans-inclusive toilets in the US indicates that reported incidents of crime in public toilets are 'exceedingly rare' irrespective of trans-inclusion policies (Hasenbush et al., 2018, p. 79). Phipps notes how the experience of rape 'becomes capital' in these arguments, 'mobilised by trans-exclusionary feminists alongside a construction of trans women as predatory, dangerous and essentially male' (Phipps, 2017, p. 310). In other instances, trans women and girls are depicted as a 'Trojan Horse whose access to women's spaces will enable predatory men to similarly enter these spaces by claiming that they are women' (Pearce et al., 2020, p. 3). In both cases this obscures the threat of harm and exclusion facing trans women (Phipps, 2016). An 'emotive politics of fear' (Phipps, 2016, p. 312) is used to exclude trans women from women-only spaces, whilst also averting any admission of cisgender women's privilege relative to trans women.

Changes to gendered facilities are presented as fast-moving and specifically catering for a negligible and ephemeral trans community. Toilet scholar Greed (2018), for example, refers to trans people as a 'teeny weeny . . . percentage of the population' for whom 'heaven and earth is being moved to accommodate'. The central role of some feminist groups in the rival campaign has led to a strategic binary positioning, placing feminism in conflict with trans justice. For instance, headlines have argued that '[t]rans rights should not come at the cost of women's fragile gains' (Ditum, 2018) and '[w]omen are abused in the name of "trans rights"' (Kirkup, 2018). As Ahmed notes, the figure of the trans activist is often constructed as 'making unreasonable demands and arguments' (2016, p. 24) as a way 'to impose a restriction on feminist speech' (2016, p. 25). Trans activism and transgender studies are also placed in opposition to 'good' scholarship. Those opposing all-gender toilets claim that there is little research supporting trans people's need for changing toilet provision (e.g. Greed, 2018, 2019). In doing this, they fail to acknowledge a growing body of scholarship documenting trans people's experiences of toilet (in)accessibility and exclusion (e.g. Blumenthal, 2014; Cavanagh, 2010; Patel, 2017; Slater & Jones, 2018; Slater et al., 2018). By overlooking these important contributions, it has been possible to construct a battle between 'objective and enlightened researchers' and 'emotional and volatile activists'.

We have identified how multiple territories of toilet politics have become a source of contestation. Trans-inclusive approaches to toilet usage and design are represented as infringing upon (cisgender) women's safety and therefore contesting fundamental feminist principles. Such claims are rarely evidenced, and in most instances fail to recognise trans women's particular vulnerabilities to violence (Phipps, 2016). Furthermore, the push for more trans-inclusive approaches to toilets is framed by some toilet scholars as an affront to their research and to the field more broadly; this is therefore also a fight for ideological ownership in toilet research, whereby historically cisgender women have been the focus of these social justice claims. In what follows, we use findings from the Around the Toilet project to explore conflicts between 'gender-critical' feminists and trans scholarship and activism. We argue that attempts to restrict trans people's access to toilets are not so much about practical concerns for women's comfort or safety, but ideologically securing the boundaries of (a particular type of cisgender) womanhood, and by doing so, denying trans 'possibility' (Pearce et al., 2020; see also Cox, 2017).

Methodology: Around the Toilet

As we have shown, in some strands of feminism, liberation for women and trans people are positioned as discrete and competing agenda. Running between April 2015 and February 2018, the Around the Toilet project was established as a response to attempts to isolate these justice movements. The project was funded by the Arts and Humanities Research Council Connected Communities programme to examine the extent to which toilets provide a safe, accessible and comfortable space for everyone, whilst centring the experiences of disabled, trans and queer people.

The project drew on collaborative and creative research design principles coming from feminist, disability studies and queer perspectives (Bailey et al., 2014; King & Cronin, 2016; Pauwels, 2015). This allowed us to work with diverse participants, organisations and stakeholder groups, some of whom were involved in initial research design. Around 30 people in the north of England participated in data collection including one-to-one interviews, group storytelling, sculpture and performance workshops. However, as Around the Toilet has been consistently outward facing, many more people engaged with the project internationally through social media (@cctoilettalk; #cctoilettalk), writing for project publications, and at public events. Although initial participants identified as trans, queer and/or disabled, the project expanded to include others who had toilet experiences to share. In particular, we sought mobile workers, toilet cleaners, parents and carers, children and young people, and people whose religion impacted upon toilet use. Audio and graphic recordings, video and fieldnotes were used to capture dialogue, as well as spatial and embodied dimensions of data. Most people who took part in interviews and workshops had some form of sustained participation, such as attending multiple activities, collaborating in later research design, joining the advisory board, becoming a co-investigator and/or participating in data analysis. Accessible project outputs made through the project (films, postcards, a zine [Jones & Slater, 2018] and interactive websites – all available at http://aroundthetoilet.com), allowed for the ongoing sharing and discussion of data with diverse audiences. Such discussions informed the dynamic and responsive research design and data analysis, which has been continuous and iterative.

Around the Toilet was given ethical approval by Sheffield Hallam University. Ethics have been integral to every methodological decision. For example, we sought to be open about structural inequalities and power dynamics within the project team, and regularly invited input from a range of expertise and experience. All participants gave informed consent around issues of anonymity and confidentiality, although consent was an ongoing process (Edwards & Mauthner, 2012). Following Cavanagh (2010) and the politics of self-definition, consent forms included a section asking participants to self-define in their own words (for example, in terms of gender, disability, race, occupation and so on). Pseudonyms and descriptions of participants' identities are used in our writing with their agreement. A project report is available with more detail on the project process, findings and recommendations (Slater & Jones, 2018).

Sites of trans (im)possibility

In the sections that follow, we explore three key themes that emerged through conversations with participants: safety, validation and sharing. These themes illustrate key sites of friction for the trans politics of the toilet, but they also reach outside of these limits. As we argue, toilet 'debates' are about so much more than the amenities themselves. Thus, we consider how toilets have been weaponised to restrict the freedom of trans people, and propose that toilets nevertheless have the potential to be sites of 'trans possibility' (Pearce et al., 2020).

The notion of 'possibility' sheds light on the ways in which lives, and ways of living, can be both nurtured and fiercely shut down by the environments we occupy. The separation of toilets – an essential resource – rests upon regulative assumptions, whereby in order to move freely, bodies are required to be socially legible, familiar and coherent (Jones et al., 2020). Restrictions around their use can therefore be received as a form of governing: defining 'which lives are livable, and which are not' (Butler, 2004, p. 4), and how those lives can be expressed and amongst whom. Through our analyses, we seek to 'imagine otherwise' (Butler, 2004), by looking to the toilet to consider how places of trans 'impossibility' can be reconstituted as locations of *possibility*. Butler (2004, p. 4) notes how an analysis of the terms under which life is constrained may 'open up the possibility of different modes of living; in other words, not to celebrate difference as such but to establish more inclusive conditions for sheltering and maintaining life that resists models of assimilation'. Possibility, as Butler (2004, p. 29) observes, 'is not a luxury'. Thus, whilst we consider how trans possibility in toilet spaces could generate the potential for exciting new explorations, conceptualisations and renegotiations of space, 'possibility' here is also simply about 'getting by'.

Safety

As we have explored, women's safety has been used by 'gender-critical' feminists and some toilet researchers to justify a continuing need for gender-separated toilets. Yet, the public surveillance required to maintain such a space meant that trans people in our research shared how toilets could be especially dangerous places for them: a location of both scrutiny and continuous risk management, whereby 'the cisgender gaze becomes brutal and controlling in order to preserve "pure womanhood"' (Patel, 2017, p. 57). Alex, a non-binary participant, said that regardless of whether they used the men's or the women's toilets, they received harassment by other toilet occupants and security guards:

> I find the way people read my gender is quite unpredictable so I get harassed and kicked out and security called on me whichever gender toilet I'm using, so I can't really find a way 'round it. I get a lot of stares all the time but sometimes people actually confront me, saying I'm in the wrong toilet.

Alex noted that all-gender, self-contained cubicles (i.e. with a private basin) were therefore their preference. In communal toilets, other users became arbiters of propriety. Alex said that their own focus steered towards how their gender was perceived by others (regardless of their own identification) in order to predict the potential for harmful encounters. Whilst it should not be Alex's responsibility to modify their appearance to stay safe, they explained the difficulty they faced in averting the risk of danger, when attempts to categorise and interpret gender are inevitably inconsistent and subjective. For Alex, safety felt especially elusive when there was no all-gender toilet provision.

Erin, a trans woman, had also been subjected to violent encounters in the toilet. In line with other studies (Cavanagh, 2010; Patel, 2017), security guards were often reported to have posed a physical danger to trans participants in our research, despite their supposed role in creating a safer environment. Erin described the anxiety she felt about entering communal toilets, knowing that she might need to deal with conflict:

> There's a consistent knot in my stomach whenever I need to cross that invisible boundary between what's doing a necessary daily thing and what's going to get me into trouble, because it has and it does. I've been toilet-policed in a lot of places . . . . Sometimes it happens from security staff in pubs and things, which is really annoying and I kind of wish I could just explain to people what's going on. I have communication issues and, even if I didn't, I know that some people just aren't that receptive to being communicated with, especially if there's some kind of dispute involved. But yeah, I've been turfed out of toilets more than once . . . and it's quite humiliating, frankly.

Erin's desire to explain her circumstances to people who she says 'aren't that receptive' and Alex's struggle to 'find a way 'round it' illustrate how attempts to find safety and accommodation are repeatedly obstructed. For many trans participants, the toilet was always a place of precarity and risk. This was compounded further by other axes of marginalisation. Patel (2017), for example, notes that whilst the gendered segregation of toilets marginalises white trans people, trans people of colour, further/differently oppressed through coloniality and racism, were at a heightened risk of violence.

Erin shared an awareness that one of the reasons she was prevented from using the women's toilets safely was due to a belief held by others that she might be a threat. She reflected, 'I wonder what . . . it takes to imagine that I want to do anything other than that: I go into the toilet, I use the toilet, wash my hands, leave.' Erin portrayed the toilet as fundamentally mundane and utilitarian, and the implication that she had predatory or otherwise deceitful intentions placed restrictions upon her freedom, as well as making her physically unsafe within public spaces.

Barcan (2010, p. 41) proposes that 'divisions, separations and disavowals' are, themselves, 'mechanisms that make people feel safe', regardless of the logic behind them. Whilst customs and norms that are rooted in categorisation can offer security and comfort for some, we must also interrogate the 'risk' that trans people are understood to pose and the nature of these fears. Patel (2017, p. 58) suggests that trans occupants in women-only toilets 'challenge the politics of feminine respectability', and thus their threat may lie in the subsequent need to reconsider the stability of our modes of social categorisation. Likewise, Pearce et al. (2020, p. 7) discuss how 'trans ideas and trans people's experiences . . . threaten the current order of things as much as they promise the possibility of renewal and change'. Thus, we are often confronted with 'those who wish to halt or reverse the profound changes in understanding and possibility heralded by the emergence of trans' (Pearce et al., 2020, pp. 7–8). Of course, a change in the way that we think about toilets may reflect/motivate a change in the way that we think about gender more broadly.

We suggest that the risk of toilet violence and surveillance curtails trans possibilities in a space which is fundamental for everyone's everyday movement. Toilets *become* dangerous to make trans identities *impossible*. Gupta (2020, p. 66) reflects on the importance of centring trans experiences spatially, noting that '[s]pace is also about what is given voice, what is allowed to flourish, the possibilities that can be articulated'. Following this, we suggest that meaningful consideration of trans identities and experiences in toilets is not only a way of facilitating safety (as important as this is), but also a way of granting trans possibility: allowing trans people to 'be'.

Belonging and (in)validation

Toilets that enable trans possibility are 'explosive because they recognize, accommodate, and, hence, legitimate the presence of a social group who customarily "make do" and remain invisible at the level of representation' (Gershenson & Penner, 2009, p. 9). Trans participants noted that coming across all-gender provisions was rare, but many participants, such as Erin, said it was a 'massive relief' and an 'acknowledgement' of their presence. Finding provisions that felt comfortable could impact trans participants' wellbeing, thus the toilet's potential to affirm identities is one way in which trans people are also rendered vulnerable. Erin, who lost her job due to negative responses from her colleagues when she started using the women's toilets at work, noted:

[Using the toilet is] a thing that everybody needs to do every day, and because of a lot of ingrained transphobia, people take issue with that. People take issue with the fact that people need to pee and take action to stop them, whether it be harassing people in toilets or, you know, sacking them or getting them in trouble with the police.

Like Alex above, Erin also preferred an all-gender toilet, not only because she felt safe to use it, but also because the toilet signalled an inclusive philosophy beyond the toilet door:

Generally [finding an all-gender toilet] tends to happen in some pretty friendly places anyway. Generally if I can see a gender neutral sign then I'm somewhere that's got pretty sound people in.

Other participants agreed that safe and comfortable toilet provision had consequences stretching beyond immediate use. A trans woman, Penny, described how her ability to work was limited by not having access to all-gender toilets. She explained that when she felt unsafe to use public toilets, she was unable to leave her home. Penny was often late for appointments because of the time she spent putting on clothes and makeup in order to feel that she would be viewed and treated as a cisgender woman. Safe and comfortable toilets allowed her to take necessary, everyday journeys away from home:

It's not like the bathroom ends at the door to the bathroom, it actually extends to everywhere and if the bathroom was just a row of cubicles with sinks outside with no gender written on them, then maybe I would be more able to just roll out of bed and engage with society without being late for work because I'm redoing my make-up for the third time. . . . What makes a toilet accessible for me in actual practicality? Being able to leave my house.

Penny was conscious that she must perform a particular type of femininity in order to be read as a woman by other toilet users and mitigate potential violence. 'Gender-critical' feminists (e.g. Jeffreys, 2014b) often argue that 'trans activists' reinforce stereotypical gender roles – for example, promoting that a woman must look and act in a particularly feminine way. In our data, however, hetero- and cisnormative systems and structures (protected by 'gender-critical' feminists and others), pressured trans people to act and present according to specific, normative gender expectations in order to keep themselves safe (see also Bender-Baird, 2016). Of course, cisgender women, too, have to meet these standards; gender non-conforming and butch cisgender women are also subject to mis-gendering and violence in women's toilets (Cavanagh, 2010; Munt, 1998). Surveillance in women-only toilets therefore reinforces the rules that gender-critical feminists claim they want to abolish. Making trans lives impossible is prioritised over and above creating spaces inclusive of all women.

Fears about violence in gender-separated toilets sometimes led trans participants to use all-gender accessible toilets. A disabled trans woman, Daisy, told us that having access to a RADAR[7] key was 'possibly the most useful thing as a trans person' because it gave her access to an all-gender toilet. Yet, trans participants without physical impairments were often aware that their need for an all-gender space may compete with the needs of those with physical impairments, whose use of the space was portrayed as more legitimate. When asked if they ever used the accessible toilet, Alex said:

Sometimes, but I don't really want to . . . I don't want to be using it and then someone might come and need to actually use it because they're actually, like, physically disabled.

There was an awareness amongst trans participants that accessible toilets were scarce and that for some disabled people they were the only physically usable option. Some cisgender participants with 'invisible' impairments also said that they modified their use of the accessible toilet because they did not 'look disabled', and so felt – or worried that others might think – that they were undeserving of the space (Jones & Slater, 2018; Jones et al., 2020). In one workshop, participants were asked to design their ideal toilet using cardboard. Together, two disabled trans participants created two cubicles sitting side-by-side. A sign read, 'free public loo' while additional signage said, 'smaller toilet' and 'bigger toilet', describing the facilities rather than prescribing the users. The bigger toilet included additional writing: 'No toilet policing!! Please use this toilet if you need to and do not question if others need to.' In contrast to 'gender-critical' feminists and their allies, Around the Toilet participants worked towards 'an alternative way of seeing the toilet, as a site where personal choice is valued, and where forms of external authorisation or governance are unneeded/unwanted' (Slater et al., 2018, p. 961).

Scarcity and the sharing of space

Whilst toilet infrastructure is sometimes built to accommodate all-gender toilets (such as private self-contained cubicles with a hand-basin), on other occasions gender-separated toilets are re-labelled as 'all-gender' as a makeshift 'retrofitting' (Dolmage, 2017). Although we argue that the former is preferable (Slater & Jones, 2018), the latter nevertheless signals that trans people have been considered within that space. Lohman and Pearce (2020) playfully refer to the adaptation of spaces for trans people's comfort and protection as '*transing*' a space. Transing a toilet brings 'the politics of trans diversity, inclusion and visibility . . . into wider public spaces as part of a commitment to trans [people's] safety' (Lohman & Pearce, 2020, p. 81), helping to create conditions that make trans lives possible. Yet, 'transed' toilets are also precarious and vulnerable to abuse. One non-binary participant, Sam, told us about an occasion when the former gender-separated toilets at their workplace were re-designated as all-gender:

> . . . someone took their lipstick and wrote 'women's' on what used to be the women's toilet [now an all-gender toilet]. This was on a Friday and by Monday the [all-gender] signs had gone and we were back to the binary toilets.

Similarly, Alex said that when using an all-gender toilet, they found that:

> . . . someone had scribbled out 'gender neutral' and written 'women' on it, like on the sign on the door that was explaining why there was gender neutral toilets. Someone had gone on it with biro and just scribbled out the gender-neutral stuff and written 'women'. There's women-only toilets round the corner if you want to go to women-only toilets, it just doesn't make sense. . . . someone's just been angry with a biro.

Alex's words highlight that the protection of women-only toilets is not simply about practical access or women's safety; there was no need for anyone to use the all-gender toilets against their wishes as there were women-only toilets nearby. The re-designation of the toilet as women-only reinstated the 'social norm' (Ramster et al., 2018, p. 69) of the gender-separated toilet, or what Patel (2017, p. 51) calls 'violent cistems': 'the systematised power which oppresses, subjugates, and marginalises transgender people'. The protection of women-only toilets is not so much about supporting women's needs as denying trans possibilities.

A culture of 'violent cistems' means that the small-scale 'transing' of toilets, as described above, can fuel larger-scale transphobia. This was the case when in April 2017, BBC Radio 4 journalist Samira Ahmed tweeted to complain that the Barbican Arts Centre in London had re-labelled a set of their gender-separated toilets – both men's and women's – as 'gender neutral with urinals' and 'gender neutral with cubicles' respectively. Despite the change to the toilets having been made six months prior to Ahmed's tweet, newspapers were quick to report women's 'outrage' over men joining the queue for the (formerly women's) toilets without urinals (e.g. Burgess, 2017; Couvée, 2017). Greed (2019, p. 910) followed this trend, arguing that the situation in the Barbican highlighted the importance of retaining women-only toilets, because 'women – who already had to queue for longer than men when these very same toilets were gender-binaried – have to share their already meagre resources even further'. Media responses largely failed to mention the gender-separated toilets available elsewhere in the building, nor studies showing that all-gender toilets reduce queuing times (Chalabi, 2019). Nowhere was it asked why men (and others previously using the men's toilets) may prefer the newly designated all-gender toilets without urinals,[8] which meant that the focus on de-legitimising trans experiences of toilets also came at the expense of others for whom toilets could also be improved.

A scarcity of toilets suitable for a range of people and needs has led to debates over who is valued, important, and deserving of designated resources. Yet, placing needs in opposition is detrimental to a range of people, particularly trans people. We maintain that generating conflict around toilet politics is often strategic. Whilst claiming to be concerned about women's needs, gender-critical feminists prioritise the de-legitimation and demonisation of trans people (particularly trans women and others who experience transmisogyny) at the expense of a thorough discussion of toilets that could include all women, as well as others who experience transphobia, queerphobia and other gender-based oppressions.

Conclusion

Women's access to safe and comfortable toilets has (rightly) been presented as a feminist issue, and part of women's broader struggles to access public space (Greed, 2010; Jeffreys, 2014a; Kogan, 2010; Penner, 2001; Ramster et al., 2018). Yet, increased trans visibility, and the possibility of improving trans people's rights in the UK have led to a transphobic backlash. 'Gender-critical' feminists claim that trans people's rights come at the expense of cisgender women's rights and, as one of few gender-separated spaces, the toilet has become a focal point of these debates (e.g. Greed, 2018, 2019; Greed & Bichard, 2012; Jeffreys, 2014a; Ramster et al., 2018).

'Gender-critical' feminists have argued that trans people using the toilet that aligns with their gender, or the implementation of all-gender toilet design, is a threat to women's safety and comfort, as cisgender women would have to share facilities with those that they position outside of womanhood (Greed, 2019; Greed & Bichard, 2012; Jeffreys, 2014a; Ramster et al., 2018). Such arguments are rarely based on empirical research, nor do they engage with trans studies or trans people's toilet experiences. Rather, they rely on a portrayal of trans women and others who experience transmisogyny as dangerous sexual predators (Phipps, 2016). In doing this, they negate, deny and perpetuate trans people's own vulnerabilities to violence in the toilet (Patel, 2017; Phipps, 2016). Trans participants in this article highlighted symbolic, epistemic and physical violence that they have experienced in communal, gender-separated toilets. They also shared how staying at home sometimes felt necessary in order to prevent harm. For many trans participants, finding an all-gender toilet (even when imperfect) made them feel considered, signalling the wider trans-inclusive politics of a space. Yet, changes to toilets do not in themselves abolish prejudice; trans-inclusive toilets were often precarious and vulnerable to becoming a site of transphobia.

We have shown how, in their insistence for a woman-only space, 'gender-critical' feminists impose a narrow definition of womanhood and 'female "oneness"' (Serano, 2007, p. 350), reinforcing normatively gendered ways of being. Some trans women participants described feeling compelled to conform to cissexist standards of femininity in an attempt to 'pass' as cisgender women, and some non-binary participants said that they mediated their gender presentation in an attempt to fit into coercive male and female categories. Arguments for women-only toilets do not only risk excluding trans women, but also some cisgender people, such as cisgender butch women who may also be misgendered in women's toilets. Such arguments also disregard the circumstances of cisgender disabled people, many of whom already use all-gender facilities (Slater & Jones, 2018).

'Gender-critical' feminists prioritise the demonisation and exclusion of trans people, even when this comes at the expense of improving toilets for all. We argue, therefore, that their concerns are not merely architectural, nor are they entirely concerned with equity or (cis) women's rights. Rather, their views are ideological: trans people's increased visibility is interpreted as dangerous because it holds the possibility of changing entrenched binary understandings of sex and gender. Thus, the fight is not so much 'about toilets' but about the contested boundaries of womanhood, tightening the reins on gender, and making trans lives impossible. This is not to say that re-thinking toilet design is unnecessary. Toilets can and should be changed for the better (Slater & Jones, 2018). In fact, we argue that toilets are contested *because* they are important, and access to safe and comfortable toilets plays a fundamental role in making trans lives possible.

Acknowledgements

Thank you firstly to the editors, Sonja, Ben and Ruth, for putting together this collection, and for their kind and considerate approach to the editorial process. We also appreciate the thoughtful feedback given to us by the anonymous reviewers. We're especially grateful to all the Around the Toilet participants, contributors and collaborators, not least Lisa Procter and Emily Cummings, whose work continues to shape and influence the project. Finally, we're thankful to Kirsty Liddiard for her contributions to conversations about this article in its early stages.

Funding

The Around the Toilet project was funded by the AHRC Connected Communities programme (AH/M00922X/1 and AH/P009557/1), and Charlotte is now funded by the Wellcome Centre for Cultures and Environments of Health (203109/Z/16/Z).

Notes

1. Quoted in Gilligan (2018).
2. Gender-separated toilets are the 'conventional' model in the UK, also known as 'sex-separated' or 'sex-segregated' toilets.
3. These are largely intended/designed for use by cisgender, non-disabled men. The requirements of trans people are often omitted in feminist toilet literature and disabled people's needs are treated as entirely distinct.
4. We suggest it is best not to assume any certainties about physiology based upon sex, gender or other identity markers.
5. Also known as 'gender neutral' or 'unisex' facilities.
6. Whilst there is no evidence of the extent to which all-gender toilets are replacing gender-separated facilities, qualitative data indicate that all-gender toilets are still found infrequently and more are needed (Slater & Jones, 2018).
7. RADAR keys, also known as NKS keys, can be applied for or bought online and offer people independent access to locked accessible public toilets across the UK. They are predominantly aimed at disabled people but also used by some non-disabled people.
8. Urinals presented problems for cisgender and trans participants. Some could not urinate in front of others, or pointed out that men's toilets often contained only one cubicle, which was not enough, especially for those who were self-conscious about occupying the cubicle for a long time (impacting particularly on those with bowel conditions, such as inflammatory bowel disease or irritable bowel syndrome). Some participants also noted that urinals did not suit a diversity in bodies (Slater & Jones, 2018; see also Orr, 2019).

References

Ahmed, S. (2016). An affinity of hammers. *Transgender Studies Quarterly, 3*(1–2), 22–34.

Bachmann, C., & Gooch, B. (2018). *LGBT in Britain: Trans report*. Stonewall.

Bailey, S., Boddy, K., Briscoe, S., & Morris, C. (2014). Involving disabled children and young people as partners in research: A systematic review. *Child: Care, Health and Development, 41*(4), 505–514.

Banks, T. (1991). Toilets as a feminist issue: A true story. *Berkeley Journal of Gender, Law & Justice, 6*(2), 263–289.

Barcan, R. (2010). Dirty spaces: Separation, concealment, and shame in the public toilet. In H. Molotch & L. Norén (Eds.), *Toilet: Public restrooms and the politics of sharing* (pp. 25–46). New York University Press.

Bender-Baird, K. (2016). Peeing under surveillance: Bathrooms, gender policing, and hate violence, *Gender, Place & Culture, 23*(7), 983–988.

Blumenthal, D. (2014). *Little vast rooms of undoing: Exploring identity and embodiment through public toilet spaces*. Rowman & Littlefield.

Burgess, K. (2017, April 6). Women queue up to condemn arts centre's unisex lavatories. *The Times*. www.thetimes.co.uk/article/women-queue-up-to-condemn-arts-centres-unisex-lavatories-jq9mswjsp (last accessed 4 June 2020).

Butler, J. (2004). *Undoing gender*. Routledge.

Cavanagh, S. (2010). *Queering bathrooms: Gender, sexuality, and the hygienic imagination.* Toronto Press.

Chalabi, M. (2019, September 6). Gender-neutral bathrooms can save women from waiting forever in line. *The Guardian.* www.theguardian.com/news/datablog/2019/sep/05/gender-neutral-bathrooms-can-save-women-from-waiting-forever-in-line (last accessed 4 June 2020).

Couvée, K. (2017, April 14). We won't stand for Barbican gender-neutral loos, say women. *Islington Tribune.* http://islingtontribune.com/article/we-wont-stand-for-barbican-gender-neutral-loos-say-women (last accessed 4 June 2020).

Cox, L. (2017). *Laverne's story. . .* http://lavernecox.com/about/ (last accessed 4 June 2020).

Ditum, S. (2018). Trans rights should not come at the cost of women's fragile gains. *The Economist.* www.economist.com/open-future/2018/07/05/trans-rights-should-not-come-at-the-cost-of-womens-fragile-gains (last accessed 4 June 2020).

Dolmage, J. (2017). From steep steps to retrofit design, from collapse to austerity: Neo-liberal spaces of disability. In J. Boys (ed.), *Disability, space, architecture: A reader* (pp. 102–115). Routledge.

Edwards, R., & Mauthner, M. (2012). Ethics and feminist research: Theory and practice. In M. Mauthner, M. Birch & J. Jessop (Eds.), *Ethics in qualitative research* (pp. 14–28), Sage.

Fair Play For Women. (2017) *Miscarriages in pub toilets. Is gender-neutral ready?* https://fairplayforwomen.com/miscarriages-pub-toilet-gender-neutral/ (last accessed 4 June 2020).

Fair Play For Women. (2018a) *Fair Play for Women guidance for responding to the GRA consultation.* https://fairplayforwomen.com/full_guide/ (last accessed 4 June 2020).

Fair Play For Women. (2018b) *It's now or never to defend female rights – here's why.* https://fairplayforwomen.com/backgrd (last accessed 4 June 2020).

Gendered Intelligence. (2019) *Background to the Gender Recognition Act.* http://genderedintelligence.co.uk/gra/background (last accessed 4 June 2020).

Gershenson, O., & Penner, B. (2009). Introduction: The private life of public conveniences. In O. Gershenson & B. Penner (Eds.), *Ladies and gents: Public toilets and gender* (pp. 1–32). Temple University Press.

Gilligan, A. (2018, July 29). Ladies' loos at City landmarks may open to trans women. *The Sunday Times.* www.thetimes.co.uk/edition/comment/corrections-clarifications-x82zqbmqx# (No longer available online due to redaction).

Greed, C. (2010). Creating a nonsexist restroom. In H. Molotoch & L. Norén (Eds.), *Toilet: Public restrooms and the politics of sharing* (pp. 117–141). New York University Press.

Greed, C. (2018, November 1). *A woman's place is to be heard: A discussion on the gender recognition act.* Paper presented at A Woman's Place UK, Bath. www.youtube.com/watch?v=aD92aLqgtTA (last accessed 4 June 2020).

Greed, C. (2019). Join the queue: Including women's toilet needs in public space. *The Sociological Review, 67*(4), 908–926.

Greed, C., & Bichard, J. (2012). 'Ladies or gents': Gender division in toilets. *Gender, Place & Culture, 19*(4), 545–547.

Gupta, K. (2020). Creating a trans space. In R. Pearce, K. Gupta, I. Moon & D. L. Steinberg (Eds.), *The emergence of trans: Cultures, politics and everyday lives* (pp. 65–67). Routledge.

Hanson, J., Bichard, J., & Greed, C. (2007). *The accessible toilet resource manual.* University College London.

Hasenbush, A., Flores, A., & Herman, J. (2018). Gender identity nondiscrimination laws in public accommodations: A review of evidence regarding safety and privacy in public restrooms, locker rooms, and changing rooms. *Sexuality Research and Social Policy, 16*(1), 70–83.

Heyes, C. (2013). Feminist solidarity after queer theory: The case of transgender. *Signs: Journal of Women in Culture and Society, 28*(4),1093–1120.

Hines, S. (2019). The feminist frontier: on trans and feminism. *Journal of Gender Studies, 28*(2), 145–157.

Jeffreys, S. (2014a). The politics of the toilet: A feminist response to the campaign to 'degender' a women's space. *Women's Studies International Forum, 45*, 42–51.

Jeffreys, S. (2014b). *Gender hurts*. Routledge.

Jones, C., & Slater, J. (2018). *Lift the lid – Around the Toilet zine*. Around the Toilet. https://issuu.com/aroundthetoilet/docs/zine_finished_web_optimized (last accessed 4 June 2020).

Jones, C., Slater, S., Cleasby, S., Kemp, G., Lisney, E., & Rennie, S. (2020). Pissed off! Disability activists fighting for toilet access in the UK. In M. Berghs, T. Chataika & Y. El-Lahib (Eds.), *Routledge handbook of disability activism* (pp. 219–231). Routledge.

King, A., & Cronin, A. (2016). Queer methods and queer practices: Re-examining the identities of older lesbian, gay, bisexual adults. In K. Browne & C. Nash (Eds.), *Queer methods and methodologies* (pp. 85–96). Routledge.

Kirkup, J. (2018). Women are abused in the name of 'trans rights'. But do MPs care? *The Spectator.* https://blogs.spectator.co.uk/2018/12/women-are-abused-in-the-name-of-trans-rights-but-do-mps-care/ (last accessed 4 June 2020).

Knight, G., & Bichard, J. (2011). *Publicly accessible toilets: An inclusion design guide*. Helen Hamlyn Centre for Design.

Kogan, T. (2007). Sex-separation in public restrooms: Law, architecture, and gender. *Michigan Journal of Gender & Law, 14*, 1–54.

Kogan, T. (2010). Sex separation: The cure-all for Victorian social anxiety. In H. Molotch & L. Norén (Eds.), *Public restrooms and the politics of sharing* (pp. 145–164). New York University Press.

Lewis, R., Sharp, E., Remnant, J., & Redpath, R. (2015). 'Safe spaces': Experiences of feminist women-only space. *Sociological Research Online, 20*(4), 1–14.

Lohman, K., & Pearce, R. (2020). DIY identities in a DIY scene: Trans music events in the UK. In R. Pearce, K. Gupta, I. Moon & D. L. Steinberg (Eds.), *The emergence of trans: Cultures, politics and everyday lives* (pp. 68–84). Routledge.

Molotch, H. (2010). Introduction: Learning from the loo. In H. Molotch & L. Norén (Eds.), *Public restrooms and the politics of sharing* (pp. 1–20). New York University Press.

Munt, S. (1998). *Heroic desire: Lesbian identity and cultural space*. Cassell.

Orr, C. E. (2019). Resisting the demand to stand: Boys, bathrooms, hypospadias, and interphobic violence. *Boyhood Studies: An Interdisciplinary Journal, 12*(2), 89–113.

Patel, N. (2017). Violent cistems: Trans experiences of bathroom space. *Agenda Empowering Women for Gender Equity, 31*(1), 51–63.

Pauwels, L. (2015). 'Participatory' visual research revisited: A critical-constructive assessment of epistemological, methodological and social activist tenets. *Ethnography, 16*(1), 95–117.

Pearce, R., Gupta, K., & Moon, I. (2020). The many-voiced monster: collective determination and the emergence of trans. In R. Pearce, K. Gupta, I. Moon & D. L. Steinberg (Eds.), *The emergence of trans: Cultures, politics and everyday lives* (pp. 1–12). Routledge.

Penner, B. (2001). A world on unmentionable suffering: Women's public conveniences in Victorian London. *Journal of Design History, 14*(1), 35–52.

Penner, B. (2013). *Bathroom*. Reaktion Books.

Phipps, A. (2016). Whose personal is more political? Experience in contemporary feminist politics. *Feminist Theory, 17*(3), 303–321.

Phipps, A. (2017). Sex wars revisited: A rhetorical economy of sex industry opposition. *Journal of International Women's Studies, 18*(4), 306–320.

Ramster, G., Greed, C., & Bichard, J. (2018). How inclusion can exclude: The care of public toilet provision for women. *Built Environment, 44*(1), 52–76.

Serano, J. (2007). *Whipping girl: A transsexual woman on sexism and the scapegoating of femininity*. Seal Press.

Slater, J., & Jones, C. (2018). *Around the toilet: A research project report about what makes a safe and accessible toilet space (April 2015–February 2018)*. Sheffield Hallam University.

Slater, J., Jones, C., & Procter, L. (2018). School toilets: Queer, disabled bodies and gendered lessons of embodiment. *Gender and Education, 30*(8), 951–965.

Slater, J., Jones, C., & Procter, L. (2019). Troubling school toilets: Resisting discourses of 'development' through a critical disability studies and critical psychology lens. *Discourse, 40*(3), 412–423.

Walkowitz, J. (1992). *City of dreadful delight: Narratives of sexual danger in late-Victorian London*. University of Chicago Press.

Woman's Place UK. (2018). *GRA consultation*. https://womansplaceuk.org/press-release-gra-consultation/ (last accessed 4 June 2020).

Author biographies

Charlotte Jones is a Postdoctoral Research Fellow at the Wellcome Centre for Cultures and Environments of Health, University of Exeter. Her main research interests lie in gender, sexuality, disability and health, and particularly the intersections of these areas. She is currently working on a collaborative project focusing on the reproductive justice concerns of people with variations in sex characteristics.

Jen Slater is a Reader in Queer Disability Studies and Education at Sheffield Hallam University. Their research draws on disability studies, queer, trans and feminist theory to consider relationships between accessibility, gender, disability and the body. Most recently, this work has been done through the Around the Toilet project a collaborative exploration of toilets as socio-cultural spaces.

The
Sociological
Review
Monographs

Sex work abolitionism and hegemonic feminisms: Implications for gender-diverse sex workers and migrants from Brazil

The Sociological Review Monographs
2020, Vol. 68(4) 178–195
© The Author(s) 2020
Article reuse guidelines:
sagepub.com/journals-permissions
DOI: 10.1177/0038026120934710
journals.sagepub.com/home/sor

Lua da Mota Stabile
Libertarian Union of Trans People and Travestis (ULTRA), Brazil

Abstract
This article investigates and analyses the main characteristics and issues involving Western hegemonic feminisms, especially so-called 'radical feminism', on the topic of sex work and trafficking in persons/migration, to understand how these discussions have influenced the main conventions, regulations and legislation on this global subject. In particular, it enables understanding of how these regulations invisibilize and, sometimes, criminalize trans* and gender-diverse people in migratory contexts. The contributions to decolonial feminism and transfeminism made by decolonial trans writers are essential to analyse and critique some of the conceptions espoused by Western hegemonic and especially trans-exclusionary feminisms that have influenced the international anti-trafficking and anti-prostitution discourse today. These discourses often affect the voluntary migration of trans* and gender-diverse sex workers, mainly from the Global South, such as in the Brazilian case.

Keywords
gender diversity, human trafficking, migration, sex work, Western feminism

This piece aims to bring a decolonial and Brazilian transfeminist critique to bear on the Western hegemonic discourse presented in many radical feminist debates, and in the leading international and national conventions and legislation on human trafficking, migration and sex work. The history of colonialism and slavery, the imposition of binary, white, heteropatriarchal and cissexist norms, and consequently the global economic model of capitalist hegemony, is essential to comprehend how these structural systems have generated enormous inequalities between and within several countries, as is the

Corresponding author:
Lua da Mota Stabile, Libertarian Union of Trans People and Travestis (ULTRA) and COLETTIVE (Collective of Trans Activists in response to the COVID-19 Socioeconomic Impacts on the Trans Population in Brazil), SCRN 702/703, Bloco G, Entrada 45, apt. 101, Brasilia-DF, Brazil, 70720-640.
Email: luastabile@gmail.com

case of Brazil. The reason to emphasize this historical and complex background is to show how trans* and gender-diverse people were relegated to sex work, as the only option for work. This subjected them to violence and social stigma, resulting in the migration of a significant part of this population to Europe, and also vulnerability to exploitation within some schemes of trafficking (Baker, 2015; Desyllas, 2007). It is also important to foreground the debate on the stigmatization of the sex work, and how the voices of trans* and gender-diverse sex workers are very often not heard by some hegemonic white (cis)feminists from the Global North.

The community of trans* and gender-diverse people, and especially people of colour, recurrently face rejection by their families, discrimination when accessing essential health services, as well as discrimination and abuses of power in public institutions and in access to the labour market across the world (Reisner et al., 2016; Whittle et al., 2008). They also do not have access to citizenship in many places, since there is rarely an unbureaucratized, fair and democratic access to the rectification of names and genders in their national documents (Hines et al., 2018). Therefore, informal work and especially sex work is often viewed as an opportunity to obtain a source of income to survive (Transgender Europe [TGEU], 2017). The choice of sex work is, then, a reflection of limited livelihood options and scarce economic resources, but also an area where trans* and gender-diverse people can build a sense of community and not have to deal with transphobia found in other areas of cis-dominated formal occupation (TGEU, 2017).

Although trans women or transfeminine people represent the large part of the trans* and gender-diverse population who perform sex work, it is important to emphasize that there is a significant participation of trans men or transmasculine people within this market as well. However, due to their invisibility, there are few academic discussions on the subject, and few specific data are found on trans men or transmasculine sex workers' migration characteristics. However, the 2015 National Survey on Transgender Discrimination in the United States found that 26.4% of respondents to the question of sexual market participation were trans men or transmasculine (Fitzgerald et al., 2015).

Brazil is a compelling case for analysis, being a country geopolitically situated in the Global South, having suffered for years under the processes of colonization and institutionalized racism by European powers, having high rates of discrimination and violence against diverse trans* and gender-diverse people, and presenting a high rate of migration of trans* sex workers to Europe. The topic of migration characteristics of trans* and gender-diverse sex workers from Brazil to Europe is also important since, in addition to the high presence of this community in several European countries, they also face significant violence on the European continent itself. Data from the Transgender Murder Monitoring project of Transgender Europe (TGEU) show that of the 32 trans* and gender-diverse individuals known to have been murdered in Italy from 2008 to 2017, 22 (i.e. 69% of all victims) were migrants, 16 of whom were from Brazil.[1] Moreover, the only trans* murder recorded in Portugal in 2008 was of a migrant from Brazil (TGEU, 2017).

The United Nations Office on Drugs and Crime notes that:

> Although trafficking from South America occurs in a smaller number of countries, it is often severe in the places where it does occur. The main destinations for South American victims are Spain, Italy, Portugal, France, the Netherlands, Germany, Austria, and Switzerland. Almost all

of this trafficking is for the purpose of sexual exploitation, and it includes transgender victims. Among South Americans, Brazilian victims have been increasingly detected in Europe. Trafficking originating in this country mainly affects the poor communities of the north (such as Amazonas, Pará, Roraima, and Amapá), rather than the richer regions of the south. (UNODC, 2010, p. 44)

Therefore, this article aims to raise some issues regarding hegemonic Western feminist discourses, especially those relating to sex work abolitionism, as they do not support the promotion and defence of sex workers' human rights. Some are even opposed to the existence of trans persons. To this end, I will use a transfeminist and decolonial perspective to understand how trans and gender-diverse people from the Global South who wish to migrate from their localities, or who end up being victims of some trafficking processes, are being affected by these discourses.

The hegemonic Western radical (cis) feminist debates on sex work and trafficking

There are several feminist debates on sex work, migration and trafficking in persons, which can vary from region to region, from country to country, from culture to culture, and from time to time. Likewise, there are a range of views on sex work among Western feminists, with a growing number that consider sex work a kind of work. However, radical and abolitionist feminisms are among the main (cis) feminist strands currently considered hegemonic in the debates of sex work and trafficking in persons internationally, which also tend to dominate discourses around policies and conventions on trafficking and sexual exploitation globally and in many countries in Europe (Pelúcio, 2011). For this reason, they have enormous influence in the decision-making and regulation processes of the leading international organizations, such as the United Nations, and of the leading national/regional organizations or institutions on the subject, mainly in the United States and Europe, regions that receive a large contingent of migrants currently (but institutional influence is increasing in Latin America).

Radical/abolitionist feminists typically hold the view that sex work is a violation of human rights, analogous to slavery, and therefore a form of sexual violence, which affects mainly women. That is, sex work, and, consequently, the trafficking of women for purposes of sexual exploitation, is the reproduction of the subordination of women by men (Bindman & Dozema, 1997; Desyllas, 2007; Halley et al., 2006; Outshoorn, 2005).

Furthermore, the abolitionist perspective categorically criticizes the process of legalization or decriminalization of sex work that has been taking place in some countries and regions. Janice Raymond (2004, p. 316), for example, highlights that:

> Some people believe that, in calling for legalization or decriminalization of prostitution, they dignify and professionalize the women in prostitution. But dignifying prostitution as work does not dignify women, it simply dignifies the sex industry. People often do not realize that decriminalization means decriminalization of the whole sex industry, not just the women in it. And they have not thought through the consequences of legalizing pimps the legitimate sex entrepreneurs or third party people in business, or the fact that men who buy women for sexual activity are now being accepted as legitimate consumers of sex.

The abolitionists then address the international trafficking of women as a consequence of the existence of prostitution, and argue that the best way to eliminate or combat it would be to abolish prostitution and the sex industry as a whole (Desyllas, 2007). Concerning the specificity of trans* and gender-diverse people, the analyses made by abolitionist feminists do not substantively or systemically address trans* issues within the specific context of sex work. But it is important to note here that this lack of attention is not something shared only by abolitionist feminists, but within most Western and hegemonic (cis)feminist accounts too. However, many abolitionists have been described by trans* activists and scholars as trans-exclusionary radical feminists (TERFs), because in addition to failing to address the specificities of trans* and gender-diverse sex workers, they have tended to debate and delegitimize, in a very transphobic and racist way, the mere existence of trans identities or expressions. For example, Raymond (1979) argues that trans* and gender-diverse people 'rape women's bodies by reducing the real female from an artifact, appropriating this body for themselves' (Raymond, 1979, p. 104).

As we shall see later, the abolitionist perspective has influenced current anti-trafficking and anti-sex work discourses throughout the world, including significant policies and conventions. Hence, it is important to note how this can affect particularly trans* and gender-diverse sex workers, when cisnormative and transphobic discourses are also tied to abolitionist feminist perspectives (Carneiro, 2016; Whittle, 2002).

The (cis)radical feminists take over the international and national regulations on trafficking in persons and sex work

In order to understand how the migration of Brazilian trans* and gender-diverse sex workers is being affected/criminalized by anti-trafficking discourses, it is necessary to provide historical context on how the international and national debates on trafficking in persons and sex work are currently structured. The hegemonic (cis)feminist debates from the Global North over the past decades have not only analysed and criticized the problem of gender-based violence through academia and activism, but also influenced the construction of policies and regulations against trafficking in persons, especially those involving sexual exploitation.

Initially, around the 1950s, opposition between different (cis)feminist positions was almost non-existent within the leading international organizations, mainly due to the invisibility of other feminist groups and demands, such as black, indigenous and trans feminists, among others. This invisibility still exists today concerning the demands of people of colour, indigenous persons, persons with disabilities, sex workers, queer and trans* feminists, as we will see later. The topics of prostitution and the human rights of women were marginalized more generally, as was the relationship between prostitution and human rights itself. Gradually these topics began to be discussed and incorporated into some international conferences, but always under the leadership of (cis)feminist groups originating in the Global North, with a focus on the Global South, which demonstrates some colonialist and imperialist thinking (Halley et al., 2006). At the United Nations, radical (cis)feminists/abolitionists have been able to be recognized and inserted more easily within the organization's debates, with the main UN operations located in the Global North (New York and Geneva). In addition, the (cis)radical/abolitionists feminists had already found in the UN a convention that could benefit their position. Considered the first international document on the subject of human trafficking and 'forced prostitution', the Convention on the Suppression of the Trafficking in Persons and of the Exploitation of Others, adopted by the UN in 1949, suggested that sex work should be illegal, irrespective of any level of consent or choice on the part of persons practising that profession. Therefore, all activities also around the subject of human trafficking and prostitution had a significant influence from the NGOs formed by (cis)radical/abolitionists feminists (Halley et al., 2006, pp. 348–356).

The final definition of trafficking in persons in the UN Protocol (2000, p. 2) on the subject, known as the Palermo Protocol, was as follows:

> 'Trafficking in persons' shall mean the recruitment, transportation, transfer or harboring or receipt of persons, by means of the threat or use of force or other forms of coercion, of abduction, of fraud, of deception, of the abuse of power or of a position of vulnerability or of giving or receiving payments or benefits to achieve the consent of a person having control over another person, for the purposes of exploitation. Exploitation shall include, at a minimum, the exploitation of the prostitution of others or other forms of sexual exploitation, forced labour or services, slavery or practices similar to slavery, servitude or the removal of organs.

Some positive aspects of the Palermo Protocol can be recognized in its changing some abolitionist perspectives from the 1949 Convention, for instance by bringing in the distinction between forced and voluntary prostitution. Moreover, the focus on working conditions rather than on women's morality and sexuality was also a necessary change (Desyllas, 2007). However, we will see later that although there are good elements to the protocol, there is still a long way to go in relation to the international debate on trafficking in persons/migrants and sex work, since the discourse, in addition to invisibilizing trans* experiences, also reproduces racism, binaries, colonialism, and dramatically affects the human dignity of migrant sex workers, by stigmatizing sex workers from the Global South as unconscious and weak women who need to be rescued or saved by the Western women from sexual exploitation (Desyllas, 2007; hooks, 2000).

However, the existence of the Palermo Protocol also did not prevent some countries from having a focus on women's sexuality in their internal regulations on trafficking in persons and prostitution. This was the case with US anti-trafficking policy, for instance. The United States Congress also approved the Victims of Trafficking and Violence Protection Act in 2000, ostensibly to combat the crime of trafficking in persons and to protect its victims. However, what was presented in the mainstream media was a policy to fight against international sex trafficking. The law passed in the United States was supported by leaders of religious groups, neoconservatives and abolitionist feminists. In the very title of the law, it is possible to identify the discourse that all trafficked people, including all women and even trans* people, are victims of trafficking and need to be rescued and protected (Desyllas, 2007). This matters on an international level because the United States has been a huge player in international relations in the past years, influencing several migration laws or regulations in other countries, especially in the Global South – although this might now be changing due to the 2020 COVID-19 crisis.

The European Union has also taken severe measures in recent years concerning border control, immigration and the fight against trafficking in persons and sexual exploitation. The European Union Framework Decision on Combating Trafficking, adopted in 2002, calls on member states to develop practical, proportionate and dissuasive policies to combat trafficking in persons. The European Union has also prioritized cooperation between police and security institutions to prevent what is considered 'one of the most dangerous threats to the EU Member States', i.e. international trafficking in persons (Europol, 2003, p. 9). Although the European Parliament has mechanisms that focus on the protection of victims of trafficking, authors such as Desyllas (2007), argue that a number of European countries have defined criminality in a way that positions 'trafficked people' as perpetrators of the crime of trafficking in persons. Consequently, migrant sex workers, mainly from the Global South, can find themselves targeted by the police or by immigration institutions because of the regulations developed to end international trafficking networks.

Sweden's abolitionist model, known as the 'Nordic Model', influences several policies and actions on sex work in various parts of Europe, including Finland, Norway, France, the United Kingdom, Ireland and the European Union itself, through the European Parliament. This model is based on the legislation criminalizing the purchase of sexual services in Sweden, which was passed in 1999. This process of criminalization was celebrated and supported by adherents to the radical/abolitionist feminist perspective, who believe it is the solution to combat international trafficking in women and sexual exploitation through prostitution. The Swedish government also stated that by adopting such legislation concerning the criminalization of the purchase of sexual services, a series of oppressions against women and children would be combated (Halley et al., 2006; Hubbard et al., 2008). Nevertheless, some national and international organizations of sex workers, such as the Red Umbrella Project (RedUP) and the Swedish Association for Sexuality Education (RFSU), are extremely critical of the Nordic Model and its results following the adoption of the Swedish legislation. Their main arguments are that sex work, as well as the international trafficking of women, did not diminish or disappear in Sweden; in fact, these practices just changed form, taking place underground in more dangerous spaces for sex workers. This has meant worsening working conditions for sex workers, with lower payments, more reliance on pimps, and higher risks to their health and safety (Global Network of Sex Work Projects [NSWP], 2015; Halley et al., 2006).

The so-called legalization model or 'Dutch Model' was applied in the Netherlands in 2000. The criminalization of bordellos was withdrawn, and a process of legalization of the voluntary commercial organization of adult prostitution began. Some other European countries have also followed this model, as is the case in Germany and Greece. Thus, sex workers gained access to retirement, social security benefits, specific healthcare, and the right to seek justice when their rights were violated (Halley et al., 2006). However, while some studies argue that women working in regulated areas of prostitution are now less marginalized, it has also been found that many sex workers in Germany remain unregistered, mostly to avoid paying taxes (Bettio et al., 2017). To return to the specific focus of this article, the Dutch legalization model still has limitations regarding the protection and regularization of sex workers who are in situations of greater vulnerability and marginality, as is the case of those who have uncertain migrant status, drug users and trans* or gender-diverse people, primarily those who are black or people of colour. Thus, marginalized communities of trans* sex workers do not have all the protection guaranteed by law, which further increases the risk of rape and abuse by both clients and police officers and agents of security and immigration (Bettio et al., 2017).

Decolonial and transfeminist perspectives on colonialisms, globalization, capitalism, migrations and trans* sex work

After this brief overview of the hegemonic feminist debate and its influences on the central discussions and norms of international organizations and of US and European Union legislation, it is necessary to highlight decolonial and transfeminist perspectives, especially with regard to the specificities of trans* and gender-diverse migrants and sex workers from the Global South. It is essential to contrast these with the discussions and debates presented above, but also to provide visibility and legitimacy to the debates and perspectives of subaltern, racialized and non-cisgender feminists on the topic at hand.

To have a serious and coherent discussion about Brazilian trans* and gender-diverse migrant sex workers, it is important to avoid reproducing frequently encountered academic narratives that treat trans* sex workers of the Global South only as victims with some mental disorder (due to past pathologization through the World Health Organization), or as metaphors used only to introduce greater social problems. It is necessary to bring to light the intersectionalities and connections between sexuality, gender, race, ethnicity, body, disability, capitalism, colonialism, legality, nation-state, and the power discourses of the medical and legal domains (Rev & Geist, 2017). Therefore, it is imperative to emphasize that the community of concern in this article comprises a huge diversity of conscious agents, navigating between different complex and valid identities, with different experiences of life.

Some feminist perspectives, such as the postcolonial or decolonial perspective, criticize the main arguments developed by (cis)radical/abolitionist and liberal/libertarian feminists, for being either orientalist or imperialist, mainly because of the way subaltern and racialized women are represented in their discourses uncritically as victims of the systems of human trafficking and/or prostitution (Baker, 2015). Decolonial writers such as Kempadoo and Doezema (1998) argue that the state, as well as capitalist, patriarchal and colonialist power relations, are key paradigms commonly overlooked or neglected in the central feminist debates of the Global North that examine how people are exposed to exploitations of sex work, migration, and trafficking in persons. Also, it is vital to recognize the self-determination, capacity and awareness of sex workers, as well as the legitimation of sex work as a platform for income generation and survival in which many people in the Global South are continually voluntarily and conscientiously engaging. Thus, contrary to the abolitionist perspective previously seen, sex work should not be regarded as a form of oppression or victimization, but rather it should be examined from a perspective of empowerment and resistance (Kempadoo & Doezema, 1998).

bell hooks (2000) and Espinosa-Miñoso (2009) also illuminate the fact that, in addition to the agency of sex workers of the Global South often being invisible, there is a constant reproduction of a Western epistemological framework by the hegemonic feminisms, which promotes a form of 'epistemicide' (Espinosa-Miñoso, 2009, p. 45). Through this, the philosophies and contributions of indigenous and native peoples, and people of African descent, among other people of colour, are erased from homogenized 'global' perspectives on gender or women (Espinosa-Miñoso, 2009; Lugones, 2008; Mignolo, 2008). This perpetuates the image of otherness for women from the Global South, especially Afro-descendants, indigenous women, lesbians, bisexual women, trans* women and sex workers (Hall, 2006). There is therefore a contrast made between the 'weak and unprotected third world women/people' and 'powerful western women' (Desyllas, 2007, p. 64; Doezema, 2002; hooks, 2000). This highlights the perpetuation of colonialism and imperialism that also substantially affects trans* and gender-diverse sex workers from the Global South.

The colonial systems that have been developed and implemented in several countries for centuries, such as in Brazil, had as a reproduction matrix the construction of a historical project of white supremacy and structures of global hierarchy (Lugones, 2008; Quijano, 1997). For instance, the postcolonial author Quijano (1997) presents the concept of 'Coloniality of Power', which principally is the process of production of global hierarchical structures, by the European colonization system of the modern era. For him, this formed the basis for structural and institutionalized oppression and violence based on gender, race, ethnicity, sexuality, religion, epistemology, language, among others, which we find in various regions of the globe. Moreover, these hierarchical structures were only possible to establish through the institutionalized racism and slavery of the native and African peoples, generating the rise of the capitalist, patriarchal and colonial system, as well as strengthening the institutionalization of nation-states and borders (Quijano, 1997, p. 117).

With inspiration from theory developed by Quijano (1997), the decolonial author Maria Lugones (2008) expresses that 'coloniality of power' as a framework of analysis also helps in the understanding that colonization brought a racist, patriarchal, heterosexual and binary mode of organization to social relations. This results in the transformation of non-white women into subordinates, and the pathologizing of any form of expression, identity and/or corporeity that deviates from the endosexual,[2] cisheteronormative and patriarchal norms regarding sexual relations, gender, affection, community, bodies, genitalia, clothing and non-Western roles or performances of gender (Lugones, 2008, pp. 77–78).

Therefore, with the colonial project that resulted in the violent incorporation of Western, white, Christian, binary, endosex and cisheteropatriarchal norms, the body diversity and expressions/identities of several gender identities or expressions were gradually exterminated and criminalized by the process of colonization (Araruna & Carneiro, 2017; Carneiro, 2016; Vergueiro, 2016). Consequently, it is possible to affirm that the decolonial perspective is very close to that of transfeminism, due to how issues of gender, sexual orientation, race and ethnicity, among others, are linked to the history of colonialism. The Brazilian decolonial and transfeminist scholar Viviane Vergueiro (2012) observes that 'it is imperative to have a matrix of decolonial and transfeminist analysis on the issues of trans* and gender-diverse people from the Global South' (Vergueiro, 2012, p. 9). According to Vergueiro (2016, p. 64):

This masking of power relations hampers the perception that supposedly scientific 'sexual dimorphism' is aligned with Euro-American ways of understanding how the world works . . . . All bodies and genders have a history, and binaries, as a Eurocentric socio-cultural normativity defines and restricts the destinies of many of them around the world.

This in turn is relevant also to migratory sex work contexts, once one can denounce the colonizing nature of some institutional and non-institutional obstacles that work against the dignity of this community. Moreover, as we have seen previously, hegemonic feminisms often have imperialist views and do not consider the colonial history of resistance from non-white women/people. For Raymond (1979), the category of women, and their respective narratives and experiences of oppression, are delimited to the genitalia. She, like other trans-exclusionary authors, argues that the trans* community has emerged as a product of the medical and pharmaceutical industry, and that the fact that transfeminine people have had male socialization or a genital organ considered socially masculine, even if for a short period, means they are hierarchically positioned above cisgender women and will never experience the oppression of cisgender women (Raymond, 1979; Whittle, 2002). Nevertheless, what the decolonial and transfeminist perspectives allow us to perceive is that the whole Eurocentric relationship between genitalia and binary sex/gender systems originates from colonial mechanisms that aim to reinforce global hierarchies based on racism/ethnocentrism (Hayward & Gossett, 2017; Lugones, 2008; Vergueiro, 2016).

It is also crucial to bring the transfeminist critique to bear on ideas defended by (cis) abolitionist/radical feminists, based on the discussions around trans* people in the sex trade, mainly in the Brazilian context. The transfeminist writer and sex worker Amara Moira (2018) emphasizes that the argument that sex work is comparable to sexual slavery or paid rape, much advocated by many (cis)radical feminists/abolitionists, only demonstrates that this view comes from people who have never exercised this job (Moira, 2018). The argument also often reveals it is used without the recognition that sex workers are able to consciously identify when they are experiencing a rape situation or not.

The 'European dream'

For trans* and gender-diverse sex workers, the migration process often starts within the country itself, when they are expelled from their homes by relatives or laid off from their jobs when they transition or assume a transsexual identity. They move to the major cities and capitals of Brazil, especially São Paulo and Rio de Janeiro, mainly because they have a huge community of trans* sex workers already installed, who help in the process of integration for new sex worker arrivals, but also, due to the ease of international migration from these cities, for which Europe is the main destination (TGEU, 2017). As indicated earlier, *Travestis*[3] and trans women represent the majority of sex workers within the trans* and gender-diverse community, so it is important to highlight the 'crisscrossing of oppression' especially for those with the *Travesti* identity (Pelúcio, 2011, p. 115). Class, gender and race paradigms are important factors for the deepening of marginalization and vulnerability of these people, especially for contexts of sexual exploitation and some exploratory schemes of trafficking in persons/migrants.

Some motivations for the migration of Brazilian trans* and gender-diverse sex workers to Europe are linked to the context of discrimination, inequality, violence, transphobia and lack of opportunities that this community faces. The quest for the European continent is very particular and characteristic of Brazilian trans* migrations, especially for trans women, *Travestis* and transfeminine people. However, many of the factors that intensify this migration are not commonly taken into consideration by organizations that fight against trafficking in persons, within hegemonic feminist debates and/or by migrant assistance organizations in Europe (Pelúcio, 2011).

Within the Brazilian trans* migratory context, economic motivators – which are those related to the desire to obtain better living and working conditions or a higher income – intersect with motives related to individuals' search for safer environments and less discriminatory places to perform sex work and express their gender identities. However, another factor motivating migration (specific to Brazilian *Travestis* and transfeminine sex workers, but relatable across trans* Latin American populations) is I will call 'the European dream' – a shared dream within the community of becoming European. Some ethnographies and analyses of the experiences of trans women and *Travestis* who migrated to Europe or dream of migrating show it is possible to find a guiding axis that refers to the symbolic, social and cultural capital they seek to acquire (Nogueira, 2017; Pelúcio, 2011; Teixeira, 2008). For a number of Brazilian trans* and gender-diverse (especially transfeminine) people, being a sex worker in Europe brings approval from the family and other sex work colleagues in Brazil, as well as offering a place where the imaginaries of 'luxury', 'wealth' and 'glamour' replace the reality of dehumanization, poverty and violation of their bodies and dignities in Brazil. There is even a phrase used among the *Travestis* in Brazil: '*Travesti* is Luxury, *Travesti* is Glamour', which is much used as an analogy between the *Travesti* identity and the European continent (Pelúcio, 2011, p. 109).

Thus, for trans* and gender-diverse people, there is a specific relationship between cultural and social status, and migration to Europe. This shows how historical, colonial legacies still have effects and consequences within the colonized countries to the present day. The European imaginary, and ideas of being European, are always related to progress, cultural, social and economic development, and evolution (Pelúcio, 2005). Countries from the Global South, such as Brazil, are positioned as inferior, with no cultural and symbolic value, mainly due to all the economic, political and social difficulties that one must face in Brazil, especially when belonging to a marginalized social group. Being a trans* sex worker in Brazil is extremely difficult due to discrimination, violence and stigma; therefore, the search for Europe or being European can be linked to the search for acceptance, respect and identity legitimacy by family, friends and society in general (Montvalon, 2014, p. 35). However, both the difficulties faced in Brazil and much of this idealized perspective on European nationality have their origin in the colonial legacy or in the effects of the international political economy, being based on the production of inequalities between the countries and within them, within the hegemonic global capitalist system (Lugones, 2008; Quijano, 1997). Therefore, the connection between colonialism, capitalism, social inequality, discrimination and territories is also crucial to understand the migratory phenomena of gender-diverse peoples from Brazil to Europe (Pelúcio, 2011, p. 111). But these paradigms can also be used to understand the existing demand within the European sex market for Latin American sex workers, which also contributes to the enormous popularity of the European continent as a migratory destination.

Brazilian sex workers represent a cheap sexual pleasure for the European imagination, which at the same time is fetishized through the characteristics of cultural difference and 'otherness' (Burgio, 2017). However, Brazilian trans* sex workers use this construction of racialized stereotypes in a strategic way to achieve success in the European sexual market. This means that there is awareness of this imagery of eroticization, which, despite being part of the colonial discourse of racial superiority, is also a way of surviving and succeeding in this field on the European continent. Pelúcio (2011) adds that:

> In the transnational sex market, many Brazilian *Travestis* are affected by these relationships and by the interweaving between notions of sexuality, gender, race, ethnicity, and nationality. But what I realize is that they are manipulating these stereotypes to promote themselves in that competitive business. They learn to play erotic games that deal with roles of power and submission, domination and passivity. Finding out that there is a dense sexual grammar that composes the codes for these encounters. (Pelúcio, 2011, p. 113)

The context of marginalization and vulnerability for sex work in Brazil, structured around exploitative relations and overseen with great vigilance by the police in an arbitrary and discriminatory way, disproportionately affects trans women and *Travestis*, since they are so often located within the sex market and because of their vulnerability to transphobic attacks and hate crimes from clients, from the state and from society (TGEU, 2017). This scenario, coupled with the state's complete failure to protect the rights of this community, means that trans women and *Travestis* are especially vulnerable to exploitative schemes for trafficking in persons. They have an enormous interest in leaving these contexts of violence in Brazil, and face significant difficulties in navigating the formal barriers that the countries of the North pose for the voluntary migration of people from the Global South (TGEU, 2017).

Therefore, we must consider the trafficking of Brazilian trans* and gender-diverse sex workers in a broader context, with attention to the particularities and specificities that these people face in the sexual market due to discrimination, violence and, in some cases, exploitation. The exploitative schemes of trafficking in persons often reveal national social issues, unequal international relations, and much greater vulnerabilities among particular marginalized groups. Some discourses and discussions end up positioning people who are trafficked as mere victims of crime, forgetting the whole social, economic and political context that puts people in that situation, often in a voluntary and conscious way, since the place of origin can be threatening to these bodies (Fernandes, 2014; Pelúcio, 2011; Teixeira, 2008).

A critique of the international anti-trafficking discourse

To analyse the migration of trans* and gender-diverse Brazilian sex workers to Europe, it is necessary to understand how the Brazilian reality of transphobia and violence obliges this community to depend on trafficking to achieve the European dream and escape the exploitative and violent environments in which they live. As such, most trans* and gen-der-diverse migrant sex workers in Europe do not consider themselves victims, or as objects that do not consent to their realities (Navas, 2013, pp. 5–6). While there is still a need to combat any kind of exploitation or marginalization, in order to understand the phenomenon of international human trafficking, it is also necessary to reflect on how the global capitalist economy is structured, and how unequal and neocolonial international relations influence social, political and economic development, creating inequalities within and between various countries (Navas, 2013; Office of the United Nations High Commissioner for Human Rights [OHCHR], 2014).

However, what we find in hegemonic international anti-trafficking discourses, espe-cially those in the Global North, which influence the attitudes of security institutions in the Global South also, is a 're-inscription of colonialism and western imperialism' through the implementation of anti-trafficking policies (Desyllas, 2007, p. 72). Some decolonial feminists, such as Kempadoo (2005) and hooks (2000), point out that the anti-trafficking agenda prioritizes criminalization, punishment and immigration control over bodies that have a specific origin and skin and, I would add, gender identity or expression. In addition, anti-trafficking discourse reproduces a racism and binarism that invisibilizes the specific issues experienced by some communities, such as trans* and gender-diverse people, in addition to defining migrant sex workers as always the vic-tims of sexual exploitation (Kempadoo, 2005). In the anti-trafficking hegemonic dis-course there is a stiffening of the binary categories of man and woman, in addition to the reinforcement of cisheteronormative gender stereotypes. In addition to sexual exploita-tion being commonly associated with sex work and trafficking, it is seen as affecting only cisgender women, disregarding the experiences and specificities of trans* and gender-diverse people, as well as cisgender men. This perception of sex work as sexual exploitation also presupposes the illegitimacy of autonomy for those working in the sex industry abroad with the intention of earning increased economic security (Frisso, 2014, pp. 80–81). The personal experience outlined below, reported in an autoethnography by the author Claudia Cojocaru (2016), offers a greater understanding of this context. According to her:

> Individuals may react to traumatic events in ways that do not always fit into neatly delimited categories. Most of the women I had contact with experienced violence to some degree, whether it was at the hands of family members, romantic partners, other men and women, pimps, clients or bar staff. Despite personally experiencing violent incidents, neither I nor most of these women would identify with disempowering and stigmatising conceptualisations of victimisation or exploitation in the sex industry. The anti-trafficking sexual humanitarian discourse lumps all women who sell sex into a common category: whether they are trafficked or not, they are invariably understood to be vulnerable, passive and witless victims. According to abolitionist logic, these women's perceived lack of agency and self-determination justifies a range of coercive interventions, from stigmatising labelling, to highly intrusive and destabilising rescue missions. (Cojocaru, 2016, pp. 19–20)

There is a common discursive construction within the hegemonic anti-trafficking debate: the connection between sexual exploitation and international trafficking with the category of 'modern slavery'. This conflation is much advocated by abolitionist feminists, by some human rights organizations, as well as by security institutions. These simplistic comparisons between trafficking and slavery reveal how the representation of migrant sex workers, particularly those from the Global South, as 'powerless victims' erases their agency and autonomy. It also omits the real purpose and context of migratory processes and conceals the truth that for many trans* and gender-diverse migrants, sex work is the main way to earn an income and achieve some degree of social mobility (Andrijasevic & Mai, 2016, p. 2). The supposed relationship between international trafficking and modern slavery also reveals discourses that try to untangle the white privilege from the actual effects of slavery on people of colour, and especially black and indigenous peoples. On this, author Julia O'Connell Davidson (2017, p. 5) states that:

> The abolition of slavery did not mark the end of race as a system of domination. It persisted, and it continues to privilege white and devastate black lives in the contemporary world. The discourse of 'trafficking as modern slavery' actively deflects attention from this. It works to minimise the scale and nature of the atrocity of transatlantic racial slavery (epitomised by the oft-repeated claim that 'there are more slaves today than at any point in human history'), and to dissociate it from the specifically anti-black racism it fostered. It thus produces a lens that occludes the relationship between white privilege and the on-going devaluation and endangerment of black lives in the US, Brazil and other former slave and colonial states.

An alternative to the anti-trafficking perspective is to remove moral lenses that stigmatize and marginalize trans* and gender-diverse sex workers, and move to a perspective of protecting all migrant workers from precarious working conditions. Several Brazilian sex worker activists and organizations have in the past recommended that it is necessary to fully regulate and legalize sex work (Prada, 2018). In 2012, Brazilian legislator Jean Willys introduced a Bill for the legal regulation of sex workers, named after Gabriela Leite, a Brazilian sex work activist who organized the first Brazilian sex workers' conference. The Bill was never approved. But since then, a growing debate has emerged among progressive sex worker activists, including trans* activists, especially through the internet and social media forums. For instance, the famous Brazilian sex work activist Monique Prada (2018) argues that:

> Regulation is a complicated thing, actually. I can't say that in any country things are going well, things are working out. The big question is that the great model that is being defended worldwide is the abolitionist model of prostitution which aims to end demand, through criminalizing the man who pays for sex. Well, that model was implemented in 1999 in Sweden, and today there are still prostitutes in Sweden. This model was implemented in France a year ago, and the reports are that the effects of this model are severe, they are strong. Spain wants to implement this model, and Brazil also wants to implement this model. We talk a lot about the Gabriela Leite Bill, but no one remembers talking about the Bill 377/11, by the Legislator João Campos, who uses feminist arguments [from radical feminists or TERFs] in a very cynical and very inappropriate way [manipulating information with fake and sensationalist news]. When we are starting to join with the fundamentalists parliamentarians' Bills, I think it is time to take a step back. (Prada, 2018, translation by author)

Therefore, there is a counter-argument to legalization, that likewise stands opposed to abolitionism. The Dutch model discussed earlier has adversely affected sex workers due to high taxes and also other restrictions, such as how places and venues are authorized. In addition, sex work ends up being authorized for people with official Dutch documentation and with certain symbolic capital. This mainly excludes trans* and gender-diverse people, especially those who are not cis-passable, migrants, people of colour, people with disabilities and the poorest.

Through legalization (as opposed to decriminalization), the total regulation of sex work by the state may culminate in several human rights violations (English Collective of Prostitutes, 2016). Regulation by the state can present many requirements to be fulfilled by sex workers, which will mainly affect trans* and gender-diverse, people of colour and/or black people. Bureaucracies that reproduce structural transphobia, and put the regulation of this category in the hands of the state, may lead to a new 'illegalities', where people cannot hope to meet the requirements of the legislation as the result of the enormous social inequality that exists in Brazil, especially among trans* people (English Collective of Prostitutes, 2016).

A demand common among most progressive sex worker activists, which I support as well, is the call to decriminalize sex work in all respects and take into account the agency, autonomy and conditions of trans* sex workers in the context of prostitution and trafficking in persons. Marginalized groups need to be able to speak for themselves, and must have their voices and demands heard, so they can prioritize their own agendas and experiences (Desyllas, 2007). Most importantly, it is vital to focus on the empowerment of vulnerable and marginalized groups, rather than on a process of rescue by the Global North (Andrijasevic & Mai, 2016).

Conclusions

This article presented a discussion of the issues, specificities and central characteristics of the migration of Brazilian trans* and gender-diverse people to Europe. As most Brazilian trans* and gender-diverse migrants on the European continent are trans women, *Travestis* or transfeminine sex workers, who often arrive in the Old World from trafficking in persons/migrants schemes or networks that support the migratory process, giving voice to these individuals in the debate on trafficking in persons and sex work has become essential. What we can conclude is that the hegemonic feminist debates on the subject of trafficking in persons and sex work, especially the abolitionist, as well as the hegemonic anti-trafficking discourse, often reproduce colonialisms, cissexisms and racism, due to the way trans* migrant sex workers from the Global South are represented. Therefore, many laws, regulation, and norms designed to confront trafficking in persons/migrants or to criminalize the purchase of sex bear hidden interest: that is, to eliminate prostitution and migrants from the Global South, especially those who deviate from moral Christian, white and cisheteropatriarchal norms. The self-determination, the capacity and the conscience of all the people positioned within the context of sexual work must be respected and it is necessary to understand that given the severe oppression of patriarchal, transphobic, colonial, state and capitalist relations, sex work and migration to the European continent reveal themselves as a search for the means of survival, resistance and independence. Sex work does not in and of itself generate victimization and is not directly associated with sexual or moral violence: rather, cases of exploitation and violence can and do happen, as in any other work or social environment. For these exploitations and violence to diminish, it is vital to promote the following: decriminalization and regulation of prostitution in all states; the protection of the economic, social and political rights of professional sex workers; efficient and targeted public policies that benefit trans* and gender-diverse people; and a more receptive perspective on migrants in the Global North. This is especially the case for those who are most vulnerable and marginalized, such as trans* and gender-diverse sex workers from the Global South.

Funding

The author received no financial support for the research, authorship, and/or publication of this article.

Notes

1. Given the lack of attention to monitoring violence towards trans* and gender-diverse populations, it is likely that the actual murder rate is much greater.
2. Endosex or endosexual is a category used to define a person who is not in any way intersex. According to the Organisation Internationale des Intersexués (OII), 'Intersex people are born with atypical sex characteristics. Intersex relates to a range of congenital physical traits or variations that lie between stereotypical definitions of male and female. That is physical differences in chromosomes, genetic expression, hormonal differences, reproductive parts like the testicles, penis, vulva, clitoris, ovaries and so on. Many different forms of intersex exist; it is an umbrella term, rather than a single category' (OII, 2012).
3. *Travesti* is a Latin American and Brazilian transfeminine gender identity. The origins of the word refer to cross-dressing, however the term was reaffirmed so much within *Travesti* communities to the point of being re-signified and understood in Brazil as related to gender identity, and not to cross-dressing per se. This identity is a quite open one, so today there are *Bichas Travestis* (Queer Travestis), there are *Travestis* who identify as both as *Travesti* and as trans women or women, there are some who identify neither as man or woman, describing themselves as only *Travestis*, in a way that sits outside the Western gender binaries (Luz, 2018).

References

Andrijasevic, R., & Mai, N. (2016). Editorial: Trafficking (in) representations: Understanding the recurring appeal of victimhood and slavery in neoliberal times. *Anti-Trafficking Review, 7*, 1–10.

Araruna, M. L. F. B., & Carneiro, T. (2017). *Autodeterminação Trans no Brasil: embates e negociações com tecnologias de gênero colonizadoras*. University of Brasília.

Baker, C. N. (2015). An examination of some central debates on sex trafficking in research and public policy in the United States. *Journal of Human Trafficking, 1*, 191–208.

Bento, B. (2018). Necrobipoder: Quem pode habitar o estado-nação [Necrobipower: Who can inhabit the nation-state]. *Cadernos Pagu, 53*, e185305. http://dx.doi.org/10.1590/18094449 201800530005

Bettio, F., Giusta, M. D., & Di Tommaso, M. L. (2017). Sex work and trafficking: Moving beyond dichotomies. *Feminist Economics, 23*, 1–22.

Bindman, J., & Doezema, J. (1997). *Redefining prostitution as sex work on the international agenda*. Anti-Slavery International. www.walnet.org/csis/papers/redefining.html (last accessed 3 June 2020).

Burgio, G. (2017). Bodies for sale: Migration and sex work. *Pedagogia Oggi, 1*, 283–296.

Carneiro, T. (2016). *Montação: Os usos da moda na comunicação da identidade de gênero de travestis e mulheres transexuais.* [Bachelor's dissertation, University of Brasília].

Cojocaru, C. (2016). My experience is mine to tell: Challenging the abolitionist victimhood framework. *Anti-Trafficking Review, 7*, 12–38.

Desyllas, M. C. (2007). A critique of the global trafficking discourse and U.S. policy. *Journal of Sociology & Social Welfare, 34*, 57–79.

Doezema, J. (2002, November 15). *The ideology of trafficking.* Paper presented at Work Conference Human Trafficking, Center for Ethics and Value Inquiry (CEVI), Ghent University.

English Collective of Prostitutes. (2016). *Decriminalisation of prostitution: The evidence. Report of Parliamentary Symposium, 3 November 2015.* http://prostitutescollective.net/wp-content/uploads/2016/11/Online-Report.pdf (last accessed 3 June 2020).

Espinosa-Miñoso, Y. (2009). Etnocentrismo y colonialidad en los feminismos latinoamericanos: complicidades y consolidación de las hegemonías feministas en el espacio transnacional. *Revista Venezolana de Estudios de la Mujer, 14*, 37–54.

Europol (2003). *Europol annual report.*

Fernandes, B. (2014). A relação das travestis e da transexuais com o tráfico de pessoas: onde termina a migração começa o tráfico de pessoas. In *Cadernos temáticos sobre tráfico de pessoas, volume 2: migração e tráfico de pessoas* (pp. 11–27). Governo Federal Brasil & UNODC.

Fitzgerald, E., Patterson, S. E., & Hickey, D. (2015). *Meaningful work: Transgender experiences in the sex trade.* National Center for Transgender Equality.

Frisso, G. M. (2014). O processo de tipificação do tráfico internacional de pessoas e a contínua negação da autonomia da mulher migrante pelo direito brasileiro. In *Cadernos temáticos sobre tráfico de pessoas, volume 2: migração e tráfico de pessoas* (pp. 60–85). Governo Federal Brasil & UNODC.

Global Network of Sex Work Projects. (2015). *New report claims the Swedish sex purchase law is ineffective.* www.nswp.org/es/news/new-report-claims-the-swedish-sex-purchase-law-ineffective (last accessed 3 June 2020).

Hall, S. (2006). *The question of cultural identity* (11th ed.). DP&A. [Brazilian edn.]

Halley, J., Kotiswaran, P., Shamir, H., & Thomas, C. (2006). From the international to the local in feminist legal responses to rape, prostitution/sex work, and sex trafficking: Four studies in contemporary governance feminism. *Harvard Journal of Law & Gender, 29*, 335–423.

Hayward, E., & Gossett, C. (2017). Impossibility of that. *Angelaki, 22*, 15–24.

Hines, S., Davy, Z., Monro, S., Motmans, J., Santos, A. C., & Van Der Ros, J. (2018). Introduction to the themed issue: Trans* policy, practice and lived experience within a European context. *Critical Social Policy, 38*, 5–12.

hooks, b. (2000). *Feminist theory: From margin to center.* South End Press.

Hubbard, P., Matthews, R., & Scoular, J. (2008). Regulating sex work in the EU: Prostitute women and the new spaces of exclusion. *Gender, Place & Culture: A Journal of Feminist Geography, 15*, 137–152.

Kempadoo, K. (2005). Mudando o debate sobre o tráfico de mulheres [Changing the debate on trafficking in women]. *Cadernos Pagu, 25*, 55–78.

Kempadoo, K., & Doezema, J. (1998). *Global sex workers: Rights, resistance, and redefinition.* Routledge.

Lugones, M. (2008). Colonialidad y género. *Tabula Rasa, 9*, 73–10.

Luz, R. (2018). *Transgêneros: os passos para a aceitação e a transição de crianças e adultos.* G1. https://g1.globo.com/profissao-reporter/noticia/2018/08/01/transgeneros-os-passos-para-a-aceitacao-e-a-transicao-de-criancas-e-adultos.ghtml (last accessed 3 June 2020).

Mignolo, W. (2008). Desobediência epistêmica: A opcção descolonial e o significado de identidade em política. *Cadernos de Letras da UFF – Dossiê: Literatura, língua e identidade, 34,* 287–324.

Moira, A. (2018). *Amara Moira: Não há feminismo sem prostitutas, não há esquerda sem prostitutas.* Mídia Ninja. http://midianinja.org/amaramoira/nao-ha-feminismo-sem-prostitutas-nao-ha-esquerda-sem-prostitutas (last accessed 3 June 2020).

Montvalon, D. P. (2014). Trans, migrantes y prostitutas en una ciudad de Francia: Dominaciones imbricadas y espacios de negociación. *Trabajo y Sociedad, 23,* 27–43.

Navas, K. M. (2013). O tráfico e a exploração sexual de travestis e transexuais como violação dos direitos humanos. *Jornada Internacional de Políticas Públicas.* www.joinpp.ufma.br/jornadas/joinpp2013/JornadaEixo2013/anais-eixo7-questoesdegeneroetniaegeracao/otraficoeaexploracaosexualdetravestisetransexuaiscomoviolacaodosdireitoshumanos.pdf (last accessed 3 June 2020).

Nogueira, S. (2017). Estudo de caso: Brasil. In *O círculo vicioso da violência: pessoas trans e gênero-diversas, migração e trabalho sexual. Série de Publicações TvT, Vol. 19.* TGEU.

O'Connell Davidson, J. (2017). Editorial: The presence of the past: Lessons of history for anti-trafficking work. *Anti-Trafficking Review, 9,* 1–12.

Office of the United Nations High Commissioner for Human Rights. (2014). *Human rights and human trafficking: Fact sheet no 36.* United Nations. www.ohchr.org/Documents/Publications/FS36_en.pdf (last accessed 3 June 2020).

Organisation Internationale des Intersexués (OII). (2012). *What it is intersex?* http://oiiinternational.com/intersex-library/intersex-articles/what-is-intersex/ (last accessed 3 June 2020).

Outshoorn, J. (2005). The political debates on prostitution and trafficking of women, social politics: International studies in gender. *State and Society, 12,* 141–155.

Pelúcio, L. (2005). Na noite nem todos os gatos são pardos: Notas sobre a prostituição travesti. *Cadernos Pagu, 25,* 217–248.

Pelúcio, L. (2011). Corpos indóceis: a gramática erótica do sexo transnacional e as travestis que desafiam fronteiras. In B. R. Magalhães, T. T. Sabatine & L. A. F. Souza (Eds.), *Michel Foucault – Sexualidade, corpo e direito* (pp. 105–132). Cultura Acadêmica, São Paulo.

Prada, M. (2018). *Regulamentar a prostituição é o melhor caminho para as mulheres?* A Casa Publica. https://apublica.org/2018/09/regulamentar-a-prostituicao-e-o-melhor-caminho-para-as-mulheres/ (last accessed 3 June 2020).

Quijano, A. (1997). Colonialidad del poder, cultura y conocimiento en America Latina. *Anuario Mariateguiano, 9,* 113–121.

Raymond, J. G. (1979). *The transsexual empire: The making of the she-male.* Beacon Press.

Raymond, J. G. (2004). Ten reasons for not legalizing prostitution and a legal response to the demand for prostitution. *Journal of Trauma Practice, 2,* 315–332.

Reisner, S. L., Poteat, T., Keatley, J., Cabral, M., Mothopeng, T., Dunham, E., Holland, C. E., Max, R., & Baral, S. D. (2016). Global health burden and needs of transgender populations: A review. *The Lancet, 388,* 412–436.

Rev, N., & Geist, F. M. (2017). Staging the trans sex worker. *TSQ: Transgender Studies Quarterly, 4,* 112–127.

Teixeira, D. B. F. (2008). L'Italia dei divieti: entre o sonho de ser europeia e o babado da prostituição. *Cadernos Pagu,* 31. www.scielo.br/scielo.php?script=sci_arttext&pid=S0104-83332008000200013 (last accessed 3 June 2020).

Transgender Europe. (2017). O círculo vicioso da violência: pessoas trans e gênero-diversas, migração e trabalho sexual. *Série de Publicações TvT, Vol. 19.*

United Nations Office on Drugs and Crime.(2010). Trafficking in persons to Europe for sexual exploitation. In *The globalization of crime: A transnational organized crime threat assessment*. United Nations Publications. No. E.10.IV.6.

UN Protocol. (2000). *Protocol to prevent, suppress and punish trafficking in persons, especially women and children, supplementing the United Nations Convention Against Transnational Organized Crime*. www.ohchr.org/en/professionalinterest/pages/protocoltraffickinginpersons.aspx (last accessed 3 June 2020).

Vergueiro, V. (2012). *For the decolonization of trans* identities*. http://abeh.org.br/arquivos_anais/D/D019.pdf (last accessed 3 June 2020).

Vergueiro, V. (2016). *Por inflexões decoloniais de corpos e identidades de gênero inconformes: uma análise autoetnográfica da cisgeneridade como normatividade*. [Master's dissertation, Federal University of Bahia, Salvador].

Whittle, S. (2002). *Respect and equality: Transsexual and transgender rights*. Cavendish Publishing.

Whittle, S., Turner, L., Combs, R., & Rhodes, S. (2008). *Transgender EuroStudy: Legal survey and focus on the transgender experience of health care*. www.pfc.org.uk/pdf/eurostudy.pdf (last accessed 3 June 2020).

Author biography

Lua Da Mota Stabile is the International Relations Officer at the Libertarian Union of Trans people and Travestis (ULTRA). Lua is a Brazilian transfeminist who identifies as *Travesti* and Bisexual. She has been fighting for LGBTI+ rights in Brazil since 2014. She is a Chevening alumni, Outright's 2019 UN Religion Fellow and former LGBTI Diversity Specialist from the UN Brazil. She has a Master's Degree in Gender and International Relations from the University of Birmingham (UK). She has academic, social and professional experience in the areas of international relations, gender identity, sex characteristics, criminalization of LGBTI people, asylum, migration and human trafficking focused on trans* and gender-diverse people.

The Sociological
Review
Monographs

The transfeminist and the liberal institution: A love story

The Sociological Review Monographs
2020, Vol. 68(4) 196–207
© The Author(s) 2020
Article reuse guidelines:
sagepub.com/journals-permissions
DOI: 10.1177/0038026120934711
journals.sagepub.com/home/sor

Jay Bernard
Writer and film programmer, UK

Abstract
As queer owned and operated spaces shut down and we increasingly find ourselves annexed to public institutions and/or private corporate spaces, how do we build truly radical community practices? This piece critically reflects on the practical aspects of organising RadFem/Trans: A Love Story – an event on feminist history and trans inclusion that took place at BFI Flare 2018. It also examines how we might to create the conditions for a better conversation, greater trans inclusion, and deeper organisational thinking.

Keywords
cultural production, feminist politics, intersectionality, LGBTQ politics, trans inclusion

In 2018 I programmed an event called 'RadFem/Trans: A Love Story' at the British Film Institute (BFI). It was part of BFI Flare, London's LGBTQ film festival and a response to the proposed changes to the Gender Recognition Act 2004. At the time, a public consultation was underway and changes which would create a simpler procedure for trans people to change the sex on their legal documentation without arbitrary and invasive scrutiny from a panel of cisgender people was being fiercely contested. As the programming season drew near, it became clear that as one of the largest LGBTQ film festivals in the world, it was imperative that Flare address the toxic war between trans-exclusionary radical feminists (TERFs) and the trans community.

In this article I discuss what it means to produce an event about an explosive and divisive topic in a public institution, where the default approach is, ostensibly, to not take sides. I examine the purpose of LGBTQ film festivals as a physical location for queer discourse distinct from but tethered to conversations online. In doing so, I compare RadFem/Trans to a previous event I programmed in 2017 entitled 'Sexit: What the Fuck is Happening with UK Porn Laws?', which focused on a raft of now repealed legislation

Corresponding author:
Jay Bernard.
Email: jaybernard@protonmail.com

which criminalised the depiction of queer and female specific sex acts. This comparison shows how the legal battle for sexual minority practices continues even as the rights of cisgender lesbian, gay and bisexual people are considered largely won.

I argue that these laws are seen as secondary, even unimportant, but that they form a basis for discrimination and self-censorship within cultural institutions and beyond (not unlike Section 28, which outlawed the teaching and promotion of homosexuality by local authorities and in schools from 1988 to 2000 in Scotland, and 2003 in England and Wales). Moreover, these laws are part of a well-established turn towards authoritarianism in the UK, in which TERFs play a crucial part. This trend threatens all sexual minorities on the logic that the oppression of one makes likely and possible the oppression of all, and creates the conditions for regressive sex and gender-based oppressions. Many TERFs deride intersectional feminism, precisely because their activities justify and necessitate it. Hence my approach to programming is to avoid single issue discussions of identity and to take broader political, social and legal conditions into account.

As trans people are derided as a recent 'trend', it is important to hear trans history, feminist politics and queer cultural production in the same breath. On this point I discuss the controversy surrounding the London Porn Film Festival, the TERF protest at London Pride, and other examples of antagonism championed by TERFs, which has transphobia, and a particular abhorrence for trans women, baked in. I discuss the successes and pit-falls of RadFem/Trans and explore how it might have worked better. I also show how it is imperative that film festivals do not simply concentrate on cinema, but take into account screen culture more generally. Often such awareness is only with regard to com-petition, such as Netflix overtaking cinema attendance. But as this is being published, we are in the midst of a global pandemic which has shifted the attention to how we consume and create media online, as well as our modes of communication, and hence how we organise. Our screens have become our main, and in some cases, only, portal to the world, where once they were portals to somewhere else. Finally, the role of programmer is examined as a position of both precarity and power. I mention all of these events together because they form part of my acknowledgement of my own practice, ambitions, limitations and naiveties as a non-binary programmer, which I will return to later. Given that it often falls to individual programmers to address (and supposedly fix) social ineq-uities, how do we negotiate the tension between our radical transfeminist politics and the liberal cultural institutions we work within?

Just do it

I proposed the RadFem/Trans session because I felt it was important for an event on the scale of BFI Flare to directly address the political conditions of the audiences we serve and the film productions we screen. This built on 'Sexit: What the Fuck is Happening with UK Porn Laws?', which I programmed in 2017 as a response to the insidious raft of legislation that had grave implications for the representation of queer sexuality and cul-ture on screen. I mention 'Sexit' at the beginning of this article not to conflate or compare struggles, but to explain how programming at film festivals, ostensibly an artistic space, can address political issues in an ongoing way, and also to highlight the problems and complexities of this being down to programming rather than structural change.

The key laws were the Audio Visual Media Act 2014, which (infamously) banned depictions of face-sitting, as well as female (but not male) ejaculation, among other acts; the Digital Economies Act 2017, which proposed age verification as a way to prevent children accessing porn, but ignored considerable privacy issues; and the Investigatory Powers Act 2016, which has since come into force and means the UK government has a record of every page we visit online for up to 12 months.

Caught in the nexus of these laws were sex workers, porn producers, activists, queer people, and basically anyone who watches adult content. Porn is figured as a minority taste when in fact it is very mainstream and a driver of technical innovation – good or bad, how we use technology has been shaped and directed by porn for centuries. Yet these laws create a pretext of criminality for the most vulnerable (sex workers themselves, who are so often queer and/or trans) while audiences consuming porn are relatively safe. What is doubly alarming is the way that the criminalisation of a small minority is then used as a pretext for the surveillance of the majority.

During Sexit, which featured obscenity lawyer Myles Jackman, and porn producers, performers and activists Jiz Lee and Pandora/Blake, we screened the very acts that were deemed illegal and showed how these laws were trampling over rights that many people did not realise existed. The Audio Visual Media Act in particular showed the continued horror of queer bodies and genitalia, and pandered to conservative feminist ideas which were anti-porn, anti-sex, anti-queer and against sex workers. None of these laws were explicitly anti-queer in the more legible manner of, say, Section 28, yet they significantly impacted queer people, complicating the notion that the UK is more enlightened than other places, such as third world or developing nations, in terms of the advancement of LGBTQ rights. This is also evident in immigration law, where queer migrants are regularly disbelieved, detained and then deported back to countries where homosexuality is a crime or culturally unacceptable.

The BFI's status as a cultural institution made it both the perfect place to challenge these laws as part of the raison d'etre of a film festival, and exemplified how class, power and privilege work to shield some from toxic laws and not others. A middle class, educated, film audience (Flare's main demographic) could theoretically watch pornographic material that contravened the law and not be seen as viable for prosecution whereas a sex worker making the same material at home could be – and technically was – under much more scrutiny. Although there were no individual prosecutions under the Audio Visual Media Act, many small, independent queer porn websites were forced offline, including Dreams of Spanking run by Pandora/Blake.

The law around obscenity is vague, which is also its power. It operates via licensing laws for venues. Technically it is not illegal to screen sexually explicit content publicly. The point at which it tips over into obscenity – which is illegal – is a grey area and highly subjective. This was exemplified by the attack on the London Porn Film Festival in April 2019, when it was forced out of its original location by Camden Council, who objected to the festival's programme. The festival then moved to a venue in the jurisdiction of Southwark where the corresponding legal department had no real understanding of obscenity laws and accepted legal assurance that the content did not contravene them. Two years prior, the Audio Visual Media Act could have been invoked, leading to the arrest and prosecution of the festival's organisers, all of whom are trans, non-binary and queer. The message? Cis, straight, conventional ideas of pornography are okay. Queer pornography by and for ourselves is not. It seems like a small point, but this thinking undergirds the demonisation of trans people as sick, predatory and perverted, and for a time was supported in British law, not through overt criminalisation, but a vague back-up tellingly couched in cultural production, and available for use by TERF organisations like Object who protested the festival.

Then do it again

The reception of 'Sexit' is what emboldened me to programme 'RadFem/Trans'. It was extremely important to me that I didn't present 'Sexit' as a debate, and this concern carried over to 'RadFem/Trans'. To debate what was essentially the exclusion of trans women, repulsion or indifference towards trans men, and an attempt to undermine the advancing of trans rights by citing sexual assault and abuse, was non-negotiable, therefore I presented the event as an examination of the feminist movement as a whole. The original copy for the event reflected this:

> The feminist movement is no stranger to controversy, from class divisions among the suffragettes to the sex wars of the nineteen eighties. Debates around race, pornography, BDSM, socialism, lesbianism, separatism and sex work have caused schisms that have both threatened to tear the movement apart and enabled a more intersectional understanding of feminist struggle. Debates around trans inclusion have raged for many years, but have recently been reignited by imminent changes to the gender recognition act, which will allow people to self-identify without medical supervision. This talk by programmer Jay Bernard and invited guests will look at a selection of archive footage, media clips and more recent films to examine how these debates have been represented in cinema and what these representations can tell us about the imaginative ways in which deep-rooted conflicts have been resolved in the past. With an attitude of exploration, openness, imaginative possibility and – most importantly – compassion, this event will ask big questions about where we are and where we hope to be.

The word 'debates' precedes a list of subjects – race, porn, sex work as well as trans inclusion. Therefore, the debate is not 'should the Gender Recognition Act be reformed?' – yes, it should – but 'how has the acknowledgement of difference broadened Feminism?'

I began the event by pointing out that the feminist movement is not monolithic, but has in fact been created and developed precisely by the kind of transformative activism happening with trans politics today. And each new era has been met by people saying the incomers are 'not feminists'. To pose the event as a debate would be to operate on the terms of the exclusionary feminists who see themselves as gatekeepers, and to entrench the idea that trans women are imposters who need to be admitted. It would leave the rich and multi-valent term 'lesbian' in their hands.

I specifically and deliberately used the full term – trans-exclusionary radical feminist – as TERF was being refigured as a slur, specifically against cis women. I felt using it would be an open goal for those who are more offended by the acronym than the reasons it was coined in the first place. I wondered whether this was cowardice. I think it was a small, pragmatic decision, but it highlighted my instinctive protection of the festival, the institution and its revenue as a paid member of the Flare team. You very quickly absorb

the unspoken and unacknowledged rules of the institution, which like the British constitution, are unwritten and rely on a complex set of educational, social and political man-
ners. This instinct is, essentially, what is learned when you are immersed in elite
institutions. It serves as a formidable inner cop when it comes to taking action that moves
beyond mere representation and begins to challenge the legal and economic structures
that make the institution what it is.

The more I discussed approaches to the issue, the more necessary it seemed to examine the whole history of how feminism had been presented on screen – which moments
had been captured and passed down to us, and how by looking at these moments, we
might see the present day more clearly as not particularly or uniquely difficult. Indeed,
we might laugh in the face of trans-exclusionary radical feminists and point out that they
are on the same side of history as racist feminists who did not wish to include or acknowledge the struggle of black women; heterosexual feminists who did not want to include
lesbians; sex worker exclusionary feminists who saw the economic and social conditions
of sex workers as a betrayal of the movement; and middle class feminists who dismissed
the concerns and lives of working class women.

The historical framing of the clips I chose were designed to illuminate our long and
fractious history and to show how long exclusionary practices have been going on. And
in my case, as a programmer, the question of how to directly speak about the intense
transphobia I was witnessing around the GRA could not be separated from a broader
discussion of how our community has documented its schisms, and more precisely, documented the exclusion of a marginal group by a more dominant one. The year-on-year
presentation of politically informed events can sometimes create the illusion of discrete
issues, yet the main programme has included films such as *Carmin Tropical, Tangerine,
Call Her Ganda* and *Lucid Noon, Sunset Blush*: all films that deal with sex work and
trans lives simultaneously, as well as other issues including class, race and economics.

I began the event in the following way:

> I suspect this topic was attractive to some people because it caused a jolt to the stomach; what,
> a talk on this rather sensitive area, which invites so much bitterness and anger, at Flare, at the
> BFI? Without bullet proof glass? But why not? And why not view it as a love story? The
> schisms that have torn people apart have also brought people together and engendered radical
> new ways of living, relating and understanding. Why not view the present as the product of a
> whirlwind romance. One that began long ago, in the nightclub of history, where, in the smoke,
> middle class women reject working class women, straight women reject lesbians, lesbians
> reject straight women, vanilla lesbians reject S/M dykes, radicals and socialists reject each
> other, anti-porn campaigners reject sex workers, cisgender people reject transgender people;
> but the contrary too. The most unlikely lovers have been making out all over the place, in
> brilliant displays of solidarity but also sometimes in disguise.

> I think we are in the middle of one of the most exciting and interesting times for feminism, both
> culturally and politically and this was exemplified just a few weeks ago on March 8th, during
> the women's strike, and again on Saturday during the latest demonstration at Yarl's Wood.
> Changes to the Gender Recognition Act are imminent, and being opposed by feminist groups
> who feel they have not been consulted, who feel threatened, while also being championed by
> trans people who have pushed for a better, less medicalised practice. The #MeToo and Times

Up campaigns have been met by hysterical claims of witch hunting and pleas for mercy by patriarchal cis men, who, (rightly, I think) fear that the feminists might treat them with the same contempt with which they have treated us. So this talk isn't only about schisms or current disagreements, the wilful misunderstanding of trans people and trans rights, nor the reduction of lesbian politics to its ugliest components. I hope that this event will be a small step towards examining and celebrating our varied herstories as they have converged and diverged; I hope that people will see themselves in the clips on screen as well as other people, and that we might make a bit of space at this festival for some conscious meditation on our collective triumphs and mistakes.

Over the course of 50 minutes, I looked at the following films: *Go Fish, Carry Greenham Home, Born in Flames, Under Your Nose, The 1982 Church Occupation in Kings Cross, A Way of Dying, Sylvia Rivera's Speech, Adventures in the Gender Trade* and *Audre Lorde in Conversation*. I selected each clip because it in some way referenced a rift, schism or disagreement within the feminist movement, and provided an opportunity to talk about how that rift was addressed if not resolved.

Go Fish includes a famous 'judgement scene', which encapsulated the thorny issue of lesbians sleeping with men, and showed the literal-minded policing of the term lesbian. Two clips from *Carry Greenham Home* depicted several women having a fight over how to run a highly politicised, activist space, as well as a clip of a working class woman talking quite lucidly about how much she had learned by living on the common and being privy to the discussions, arguments and ideas formed there. *Born in Flames* showed a similar discussion between two women who had opposing views of how an activist 'women's army' had responded to rape – one being radical, and the other more pragmatic.

Under Your Nose showed the little-known history of the black LGBT centre in London, which showed how the demise of political blackness as a concept revealed and entrenched key differences between black and Asian communities, as well as different faith communities. This felt particularly relevant given the re-emergence of political blackness as an issue within organising communities, but also because the film highlighted the complexity of the term's history, and that there was always opposition to its use despite widespread currency. The *1982* footage depicting the occupation of a church in King's Cross by the English Collective of Prostitutes was followed by footage of Selma James in a brilliant battle with a vicious news anchor, who aims to undermine her allyship and the occupation itself by pointing out that she is not a sex worker. The anchor also accuses the occupation of inviting more violence from the police, in a uniquely liberal approach to concern.

The third part of the screening looked more explicitly at gender identity. *A Way of Dying*, by Mijke van der Drift, depicted two trans people enacting and coming to terms with violence and death. *Sylvia Rivera's Speech* showed how the white, middle class, cisgender Lesbian and Gay Movement was being called out for the co-option of trans women's work before the dust of Stonewall had even settled. Finally, a clip from *Adventures in the Gender Trade* depicted Kate Bornstein, Justin Bond and Patrick Califia discussing, explicitly, the essentialism, gender binaries and forms of bigotry in feminism in the 1990s. It was especially important to end with this clip, because it showed how long the exclusion of trans women from lesbian and feminist spaces had been happening, and served to show that trans people are not a trend invented on the internet.

Once the clips had been shown, I directed the audience to pens and paper below their seats. I asked them that, given the trip through history we had taken, they write down what they hoped the future of our community was, and how people might view that historical moment. Then I asked them to turn to their neighbour and discuss what they had written, which felt like the risky and important bit: I wanted to re-frame the debate, if only for that evening and with the people in that room. There was no vetting, no division – people had to take the risk of potentially speaking honestly to someone with whom they passionately disagree. This automatically changes how you phrase things and what you are willing to discuss. Online debates, where much of the anxiety and pain that had informed RadFem/Trans in the first place, are notoriously toxic precisely because we forget that there are people on the other side. Digital platforms manipulate discussion and encourage division as a simplistic marker of engagement, while at the same time personalising the content of our timelines so that we experience an echo-chamber: content that reflects our previously held views and gets us riled so that we comment, like and click, thus creating a perfect, profitable, circle.

During the final section of the evening I sat down with a panel formed by myself, KUCHENGA, Camille Kumar and Sarah C – all activists, writers and organisers. I deliberately chose an all-Black and People of Colour (BPOC) panel to address the relative lack of BPOC representation in the films and to continue showing that this event was not simply about trans exclusion, but how it intersected with race and other factors. Prior to the event, we had met in the delegate centre of the BFI and worked out what to do if there was any disruption (as moderator, I reassured them that I would take the heat). Our voices were low, and then we walked to the auditorium with a strange solemnity.

All things considered, the event went very well. But then something happened: as people were leaving the auditorium, and as I was chatting on the stairs with people who had attended, the fire alarm went off. It was extremely surreal and at the back of my mind I wondered if a TERF or two had intended to disrupt my event. The BFI reported that CCTV showed some young people had pulled the alarm in a corridor that they had gained access to. This was a relief, but the coincidence was unsettling. While we waited outside in the cold, several people came up to me and talked about their views on the evening. Two comments in particular stand out.

The first was a woman who said she had enjoyed the clips and especially the one of 'that guy talking to the crowd'. She meant Sylvia Rivera. I pointed out that Sylvia Rivera was not 'a guy', but she looked at me with a strange smile and did not respond. This brought home something programmers constantly experience: the gulf between what we think we are putting on the screen and what audiences are taking away.

Second, a trans man who I have known for several years pointed out that trans men are always left out of the discussion. This felt like an important oversight. Although I had included *Adventures in the Gender Trade*, specifically to point out Patrick Califia's journey from trans-exclusionary feminist to S&M advocate and trans man, I had prioritised women-identified people, and saw myself as a non-binary person as a mediating presence. But I had inadvertently replicated the silencing and invisibilisation of trans men that the media perpetuate. For example, in the same year Channel 4, as part of a series of misguided and opportunistic TV programmes, hosted a 'debate' with Germaine Greer and Caitlyn Jenner as the main act. The sole masculine-presenting non-binary participant was mostly ignored and their experiences of being aggressively policed in women's toilets was met with incuriosity.

Now what?

A little while later, I was part of a group that drafted and published an open letter on *The Independent* newspaper's website (Bernard et al., 2018a), criticising the interruption of London Pride by lesbians who were calling for the 'L' (for lesbian) to be removed from the LGBT acronym, and thereby disassociated from the 'T' (for trans).[1] The action at Pride felt like an attack on history; the formation of the acronym had come about because of decades of queer activism, in which each letter symbolised the political organisation and mobilisation, not the newness, of that group. The solidarity statement, which was signed by 125 people, read:

> We are a group of feminists, many of whom identify as lesbian or whose politics were influenced by lesbian culture. We are cisgender, we are non-binary and we are trans. We have all benefited from the deep analysis, radical lifestyle and astonishing bravery of the lesbian feminists who came before us – actions that we understood to be about dismantling the patriarchy, liberating all women from gendered oppression and reimagining the future.

> We were dismayed to see Pride in London being hijacked by a fringe group determined to divide the LGBTQIA+ community along the issue of trans rights, particularly rights for trans women.

> This cannot stand.

> We restate our support for trans people everywhere. Transitioning in a transphobic society is a brave – sometimes medical – decision. It is not a fad. We have a long way to go in defeating sexism, homophobia and transphobia. We have a long way to go to defeat the systems of class, border control and racism that reinforce them. But we know bigotry when we see it. We recognise the difference between critique and hatred. . . .

> Trans women are an essential part of an intersectional and successful feminist struggle. The astonishing campaign in Ireland to legalise abortion patently understood that abortion rights and trans rights go hand in hand (Redmond, 2018). . . .

> There are many other campaigns and acts of solidarity we can be engaged in, including:

> Speaking up for trans rights and helping reform the Gender Recognition Act (Government Equalities Office, 2018)

> Letter-writing to LGBTQI prisoners through Bent Bars project (2011) . . .

> Donating to Action for Trans Health (2018)

Either you work for the liberation of all or you work for the liberation of no-one. (Bernard et al., 2018b)

One can critique the lumping together of all sexually diverse people (besides straight people, though they are included in some extended versions of the acronym as 'allies') beneath a single umbrella. We can also critique LGBT as a marker of liberal values aligned along the axis of sexuality and sexual identity only – hence newer terms such as QTIPOC (Queer, Trans, Intersex People of Colour) and BIPOC (Black, Indigenous, People of Colour). We can also critique the acronym for not being inclusive enough; intersex, asexual and pansexual identities are rarely included, yet all, particularly the first, have growing movements behind them. But we can also see the acronym as an attempt at solidarity; an unusually public, mutable and messy one at that. This was the point behind the final line of the statement: critiquing how we organise is different to wanting to break up the acronym because one objects to other people within it.

As the letter was being published (and greatly cut down by editors) I worried about whether it was wise, as someone who works for a very public festival, to nail my colours so firmly and publicly to the wall. But the answer is best summarised by something Mijke van der Drift, whose film I had excerpted during the talk, wrote in a piece called 'The Gentrification of Politics' about trans femmes being punished for speaking up or attempting to move freely in certain spaces:

> The worst is when spaces of expression, such as queer cultural festivals claim to be 'neutral and welcome everybody'. This literally means they will be mainstream and have a high chance of having offensive material, screenings and debates. (van der Drift, 2017, pp. 19–20)

The piece describes the process of gentrification in which offensive, toothless films are screened at the expense of trans femmes 'because they are beautiful', and in turn:

> . . . gentrify the debate away from . . . structural trans-misogyny, racism and by being such single-issue approaches [that they] manage to turn away from 5 decades of political organising aiming for an understanding of interlocking oppressions, interlocking solutions, multi-layered critique[.] (van der Drift, 2017, pp. 20–21)

It ends with the following challenge:

> The question to platforms, festivals and spaces is how one can centre the reasonability that is radicalism relieving [the] pressure of adaptability and disposability of trans femmes, and shift the centre of discomfort from the margin to the middle. Part of the answer lies in modesty when claiming one is already there. (van der Drift, 2017, p. 23)

I questioned whether I should back the letter precisely because I was worried about being seen to present 'radicalism' as reasonable. This is a line that programmers and cultural curators in mainstream institutions regularly have to tow. For a start, this line is tacit. Second, it is exacerbated by the contradictory role programmers have, being powerful in the context of the festival and yet powerless in the larger arena of the institution. Flare takes place within the BFI, therefore I am associated with the BFI. Yet I am not employed by the BFI, have zero employment benefits and grace its offices for only one day per week, five months of the year. I am in fact a consultant; and this precarity is part of why I am able (and encouraged) to put on events such as RadFem/Trans, and why I will inevitably fail at bringing about the kinds of changes I wish to see. This combination of association with radical ideas without commitment to integrating them is the problem many black, queer, disabled, sex-working, migrant and otherwise marginal cultural producers face. Commitment would mean refusing to check passports (as is currently required as part of the Conservative government's drive to make immigration officials of all administrative workers). It would mean white, cis, able-bodied, middle and upper class people at the top resigning their privilege and pay packet in order to make room for others. It would mean fundamental structural change. And that is not going to happen via programming. Yet I must also eat. Frustration or starvation? I take the former. It is precisely because I am not an employee at the BFI that I am able to continue to work there. I have watched many others burn out and leave.

The economics of film festivals is the subject of another paper. However, the work expected of programmers (and generally freelancers from marginal communities) is often integral to the institution acknowledging our presence at all. The core of the machine is unchanged by events such as RadFem/Trans, and yet the exhaustion (stress, fear, risk) of producing such an event is part of the reason you are there in the first place. Yet to not do this work results in nothing happening at all, or it being undertaken by well-meaning but uninformed cultural producers who have no clue about the material realities of our lives. How to get at the core?

Some might argue this is not necessarily a bad thing, especially if such cultural producers can amplify the message. In that respect film festivals are a stealthy cultural front and political thermometer, particularly for countries in which queer and trans people face more danger. It is easy to criticise and dismiss something others would die for.

Moreover, to return to an earlier point: the phenomenon of someone from one group standing in to represent members of another is partly down to the structural rigidity of our institutions. We have no trans femme people on our programming team, nor in the broader team that delivers the festival. For many years I was the sole person of colour on the programming team, until Tara Brown joined as an assistant programmer for 2020,[2] a scheme we will be continuing in the future. We do however have two programmers who identify with and care about trans politics, therefore we stand in during a range of events which, because of our marginalisation in one form, makes us sensitive to another. Earlier I mentioned my 'practice, ambitions, limitations and naiveties as a non-binary programmer'; the fact that I pass as both cis and trans, the fact that I am skinny and can pull off jeans from Topman, my educational privilege and the fact that I am able-bodied interlock with my blackness, my immigrant family background and working class experience in such a way that I am the perfect minority: well-spoken, well-dressed, well-versed in film and literature.

I would hope that my programming ethic was as 'interlocking' as van der Drift's piece outlined. But I am also the same programmer who was called out for the lack of disabled people in the festival; who was asked by a Turkish woman where the black British trans people were in my programme that stretched back to the early 1990s – I had not even thought of including *The Crying Game*.

The festival might have a new remit in our age of digital debate and exchange: to be a site in which our history is constantly explored and shown, contrary to the film industry imperative to always be new. It might become a site for contesting production conditions and values, where we continue to be critical of all-white, all-cis crews making the most successful queer films. Where people don't grow up thinking that sex work, queerness, race and disability have 'never been explored' because films are screened once, do not get proper distribution, are victims of some unfavourable algorithm, then fade away.

Art is important in and of itself, but this cannot distract from the fact that it is produced and those conditions must change alongside broader social changes that emerge from the pandemic. It cannot be that year after year programmers must present discussions and panels because no film submission addresses legal battles or the TERF wars. It might even be that physical film festivals disappear altogether, though I would be cautious about seeing such a development as 'progress'.

As everything changes, this might be something we see with COVID-19, where screen culture has become a central, global issue. We must continue to think deeply about how we engage with cultural institutions, how we build platforms that serve our needs and how we preserve and disseminate the cultural histories of trans people in a way that draws from multiple sources of radical thought and praxis.

I do not know, as a programmer, how to address this other than peppering the programme with the approach I do have at my disposal: events such as RadFem/Trans that do not mimic the combative, amnesiac tone of the mainstream, but attempt to speak multiply, from the intersections; to always begin from a position of collectivity, not individual identity.

Funding

The author received no financial support for the research, authorship, and/or publication of this article.

Notes

1. Of course, BFI Flare itself had changed its name from the London Lesbian and Gay Film Festival to reflect a shifting cultural and political terrain. In 2020, it also added I for intersex to all official publicity.
2. Unfortunately, this edition of the festival was cancelled due to COVID-19.

References

Action for Trans Health (2018). *Action for trans health. Campaigning for democratic healthcare.* https://actionfortranshealth.org.uk (last accessed 12 June 2020).

Bent Bars Project (2011). *Bent bars project: A letter writing project for lesbian, gay, bisexual, transgender, transsexual, gender-variant, intersex, and queer prisoners in Britain.* www.bentbarsproject.org (last accessed 12 June 2020).

Bernard, J., Jamal, N., Nkonde, N., Taylor-Stone, C., Balani, S., Yeung-Kurylowski, H., Widyaratna, K., Rogers, A. B., Gragnon, O., Shreir, D., Conrad, C. A., Frankland, E., Carty-Williams, C., Taylor, J., Barker, J., Shin, S., Suffee, Z., Hans, S., Ostrowska, A., . . . Riley, C. (2018a, July 11). As feminists of all genders, we stand with trans people. *The Independent.* www.independent.co.uk/voices/letters/transgender-rights-pride-london-anti-trans-transphobic-protest-lgbt-brexit-boris-johnson-jeremy-hunt-a8442841.html (last accessed 12 June 2020).

Bernard, J., Jamal, N., Nkonde, N., Taylor-Stone, C., Balani, S., Yeung-Kurylowski, H., Widyaratna, K., Rogers, A. B., Gragnon, O., Shreir, D., Conrad, C. A., Frankland, E., Carty-Williams, C., Taylor, J., Barker, J., Shin, S., Suffee, Z., Hans, S., Ostrowska, A., . . . Riley, C. (2018b). *Feminist solidarity: Cis and trans people will not be divided!* https://solidaritystatement650530505.wordpress.com/ (last accessed 12 June 2020).

van der Drift, M. (2017). Gentrification of politics. In A. B. Silvera, C. Weerawardhana, C. Hunter, Edinburgh Action for Trans Health, KUCHENGA, van der Drift, M., Mukund, N. Raha, Odete, *Radical Transfeminism* (pp. 19–23). Sociopathic Distro.

Government Equalities Office. (2018). *Reform of the Gender Recognition Act.* https://consult.education.gov.uk/government-equalities-office/reform-of-the-gender-recognition-act/ (last accessed 12 June 2020).

Redmond, S. (2018). *An open letter to the organisers of the 'we need to talk tour' from a group of feminists in Ireland.* Feminist Ire. https://feministire.com/2018/01/22/an-open-letter-to-the-organisers-of-the-we-need-to-talk-tour-from-a-group-of-feminists-in-ireland/ (last accessed 12 June 2020).

Author biography

Jay Bernard is a writer and film programmer from London. They have worked at BFI Flare, London's LGBTQIA film festival since 2015. Their short film *Something Said*, an essay film about physical transformation and Black British history has screened in the UK and internationally, including Sheffield Doc Fest, CinemAfrica, Aesthetica and Leeds International Film Festival.

The
Sociological
Review
Monographs

Afterword: TERF wars in the time of COVID-19

The Sociological Review Monographs
2020, Vol. 68(4) 208–214
© The Author(s) 2020

Article reuse guidelines:
sagepub.com/journals-permissions
DOI: 10.1177/0038026120934712
journals.sagepub.com/home/sor

**$SAGE

Ruth Pearce
University of Leeds, UK

Sonja Erikainen
Centre for Biomedicine, Self and Society, University of Edinburgh, UK

Ben Vincent
Open University, UK

Keywords
coronavirus, COVID-19, discrimination, transgender, transphobia

We conceived of this collection at a different time.

As an editorial team, we were spurred to action in 2018. The catalyst for this was the rapidly growing number of publications which spread fear and misinformation about trans and non-binary people and the supposed danger that we pose to women, children, and the established moral order, especially that of the 'West'. An untold number of these were published (and continue to be found) in the mainstream media, bringing ideas from the far-right and from trans-exclusionary branches of feminism alike to a mass audience. We were also concerned by the growing anti-trans sentiment within academia, disseminated primarily in conference proceedings, blog posts, and though predatory publishers, but also increasingly through 'respectable' academic outlets. We wanted to provide a thoughtful, well-evidenced response, which would address anti-trans arguments head-on, while also moving the conversation forward.

Working in the fields of trans, feminist and intersex studies, the TERF wars have always been a frustrating distraction for us, rather than an interest as such. As researchers, we have sought to address inequalities and abuses of power in arenas such as healthcare, education and sports; as activists, we have fought for abortion rights, bodily autonomy and self-determination, fair pay, equal rights to sport participation and physical activity, wealth redistribution, open borders, and freedom from sexual violence.

Corresponding author:
Ruth Pearce, School of Sociology and Social Policy, University of Leeds, Woodhouse Lane, LS2 9JT, UK.
Email: r.pearce1@leeds.ac.uk

Similarly, each of the contributors to this collection has made an impressive contribution to political struggles: not simply through their writing, but also through arts, culture and public protest. There has been much to struggle against in recent years, from the emerging climate crisis, to the resurgence of nationalist and neo-fascist movements, to the continued marketisation and commodification of work, education and leisure. All of this has been framed by the continued impact of the 2007–8 global economic crash, and the subsequent scapegoating of migrants, racialised minorities and the working classes.

Amidst the tumultuous chaos of the early 21st century, the TERF wars have remained ever-present, woven through endless threads on social media, a constant interference on the television and radio. Within trans and feminist communities, these incessant, fruitless debates sap our energy and interfere with our ability to focus on the tasks at hand. While the TERF wars have become far too convoluted and extensive to summarise (let alone analyse) within a single volume, we felt that at the very least this collection could serve as our reply to many trans-exclusionary arguments. Something to point to, so we can say, 'this is what we have to say about that', and then all get on with more pressing matters.

We are putting the final touches to this collection in the spring of 2020, during a global pandemic the likes of which have not been seen for over a century. 2018 feels a world away; and yet, many of the most disturbing developments of recent months are of course a consequence of the events of the 2010s. At this juncture, it feels necessary to reflect on what has changed with the coming of the COVID-19 crisis – and what has not.

Marginalised social groups and individuals have been disproportionately affected by the pandemic. We can see this in the devastating increase in domestic abuse against women and children across the world (Dalton, 2020), the shock experienced within informal economies such as sex work (Hurst et al., 2020), and the horrifyingly disproportionate death rate for Black, Asian, and minority ethnic populations and low income communities in the Global North (e.g. Office for National Statistics [ONS], 2020; Yancy, 2020). This unnecessary suffering is the consequence of long-term systemic inequalities, compounded in many countries by years of underinvestment, cuts and privatisation of public services. Trans and non-binary communities, too, are in an especially precarious situation. The impact will be most pronounced for individuals whose social positions sit at the intersection of multiple forms of marginalisation, including trans people of colour, disabled and elderly trans people, and trans people who are low income, immigrants, refugees, or homeless. As several major human rights organisations have observed, trans and non-binary people as a group are more at risk of exposure to the virus and of developing severe symptoms (e.g. Human Rights Campaign, 2020; Transgender Europe [TGEU], 2020; UN Human Rights, 2020). This is because they (we) are more likely to have existing health conditions and face barriers to healthcare access, such as a reluctance to seek healthcare when needed due to fears and experiences of discrimination. Trans and non-binary people are also more likely to be disproportionately impacted by the socioeconomic effects of the crisis, being overrepresented in precarious and low income employment, as well as being disproportionately unemployed, and more likely to live in unstable housing conditions (Human Rights Campaign, 2020; TGEU, 2020).

As healthcare systems become overloaded, trans-specific services are already being deprioritised or interrupted, negatively affecting mental health and suicide risk. In the

UK there has been a chaotic response from gender identity clinics: many individuals have found their appointments cancelled, surgeries delayed, and their hormone prescriptions suddenly more difficult to access. For example, the Leeds and Aberdeen gender clinics suspended all services after staff were redeployed in response to the COVID-19 crisis; notably, the Leeds clinic initially failed to inform most patients that their appointments had been postponed. Concurrently, trans people in general and trans youth in particular are at increased risk of domestic violence and abuse at home due to stay-at-home restrictions (UN Human Rights, 2020). There have also been reports of increasing transphobic rhetoric in some countries as well as police abuse of COVID-19 directives to target and attack LGBTIQ+ individuals and organisations (UN Human Rights, 2020). Some countries, such as Panama, Peru and Colombia, have implemented gender-segregated quarantine rules, which mean that men and women are allowed in public on different days, the effect of which has been that trans and non-binary people have been subjected to harassment, abuse, fines and police violence, especially when their identification documents' gender markers have not been consistent with their gender identity and presentation (Perez-Brumer & Silva-Santisteban, 2020). On a more mundane note, it is important to observe our increasing reliance on the Internet for work and leisure while many nations are in lockdown. In many online spaces, especially within the Anglophone world, unmoderated transphobic rhetoric and hate speech has been on the rise over the last few years (Brandwatch & Ditch The Label, 2019; Colliver et al., 2019). All of this makes it challenging for trans people to survive and live, let alone thrive enough to have the extra capacity required to debate and argue about conceptual questions around sex, gender and feminism, or to defend one's right to an empowering and self-defined gendered existence.

Yet, these debates have not only continued to rage in the mainstream press and on social media,[1] but also within legislatures. In a couple of last-minute edits to the introductory essay for this collection, we noted the tabling of a new anti-trans law by the Hungarian government of Viktor Orbán, and a series of concerning pronouncements from UK Women and Equalities Minister Liz Truss. The similarities and differences in discourse within the two countries is important. In both cases, government figures appear to be taking advantage of the pandemic to push back on formal recognition of trans people, through centring 'biological' sex as a determining factor of social and legal identity. In Hungary, this move is the latest in a highly public culture war. The increasingly authoritarian government has sought to uphold traditional 'family values' in opposition to 'gender ideology', for instance through banning gender studies programmes in universities. Feminist commentators such as Eileen Boris have observed that this is part of a wider essentialist agenda on the part of religious and social conservatives:

> The Hungarian ban . . . belongs to a larger rollback against dissenting intellectuals and defense of traditional values, in which women's place is having children for the nation. 'When our girls give birth to our grandchildren, we want them to regard it as the defining moment of their self-realization', Hungarian Parliament President Laszlo Kover of the ruling party declared. 'Gender madness' can only lead to the decay of civilization as it is part and parcel with sexual deviancy. The government proclaims a form of gender essentialism, declaring that 'people are born either men or women'. (Boris, 2019, p. 688)

Many of these concepts – such as the idea that 'people are born either men or women', or the notion that women and girlhood are defined by reproductive capacity – will be familiar to those who have been following the TERF wars in the UK. The difference is that in the UK, appeals to religious and social conservative values have been less successful in recent decades; we have therefore seen a laundering of anti-gender talking points through forms of 'respectable' middle-class feminism. A recent essay on UK transphobia in the time of pandemic from trans blog *The right lube* observes that:

> We cannot talk about the presence of TERFs without talking about the English class system. The Karens of Mumsnet are a gender in themselves: a gender of whiteness, a gender of the absurd and rigid English class system. Transphobia is a sense-making process of gender for and by the upper middle classes. Transphobia, posing as feminism filtered through family values, is a perfect potion to split solidarity between the middle and working classes and push social conservatism. (*The right lube*, 2020)

An example of how the concept of 'biological' sex is mobilised by those campaigning to define womanhood on this basis in the UK can be seen in the quotation below from Suzanne Moore, writing for liberal newspaper *The Guardian*:

> Female is a biological classification that applies to all living species. If you produce large immobile gametes, you are female. Even if you are a frog. This is not complicated, nor is there a spectrum . . . . Female oppression is innately connected to our ability to reproduce. Women have made progress through talking about biological menstruation, childbirth and menopause. We won't now have our bodies or voices written out of the script. . . . You either defend women's rights as sex-based or you don't protect them at all. (Moore, 2019)

It is not a coincidence that this notion of 'sex-based' rights, along with Moore's assertion that 'shocking' numbers of 'teenage girls' are transitioning, has been echoed in Conservative minister Liz Truss's recent statements. These include support for 'the protection of single-sex spaces', 'checks and balances' for trans adults, and 'making sure that the under 18s are protected from decisions that they could make' (Truss, 2020). Nor is it a coincidence that any formal policy proposals that follow from these statements are likely to disproportionately affect cis women as well as trans and non-binary people, through tying legal definitions of womanhood to reproductive capacity and undermining adolescents' right to consent to medical treatment (a move that will most likely also impact on teenagers' current legal right to confidentially access contraception, abortions and domestic violence services). This, ironically, is the front through which the war on women is being fought in the UK, as well as the war on trans existence, including – *especially* – during the COVID-19 crisis.

The TERF wars, now more than ever, are a vexing diversion away from the more pressing priorities for most women as well as trans and non-binary people, including equitable access to basic needs like healthcare, housing, employment and education. Moreover, they are both a consequence of and a distraction from the dangerous growth of nationalist sentiments across the world, as represented by authoritarian rulers such as Orbán, and the concurrent resurgence of interest in pseudoscientific concepts such as eugenics and phrenology among white elites; a connection referenced in the cover art for this collection.[2] The contributions this collection brings together are therefore – and regrettably – just as timely and relevant today as they were in 2018 when the collection was first conceived.

In these frightening times, we find hope in the lessons of the past, the solidarities of the present, and the possibilities of the future. As Jay Bernard and Cristan Williams wisely observe in their respective contributions to this collection, trans and non-binary people are always already a part of our cultures, *especially* our feminist and LGBTIQ+ cultures. Across the world, trans and feminist activists are forging alliances on the basis of our shared interests, fighting back against oppressive patriarchal systems and organising amidst the pandemic. We can see this in the work of groups such as South African advocacy organisation Iranti, which has built a united lesbian, trans and intersex alliance against gender-based violence, and in the contributions of activists such as trans feminist student leader Emilia Schneider, an organiser in Chile's 2019–20 protests against neoliberal governance. In the UK, transfeminist autonomous care organisation Queercare have helped to pioneer the grassroots mutual aid response to the COVID-19 crisis, with their resources cited prominently by National Health Service bodies and the national support network Covid-19 Mutual Aid UK.

In our future work, we will continue to take strength and inspiration from such examples. We will once again look beyond the TERF wars, focusing instead on the lessons we can learn from those who stand united against oppression on the basis of sex and gender. We encourage you to do the same.

Funding

This scholarship was supported in part by the Wellcome Trust (grant number 209519/Z/17/Z).

Notes

1. One particularly prominent example from the UK involved complaints about trans women delivering food as part of a queer mutual aid group.
2. Biometrics and the use of technologies such as facial recognition as means of profiling, classification and surveillance can be seen as part of the historical trajectory of fields like phrenology as well as physiognomy (Bueno, 2019). Alongside tools such as magnetic resonance imagining, such approaches to biologically mapping the body (and the brain) have been claimed to biologically locate social attributes and emotive states such as disgust (Schermer, 2008). Echoes of phenological logics can also be seen in some 'incel' discourse online. Eugenic logics are arguably echoed within fields such as epigenetics (Gillies et al., 2016); although of course, the necropolitical devaluing of Black bodies (as evidenced for example in heightened COVID-19 death rates) and continued state sterilisation of trans people in many contexts, indicates that eugenic thinking never really went away (Gill-Peterson, 2018; Honkasalo, 2020).

References

Boris, E. (2019). Gender troubles, Redux. *Women's History Review, 28*(4), 686–691.

Bueno, C. C. (2019). Face revisited: Using Deleuze and Guattari to explore the politics of algorithmic face recognition. *Theory, Culture & Society, 37*(1), 73–91.

Colliver, B., Coyle, A., & Silvestri, M. (2019). The 'online othering' of transgender people in relation to 'gender neutral toilets'. In K. Lumsden and E. Harmer (Eds.), *Online othering: Exploring digital violence and discrimination on the web* (pp. 215–237). Palgrave Macmillan.

Brandwatch, & Ditch The Label (2019). *Exposed: The scale of transphobia online.* Brandwatch. www.brandwatch.com/reports/transphobia/ (accessed 24 May 2020).

Dalton, S. (2020). When staying at home can mean danger. *Concept: The Journal of Contemporary Community Education Practice Theory, 11*(suppl). http://concept.lib.ed.ac.uk/article/view/4371/5961

Gill-Peterson, J. (2018). *Histories of the transgender child.* University of Minnesota Press.

Gillies, V., Edwards, R., & Horsley, N. (2016). Brave new brains: Sociology, family, and the politics of knowledge. *The Sociological Review, 64*(2), 219–237.

Honkasalo, J. (2019). In the shadow of eugenics: Transgender sterilization legislation and the struggle for self-determination. In R. Pearce, I. Moon, K. Gupta & D. L. Steinberg (Eds.), *The emergence of trans: Cultures, politics, and everyday lives* (pp. 17–33). Routledge.

Human Rights Campaign. (2020). *How transgender and non-binary communities around the world are being impacted by COVID-19.* www.hrc.org/blog/how-transgender-and-non-binary-communities-are-impacted-by-COVID19-globally (accessed 24 May 2020).

Hurst, L., Martinez, M. R., & Monella, L. M. (2020). *'It's a contact job': Sex workers struggle amid the coronavirus crisis.* Euronews. www.euronews.com/2020/04/16/it-s-a-contact-job-sex-workers-struggle-amid-the-coronavirus-crisis (accessed 24 May 2020).

Moore, S. (2019, March 2). Women have the right to organise. We will not be silenced. *The Guardian.* www.theguardian.com/society/commentisfree/2020/mar/02/women-must-have-the-right-to-organise-we-will-not-be-silenced

Office for National Statistics. (2020). *Coronavirus (COVID-19) related deaths by ethnic group, England and Wales: 2 March 2020 to 10 April 2020.* www.ons.gov.uk/peoplepopulationand-community/birthsdeathsandmarriages/deaths/articles/coronavirusrelateddeathsbyethnicgrou penglandandwales/2march2020to10april2020 (accessed 24 May 2020).

Perez-Brumer, A., & Silva-Santisteban, A. (2020). COVID-19 policies can perpetuate violence against transgender communities: Insights from Peru. *AIDS and Behavior.* Advance online publication. https://doi.org/10.1007/s10461-020-02889-z

Schermer, M. (2008). A new phrenology? *Scientific American, 298*(5), 46–48.

The right lube. (2020). *Transphobia in the UK: Why is the UK media so transphobic? . . .Why wouldn't it be?* www.therightlube.co.uk/transphobia-in-the-uk (accessed 24 May 2020).

Transgender Europe. (2020). *COVID-19 and trans people.* https://tgeu.org/covid-19/trans-people/ (accessed 24 May 2020).

Truss, L. (2020). *Minister for Women and Equalities Liz Truss sets out priorities to Women and Equalities Select Committee.* GOV.UK. www.gov.uk/government/speeches/minister-for-women-and-equalities-liz-truss-sets-out-priorities-to-women-and-equalities-select-commit-tee (accessed 24 May 2020).

UN Human Rights. (2020). *COVID-19 and the human rights of LGBTI people.* www.ohchr.org/Documents/Issues/LGBT/LGBTIpeople.pdf (accessed 24 May 2020).

Yancy, C. W. (2020). COVID-19 and African Americans. *JAMA: The Journal of the American Medical Association.* Advance online publication. https://doi.org/10.1001/jama.2020.6548

Author biographies

Ruth Pearce is a Visiting Researcher in the School of Sociology and Social Policy at the University of Leeds. Her work explores issues of inequality, marginalisation, power and political struggle from a trans feminist perspective. Ruth is the author of *Understanding Trans Health* (Policy Press,

2018), and co-editor of *The Emergence of Trans* (Routledge, 2020). She blogs about her work and interests at http://ruthpearce.net

Sonja Erikainen is a research fellow at the University of Edinburgh Centre for Biomedicine, Self and Society, where their interdisciplinary research focuses on social, historical and ethical issues around biomedicine and scientific knowledge production. Their research and publications cover areas including gender and sport science, hormones in scientific and popular cultures, and the promissory futures of science. They are the author of *Gender Verification and the Making of the Female Body on Sport: A History of the Present* (Routledge, 2020).

Ben Vincent (they/them) has a PhD in Sociology from the University of Leeds, which followed degrees in biological natural sciences and multidisciplinary gender studies, from the University of Cambridge. Their first book, *Transgender Health*, was highly commended at the BMA Medical Book Awards. They are the author of *Non-Binary Genders: Navigating Communities, Identities, and Healthcare*, and co-editor of the collection *Non-Binary Lives*. They are online via @gender-ben on Twitter.

Acknowledgements

The Sociological Review Monographs
2020, Vol. 68(4) 215–216
© The Author(s) 2020
Article reuse guidelines:
sagepub.com/journals-permissions
DOI: 10.1177/0038026120938302
journals.sagepub.com/home/sor

Ben Vincent

I wish to open with how this project was catalysed. In 2018 I was invited to review a collection on trans youth edited by Heather Brunskell-Evans and Michele Moore. While the review did not occur, the trans-antagonistic content proved inspirational, and drove what became this collection. My first thanks go to my colleagues at the Open University – Ev Callahan, my fantastic fellow fellow, Richard Holti, for being an exceptionally supportive project lead, and Jo Brewis for invaluable support of this project. I would also like to thank the various peer reviewers who generously gave of their time and expertise to assist us and the contributors to this collection. Thank you to Steve Brown for providing valuable information, resources, and flexibility as editor of the *Sociological Review Monograph Series*. I'm also really grateful to everyone who contributed to our related project workshop in December 2019, with special gratitude to CN Lester for the deeper friendship and music making since then! My most heartfelt thanks go towards Ruth and Sonja, without whom this collection would not have happened. A more enriching, productive, and enjoyable collaboration I cannot imagine, and I am profoundly humbled to count such wonderful people as my dear friends.

Sonja Erikainen

I wish to thank my colleagues at the Centre for Biomedicine, Self and Society, and especially my mentors, Sarah Chan and Sarah Cunningham-Burley, for supporting my work even during my more provocative moments, which has allowed me to do my part in bringing together this wonderful collection. I am also entirely indebted to all the authors who have contributed their work, and to my two co-editors without whom this book would, of course, never have even been conceptualised let alone materialised.

Ruth Pearce

Thanks to my former colleagues at the School of Sociology and Social Policy and the Centre for Interdisciplinary Gender Studies at the University of Leeds, where I did the majority of my work on this project. I am especially grateful to Karen Throsby for her mentoring and steadfast commitment to feminist scholarship, Sally Hines for being an amazing PI and providing me with the time and space to work on my own projects, and Karen Cuthbert for our mutual venting sessions. I am also deeply thankful to Bobby S. Sayyid and Jodie Dyson for taking the harassment that I and others faced as trans studies scholars incredibly seriously, and for committing the School to fully supporting our research.

Thanks must go too to Kirsty Lohman, whose determined support I am always grateful for, and Sophie Wilson, whose good humour, fine company, and excellent taste in BreadTube helped me through many hours of bashing away at my laptop in our flat.

I am incredibly honoured and humbled by the range of contributions we have received for this collection. Thank you to all the authors, to my co-editors Sonja and Ben, and to every trans feminist activist and scholar who has inspired us to fight for a better world. Here's to a future where this book is no longer necessary or relevant.